DECADENCE

Manchester University Press

Decadence

AN ANNOTATED ANTHOLOGY

edited by

Jane Desmarais and Chris Baldick

Manchester University Press

Published by Manchester University Press
Altrincham Street, Manchester M1 7JA
www.manchesteruniversitypress.co.uk

British Library Cataloguing-in-Publication Data is available

ISBN 978 07190 7550 6 hardback
ISBN 978 07190 7551 3 paperback

First published 2012

Typeset in 10.5/12.5pt Warnock
by Servis Filmsetting Ltd, Stockport, Cheshire

CONTENTS

ACKNOWLEDGEMENTS

Over the course of several years in preparing this book, we have both degenerated somewhat, but not lapsed into such decadence as to forget the numerous debts of gratitude we have incurred. In the first place we thank our illustrious translators and co-translators, Derek Mahon, Martin Sorrell, and Frank Krause. We are also grateful for specialist advice given on particular texts and explanatory notes by fellow scholars, notably Peter Coles, Sally Collins, Barbara Goff, Steven Halliwell, Diana Holmes, Joseph Holt, Isobel Hurst, Katy Layton-Jones, Lisa Rodensky and Brian Stableford. We wish to thank also the anonymous editorial adviser to the Press, whose judicious intervention has helped to clarify the arrangement of our selections.

For permission to reprint texts under copyright, we are grateful to Jacqueline Baldick (for the Estate of Robert Baldick), the Punch Library, Brian Read (for the Estate of Arthur Symons), and Romana Severini Brunori (for the Estate of Rachilde).

INTRODUCTION

If we speak of being decadent in our own times, we will refer usually to some form of private self-indulgence: lounging around eating too many chocolates, or perhaps idly soaking in a bath rather than taking a brisk shower. In reaching for that word when speaking of our moments of pampered indolence, we will perhaps summon some mental image of wealthy ancient Romans lolling on couches while being fed grapes by their slaves. In so doing, we revive, however fleetingly, a long and rich tradition of cultural and historical imagination with which this book is concerned: one in which private pleasure and the fate of civilisations are ominously linked. Our everyday notion of decadence involves a slightly guilty sense that luxury, like pride, comes before a fall.

In the later nineteenth century, however, Decadence was an idea with a far greater provocative power and cultural resonance than it has in our current looser usage. This anthology is devoted to Decadence in that older and stricter sense, by which we refer to an important tendency in nineteenth-century literature and art, especially in France but later in England and elsewhere, which embodied a peculiar post-Romantic form of protest against modern civilisation and against inherited literary and cultural assumptions. We call this a tendency rather than a movement or school, for reasons we indicate below; and sometimes we refer to it as a tradition, although as traditions go it is subject to discontinuity, intermittence, and bifurcation into relatively distinct French and English versions.

Bringing this literary-artistic tendency under anything like a stable definition is notoriously difficult, and we shall not attempt to do that here. The primary purpose of this book is to make available some of the more important materials which exhibit the characteristic effects of Decadent writing, and upon which a provisional definition might be attempted – or abandoned. Several of the studies listed in our Select Bibliography consider these problems of definition at considerable length, taking into account complicated overlappings with neighbouring tendencies (Pre-Raphaelitism, Aestheticism, Dandyism, the French Parnassian school, Impressionism, Symbolism) from which Decadence is never fully disentangled. Other problems that obstruct the quest for definition here include the rather different cultural associations that 'decadence' carries in French and in English-language contexts. The most we can offer here is a preliminary indication of some of the important evolving senses of the term 'decadence' and its more significant applications to literature, art, and cultural attitudes in the periods covered here.

Unlike a number of previous anthologies of Decadent writing, ours does not confine itself to the last years of the nineteenth century, known as the *fin-de-siècle* period. The Decadent tradition does indeed reach a kind of defining culmination at that time, but we are keen to give our readers fuller opportunities to trace its earlier evolution from the 1830s, and to see the connections between the proto-Decadent poetry of the 1850s and 1860s and the later work of the century's *fin* itself. Unusually, we dedicate a special section to writings from and about ancient Rome, for reasons that we justify below.

The Roman heritage

The historical resonance of the term 'decadence' is best understood in the context of the academic study of the Latin language and its literature. Before there was decadence in any sense applicable to individual tastes, habits, or self-indulgences, there was something known as 'the' decadence, which was not a disposition but a *period* of alleged linguistic and literary decline. Differences between golden ages of literature and inferior succeeding periods had been noted and discussed in antiquity; but, among classical scholars in the nineteenth century, such distinctions had become codified into a dogma imbibed by rote-learning in school: that true classical Latin was to be found in the periods of the late republic and the early (i.e. Augustan) empire, thus approximately 80 BCE to 14 CE, virtually all later Latin writings being inferior, corrupted by gaudiness, neologism, and incoherence, and thus unworthy of serious study. This standpoint is to be found in Désiré Nisard's (1806–88) *Cultural-Critical Studies of the Latin Poets of the Decadence* (*Etudes de moeurs et de critique sur les poètes latins de la décadence*, 1834) (see pp. 75–8), both in its title and in its 'classicist', or properly Neoclassicist arguments.

When writers of the new Romantic school, led by Théophile Gautier in the 1830s and followed by Charles Baudelaire and others, began to affect admiration for Latin writing of 'la décadence', they were declaring their resistance to the deeply entrenched Neoclassical tradition in French literary culture. Their successors at the end of the century defended what had by then become known as the Decadent (or Symbolist) school in similar terms of defiance against the stranglehold of 'classicist' codes of imitation, as can be seen in Remy de Gourmont's essay on Mallarmé (see pp. 275–83).

To favour the style of Latin 'decadent' literature, then, was in the first place a literary or linguistic provocation, rather than a confession of personal laxity or depravity.

In French contexts, the idea of decadence as it expanded beyond these academic senses was necessarily coloured too by political associations. French history through the nineteenth century was marked by major constitutional alternations between successive forms of Empire and Republic, both terms being variously interpreted and fought over in terms of Roman history. Commonplace parallels between ancient Rome and modern Paris as equivalent centres of world civilisation could be pursued in a number of directions. Especially after the humiliating collapse of France in 1870 – militarily at the hands of Prussian invasion, socially in the Paris Commune – adopting the identity of a 'decadent' was a socially critical posture that implicitly accused French society itself of exhaustion or decrepitude. To be 'decadent' in this sense was no indication of one's own indolence or perversity, but a way of declaring oneself a citizen-subject of a bankrupt or doomed civilisation.

One reason why it has been impossible to stabilize any definition of Decadence is that these specific French associations of the term were garbled or lost in translation as they crossed the Channel. In the far more moralistic climate of Victorian Britain, 'decadence' spelt spinelessness or depravity: either that of the more violent and sexually perverted Roman emperors or that of the modern erotomaniac Parisian. To put the point perhaps too simply, where discussions of Decadence in France revolved around matters of language and style, in Britain they came down to matters of moral failure.

In so far as 'decadence' shifted from a term of linguistic history to a term of moral valuation (as it did to a limited degree in France too), its primary referent was Roman. Our book includes a section of extracts from a few Roman writers themselves, the reason for this being that the moral implications of the larger idea of Decadence originate with them. Roman literature itself, even before its supposed period of literary decadence, had repeatedly offered a powerful narrative or simplified 'myth' of its own society's decline: this self-diagnostic story, in contrasting starkly the clean-living virtues of early Roman history with the corrupting luxuries of its imperial era, amounts to nothing less than the *invention* of 'decadence' as a key trope in the moral interpretation of history.

Earlier cultures, notably the Greek, had also assumed that their own times were inferior to former golden and silver ages of peace, plenty and heroism; but the Roman writers went beyond such mythological nostalgia to construct a more specifically historical and more pointedly moral measure of their fall from former glories. On this widely agreed account, the earliest Romans had built their city-state and expanded its power through

Italy on the basis of their virtuously simple lives of hard agricultural work, frugality, chastity, and military self-discipline; these virtues having been vindicated in recorded times by victory in the three wars against Carthage (the 'Punic wars') waged in the third and second centuries BCE. More recently, though, whether in the civil wars and dissensions of the late republican age or under the relative stability and prosperity of the early imperial era, the sturdy farmer-warrior breed of those days, raised by faithfully fertile and disciplinarian matrons, had given way to the indolently pleasure-seeking and sexually dissolute citizen who was scandalously unfit to take arms in defence of Rome's power.

Presented in the form of pseudo-history, this myth was most influentially propounded under the long reign (31 BCE–14 CE) of the first emperor Augustus by the historian Livy (Titus Livius, 59 BCE–17 CE) in his enormous *History of Rome from its Foundation* (*Ab urbe condita libri*), which idealised the earliest Romans as rugged primitives to whom pleasure, let alone self-indulgence, was either repugnant or entirely unknown. The same myth reappears in contemporary poetry, notably in Horace's ode 'Delicta maiorum' (book III, ode vi, published 23 BCE), which hymns his forebears of the Punic-war period:

> Theirs was a hardy soldier-brood,
> Inured all day the land to till
> With Sabine spade, then shoulder wood
> Hewn at a stern old mother's will.[1]

Not every Roman author cultivated this kind of nostalgic primitivism: Ovid, for example, was an explicit dissenter from it.[2] The conviction that Rome had been corrupted by peace, luxury, and foreign manners, however, persisted powerfully into the literature of the Latin 'decadence', and is clearly exhibited in the excerpts we provide from Juvenal's *Sixth Satire*.

The Decadent outlook

When, in 1892, Oscar Wilde left his lecture tour in the United States for Paris to get an *à la mode* haircut in the style of Nero,[3] Decadents were trading fairly liberally on notions of Roman licence and style. Earlier in the century, writers had used the Romans as examples of what might happen if modern civilisation developed too quickly, but, from about 1890, there is a tendency among Decadents especially to caricature the extravagance and debauchery of the Romans and indulge in refined self-parody. Wilde's was a typical Decadent pose at the *fin de siècle*, and the conservative press had great fun with the effeminate and languid dandyism of the period. We devote a section of the anthology to late nineteenth-century parodies and pastiches of Decadence, especially its fascination with feminine cosmetics and oriental perfumes, buttonholes and hot-house flowers.

In the late nineteenth century, literary Decadence represented a hedonistic embrace of self-destructive indulgence and a glorification of our ephemeral human sensibility. The Decadent was a connoisseur of the passing cloud. Flux and ephemera and temporary sensations, particularly in luxurious material consumption and sexual excess, were subjects treated by Decadents on both sides of the English Channel. Living at a time in history when political, cultural, and scientific revolutions had swept across Europe, when social change seemed to be accelerating towards a state of affairs of which no one could be fully certain, these writers resisted the clamour of 'Progress', and in their work we repeatedly encounter images of anxiety, boredom, destruction, and death. Rather than eternal bounty, Nature is represented as a figure of treacherous transience. Ripening and rotting, individuals must prepare themselves for death, burning hard like a gemlike flame (to borrow Walter Pater's phrase), which then flickers and disappears. There is beauty, but it exists only because there is contrasting ugliness and squalor. The Decadents, disgusted by metropolitan landscapes of overcrowding and poverty, and revolted by the impact of industrialisation and most aspects of the new commercial culture, found in vice and sin a convenient way to shock the bourgeois and resist moralism.

Decadents in France rejected both the Romantic and the picturesque attitudes towards nature and the idea that external nature has a moral life. Theirs was an urban and interior aesthetic. They preferred the wilder manifestations of nature to be held strictly in abeyance. From the 1830s in France, the Decadent view of nature reflected a cultural energy that was directed towards new, densely populated urban areas such as Paris, where there was little natural beauty. The countryside held little interest for Decadents. For them, nature was the oppressor of humanity, and natural beauty only a reminder that states of perfection are subjective and fleeting. This was the view of Charles Baudelaire, whose jaundiced and soul-weary denunciations of modernity and modernization in the mid-nineteenth century were articulated through images that inverted conventional notions of the natural and ideal. Not for him the decorous forms of flower poetry, with its roots in pastoral verse and prayer. Instead, *Les Fleurs du mal*, in which all bloom (in both botanical and sexual sense) is blighted. In nature Baudelaire sees only the tedious circuitry of the life cycle that ends in corruption and death.

The shocking paradoxes of Decadence find their most original expression in the work of Baudelaire, and in the section of this book devoted to Decadent Verse we offer a generous selection of his poems. The dissonance and contradiction in his work, studied by many as a pillar of modernist aesthetics, is primarily and principally, but not exclusively, Decadent.

Frank Pearce Sturm asserted as much in 1906: 'Baudelaire *is* decadence; his art is not a mere literary affectation, a mask of sorrow to be thrown aside when the curtain falls, but the voice of an imagination plunged into the contemplation of all the perverse and fallen loveliness of the world'.[4]

By the mid-nineteenth century, Decadence is not a term used merely to describe a writer's exuberant stylistic flourishes, as Nisard uses it in his *Cultural-Critical Studies*. It has become, principally through the work of Baudelaire, a paradoxical perspective on the rapid changes of the modern world. This is Gautier's view in his prefatory notice to *Les Fleurs du mal* in 1868, in which he connects the poet's work to both a romantic and a modern obsession with expressing the ineffable and exploring the fleeting shades of the unconscious and the dark side of human nature. Post-Enlightenment people are nervous, self-conscious, attracted to sensations and with a taste for the unnatural. Perversity and paradox; these, according to Gautier, are qualities special to Baudelaire, and they become defining qualities of Decadent poetry at the *fin de siècle*.

Literary Decadence in the nineteenth century was almost exclusively a male preserve. There were Decadent women writers, and we include works by two of them here – Rachilde and Kate Chopin – but, on the whole, the tradition is dominated by an elite metropolitan circle of highly educated, upper-middle-class male writers. Readers will no doubt be struck by this, and by the preoccupation of these writers with decadent women or *femmes fatales*. Decadent woman is the antithesis of the submissive and dutiful minor character found in so many Victorian novels, but is sexually dominant and socially independent of men, whom she uses for her own personal pleasure and gain. Decadent woman is confidently sexual, even over-sexed, and her sexuality is often perverse or corrupting. She is at times diseased. In *Against Nature*, for example, the hero, Des Esseintes, has a nightmare about the Nidularium plant, a symbol of female sexuality corrupted by the Pox. The principal model of Decadent woman in the nineteenth century is the *femme fatale*; vampires, demons, sphinxes, sirens, and priestesses may be classed as sub-categories.

Towards real women, Decadent authors expressed a horror of their reproductive capabilities and their sexual appetites; towards the ideal of womanhood, an ideal embodying beauty and femininity, they expressed fascination. This was a defining contradiction in the Decadent perception of women. As Asti Hustvedt has noted, Decadents abhorred the natural and procreative female body, but they were attracted by all things 'feminine', including jewels, clothes, and perfume.[5] Decadents self-consciously cultivated an image of effeminacy for themselves; it was part of a pose gifted to them by the responses of hostile contemporary critics, who ridiculed them for their effeminate ways and sexual ambiguity. In an anonymous article in *Le Décadent* of 1886, for example, Decadence is perversely defined as a form of social progress in which conventional notions of masculinity are outmoded. The author describes how the Decadents, 'precursors of the society of the future, are close to the ideal type of perfection. . . . Man is growing more refined, more feminine, more divine.'[6]

Decadence, decadentism, décadisme

Decadence is a complex terrain: its diversity and resistance to classification have already been mentioned here. Apart from the indefiniteness of the term itself, decadent self-mockery and the proliferation of parodies and spoofs at the *fin de siècle* bring further confusion: in some cases, the original and the spoof are so closely aligned that the object of parody is lost to view – which is invariably the point.

In France, where the decadent tradition reached a peak in the 1880s, there were two associated concepts, *décadence* and *décadentisme*. The first is a historical and material signifier, and refers to the process of decline and decay, as we might find in civilisations or buildings (deriving from the Latin term *de + cadere*, to fall away from). The second, rarer usage, *décadentisme*, refers to a style or an aesthetic, and is a correlate of terms like Symbolism or Parnassianism, which refer to a particular movement or school of writers. *Décadisme* is another, but rarely used variant, coined by Anatole Baju in the late 1880s and famously cited by Paul Verlaine in *Le Figaro* of 4 April 1891 as an alternative to the term 'symbolisme'. It is worth noting that the distinction between the historical and the aesthetic is maintained in other Romance languages. In Italian, *decadenza* refers to a period when moral and intellectual standards decline, and *decadentismo* to the poetry of sensation of poets like the Milanese *scapliagliati* and, most notably, Gabriele d'Annunzio, who preferred an aesthetic of musicality to argument and content. In English, although there is no lexical distinction between Decadence as an historical period and Decadence as a literary phenomenon, the French spelling is often retained when referring to the literary tradition.

In the nineteenth century the French term *décadence* was used by various European writers, artists, philosophers, and critics, as a way of pinning the term to its French cultural roots. It was used by all kinds of artists, writers and philosophers to suggest sophistication. Nietzsche used it in this way (usually in a pejorative sense that he applied to Christianity itself), and so did the artist, Aubrey Beardsley, though his positive embrace of French sophistication was also intended as a provocation to the old guard who disliked his work. While 'Frenchness' in the late nineteenth century was for many English critics synonymous with lax morals and social and sexual deviance, for a few its use connoted a modern outlook and was a sign to others that cross-cultural influences were to be welcomed.

English Decadence

Decadence in England was centred upon a small number of writers and artists, a selection of fashionable cafés, like St James's (known as 'Jimmy's') in Piccadilly, and a couple of publishing houses, the Bodley Head run by John Lane and the eccentric establishment of Leonard Smithers in Bond Street. At the end of the nineteenth century, the term 'decadence' was a fashionable epithet in London literary circles and connoted 'Frenchness' and moral laxity. Its two living symbols, Oscar Wilde and Aubrey Beardsley, consciously cultivated a continental and decadent persona, deliberately to clash with the prevailing nationalistic ideal in British culture. 'Beardsley is a Decadent, and must do as the Decadents do', sighed the *Magazine of Art*, 'nations ripe and ripe [*sic*], and when they rot and rot, decadence is the tale that hangs thereby'.[7]

Decadence became the byword for anything and everything that was frivolous, exotic, or unconventional. More significantly, 'decadent' was held to describe 'whatever currents in the art and literature of the time' that seemed 'new, strange, disquieting, or immoral'.[8] In France at the *fin de siècle*, the term had lost some of its original protesting resonance and had become subsumed under the notional auspices of Symbolism, but, in England, it was being utilised as a convenient critical tool with which to effect moral rather than literary or artistic censure. In Germany, it was mobilised most significantly by Max Nordau to pathologise the achievements of the avant-garde, but by the time the English translation of *Entartung* (*Degeneration*), appeared in 1895, decadence was increasingly associated with degeneration. The currency of the term at this time was undoubtedly 'lavish', as one critic has observed,[9] but it had become, as a consequence, increasingly worthless.

Arthur Symons: 'refinement upon refinement'

'No English writer has a better claim to recognition as an interpreter of the Decadence in recent English literature than Arthur Symons's, so trumpeted Holbrook Jackson in his retrospective study of *The Eighteen Nineties* published in 1913: 'He of all the critics in the Eighteen Nineties was sufficiently intimate with the modern movement to hold, and sufficiently removed from it in his later attitude to express, an opinion which should be at once sympathetic and reasonably balanced.' [10] The poet, translator, editor, and critic Arthur Symons (1865–1945) – foregrounded in this anthology as the chief spokesman for Decadence in England – revised his classic review of the concept of Decadence over a period of fifteen years, between 1893 and 1908. He attempted a first review of literary Decadence in 1893 in an article for *Harper's New Magazine*,[11] and then later revised it in *The Symbolist*

Movement in Literature in 1899. In 1908, he was drawn to comment on Decadence again, but by this time he was preoccupied with the notion of a social decadence and was seriously disillusioned with a self-destructive materialistic world.

In the *Harper's* article, Symons begins by claiming that Decadence is the 'latest movement in European literature' and that it embraces Impressionism and Symbolism, thereby representing a desire for 'the very essence of the truth' in that one seeks to represent the visible truth and the other the spiritual truth of the world. Decadence, Symons argues, has all the hallmarks of the literature of the ends of great periods – the Greek, the Latin – and as the preoccupation of the writers living at these times was with the morbid and unhealthy, so modern writers concentrate on the unhealthy and corrupt. Decadence is 'an intense self-consciousness, a restless curiosity in research, an over-subtilizing refinement upon refinement, a spiritual and moral perversity'. It is 'a new and beautiful and interesting disease', Walter Pater and W. E. Henley being the English counterparts to the French writings of the Goncourts (*Préfaces et Manifestes*) and Flaubert through to Verlaine and Mallarmé to the dramatic work of the Belgian Maurice Maeterlinck (*La Princesse Maleine*) and to Huysmans's novel *A Rebours*.

Symons explains that Decadence was created in France out of a 'morbid curiosity of form' and the stylistic innovations of the brothers Goncourt, who were keen to make language express the subtleties and detail of the 'actual impression'. Symons's preoccupation with the plastic qualities of language and the ability of Decadent writers in particular to use language so subtly that their words may be said to paint a picture, prefigures the debates among Formalist critics in the early twentieth century, such as the Bloomsbury writers Roger Fry and Clive Bell. In Symons's view, Decadence is about the use of language to suggest to the reader certain ideas, feelings, and impressions. What Decadent writers do, he argues (as had been precisely the complaint of Nisard sixty years earlier), is luxuriate in the suggestiveness of language rather than adhere to the rhetorical conventions that govern grammar and usage. Unlike Gautier, Symons is concerned not so much with the moral content of Decadent writing (indeed, he had to defend publicly his own work several times against the moralising critics) as with the *aesthetic* of decadence, the way that Decadence borrows from the others arts, including painting and music, to create impressions and insights that imitate direct experience of the subject itself. This is what he is describing when he refers to French writers' 'over-subtilizing refinement upon refinement'.

Decadence and the modern tradition

Although we devote much space in this book to the antecedents of full-blown Decadent writing, we have not been able to continue the story of its later legacy in the twentieth century, except in a short extract from Marcel Proust. It is important to remember, though, that in addition to its own intrinsic fascinations, Decadent writing has a further claim upon our attention in that it contributed powerfully to that revaluation of literary values that we call the modern tradition, or more narrowly 'modernism'. The debt owed by major twentieth-century writers to the Decadent/Symbolist tendency in the nineteenth century has been acknowledged since such pioneering studies as Edmund Wilson's *Axel's Castle* (1931) and Frank Kermode's *Romantic Image* (1957). The role of Arthur Symons in introducing the principles of French Symbolism to the English-speaking world was honoured by W. B. Yeats and T. S. Eliot, while both Eliot and Ezra Pound praised Remy de Gourmont as the most inspiring critic of his time. In a different way, Water Pater's work was a lasting influence upon Virginia Woolf and the broader Bloomsbury Group. The themes and motifs of literary Decadence can be heard echoed across a wider range of major early twentieth-century writers, including Thomas Mann, André Gide, Stefan George (represented here by two early poems), D. H. Lawrence, F. Scott Fitzgerald, Aldous Huxley, Noël Coward, W. H. Auden, Christopher Isherwood, Evelyn Waugh, and countless minor figures. The afterlife of Decadence is by no means exhausted in the later twentieth century either, but is revived in (to take only two very different cases) the work of the British novelist Angela Carter (1940–92) and in that of the Irish poet Derek Mahon – whose new translations we are privileged to include in this volume.

We have arranged our selected texts in distinct sections, each preceded by a brief headnote and concluded with detailed explanatory notes. The first section, 'Prefaces, manifestos, and declarations', presents texts from the 1830s to the 1890s that express the conscious positions of the 'decadent' movement. The second section, 'The matter of Rome', gathers extracts from satirists and historians who defined the Roman Empire as a 'decadent' civilization in ways that writers in the nineteenth century were to echo and admire. The third and fourth comprise the most substantial elements of the book, devoted to decadent verse and prose writings respectively. The verse section exhibits the tradition from Baudelaire and Swinburne through to the early 1900s; the prose section takes us from Poe and Gautier to Proust, with plentiful selections from the 1880s. The fifth section is devoted to critical responses, discussions of the term 'decadence' itself, and diatribes against the evils of the Decadent tradition. The final section continues with responses of a parodic nature. The range of material chosen reflects our conviction that literary Decadence was not a brief episode confined largely to the 'Nineties', but a strong tradition persisting from the 1830s to the early twentieth century, and that the distinctive qualities of Decadent writing emerge more clearly if presented together with examples of its elective antecedents in antiquity and contemporary critical reactions. Our approach to annotation has been selective. We have assumed some knowledge of English and French language and literature and the arts and have therefore mostly reserved our glosses for less familiar individuals, slang words or words essential to understanding a passage.

The anthology brings together mainstream and marginal Decadent texts, most of which are represented here in translation. We have followed the preferences of our translators in giving translations or not of titles of French poems. Older out-of-copyright translations have been preferred wherever possible; in all other cases the editors have tried to locate the best translation for the purpose, seeking new translations where none exist. Derek Mahon obliges us with three new translations, including Baudelaire's 'Le Poison', Mallarmé's 'Plainte d'automne' and the parodic 'Decadent Ball', and Martin Sorrell translates Mallarmé's 'Le Tombeau de Charles Baudelaire' and Verlaine's 'Crépuscule du soir mystique'. The editors also contribute their own translations and revisions of older translations.

Notes

1 John Conington, *The Odes and Carmen Saeculare of Horace Translated into English Verse* (3rd edn., London: Bell & Sons, 1892), p. 75.
2 See *Ars Amatoria* iii, 107ff.
3 See Karl Beckson, *London in the 1890s: A Cultural History* (New York and London: W. W. Norton, 1992), p. 43.
4 *The Poems of Charles Baudelaire*, selected and translated from the French, with an introductory study by F. P. Sturm (London: Walter Scott, 1906), p. 216.
5 Asti Hustvedt, (ed.), *The Decadent Reader: Fiction, Fantasy, and Perversion from fin-de-siècle France* (New York: Zone Books, 1999), p. 18.
6 Quoted in Philippe Jullian, *Dreamers of Decadence: Symbolist Painters of the Eighteen Nineties*, translated by Robert Baldick (London: Pall Mall Press, 1971), p. 46.
7 Margaret Armour, 'Aubrey Beardsley and the Decadents', *Magazine of Art*, 20 (November 1897), pp. 10 and 11.
8 Wendell V. Harris, 'Identifying the Decadent Fiction of the 1890s', *English Literature in Transition*, 5, 5 (1962), 1.
9 Ibid.
10 Holbrook Jackson, *The Eighteen Nineties* (London: Grant Richards, 1913), p. 50.
11 See below, pp. 251–62.

1

PREFACES, MANIFESTOS, AND DECLARATIONS

Decadence cannot properly be described as a school or a movement. Walter Pater's 'Conclusion' to *The Renaissance* was adopted unofficially as a manifesto by young English Decadents in the 1880s and 1890s, but it was never intended as such, and the only attempt to establish a school of Decadence was in France in 1886: it lasted two years. Many so-called French Decadents – Baudelaire, Verlaine, Mallarmé, Huysmans – eschewed the title of 'decadent'; and English Decadents – Beardsley, Wilde, Symons – equally suspicious of such labels, tended to cultivate decadent personas in order to attract publicity. However, in spite of the unwillingness of individual writers to commit themselves to a school or a single manifesto, there are a number of key texts from the 1830s to the 1890s that express the conscious positions of the Decadent tradition, and a selection of these is presented here.

One of the most positive, enduring formulations about amoral aesthetics is made by Théophile Gautier (1811–72) in his 'Préface', published originally as an attack on *Le Constitutionnel* for criticising his articles in *La France littéraire,* and published as the 'Préface' to *Mademoiselle de Maupin* (1835), a modern novel about gender, identity, and aesthetics.[1] In the 'Préface', Gautier vigorously and indignantly denounces nineteenth-century bourgeois morality and literary prejudice, and praises the element of uselessness in art. He was at odds with the prevailing liberal-utilitarian cultural attitudes and declared uselessness to be intrinsic to beauty and to a true appreciation of art, the significance of which should be unhindered by the search for moral messages. His modern free-thinking attack on the hypocrisy of the moralising critics and his assertion of art for art's sake (*l'art pour l'art*) were a great influence on English Decadents later in the century, and in Oscar Wilde's (1854–1900) 'Preface' to *The Picture of Dorian Gray* (1891) we find an explicit acknowledgement of Gautier's anti-utilitarian ideas. Wilde concludes his 'Preface' with the assertion: 'All art is quite useless.'

Charles Baudelaire (1821–67) declared the concept of literary Decadence to be meaningless, 'a gigantic yawn' ('un baillement emphatique').[2] Like Gautier, the perfect magician ('le parfait magicien'), his essays, reviews, and poetry represented a shock to the orthodoxies of contemporary French literary culture. In romantic pursuit of Beauty and the higher forms of Imagination, Baudelaire looked to the modern spectacle of contemporary Paris and the heroism of modern life ('l'héroïsme de la vie moderne'); in the fashion and manners of individuals swarming the crowded boulevards he found aesthetic pleasure and inspiration. He drew particular attention to the women who made themselves up to be seen as they strolled along the new boulevards. Finery ('La parure'), Baudelaire writes in 'In Praise of Make-Up' ('Eloge du maquillage', published as a section of his essay 'The Painter of Modern Life' ('Le Peintre de La Vie Moderne'), 1863), is 'one of the signs of the primitive nobility of the human soul' ('comme un des signes de la noblesse primitive de l'âme humaine'). For Baudelaire, adornment and artifice were the means of trumping nature, of using human and material progress to defeat the natural forces that overwhelm us all in the end.

In spite of Baudelaire's refusals to ride bandwagons, many writers and critics adopted him as the figurehead of literary Decadence. This was principally due to the controversy over the first edition of his volume of poetry *Les Fleurs du mal,* which was confiscated under French obscenity laws in 1857. The dissonance and contradiction in Baudelaire's poetry, the shocking juxtapositions of word and image, the references to sadism and lesbianism, which inspired one journalist to call his poetry 'carcass literature' ('la littérature-charogne'),[3] were regarded as essentially Decadent. Baudelaire was blamed by rear guard critics for cultural degeneration. In his long, polemical work, *Entartung,* for example, first translated into English as *Degeneration* in 1895, Max Nordau argues that the cross-fertilisation of continental ideas leads to diminished cultural vitality throughout Europe, the source of which, he claimed, was found in France.

Nordau traces the line of decadent heredity from the French Romantic school to the Parnassians to the Decadents, and to the 'School of Baudelaire', but this reference was typically inaccurate. Literary Decadence was not organised in the way that he suggests. There was one short-lived attempt in the mid-1880s by Anatole Baju (1861–1903) to give some coherence to the work of Decadents, but the project did not survive beyond 1888. On 10 April 1886, Baju launched the first number of the fortnightly journal *Le Décadent,* and its appearance sparked a heated debate among competing journals about the new literature and its proper designation. There ensued much verbal duelling among editors and writers of *Le Symboliste, Le Scapin, La Renaissance, La Vogue,* and *La Revue Indépendant* about the difference between Decadence and Symbolism.[4] Paris was in a publishing ferment. *Le Décadent* was a shooting star in the firmament of the Paris publishing world, and Baju made what we might call a typical Decadent move by co-opting the term 'decadent', with all its negative connotations, for the journal and its contributors. But by the late 1880s, 'décadence' had come to connote a negative idea, and it was a source of parody and lampoon in the popular press. Being pulled by admirers and detractors in different directions, Decadence was a term going nowhere fast, and its life through *Le Décadent* was abrupt and uneventful. *Le Décadent* faltered after the first few issues, its contents eventually being merged with a more Symbolist aesthetic under the more sober title of *La France littéraire et artistique.*

The French may have fallen out of love with literary Decadence by the 1880s, but by this time it had found a new base in London and was generating considerable interest there among Francophile aesthetes. Swinburne had promoted Baudelaire in England as early as 1862, with his review of *Les Fleurs du mal* in the *Spectator* on 6 September, but English Decadence was set in motion by Walter Pater's (1839–94) 'Conclusion' to *The Renaissance.* Pater's suggestive 'Conclusion' seemed to define the Decadent quest, the dark side of Romanticism, derived from Poe, Baudelaire, and other writers who defined it in terms of strange sins transfigured by beauty, but it was omitted in the second edition after colleagues at Oxford suggested that it might foster wrong ideas in young minds. The version of the 'Conclusion' we have used here is the first unamended version, adapted from an earlier essay on William Morris (1868). The impact of the 'Conclusion' on young *fin-de-siècle* writers, its exhortation to live life subjectively and intensely, was so extraordinary that it was appropriated as the unofficial manifesto of Decadence, and among English Decadents we find liberal tributes to Pater's decadent ideas. Wilde told W. B. Yeats: 'It is my golden book; I never travel anywhere without it; but it is the very flower of decadence: the last trumpet should have sounded the moment it was written.'[5]

In the 1890s, a tradition of literary Decadence emerges, with a continuity of ideas going back to the work of Gautier, Baudelaire, and Pater. Arthur Symons (1865–1945) becomes its interpreter and spokesman. Symons's, 'Preface' to the second edition of *Silhouettes* restates Gautier's philosophy in his 1834 'Preface', in which he denies that the value of art is to be measured entirely by its morality, and affirms his discipleship to Pater. Symons articulates common Decadent concerns – 'the lighter and the more fleeting emotions', 'the beauty and strangeness and curiosity of the visible world', 'the blush of rouge', 'the most factitious town landscape' – each one underpinned by a proto-modernist assertion of the autonomy of art: 'And if Patchouli pleases one, why not Patchouli?'

THÉOPHILE GAUTIER

From Preface to *Mademoiselle de Maupin*

To claim that a man is virtuous because he has written a moral fable is just as nonsensical as saying he is a drunkard because he describes revelries or that he is a rake because he writes about debauchery. Every day we can see the opposite is true. It is only the characters in a story who speak, not the author: his hero may be an atheist, but that does not mean he is atheistic. If he shows us bandits behaving and speaking as bandits do, he is still not a bandit himself. On that basis, we would have to guillotine Shakespeare, Corneille, and all the tragedians, as they have perpetrated more murders than Mandrin and Cartouche.[6] We have not done this, though, and I do not believe we shall for some time to come, however virtuous and moralising the critics become. It is one of the obsessions of these narrow-minded little hacks always to substitute the author for his work, and to revert to personalities so as to give their wretched ramblings some feebly scandalous appeal, because they know nobody would read them if they contained only their personal opinions.

We can hardly see the point of all these squawkings, or what is to be gained from all these ill-tempered yelps, which encourage would-be authorities to behave as the Don Quixotes of morality and as policemen of literature, arresting and beating up every passing idea in a book in the name of virtue, as if its cap were not straight or its skirt worn too high. The whole business is most peculiar.

Whatever may be said about it, the age is immoral (if that word means anything, which we very much doubt), and for proof we need look no further than the quantity of immoral books that it generates, and the success these enjoy. It is our standards of behaviour that set the examples followed in books, not the other way round. The Regency period produced Crébillon; it was not Crébillon who produced the Regency.[7] Boucher's little shepherdesses were overpainted and underdressed because the aristocratic ladies of the time were overpainted and underdressed. Pictures take after their models, not models after the pictures. Somebody has said, somewhere or other, that literature and the arts influence manners. Whoever he may be, he is certainly an almighty fool. It is like saying it is peas that make the spring grow, when we know to the contrary that peas grow because it is springtime, just as cherries grow because it is summer. It is trees that bear fruit, and certainly not the fruit that bears trees, this being an eternal law that never changes under its variable forms. One century follows another, each one bearing its fruit, which is unlike the fruit of the preceding centuries. Books are the fruit of manners.

Aside from the moralising journalists, something else has sprung up under this torrent of sermons, as under a summer shower in a park: between the planks of the Saint-Simonian[8] platform has grown a row of little mushrooms, of a new species whose natural history we shall outline. These are the utilitarian critics, a pitiful breed who cannot see past their noses, even though these are too short to support spectacles.

Whenever an author launched on to their desks a book of any

description, poetry, or fiction, these gentlemen would settle back nonchalantly in their easy-chairs, balancing them on their back legs and, poised with a knowing air, would ask with a swagger: 'What use is this book? How can we apply it to the task of raising the moral standard and the welfare of the largest and poorest class of society? What? Not a word here about the needs of society, nothing here of a civilising or progressive tendency? How is it that instead of taking an integrated view of humanity and tracing the stages of providential and regenerative ideals through the events of history, novels and poems are still appearing that lead us nowhere, and fail to guide this generation along the path to the future? How can anyone be concerned with form, style, or rhyming when confronted with such weighty questions? As for us, what do we care for rhyme or style or form? The really relevant issue (*they are so immature, these poor pups*) is that Society is sick, it is writhing in mighty agonies (*in other words, nobody wants to subscribe to utilitarian journals*). It falls to the poet to seek the cause of this malaise and to heal it. He will discover a remedy by identifying himself heart and soul with humanity (*philanthropic poets? that would be a rare treat!*). We await this poet, we summon him with all our prayers. When he appears, he shall win the crowd's applause, the palms, the wreaths, the state banquets . . .'

All well and good; but since we hope our reader will stay awake to the end of this cheerful Preface, we shall go no further with this strictly faithful imitation of the utilitarian style, which is by its nature pretty soporific, capable of outdoing laudanum or academic speeches . . .

No, you morons; no, you bloated cretins! A book will not make jellied soup; a novel is not a pair of waterproof boots; a sonnet is not a syringe; a stage-play is not a railway, essentially civilising as all these items may be, leading mankind along the path of progress.

By the bowels of all the Popes, past, present and future, no – two hundred thousand times no! You cannot make a cloth cap out of a metonymy; you cannot put on a simile instead of a slipper; you cannot use an antithesis as an umbrella; and regrettably you cannot slap a few flashy rhymes around your belly as a waistcoat. I am deeply convinced that an ode is too flimsy to serve as winter clothing: its strophe, antistrophe and epistrophe[9] would leave you no better dressed than that cynic's wife who, so the story goes, contented herself with her virtue alone for a chemise, and went about stark naked. (On the other hand, the celebrated M. de La Calprenède, when asked once what his coat was made of, replied '*Silvandre*', this being the title of the successful play he had recently staged.)[10] Such reasoning can only make us shrug our shoulders above our heads, higher than the English hunchback Richard III. Yet people who claim to be economists aiming to reconstruct society from top to bottom do come out with this kind of drivel in all seriousness.

A novel is useful in two ways: one material, the other spiritual, if one can apply such a term to novels. The material use is, in the first place, a few thousand francs in the author's pocket, as ballast that prevents him being carried off by the wind or by the devil. For the publisher it means a fine thoroughbred horse that prances and trots ahead of his gig of ebony and steel, as Figaro puts it. For the papermaker, it will be a new mill beside some stream or other, probably spoiling a beauty-spot. For the printers, a few tons of logwood to help moisten their throats every week. For the reading-room, heaps of small-change covered in truly proletarian verdigris, an amount of grease sufficient, if gathered and exploited, to put the whaling trade out of business. The usefulness of novels in the spiritual sense is that, while reading them, we fall asleep and we do not read virtuous, progressive, or utilitarian journals, which are the equivalent of indigestible and stupefying drugs. Taking that into account, how could anyone claim that novels make no contribution to civilisation?

I shall make no mention here of tobacconists, grocers, or vendors of potato-fries, who have a strong interest in this branch of literature, since the paper it is printed on is generally of a higher quality than newsprint.

Listening to the republican and Saint-Simonian gentlemen sounding off is really enough to make us double up with laughter. I would like to know, in the first place, what exactly they mean by this great hulking noun with which they daily fill up the emptiness of their columns, and which they employ as their sacred shibboleth: Utility. What kind of word is this, and what can it apply to?

There are two kinds of utility, and the sense of the term is always relative. What is useful to one person is useless to another. Let us say you are a shoemaker, while I am a poet. It is useful for me to have my second line rhyme with my first, so a rhyming dictionary is of real use to me, but to you it would be of no use except to cobble a pair of old boots. It would also be fair to say that your paring-knife would not get me very far in composing an ode. To this you will object that a poet is inferior to a cobbler, in that people could do without one better than the other. Without intending any disparagement of the shoemaker's illustrious profession, which I hold in as much esteem as that of constitutional monarch, I humbly submit that I would rather leave my shoe poorly stitched than my line poorly rhymed, and that I would willingly do without shoes before I would go without poems. As I hardly ever go out, and can walk more easily on my head than on my feet, I wear out fewer shoes than a virtuous republican who spends his time scuttling from one ministry to another in the hope of some job falling his way.

I am aware that there are people who prefer mills to churches, and feeding their bodies to feeding their souls. To such people I have nothing to say. They deserve to be economists in this world, and in the next.

Is there anything absolutely useful in this world, or in this life? First of all, there is very little use in our being in this world or in being alive. I challenge the wisest among us to tell us what purpose we serve, unless it be not subscribing to the *Constitutionnel*[11] or any kind of paper whatsoever. And then, if we grant the utility of our existence *a priori*, what is really useful to sustain it? Strictly speaking, some soup and a piece of meat twice a day is all we need to fill our stomachs. A man can manage with a coffin two feet wide and six feet long when he is dead, and hardly needs much more space than that when alive. A hollow cube seven or eight feet each way, with a vent to breathe through, a single cell in the beehive: he needs no more than that for lodging and to keep the rain off his back. A blanket wrapped properly around his body will protect him from the cold as well as, or better than, the most elegant and smartly cut frock-coat from Staub's.[12] With that, he will be able to survive, in the strict sense. People say one can live on twenty-five sous a day; but then, staving off death is not living, and I cannot see how a town organised on utilitarian lines would be any more enjoyable to live in than Père Lachaise cemetery.

Nothing beautiful is indispensable to life. Were we to get rid of all the flowers, the world would not suffer materially, but then who would want to abolish flowers? I would sooner give up potatoes than roses, and I believe there is only one utilitarian in the world who could dig up a bed of tulips to plant cabbages.

What use is the beauty of women? For an economist, any woman will do, so long as she is medically fit to produce children. What use is music? What use is painting? Who would be so crazy as to prefer Mozart to Carrel,[13] or Michelangelo to the inventor of white mustard? Nothing is truly beautiful unless it is useless. Everything useful is ugly, because it expresses some need, and man's needs, like his poor weak nature, are ignoble and ugly. The most useful place in a house is the lavatory.

Speaking for myself, and without meaning to offend these gentlemen, I am one of those for whom the superfluous is a necessity. I value things and people in inverse proportion to the purposes they serve for me. In preference to a certain pot that is useful to me, I like a Chinese vase decorated with dragons and mandarins, which is of no use to me at all; and among my talents the one I value the most is that of being baffled by word-puzzles and charades. I would quite happily renounce my rights as a Frenchman and a citizen to be able to see a genuine Raphael picture, or a beautiful woman naked: Princess Borghese when she posed for Canova, say, or Julia Grisi[14] slipping into her bath. I would personally agree most willingly to the restoration of that cannibal Charles X, if he brought me back from his Bohemian castle a case of Tokay or Johannisburg; and I could reconcile myself to the widening of the franchise if some streets could also be widened, and some other things narrowed. Not that I am a dilettante, but I do prefer the sound of fiddles and tambourines to that of the President's little bell. I would sell my trousers to have a ring for my finger, and my bread for a bit of jam. The most suitable occupation for a civilised man seems to me to be doing nothing, or smoking his pipe or cigar in a pensive fashion. I also have a high regard for skittle-players, as well as accomplished versifiers. As you can see, the principles of utilitarianism are very far from my own, so I shall never become editor of a virtuous periodical – unless I undergo a conversion, which would be rather amusing.

Instead of establishing public prizes to reward virtue, I would prefer to imitate that great misunderstood philosopher Sardanapalus[15] by awarding a lavish bounty to whoever could come up with a new pleasure, since delight seems to me to be the goal of life, and the only useful thing in the world. God has willed it thus, He who created women, perfumes, sunlight, beautiful flowers, good wines, frisky horses, greyhounds, and angora cats; He who said not to his angels 'Be virtuous' but 'Be loving'; He who gave us sensitive lips so as to kiss women, eyes that can look up to see the light, a subtle sense of smell to inhale the perfume of flowers, sturdy thighs to grip the flanks of stallions and so fly swifter than thought (with no need for railways or steam-boilers), and delicate hands to stroke greyhounds' sleek heads, cats' velvety backs, and the smooth shoulders of creatures unacquainted with virtue; and Who, to conclude, has granted to us alone the triply glorious privilege of drinking without being thirsty, of striking lights, and of making love in all seasons, which distinguishes us from the brutes far better than the habit of reading newspapers or drawing up charters.

My God! What a stupid thing is this so-called perfectibility of mankind that they are forever dinning into our ears! It amounts really to saying that man is a machine that can be improved upon, so that if a gear could be adjusted here or a counterweight placed just so there, it could run more smoothly or conveniently. When they get to the point at which man can have a double stomach so he can ruminate like an ox, or eyes at the back of his head so he can see, like Janus, people poking their tongues at him behind his back (and inspect his 'baseness' in a less awkward posture than that of the Athenian Venus Callipyge),[16] or wings fixed to his shoulder-blades so he no longer has to pay six sous to get on a bus, or when they have made a new organ for him, that would be more like it: 'perfectibility' would begin to mean something. But ever since they started on this perfecting, what have they managed that had not been done just as well or better before the days of the Flood?

Have we attained the capacity to drink more than they did in the times of benighted barbarism (as we used to say)? Alexander, the dubious friend of the handsome Hephaestion, did not drink too badly, even though in his day there was no *Journal of Useful Knowledge*,[17] and I cannot think of a utilitarian who could drain the great goblet he called Hercules's cup without becoming more sozzled and bloated than a hippopotamus or than Lepeintre the Younger.[18] Marshal de Bassompierre,[19] who drained his huge top-boot in toasting the health of the Swiss cantons, seems to me singularly admirable in his fashion, and unlikely to be outdone.

Which of the economists will expand our stomachs to hold as many beefsteaks as Milo of Crotona, who ate an ox? The menu at the Café Anglais, or at Véfour's or at any other famous restaurant you could name, seems to me pretty meagre and hardly very exclusive compared with the menu of Trimalchio's feast.[20] At whose table these days do they serve up a wild boar sow with her litter of twelve on a single platter? Who has eaten eels and lampreys fattened on human flesh? Do you really believe Brillat-Savarin has improved upon Apicius?[21] And what of stout Vitellius,[22] devourer of offal? Would he be able to find enough at Chevet's to fill his famous Shield of Minerva with pheasants' and pigeons' brains, flamingoes' tongues and scarfish livers? The oysters you can have at the Rocher de Cancale are really something rather refined compared with the oysters of Lucrinus, for which a sea was specially created.[23]

The townhouses built around Paris by the Regency gentry are pitiful little cottages when compared with the villas of the Roman patricians at Baiae, at Capri, and at Tibur. The titanic magnificence of those great voluptuaries who built eternal monuments for the pleasures of a day ought to make us prostrate ourselves before the genius of the ancient world, and strike out forever from our dictionaries the word 'perfectibility'.

Has anyone invented a single new cardinal sin? Woefully, there are still only seven of them (the tally of a righteous man's daily lapses), just as before, which is all rather feeble. After a century of progress at this rate, I still don't think any lover could repeat the thirteenth labour of Hercules.[24] Could we oblige our divinity with a single effort unseen in the days of Solomon?[25] Quite the opposite view is held by plenty of eminent authorities and most respectable ladies who claim that gallantry is on the decline.

So what does all this chatter about progress amount to? I know that you will tell me we have an Upper Chamber and a Lower Chamber, and that people are hoping everyone will have the vote before long, and that the number of representatives will be doubled or trebled. Do you think there are too few errors of French committed in the legislature, and that there are not enough legislators to get through the miserable job they have to handle? I find it hard to understand the usefulness of cooping up two or three hundred provincial types in a wooden shed with a ceiling painted by Fragonard so that they can fumble and tinker with any number of ridiculous and ghastly little laws. What difference does it make if it is a sword, a sprinkler, or an umbrella that rules over you?[26] One way or another it is still a stick, so it amazes me that progressive men should be debating the choice of a rod for their own backs, when it would be far more progressive and less expensive just to break it up and throw the pieces to the devil.

1834; translated by Chris Baldick, 2011

CHARLES BAUDELAIRE

In Praise of Make-Up

There is a song, so trivial and inept that I scarcely dare quote it in a work that makes some claim to be serious, but it conveys perfectly, in Vaudeville style, the aesthetic of unthinking people: 'Nature embellishes beauty!' Presumably the poet, if he had been able to speak French properly, would have said: Simplicity embellishes beauty! which is the same as this truth of a quite unexpected kind: Nothing embellishes what is.

Most of the errors made about beauty come from false eighteenth-century conceptions about ethics. At that time, nature was understood to be the basis, source, and type of all possible good and beauty. The denial of original sin played no small part in the general blindness of that period. If, however, we stick to the simple, visible facts, to the experience of all ages, and to the *Gazette des Tribunaux*,[27] we will see that nature teaches us nothing, or next to nothing; other than compelling man to sleep, drink, eat, and protect himself as best he can against inclement weather. It is nature, let us not forget, that drives man to kill his brother, to eat him, imprison and torture him; for, as soon as we leave behind the realm of needs and necessities for that of luxury and pleasure, we see that nature can counsel nothing but crime. This infallible nature has created parricide and cannibalism and a thousand other abominations, which delicate feeling and modesty prevent our mentioning. It is philosophy (the right kind) and religion that command us to look after our poor and infirm parents. Nature (which is none other than the voice of our own self-interest) orders us to kill them. If you consider and analyse everything that is natural, all the actions and desires of pure natural man, you will find nothing but hideousness. Everything that is beautiful and noble is the product of reason and calculation. Crime, for which the human animal developed a fond taste in his mother's womb, is by origin natural. Virtue, on the other hand, is artificial, supernatural, since in every age and in every country gods and prophetesses have been required to teach it to bestial humanity, and since man, by himself, would have been powerless to discover it. Evil happens without effort, naturally, and fortuitously; good is always the product of some art. All I say about nature, as a bad counsellor in matters of ethics, and about reason, as the true reformer and redeemer, can be applied to the realm of beauty. And so I am led to regard finery as one of the signs of the primitive nobility of the human soul. Those races of people that our confused and perverted civilisation pleases to call savage, with a laughable sense of pride and complacency, comprehend, just as children do, the high spiritual quality of dressing-up. The savage and the infant show their disgust for the real by their naive desire for things that glitter, for brightly coloured feathers, for shimmering fabrics, for the superlative majesty of artificial shapes, thereby proving unwittingly the immateriality of their souls. Woe to him, who, like Louis XV (who was not the product of a true civilisation, but of a recurrence of barbarism), pushes depravity to the point of only enjoying nature plain and simple.

Fashion must therefore be thought of as a symptom of the taste for the ideal that floats on the surface in the human brain, above all the earthly and disgusting things accumulated by natural life, as a sublime distortion of nature, or rather as a permanent and continual attempt to reform nature. And so, likewise, it has been judiciously observed (without knowing the reason) that every fashion has its charm, that is to say, each one is relatively charming, being a new attempt, more or less successful, at being beautiful, or an imperfect approximation of an ideal, the desire for which constantly teases the ever-unsatisfied human mind. If we really want to enjoy fashions, then we should not look upon them as dead things; we might as well admire a dead monk's cast-offs hung up, limp and inert, like the skin of St Bartholomew,[28] in the cupboard of a second-hand clothes shop. We should picture them as living beings, imbued with life by the beautiful women who wore them. Only then can we understand their meaning and value. So if our aphorism 'Every fashion has its charm', strikes you as being too absolute, you could say without fear of contradiction: 'They all once had their proper charm.'

Woman is well within her rights, and even has a kind of duty to keep up a magical and supernatural appearance; she must astonish and she must delight; idol that she is, to be adored she must be adorned. And so it follows, that she must borrow from all the arts the means of raising herself above nature all the better to conquer the hearts and dazzle the wits of men. It hardly matters that the artificiality of her tricks is obvious to all, so long as their effect is clearly successful and still irresistible. These reflections lead the philosopher-artist to find ready justification for the ways in which women through the ages fortify and, so to speak, deify their fragile beauty. These ways are countless; but, to restrict ourselves to what we now commonly call make-up, who can fail to see that the use of rice-powder, so foolishly denounced by naive philosophers, has as its purpose and result to cover all the blemishes that nature has so outrageously sprinkled across the complexion, and to create an abstract unity of texture and colour in the skin, and that this uniformity, like that produced by tights, immediately renders the human being like a statue, that is to say, like a divine and superior being? As for black eyeliner, and rouge defining the upper part of the cheek, although their use is based on the same principle, on the need to outdo nature, it results in the satisfaction of a quite opposite need. Red and black represent life, a supernatural and excessive life; black outlines round the eyes give a deeper and stranger look, give the eye the definite appearance of a window open on infinity; rouge which creates a fiery glow on the cheek bones makes the pupils shine brightly, and gives a lovely woman's face the mysterious passion of a priestess.

Thus, if I have been properly understood, putting make-up on is not to be done with the vulgar, unworthy intention of imitating fair nature, or competing with youth. Besides, I have pointed out already that artifice does not embellish ugliness and can only serve beauty. Who would dare assign to art the fruitless function of imitating nature? Make-up has no need of concealment, no need to avoid discovery; it can, on the contrary, flaunt itself, if not with affectation, at least with a sort of candour.

I allow people whose weighty seriousness prevents them from looking for beauty in its subtlest manifestations, to laugh at my thoughts and to condemn their puerile solemnity; their harsh judgements have no effect on me; I am content to make my appeal to true artists, and to women who have received at birth a spark of that sacred fire which they use to illuminate their whole being.

1863; translated by Jane Desmarais, 2011

WALTER PATER

Conclusion to *The Renaissance*

Λέγει που Ἡράκλειτος ὅτι πάντα χωρεῖ καὶ οὐδὲν μένει[29]

To regard all things and principles of things as inconstant modes our fashions has more and more become the tendency of modern thought. Let us begin with that which is without – our physical life. Fix upon it in one of its more exquisite intervals, the moment, for instance, of delicious recoil from the flood of water in summer heat. What is the whole physical life in that moment but a combination of natural elements to which science gives their names? But these elements, phosphorus and lime and delicate fibres, are present not in the human body alone: we detect them in places most remote from it. Our physical life is a perpetual motion of them – the passage of the blood, the wasting and repairing of the lenses of the eye, the modification of the tissues of the brain by every ray of light and sound – processes which science reduces to simpler and more elementary forces. Like the elements of which we are composed, the action of these forces extends beyond us; it rusts iron and ripens corn. Far out on every side of us these elements are broadcast, driven by many forces; and birth and gesture and death and the springing of violets from the grave[30] are but a few out of ten thousand resulting combinations. That clear perpetual outline of face and limb is but an image of ours under which we group them – a design in a web, the actual threads of which pass out beyond it. This at least of flame-like our life has, that it is but the concurrence, renewed from moment to moment, of forces parting sooner or later on their ways.

Or if we begin with the inward world of thought and feeling, the whirlpool is still more rapid, the flame more eager and devouring. There it is no longer the gradual darkening of the eye and fading of colour from the wall, – the movement of the shore side, where the water flows down indeed, though in apparent rest, – but the race of the midstream, a drift of momentary acts of sight and passion and thought. At first sight experience seems to bury us under a flood of external objects, pressing upon us with a sharp importunate reality, calling us out of ourselves in a thousand forms of action. But when reflection begins to play upon those objects they are dissipated under its influence; the cohesive force is suspended like a trick of magic; each object is loosed into a group of impressions, – colour, odour, texture, – in the mind of the observer. And if we continue to dwell on this world, not of objects in the solidity with which language invests them, but of impressions unstable, flickering, inconsistent, which burn and are extinguished with our consciousness of them, it contracts still further; the whole scope of observation is dwarfed to the narrow chamber of the individual mind. Experience, already reduced to a swarm of impressions, is ringed round for each one of us by that thick wall of personality through which no real voice has ever pierced on its way to us, or from us to that which we can only conjecture to be without. Every one of those impressions is the impression of the individual in his isolation, each mind keeping as a solitary prisoner its own dream of a world.

Analysis goes a step further still, and tells us that those impressions of the individual to which, for each one of us, experience dwindles down, are in perpetual flight; that each of them is limited by time, and that as time is infinitely divisible, each of them is infinitely divisible also; all that is actual in it being a single moment, gone while we try to apprehend it, of which it may ever be more truly said that it has ceased to be than that it is. To such a tremulous wisp constantly re-forming itself on the stream, to a single sharp impression, with a sense in it, a relic more or less fleeting, of such moments gone by, what is *real* in our life fines itself down. It is with the movement, the passage and dissolution of impressions, images, sensations, that analysis leaves off, – that continual vanishing away, that strange perpetual weaving and unweaving of ourselves.

Philosophiren, says Novalis, *ist dephlegmatisiren, vivificiren.*[31] The service of philosophy, and of religion and culture as well to the human spirit, is to startle it into a sharp and eager observation. Every moment some form grows perfect in hand or face; some tone on the hills or sea is choicer than the rest; some mood of passion or insight or intellectual excitement is irresistibly real and attractive for us, – for that moment only. Not the fruit of experience, but experience itself, is the end. A counted number of pulses only is given to us of a variegated, dramatic life. How may we see in them all that is to be seen in them by the finest senses? How can we pass most swiftly from point to point, and be present always at the focus where the greatest number of vital forces unite in their purest energy?

To burn always with this hard gem-like flame, to maintain this ecstasy, is success in life. Failure is to form habits; for habit is relative to a stereotyped world; meantime it is only the roughness of the eye that makes any two persons, things, situations, seem alike. While all melts under our feet, we may well catch at any exquisite passion, or any contribution to knowledge that seems, by a lifted horizon, to set the spirit free for a moment, or any stirring of the senses, strange dyes, strange flowers, and curious odours, or work of the artist's hands, or the face of one's friend. Not to discriminate every moment some passionate attitude in those about us, and in the brilliance of their gifts some tragic dividing of forces on their ways is, on this short day of frost and sun, to sleep before evening. With this sense of the splendour of our experience and of its awful brevity, gathering all we are into one desperate effort to see and touch, we shall hardly have time to make theories about the things we see and touch. What we have to do is to be for ever curiously testing new opinions and courting new impressions, never acquiescing in a facile orthodoxy of Comte, or of Hegel,[32] or of our own. Theories, religious or philosophical ideas, as points of view, instruments of criticism, may help us to gather up what might otherwise pass unregarded by us. *La philosophie, c'est la microscope de la pensée.*[33] The theory, or idea, or system, which requires of us the sacrifice of any part of this experience, in consideration of some interest into which we cannot enter, or some abstract morality we have not identified with ourselves, or what is only conventional, has no real claim upon us.

One of the most beautiful places in the writings of Rousseau is that in the sixth book of the 'Confessions',[34] where he describes the awakening in him of the literary sense. An undefinable taint of death had clung always about him, and now in early manhood he believed himself stricken by mortal disease. He asked himself how he might make as much as possible of the interval that remained; and he was not biassed by anything in his previous life when he decided that it must be by intellectual excitement, which he found just then in the clear, fresh writings of Voltaire. Well, we are all *condamnés*, as Victor Hugo says: *les hommes sont tous condamnés à morte avec des sursis indéfinis*:[35] we have an interval, and then our place knows us no more. Some spend this interval in listlessness, some in high passions, the wisest in art and song. For our one chance is in expanding that interval, in getting as many pulsations as possible into the given time. High passions may give one this quickened sense of life, ecstasy and sorrow of love, political or religious enthusiasm, or the 'enthusiasm of humanity'.[36] Only, be sure it is passion, that it does yield you this fruit of a quickened, multiplied consciousness. Of this wisdom, the poetic passion, the desire of beauty, the love of art for art's sake,[37] has most; for art comes to you professing frankly to give nothing but the highest quality to your moments as they pass, and simply for those moments' sake.

1873

ANATOLE BAJU

The School of Decadence

Literature and manners

Life is the great generating force of all literature. It determines movements in Thought: Take a look at other developments in literature, they are all the result of changing ways of life or of a social transformation.

As nothing stays the same for ever and progress propels life ever forward, so there is a new literary form for each stage in the development of society. Men are incapable of eternalising any literary movement whatsoever; even when they do manage to hold new ideas in check, then disgust with the past and an eager anticipation of the unknown are enough to provoke a change in form.

Literature is indeed the soul of society. It reflects all its ideas, and is more than its flesh, more than its blood: literature is the breath which expresses the life of society.

Monuments are not always such a faithful and powerful record of their times. The written thought embraces an entire epoch, summarises all of its trends, and is the unique source of this lived, living, breathless life that we love, and that shakes us to the core of our being with electric and vibrant commotion.

Naturalism was the exact image of this bastard society falsely called republican; it represented it as it is. Those who find Naturalism outrageous have only our epoch to blame because Naturalism merely reflects our vices without exaggerating them. It is indeed the literature of these dog-eat-dog times when governments and men of all classes, driven by gluttony, give themselves up to their basic instincts, with reckless abandon, like the Roman emperors with their slaves, at the close of some monstrous and abominable orgy.

But today we recognise ourselves; we know that the appetites of some individuals are more easily subdued by hunger than by food: each one takes up his position and the world establishes its old equilibrium. Heavy, slumbering impotence and disgust are spreading over the planet; the honest man exasperated by the triumph of Evil and beaten by an all-powerful hostile destiny, is brought to his knees by lassitude, torpor, and ennui.

The consequence of this situation and the separation of the classes must be a new literature, corresponding to the mentality of society.

Modern spleen

Our age is not sick; it is tired, and above all nauseated. The noblest efforts of philanthropy have failed through the fault of those whose destiny it should have improved. How many men, pushing self-denial to the point of withdrawing from the world, have worked for the good of humanity and have only been mocked by it!

Everything that has been done to raise the moral and intellectual standards of the masses has been fruitless. How strange the society of the future! all the aristocracy will do is become more refined as civilisation progresses, while the lower classes, debasing themselves even more, will discover every possible kind of infamy and unknown depravity.

Faced with these lamentable successes, the man of intellect feels a profound disgust, and incurable, inescapable Dejection [*spleen*] grinds him down, like the vault of a church that has fallen upon his shoulders. Oh! this Dejection is not the spleen of emperors jaded with power, women and orgies: it is darker, more intense, more incurable, since it leads man to curse existence, to call upon Death and to wish for Nothingness.

We must not infer from what has gone before that modern man is sad, a pessimist in the true sense of the word. On the contrary, he is happy, or, if he is not really, then he knows how to renounce his ruling despair in the face of this highly superficial world. Overcome by fatality, he knows that he is mortally wounded; but, stronger in his defeat than the victor who broke him, he represses his pain in the depths of his soul and hides it beneath a semblance of gaiety, a sublime challenge that he throws to destiny to demonstrate that while it may destroy his efforts, it cannot destroy his indomitable and fearless pride!

It is while isolated even within the crowd, when the thinker is abstracting from the existence of material beings which pulse around him, when in the solitude of his mind he submerges himself in a unified contemplation of the world, that this immense and terrifying Dejection overcomes him and forces him to show a yearning for Nothingness, which is humiliating for him, and dishonourable for divinity. Oh! he suffers intensely from this atrocious illness whose effects are all the more terrible because the causes are completely unknown, or perhaps do not even exist.

Faced with this proof of his powerlessness, seeing his intelligence crushed to death by the cog-wheels of ignorant destiny, man is disgusted by life, and the nausea he feels about an automaton-like existence animated by blind forces transposes itself to his writings and gives decadent literature a heavy or light-hearted form, according to whether he expresses the bitterness of his woes or the bitter irony of his intolerable despair.

Decadence [Décadisme]

Decadent literature sums up the spirit of our times, that is to say, the spirit of the intellectual elite of modern society. When it comes to Art, we cannot take into account the multitude, which does not think, and which can be counted only in the numerical sense. The intellectually elevated public, the only one that matters and whose approval is true validation, has had enough of all these false emotions, these vulgar stirrings, these banal conventions of an imaginary world, perpetrated by previous literary movements in order to stimulate the senses.

This elite is tired of all the romantic and naturalist rubbish which sometimes captivates the imagination, but which is powerless in preventing the heart becoming numb.

What it wants is life; it is thirsty for the intensity of life shaped by progress, it needs to get drunk on it; it wants to condense a number of human lives into one only, its own, to extract its life-blood and to set itself aquiver. By a bizarre contradiction, but which, however, explains the effect of despair, the need to live is the characteristic of these times in which we seem to have acquired the sombre and shocking certitude of Nothingness.

Decadent literature promotes itself as the reflection of this splenetic world. It only takes that which is directly concerned with life. No descriptions: take everything as read. Just a quick summary giving the impression of objects. No depiction, but make us feel: give our heart the sensation of things, whether by new constructions, or by symbols evoking the idea with greater intensity by comparison. Synthesise the subject-matter, but analyse the heart.

This programme is so simple and very much in harmony with modern life. Today, we have seen everything, we know everything, we have felt all the emotions; we have an unbridled need for new sensations. Now, we have examined all the parts, we have to consider the whole.

Given the relentless progress of things, man needs to enjoy a lot in a short space of time. He can no longer read long adventure novels full of endless descriptions.

What do unlikely heroes matter to him? he is a man. What do descriptions do for him? he has a deadened heart which needs to throb. What he wants is contact with the thrills of life in order to electrify own existence.

Writers who have been impregnated with the spirit of this *fin de siècle* have to be brief and narrate the intimate struggles of the Heart, the only thing that interests man, and which he doesn't know, will never know, because the human heart is as vast as Infinity.

Sad to say, but humanity cannot be reduced to a few general types motivated by the same rules, and obeying the same influences. Just as all men have the same form, but differ according to characteristics, so, to portray all hearts, would take as many monographs as there are individuals.

Eternity, the Human Heart and Infinity are three things which man will never completely understand, three mysteries which will ever defy Science and which are the irrefutable proof of human impotence.

1887; translated by Jane Desmarais, 2011

GEORGE MOORE

Confessions of a Young Man: from chapter 9

Respectability! – a suburban villa, a piano in the drawing-room, and going home to dinner. Such things are no doubt very excellent, but they do not promote intensity of feeling, fervour of mind; and as art is in itself an outcry against the animality of human existence, it would be well that the life of the artist should be a practical protest against the so-called decencies of life; and he can best protest by frequenting a tavern and cutting his club. In the past the artist has always been an outcast; it is only latterly he has become domesticated, and judging by results, it is clear that if Bohemianism is not a necessity it is at least an adjuvant. For if long locks and general dissoluteness were not an aid and a way to pure thought, why have they been so long his characteristics? If lovers were not necessary for the development of poet, novelist, and actress, why have they always had lovers – Sappho, George Eliot, George Sand, Rachel, Sara? But good Mrs. Kendal suckles her child by day and plays Rosalind at night.[38] Truly a ridiculous endeavour! for to realize the transformation, a woman must have sinned; only through sin may we learn the charm of innocence. A woman must have had more than one lover to play Rosalind, and if she has been made to wait in the rain and been beaten she will have suffered enough, and through suffering qualified herself for the part. Sara makes no pretence to virtue, but she introduces her son to an English duchess, and throws over a nation for the love of Richepin. She can, therefore, say as none other –

> 'Ce n'est plus qu'une ardeur dans mes veines cachée,
> C'est Vénus tout entière à sa proie attachée.'[39]

Swinburne, when he dodged about London, a lively young dog, wrote 'Poems and Ballads' and 'Chastelard'; since he has gone to live at Putney, he has contributed to the *Nineteenth Century*, and published an interesting little volume entitled, 'A Century of Rondels,' in which he continued his plaint about his mother the sea.[40]

Respectability is sweeping the picturesque out of life; national costumes are disappearing. The kilt is going or gone in the highlands, and the smock in the southlands, even the Japanese are becoming Christian and respectable; in another quarter of a century silk hats and pianos will be found in every house in Yeddo.[41] Too true that universal uniformity is the future of the world; and when Mr. Morris speaks of the democratic art to be when the world is socialistic,[42] I ask, whence will the unfortunates draw their inspiration? To-day our plight is pitiable enough – the duke, the jockey-boy, and the artist are exactly alike; they are dressed by the same tailor, they dine at the same clubs, they swear the same oaths, they speak equally bad English, they love the same women. Such a state of things is dreary enough, but what unimaginable dreariness there will be when there are neither rich nor poor, when all have been educated, when self-education has ceased. A terrible world to dream of, worse, far worse, in darkness and hopelessness than Dante's lowest circle of hell. The spectres of famine, of the plague, of war, etc., are mild and gracious symbols compared with that menacing figure, Universal Education, with which we are threatened, which has already eunuched the genius of the last five-and-twenty years of the nineteenth century, and produced a limitless abortion in that of future time. Education, I tremble before thy dreaded name. The cruelties of Nero, of Caligula, what were they? – a few crunched limbs in the amphitheatre; but thine, O Education, are the yearning of souls sick of life, maddening discontent, all the fearsome and fathomless sufferings of the mind. When Goethe said 'More light,' he said the wickedest and most infamous words that human lips ever spoke.[43] In old days, when a people became too highly civilised the barbarians came down from the north and regenerated that nation with darkness; but now there are no more barbarians, and sooner or later I am convinced that we shall have to end the evil by summary edicts – the obstruction no doubt will be severe, the equivalents of Gladstone and Morley[44] will stop at nothing to defeat the Bill; but it will nevertheless be carried by patriotic Conservative and Unionist majorities, and it will be written in the Statute Book that not more than one child in a hundred shall be taught to read, and no more than one in ten thousand shall learn the piano.

Such will be the end of Respectability, but the end is still far distant. We are now in a period of decadence growing steadily more and more acute. The old gods are falling about us, there is little left to raise our hearts and minds to, and amid the wreck and ruin of things only a snobbery is left to us, thank heaven, deeply graven in the English heart; the snob is now the ark that floats triumphant over the democratic wave; the faith of the old world reposes in his breast, and he shall proclaim it when the waters have subsided.

1888

OSCAR WILDE

Preface to *The Picture of Dorian Gray*

The artist is the creator of beautiful things.

To reveal art and conceal the artist is art's aim.

The critic is he who can translate into another manner or a new material his impression of beautiful things.

The highest, as the lowest, form of criticism is a mode of autobiography.

Those who find ugly meanings in beautiful things are corrupt without being charming. This is a fault.

Those who find beautiful meanings in beautiful things are the cultivated. For these there is hope.

They are the elect to whom beautiful things mean only Beauty.

There is no such thing as a moral or an immoral book. Books are well written, or badly written. That is all.

The nineteenth century dislike of Realism is the rage of Caliban seeing his own face in a glass.

The nineteenth century dislike of Romanticism is the rage of Caliban not seeing his own face in a glass.

The moral life of man forms part of the subject-matter of the artist, but the morality of art consists in the perfect use of an imperfect medium.

No artist desires to prove anything. Even things that are true can be proved.

No artist has ethical sympathies. An ethical sympathy in an artist is an unpardonable mannerism of style.

No artist is ever morbid. The artist can express everything.

Thought and language are to the artist instruments of an art.

Vice and virtue are to the artist materials for an art.

From the point of view of form, the type of all the arts is the art of the musician. From the point of view of feeling, the actor's craft is the type.

All art is at once surface and symbol.

Those who go beneath the surface do so at their peril.

Those who read the symbol do so at their peril.

It is the spectator, and not life, that art really mirrors.

Diversity of opinion about a work of art shows that the work is new, complex, and vital.

When critics disagree the artist is in accord with himself.

We can forgive a man for making a useful thing as long as he does not admire it. The only excuse for making a useless thing is that one admires it intensely.

All art is quite useless.

1891

Phrases and philosophies for the use of the young

The first duty in life is to be as artificial as possible. What the second duty is no one has as yet discovered.

Wickedness is a myth invented by good people to account for the curious attractiveness of others.

If the poor only had profiles there would be no difficulty in solving the problem of poverty.

Those who see any difference between soul and body have neither.

A really well-made buttonhole is the only link between Art and Nature.

Religions die when they are proved to be true. Science is the record of dead religions.

The well-bred contradict other people. The wise contradict themselves.

Nothing that actually occurs is of the smallest importance.

Dullness is the coming of age of seriousness.

In all unimportant matters, style, not sincerity, is the essential. In all important matters, style, not sincerity, is the essential.

If one tells the truth, one is sure, sooner or later, to be found out.

Pleasure is the only thing one should live for. Nothing ages like happiness.

It is only by not paying one's bills that one can hope to live in the memory of the commercial classes.

No crime is vulgar, but all vulgarity is crime. Vulgarity is the conduct of others.

Only the shallow know themselves.

Time is a waste of money.

One should always be a little improbable.

There is a fatality about all good resolutions. They are invariably made too soon.

The only way to atone for being occasionally a little over-dressed is by being always absolutely over-educated.

To be premature is to be perfect.

Any preoccupation with ideas of what is right or wrong in conduct shows an arrested intellectual development.

Ambition is the last refuge of the failure.

A truth ceases to be true when more than one person believes in it.

In examinations the foolish ask questions that the wise cannot answer.

Greek dress was in its essence inartistic. Nothing should reveal the body but the body.

One should either be a work of art, or wear a work of art.

It is only the superficial qualities that last. Man's deeper nature is soon found out.

Industry is the root of all ugliness.

The ages live in history through their anachronisms.

It is only the gods who taste of death. Apollo has passed away, but Hyacinth, whom men say he slew, lives on. Nero and Narcissus are always with us.

The old believe everything: the middle-aged suspect everything: the young know everything.

The condition of perfection is idleness: the aim of perfection is youth.

Only the great masters of style ever succeed in being obscure.

There is something tragic about the enormous number of young men there are in England at the present moment who start life with perfect profiles, and end by adopting some useful profession.

To love oneself is the beginning of a life-long romance.

1894

ARTHUR SYMONS

Preface to the second edition of *Silhouettes*: Being a Word on Behalf of Patchouli

An ingenious reviewer once described some verses of mine as 'unwholesome', because, he said, they had 'a faint smell of Patchouli about them'.[45] I am a little sorry he chose Patchouli, for that is not a particularly favourite scent with me. If he had only chosen Peau d'Espagne, which has a subtle meaning, or Lily of the Valley, with which I have associations![46] But Patchouli will serve. Let me ask, then, in republishing, with additions, a collection of little pieces, many of which have been objected to, at one time or another, as being somewhat liberately frivolous, why art should not, if it please, concern itself with the artificially charming, which, I suppose, is what my critic means by Patchouli? All art, surely, is a form of artifice, and thus, to the truly devout mind, condemned already, if not as actively noxious, at all events as needless. That is a point of view which I quite understand, and its conclusion I hold to be absolutely logical. I have the utmost respect for the people who refuse to read a novel, to go to the theatre, or to learn dancing. That is to have convictions and to live up to them. I understand also the point of view from which a work of art is tolerated in so far as it is actually militant on behalf of a religious or moral idea. But what I fail to understand are those delicate, invisible degrees by which a distinction is drawn between this form of art and that; the hesitations, and compromises, and timorous advances, and shocked retreats, of the Puritan conscience once emancipated and yet afraid of liberty. However you may try to convince yourself to the contrary, a work of art can be judged only from two standpoints: the standpoint from which its art is measured entirely by its morality, and the standpoint from which its morality is measured entirely by its art.

Here, for once, in connection with these 'Silhouettes', I have not, if my recollection serves me, been accused of actual immorality. I am but a fair way along the 'primrose path', not yet within singeing distance of the 'everlasting bonfire'.[47] In other words, I have not yet written 'London Nights',[48] which, it appears (I can scarcely realise it, in my innocent abstraction in aesthetical matters), has no very salutary reputation among the blameless moralists of the press. I need not, therefore, on this occasion, concern myself with more than the curious fallacy by which there is supposed to be something inherently wrong in artistic work which deals frankly and lightly with the very real charm of the lighter emotions and the more fleeting sensations.

I do not wish to assert that the kind of verse which happened to reflect certain moods of mine at a certain period of my life is the best kind of verse in itself, or is likely to seem to me, in other years, when other moods may have made me their own, the best kind of verse for my own expression of myself. Nor do I affect to doubt that the creation of the supreme emotion is a higher form of art than the reflection of the most exquisite sensation, the evocation of the most magical impression. I claim only an equal liberty for the rendering of every mood of that variable and inexplicable and contradictory creature which we call ourselves, of every aspect under which we are gifted or condemned to apprehend the beauty and strangeness and curiosity of the visible world.

Patchouli! Well, why not Patchouli? Is there any 'reason in nature' why we should write exclusively about the natural blush, if the delicately acquired blush of rouge has any attraction for us? Both exist; both, I think, are charming in their way; and the latter, as a subject, has, at all events, more novelty. If you prefer your 'new-mown hay' in the hayfield, and I, it may be, in a scent-bottle, why may not my individual caprice be allowed to find expression as well as yours? Probably I enjoy the hayfield as much as you do; but I enjoy quite other scents and sensations as well, and I take the former for granted, and write my poem, for a change, about the latter. There is no necessary difference in artistic value between a good poem about a flower in the hedge and a good poem about the scent in a sachet. I am always charmed to read beautiful poems about nature in the country. Only, personally, I prefer town to country; and in the town we have to find for ourselves, as best we may, the *décor* which is the town equivalent of the great natural *décor* of fields and hills. Here it is that artificiality comes in; and if any one sees no beauty in the effects of artificial light, in all the variable, most human, and yet most factitious town landscape, I can only pity him, and go on my own way.

That is, if he will let me. But he tells me that one thing is right and the other is wrong; that one is good art and the other is bad; and I listen in amazement, sometimes not without impatience, wondering why an estimable personal prejudice should be thus exalted into a dogma, and uttered in the name of art. For in art there can be no prejudices, only results. If we are to save people's souls by the writing of verses, well and good. But if not, there is no choice but to admit absolute freedom of choice. And if Patchouli pleases one, why not Patchouli?

1896

Notes

1 'Préface de *Mademoiselle de Maupin*' was published in the May 1834 issue of *La France littéraire*, chiefly as a polemic against *Le Constitutionnel* but also as – in its final paragraph – publicity for the forthcoming novel, which came out in two volumes: the first in late 1835, the second in 1836.

2 Charles Baudelaire, *Notes nouvelles sur Edgar Poe*, 1857, in *Oeuvres complètes, tome II*, ed. C. Pichois (Paris: Gallimard, 1976), p. 319.

3 Alphonse Duchesne, in *Le Figaro*, 20 September 1859.

4 For the controversial debates about Decadence and Symbolism, see M. Pakenham (ed.), *Les Premières armes du symbolisme* (Exeter: University of Exeter Press, 1973).

5 W. B. Yeats, *Autobiographies*, eds William H. O'Donnell and Douglas N. Archibald (New York: Scribner, 1999), p. 124.

6 Pierre Corneille (1606–84) French dramatist; Louis Mandrin (1724–55) and Louis Dominique Bourguignon, called Cartouche (1693–1721), well-known eighteenth-century bandits.

7 The Regency refers to the period 1715–23, and the government of Philippe d'Orléans. Claude Jolyot Crébillon (1707–77) was the author of tales about the moral depravity of this period.

8 Claude-Henri de Rouvroy, comte de Saint-Simon (1760–1825), French utopian philosopher and economist.

9 A metonymy is a figure of speech in which the attribute of a thing is substituted for the thing itself; 'stage' for 'theatre', for example. Strophe, antistrophe, and epistrophe are the three parts of a Pindaric ode, the first two of which are identical in structure.

10 Gauthier de Costes, sieur de La Calprenède (1609–63), minor dramatist, author of *Silvandre*. The unreliable anecdote derives from Evrard Titon de Tillet's *Parnasse françois* (1732), in which *Sylvandre* is referred to as 'un roman'.

11 A liberal, anticlerical daily newspaper published in Paris from 1815 to 1914.
12 A famous German tailor's in Paris, mentioned by Balzac in *Un Grand homme de province à Paris* (1839).
13 Armand Carrel, journalist who founded the newspaper *Le National* in 1830 and who opposed the July Monarchy (1830–48).
14 Rafaello Sanzio, known as Raphael (1483–1520), Italian Renaissance painter; Princess Marie-Pauline Borghese (1780–1825), sister of Napoleon who famously posed for Antonio Canova's (1757–1822) sculpture of *Venus Victrix* (1804–8); Giulia Grisi (1812–69), Italian singer famed for her beauty.
15 Legendary ruler mentioned by unreliable ancient Greek sources as the last king of Assyria (thus sixth century BCE) and as an effeminate voluptuary. Lord Byron wrote a play, *Sardanapalus* (1821), about his downfall.
16 A statue from the Hellenistic era, depicting a woman looking over her shoulder at her own partially uncovered buttocks.
17 *Journal des connaissances utiles*, first called *L'Indépendant*, founded in 1815.
18 Emmanuel-Augustin Lepeintre (1788–1847), French vaudeville actor.
19 François, Baron de Bassompierre (1579–1646), French courtier and friend of Henri IV.
20 Milo of Crotona, Olympic victor known for his Herculean strength; Trimalchio: An ostentatious nouveau-riche character in Petronius's *Satyricon* (see pp. 44–51).
21 Anthelme Brillat-Savarin (1755–1826), French gastronome, author of *La Physiologie du goût* (*The Physiology of Taste*) (1825); Apicius, proverbial gourmet who lived in the reigns of Augustus and Tiberius, at the beginning of the first millennium.
22 Roman emperor (15–69 CE).
23 *Café Anglais . . . Véfour's . . . Chevet's . . . Rocher de Cancale . . . Lucrinus*: the first three were famous expensive Paris cafés in Gautier's day. Le Rocher de Cancale was a famous restaurant during the July Monarchy, named after Cancale in Brittany and famed for its oysters. Lucrinus is a lake close to the sea in the bay of Baiae famous for its oysters and shellfish.
24 In Greek legend, the impregnation by Hercules of King Thespius's daughters – all fifty of them – in the course of a single night. Although this feat was strictly a reward for slaying the local monster, it is jocularly known as the hero's thirteenth labour.
25 Although renowned for his wisdom, King Solomon, the Bible tells us, 'loved many strange women', to the number of seven hundred wives and three hundred concubines, some of whom lured him into the worship of their false gods, even including 'Molech, the abomination of the children of Ammon' (I Kings 11: 1–8).
26 These are metonyms (cf. n. 9) for Army, Church, and the civil service or state bureaucracy.
27 A daily law journal, founded in 1825, containing descriptions of crimes and trials.
28 One of the twelve apostles of Jesus who was flayed before being crucified upside-down.

29 Greek epigraph: Heraclitus says, 'All things give way: nothing remaineth' (cited by Socrates in Plato's *Cratylus*).

30 See *Hamlet*, V.i.232–4, where Laertes says: 'Lay her i' th' earth; / And from her fair and unpolluted flesh / May violets spring!'

31 Novalis, pseudonym of Baron Friedrich von Hardenberg (1772–1801); 'To philosophize is to cast off inertia, to vitalize': quotation from 'Fragmente 2', *Werke* 3, 64 (Heidelberg, 1957).

32 Auguste Comte (1798–1857), French positivist philosopher; Georg Wilhelm Friedrich Hegel (1770–1831), German idealist philosopher.

33 'Philosophy is the microscope of thought.' From Victor Hugo, *Les Misérables*, pt 5, vol. I, bk 2, ch. 2, misquoted with 'le microsope' feminised.

34 *Les Confessions* appeared posthumously in two parts (1782, 1789), the sixth book falling within the first part.

35 'Men are all condemned to death with indefinite reprieves', from Hugo, *Le Dernier jour d'un condamné* (1832).

36 A formulation taken from Comte's *Système de politique positive* (1851–54) and the title of one of the chapters of John Robert Seeley's book on Christ's humanity, *Ecce Homo* (1866).

37 Pater derives this phrase from the Preface to Gautier's *Mademoiselle de Maupin* (1835) (see pp. 15–22 above).

38 Rachel (who used that name only) and Sarah Bernhardt were the great French actresses who became international stars in the 1840s/50s and the 1870s/80s respectively. Each redefined the classical role of Racine's *Phèdre* (Rachel in 1843, Sarah in 1874 and 1879), and each had an illegitimate son as well as numerous lovers. By contrast, the respectable English actress Mrs (Madge) Kendal had five legitimate children by her husband and fellow-actor W. H. Kendal; she played Shakespeare's Rosalind in 1871 and 1885.

39 Jean Richepin (1849–1926) was a French poet, playwright, and novelist who wrote and produced three plays, including a translation of *Macbeth*, as vehicles for Sarah Bernhardt in the early 1880s, and was intermittently her lover at that time. The verse quotation here is the most famous couplet from Jean Racine's tragedy *Phèdre* (1677), in which the eponymous queen describes her incestuous feelings for her stepson: 'It is no longer a passion hidden in my veins: it is Venus herself fastened to her prey'. Inexplicably, Moore manages to misquote the first line, of which the opening phrase should read 'Ce n'est plus une ardeur'.

40 Algernon Charles Swinburne (1837–1909), the English poet. His early works, including the verse tragedy *Chastelard* (1865) and especially *Poems and Ballads* (1866), from which some poems are reprinted below (pp. 100–16), provoked critical outrage for their pagan erotic, and specifically masochist tendencies; but his friends persuaded him to treat less controversial subjects in later writings such as *A Century of Roundels* (1883). In 1879, Theodore Watts, later known as Watts-Dunton, installed Swinburne in his home in the south-west London suburb of Putney, keeping him under virtual house-arrest in order to cure him of his dangerous alcoholism. The *Nineteenth Century*, founded in 1877, was a serious monthly periodical devoted to intellectual debate.

41 Variant spelling of Edo, the original name of the Japanese capital city, renamed Tokyo in 1868.
42 The English poet, craftsman, and designer William Morris (1834–96) gave several public lectures on the future of art under socialism in the 1880s, and published these in *Hopes and Fears for Art* (1882) and *Signs of Change* (1888).
43 The dying words attributed to the great German writer J. W. von Goethe (1749–1832) have been much disputed. He is supposed to have said 'Mehr Licht!' ('More light!'), which is often taken, as here, to be a battle-cry of Enlightenment. Some accounts suggest that he was simply asking for the window-shutters to be opened.
44 William Ewart Gladstone (1809–98), the great Liberal statesman, was Prime Minister four times between 1868 and 1894, although not at the time Moore wrote the *Confessions*. The Elementary Education Act (1870) which established universal schooling was enacted under his administration. John Morley (1838–1923), a literary journalist and biographer before entering Parliament in 1883, was a close supporter of Gladstone, serving as Chief Secretary for Ireland in 1886; he later wrote the first biography of Gladstone.
45 The reviewer has not been traced, and is possibly an invention of Symons's.
46 Patchouli, peau d'Espagne and lily of the valley: heady floral perfumes for women with connotations of exoticism and sensuousness.
47 'primrose ... bonfire': idioms taken from Shakespeare: *Hamlet*, I:iii; and *Macbeth*, II:iii.
48 Symons's third and most scandalous collection of poems, published in 1895 by Leonard Smithers.

2

THE MATTER OF ROME

'All roads lead to Rome' says the medieval proverb; and the study of Decadence tends to confirm that claim. The Roman Empire's decline, and thus in the primary sense of the term its *décadence*, was the inescapable point of historical reference for all the extended and enriched meanings of the Decadent idea in the nineteenth century and beyond. Other collapsed civilisations had been remembered for their excessive luxury, corruption, depravity, or cruelty, but Rome eclipsed them all as the defining model of a prosperous and powerful civilisation apparently devoured by its own appetites. In the imaginative life of the French and British empires of the nineteenth century, the ominous story of Rome held an exemplary primacy, for a number of interlinked reasons.

In the first place, as we have indicated in our Introduction above, Roman writers may be said to have 'invented' decadence as part of their repeated myth of ancestral virtue and of subsequent moral enfeeblement. Second, in the broadest of historical schemes the decline of Rome was understood in modern times to have been both a disaster and a providential blessing in that Christendom itself, including the emergence of all the modern European nations, owed its power to the disintegration of the ancient empire, permitting the birth of a spiritually 'higher' phase of civilisations. In the third place, Latin, for centuries the international language of the Church, was still the basis of secular humanistic education; so that the most accomplished men (and a few women) of the educated classes in the nineteenth century were in a position to venture beyond the largely wholesome school texts of Roman literature's 'Golden Age', a period usually defined as 83 BCE–14 CE and thus including Virgil, Livy, Ovid, and Horace. They could sample the more colourful productions of the post-Augustan phase of Roman writing that had become known as 'the decadence' of Latin, in prose fiction (Petronius, Apuleius), verse satire (Juvenal, Martial), and biographical history (Tacitus, Suetonius, and the *Augustan History*). Leading figures in the Decadent tradition, including Théophile Gautier, Charles Baudelaire, and Joris-Karl Huysmans, boasted a special affection not only for the writings of the Latin 'decadence' broadly conceived but for the works of the 'Late Latin' period which corresponds to the early Christian era. Such a preference, in the context of French cultural antagonisms, was clearly a renewed repudiation of classicism, and a reassertion of a familiar Romantic attraction to the medieval Christian inheritance.

The passages we have chosen from Roman authors display the nostalgic primitivism commonly found among them, as in the opening of Juvenal's *Sixth Satire*, and in its later comments on the corruptions of peace, luxury, and foreign manners. As the unbridled misogyny of Juvenal's satire helps to show, the problem of imperial Roman modernity was understood literally as a problem of breeding. In the crudest terms suggested by Juvenal, if the wives of upper-class Roman citizens are spending their time drunkenly fornicating with actors, gladiators, and bisexual slaves, how can they be trusted to raise legitimate children, let alone warriors? Long before Juvenal's time the emperor Augustus himself had been so worried by the falling birthrate among the higher citizenry that he had enacted the Julian Law of 18 BCE, awarding tax-breaks to fathers of three or more children in an effort to replenish a declining race.

The severely masculinist ideology of Rome shaped not only the condemnation of sexual excess among women but the ways in which the personal conduct of men was to be judged and to be linked to its political contexts. The nostalgic cult of primitive Roman virtue was a celebration of manly self-discipline as well as of chaste matronly fecundity, and it had significant political implications. Already under Augustus and increasingly under his more terrifying successors, the oligarchic senatorial families which had shared power under the defunct Roman Republic consoled themselves in their increasing impotence by nursing an idealised memory of the Republic as a lost order of true masculine dignity. It had been the boast of free-born citizens under the Republic that they governed themselves as men, whereas the inhabitants of other lands grovelled in effeminately servile abasement before tyrants. Under the Empire, of course, such claims became shamefully hollow as the once-proud patricians flattered the latest emperor for fear of arbitrary murder and expropriation. Their retaliation came in literary form, as history or biography or satire, these genres being in Roman times scarcely distinguishable one from another, or indeed from luridly pornographic fiction.

A Roman author could heap all kinds of ignominy upon a safely dead ruler, in terms that often threw the shame of emasculation back upon the imperial head. Those writing a century or so after Augustus's time, including Juvenal and the historians Tacitus and Suetonius, could look back upon an emperor such as Caligula or Nero who had terrorised the senatorial class and paint him as both a military weakling and an effeminate pervert. Indeed these two charges amounted under the masculinist code to the same thing: a leader whose negligence had led to shameful military losses in some remote province could be nothing other than the sort of half-man who would dress in women's clothing, let himself be sodomised by filthy gladiators, and play musical instruments in public. Whether the said emperor had ever actually done anything of these kinds, or had even been responsible for military setbacks, was not a question that troubled these writers, the most important consideration being salvaging the myth of ancestral manliness.

Power wielded by an individual unconstrained by patrician families was to such writers both terrifying and shameful, and so it had to be repudiated as un-Roman, feminised, and foreign, associated with such unmanly peoples as the Greeks (especially detested by Juvenal) or Asiatics. The extravagant legends visited upon the memory of the young third-century emperor Elagabalus are particularly significant in this regard: he was the first emperor of Rome to have emerged from an 'Asiatic' background, having been born and raised in the province of Syria. Accordingly, the tall tales told about him in the *Augustan History* and elsewhere are marked by relentless emphases on effeminacy that most probably derive from popular prejudices about easterners. The last thing the reader should expect from the imperial Roman historians and biographers is responsible treatment of evidence. Quite a few passages of Tacitus and Suetonius are incidentally credible, but much, especially on the biographical side, appears to be based on rumours put about by their subjects' political enemies. As for the later *Augustan History*, and the excerpted section below on Elagabalus in particular, it is an incoherent farrago of slanderous inventions.

These lives of emperors may tell us little that is truthful about the real historical personages they treat, but they do reveal much of what Romans of that period imagined unfettered power to involve, which has two commonly represented aspects. In the first place there are depravities of sexual conduct, extending to alleged incest and pederasty, most of which we should read as metaphors of perceived political monstrosity. In the second place we find accounts of incredible extravagance or luxury in which the limits imposed by Nature herself are exceeded: artificial lakes are dug and filled with wine, buildings are made from imported snow on midsummer, and so forth.

This second aspect of the imagined excesses of boundless wealth had a special significance in the nineteenth century, which saw itself as an age of hitherto unimaginable abundance generated by industrial and technological power. Yet to the literary sceptics who launched the Decadent movement, such power was wasted on the production of tediously useful items such as steam-boilers and waterproof garments. Why, asked Théophile Gautier in his Preface to *Mademoiselle de Maupin* (see p. 20–21 above), in such an age of supposedly miraculous progress, had nobody yet invented a new sin, or even a new pleasure? Those who were acquainted with Suetonius or with the *Augustan History* would perhaps see that Gautier was alluding to those sources in which the Roman emperors Tiberius and Elagabalus are credited with inventing new sexual perversions. More directly, Gautier compares the unimaginative culinary fare of even the best Parisian restaurants of his time with the wondrously extravagant dishes served up at Trimalchio's banquet in Petronius's *Satyricon*. Considering the great pleasure-houses built by the Roman emperors and their wealthy peers at Baiae, Gautier concludes: 'The titanic magnificence of those great voluptuaries who built eternal monuments for the pleasures of a day ought to make us prostrate ourselves before the genius of the ancient world . . .' Here and in the writings of Gautier's followers, the 'decadent' Romans who had been held up for centuries as villains of profligacy are redeemed as heroes of the human imagination, who offered a lesson to the nineteenth century in the right uses of immense wealth: that it should be dedicated to the extension of delight rather than to trivial utility.

A few notes are in order here on the dates of the authors and writings represented in this section of the book, in so far as we are able to establish or guess at them. The *Satyricon*, a semi-satirical picaresque novel in prose with occasional verse, has survived only in fragments, the most important of which is the episode of Trimalchio's feast. It dates from about 60 CE, and its author, Petronius Arbiter, was probably the courtier favoured by the emperor Nero as his adviser on matters of taste (*elegantiae arbiter*) and who, as Tacitus records in his *Annals*, committed suicide in 65 CE upon being falsely accused of treachery; his date of birth is unknown. The *Sixth Satire*, which is the longest of Juvenal's sixteen satirical poems, dates from about 117 CE. Juvenal (Decimus Junius Juvenalis) was the greatest and the most caustic of Roman satirists; the best guess we can make about his dates is *c.* 55–*c.* 140 CE. Suetonius was born in about 70 CE, and became a secretary in the palace of the emperor Hadrian, until dismissed in 121 or 122. His *Lives of the Caesars* (*De vita Caesarum*) dates probably from about 125; his date of death is unknown. The *Augustan History* (so named by scholars in the seventeenth century) is a puzzling text: a collection of biographies of second- and third-century Roman emperors, apparently by six different authors of the early fourth century, it is more likely to be the work of a single anonymous late fourth-century forger, and its contents are for the most part fictitious. The extract from Gautier is from a lengthy commemorative tribute prefacing the posthumous third (1868) edition of Baudelaire's *Les Fleurs du mal*; this is followed, as it is immediately in that part of Gautier's essay, by Baudelaire's note (usually omitted from English editions) to his own Latin poem.

PETRONIUS ARBITER

From *The Satyricon*

[From the episode of Quartilla's party]

We should have cried out for help in our unhappy plight, but there was no one to hear us, and besides Psyche pricked my cheeks with her hair pin every time I tried to call upon my fellow countrymen for succour, while at the same time the other girl threatened Ascyltos with a brush dipped in satyrion.[1] Finally there entered a catamite, tricked out in a coat of chestnut frieze, and wearing a sash, who would alternately writhe his buttocks and bump against us, and beslaver us with most evil-smelling kisses, until Quartilla, holding a whalebone wand in her hand and with skirts tucked up, ordered him to give the poor fellows quarter. Then we all three swore the most solemn oaths the horrid secret should die with us.

Next a company of wrestlers appeared, who rubbed us over with the proper gymnastic oil, which was very refreshing. This removed our fatigue (we resumed the dinner clothes that we had taken off) and we were then conducted into the adjoining room, where the couches were laid and all preparations made for an elegant feast in the most sumptuous style. We were requested to take our places, and the banquet opened with some wonderful hors d'oeuvres, while the Falernian[2] flowed like water. A number of other courses followed, and we were all but falling asleep, when Quartilla cried, 'Come, come! can you think of sleep, when you know this livelong night is owed to the service of Priapus?'[3]

Ascyltos was so worn out with all he had gone through he could not keep his eyes open a moment longer, and the waiting-maid, whom he had scorned and slighted, now proceeded to daub his face all over with streaks of soot, and bepaint his lips and shoulders, as he lay unconscious.

I too, tired with the persecutions I had endured, was just enjoying forty winks, as they say, while all the household, within doors and without, had copied my example. Some lay sprawling about the diners' feet, others propped against the walls, while others snored head to head right on the threshold. The oil in the lamps had burned low, and they shed a feeble, dying light, when two Syrian slaves came into the banquet-room to crib a flagon of wine. As they were greedily fighting for it and scuffling amongst the silver, it parted and broke in two. At the same moment the table with the silver plate collapsed, and a goblet falling from perhaps a greater height than the rest, struck the waiting-maid who was lying exhausted on a couch underneath and cut her head open. She screamed out at the blow, at once discovering the thieves and awakening some of the drunkards. The Syrians, thus caught in the act, threw themselves with one accord onto a couch, and started snoring as if they had been asleep ever so long.

By this time the chief butler had wakened up and put fresh oil into the expiring lamps, while the other slaves after rubbing their eyes a bit, had resumed their posts, and presently a cymbal-player came in and roused us all up with a clash of her instruments. So the banquet was resumed, and Quartilla challenged us to start a fresh carouse, the tinkle of the cymbals still further stimulating her reckless gaiety.

The next to appear is a catamite, the silliest of mankind and quite worthy of the house, who beat his hands together, gave a groan, and then spouted the following delightful effusion:

'Who hath a pathic lust,
With Delian[4] vice accurst;
Who loves the pliant thigh,
Quick hand and wanton sigh;
Come hither, come hither, come hither,
   Here shall he see
   Gross beasts as he,
Lechers of every feather!'

Then, his poetry exhausted, he spat a most stinking kiss in my face; before long he mounted on the couch where I lay and exposed me by force in spite of my resistance. He laboured hard and long to bring up my member, but in vain. Streams of gummy paint and sweat poured from his heated brow, and such a lot of chalk filled the wrinkles of his cheeks, you might have thought his face was an old dilapidated wall with the plaster crumbling away in the rain.

I could no longer restrain my tears, but driven to the last extremity of disgust, 'I ask you, lady,' I cried, 'is this the "night-cap" [*ambasicoetas*] you promised me?' At this she clapped her hands daintily, exclaiming. 'Oh you clever boy! what a pretty wit you have! Of course you didn't know "night-cap" is another name for a catamite?' Then, that my comrade might not miss his share too, I asked her, 'Now, on your conscience, is Ascyltos to be the only guest in the room to keep holiday!' 'So?' she cried, 'why! let Ascyltos have his "nightcap" too!' In obedience to her order, the catamite now changed his mount, and transferring his attentions to my friend, set to grinding him under his buttocks and smothering him with lecherous kisses.

[From the episode of Trimalchio's feast]

Well! at last we take our places, Alexandrian slave-boys pouring snow water over our hands, and others succeeding them to wash our feet and cleanse our toe nails with extreme dexterity. Not even while engaged in this unpleasant office were they silent, but sang away over their work. I had a mind to try whether all the house servants were singers, and accordingly asked for a drink of wine. Instantly an attendant was at my side, pouring out the liquor to the accompaniment of the same sort of shrill recitative. Demand what you would, it was the same; you might have supposed yourself among a troupe of pantomime actors[5] rather than at a respectable citizen's table.

Then the preliminary course was served in very elegant style. For all were now at table except Trimalchio, for whom the first place was reserved, – by a reversal of ordinary usage. Among the other hors d'oeuvres stood a little ass of Corinthian bronze with a packsaddle holding olives, white olives on one side, black on the other. The animal was flanked right and left by silver dishes, on the rim of which Trimalchio's name was engraved and the weight. On arches built up in the form of miniature bridges were dormice seasoned with honey and poppy-seed. There were sausages too smoking hot on a silver grill, and underneath (to imitate coals) Syrian plums and pomegranate seeds.

We were in the middle of these elegant trifles when Trimalchio himself was carried in to the sound of music, and was bolstered up among a host of tiny cushions, – a sight that set one or two indiscreet guests laughing. And no wonder; his bald head poked up out of a scarlet mantle, his neck was closely muffled, and over all was laid a napkin with a broad purple stripe or laticlave, and long fringes hanging down either side. Moreover he wore on the little finger of his left hand a massive ring of silver gilt, and on the last joint of the next finger a smaller ring, apparently of solid gold, but starred superficially with little ornaments of steel. Nay! to show this was not the whole of his magnificence, his left arm was bare, and displayed a gold bracelet and an ivory circlet with a sparkling clasp to put it on.

After picking his teeth with a silver toothpick, 'My friends,' he began, 'I was far from desirous of coming to table just yet, but that I might not keep you waiting by my absence, I have sadly interfered with my own amusement. But will you permit me to finish my game?' A slave followed him in, carrying a draught-board of terebinth wood and crystal dice. One special bit of refinement I noticed; instead of the ordinary black and white men he had medals of gold and silver respectively.

Meantime, whilst he is exhausting the vocabulary of a tinker over the game, and we are still at the hors d'oeuvres, a dish was brought in with a basket on it, in which lay a wooden hen, her wings outspread round her as if she were sitting. Instantly a couple of slaves came up, and to the sound of lively music began to search the straw, and pulling out a lot of pea-fowl's eggs one after the other, handed them round to the company. Trimalchio turns his head at this, saying, 'My friends, it was by my orders the hen was set on the peafowl's eggs yonder; but by God! I am very much afraid they are half-hatched. Still we can but try whether they are still eatable.' For our part, we take our spoons, which weighed at least half a pound each, and break the eggs, which were made of paste. I was on the point of throwing mine away, for I thought I discerned a chick inside. But when I overheard a veteran guest saying, 'There should be something good here!' I further investigated the shell, and found a very fine fat beccafico[6] swimming in yolk of egg flavoured with pepper.

Trimalchio had by this time stopped his game and been helped to all the dishes before us. He had just announced in a loud voice that any of us who wanted a second supply of honeyed wine had only to ask for it, when suddenly at a signal from the band, the hors d'oeuvres are whisked away by a troupe of slaves, all singing too. But in the confusion a silver dish happened to fall and a slave picked it up again from the floor; this Trimalchio noticed, and boxing the fellow's ears, rated him soundly and ordered him to throw it down again. Then a groom came in and began to sweep up the silver along with the other refuse with his besom.

He was succeeded by two long-haired Ethiopians, carrying small leather skins, like the fellows that water the sand in the amphitheatre, who poured wine over our hands; for no one thought of offering water. After being duly complimented on this refinement, our host cried out, 'Fair play's a jewel!' and accordingly ordered a separate table to be assigned to each guest. 'In this way,' he said, 'by preventing any crowding, the stinking servants won't make us so hot.'

Simultaneously there were brought in a number of wine-jars of glass carefully stoppered with plaster, and having labels attached to their necks reading:

Falernian; Opimian Vintage
One Hundred Years Old.

Whilst we were reading the labels, Trimalchio ejaculated, striking his palms together, 'Alackaday! to think wine is longer lived than poor humanity! Well! bumpers then! There's life in wine. 'Tis the right Opimian, I give you my word. I didn't bring out any so good yesterday, and much better men than you were dining with me.'

So we drank our wine and admired all this luxury in good set terms. Then the slave brought in a silver skeleton, so artfully fitted with its articulations and vertebrae were all movable and would turn and twist in any direction. After he had tossed this once or twice on the table, causing the loosely jointed limbs to take various postures, Trimalchio moralized thus:

Alas! how less than naught are we;
  Fragile life's thread, and brief our day!

What this is now, we all shall be;
Drink and make merry while you may.

Our applause was interrupted by the second course, which did not by any means come up to our expectations. Still the oddity of the thing drew the eyes of all. An immense circular tray bore the twelve signs of the zodiac displayed round the circumference, on each of which the Manciple or Arranger had placed a dish of suitable and appropriate viands: on the Ram ram's-head pease, on the Bull a piece of beef, on the Twins fried testicles and kidneys, on the Crab simply a Crown, on the Lion African figs, on a Virgin a sow's haslet, on Libra a balance with a tart in one scale and a cheese-cake in the other, on Scorpio a small sea-fish, on Sagittarius an eye-seeker, on Capricornus a lobster, on Aquarius a wild goose, on Pisces two mullets. In the middle was a sod of green turf cut to shape and supporting a honeycomb. Meanwhile an Egyptian slave was carrying bread round in a miniature oven of silver, crooning to himself in a horrible voice a song in praise of wine and laserpitium.[7]

Seeing us look rather blank at the idea of attacking such common fare, Trimalchio cried, 'I pray you gentlemen, begin; the best of your dinner is before you.' No sooner had he spoken than four fellows ran prancing in, keeping time to the music, and whipped off the top part of the tray. This done, we beheld underneath, on a second tray in fact, stuffed capons, a sow's paps, and as a centrepiece a hare fitted with wings to represent Pegasus. We noticed besides four figures of Marsyas,[8] one at each corner of the tray, carrying little wine-skins which spouted out peppered fish-sauce over the fishes swimming in the Channel of the dish.

We all join in the applause started by the domestics and laughingly fall to on the choice viands. Trimalchio, as pleased as anybody with a device of the sort, now called out, 'Cut!' Instantly the Carver advanced, and posturing in time to the music, sliced up the joint with such antics you might have thought him a jockey struggling to pull off a chariot-race to the thunder of the organ. Yet all the while Trimalchio kept repeating in a wheedling voice, 'Cut! Cut!' For my part, suspecting there was some pretty jest connected with this everlasting reiteration of the word, I made no bones about asking the question of the guest who sat immediately above me. He had often witnessed similar scenes and told me at once, 'You see the man who is carving; well; his name is Cut. The master is calling and commanding him at one and the same time.'

Unable to eat any more, I now turned towards my neighbour in order to glean what information I could, and after indulging in a string of general remarks, presently asked him, 'Who is that lady bustling up and down the room yonder?' 'Trimalchio's lady,' he replied; 'her name is Fortunata, and she counts her coin by the bushelful! Before? what was she before? Why! my dear Sir! saving your respect, you would have been mighty sorry to take bread from her hand. Now, by hook or by crook, she's got to heaven, and is Trimalchio's factotum. In fact if she told him it was dark night at high noon, he'd believe her. The man's rolling in riches, and really can't tell what he has and what he hasn't got; still his good lady looks keenly after everything, and is on the spot where you least expect to see her. She's temperate, sober and well advised, but she has a sharp tongue of her own and chatters like a magpie between the bed-curtains. When she likes a man, she likes him; and when she doesn't, well! she doesn't.

'As for Trimalchio, his lands reach as far as the kites fly, and his money breeds money. I tell you, he has more coin lying idle in his porter's lodge than would make another man's whole fortune. Slaves! why, heaven and earth! I don't believe one in ten knows his own master by sight. For all that, there's never a one of the fine fellows a word of his wouldn't send scutting into the nearest rat-hole. And don't you imagine he ever buys anything; every mortal thing is home grown, – wool, rosin, pepper; call for hen's milk and he'd supply you! As a matter of fact his wool was not first rate originally; but he purchased rams at Tarentum and so improved the breed. To get home-made Attic honey he had bees imported direct from Athens, hoping at the same time to benefit the native insects a bit by a cross with the Greek fellows. Why! only the other day he wrote to India for mushroom spawn. He has not a single mule but was got by a wild ass. You see all these mattresses; never a one that is not stuffed with the finest wool, purple or scarlet as the case may be. Lucky, lucky dog!'

[. . .]

For when the tables had been cleared with a flourish of music, three white hogs were brought in, hung with little bells and muzzled. One, so the nomenclator informed us, was a two year old, another three, and the third six. For my part, I thought they were learned pigs, come in to perform some of those marvellous tricks you see in circuses. But Trimalchio put an end to my surmises by saying, 'Which of the three will you have dressed for supper right away? Farmyard cocks and pheasants and suchlike small deer are for country folks; my cooks are used to serving up calves boiled whole.'

So saying, he immediately ordered the cook to be summoned, and without waiting for our choice, directed the six year old to be killed. Then speaking loud and clear, he asked the man, 'What decuria[9] do you belong to?'

'To the fortieth', he replied.

'Bought,' he went on, 'or born in my house?'

'Neither,' returned the cook, 'I was left you by Pansa's will.'

'Then mind you serve the dish carefully dressed; else I shall order you to be degraded into the decuria of the outdoor slaves.'

And the cook, thus cogently admonished, then withdrew with his charge into the kitchen.

But Trimalchio, relaxing his stern aspect, now turned to us and said, 'If you don't like the wine, I'll have it changed; otherwise please prove its quality by your drinking. Thanks to the gods' goodness, I never buy it; but now I have everything that smacks good growing on a suburban estate of mine. I've not seen it yet, but they tell me it's down Terracina and Tarentum way. I am thinking at the moment of making Sicily one of my little properties, that when I've a mind to visit Africa, I may sail along my own boundaries to get there.

'But tell me, Agamemnon, what question formed the subject of your declamation to-day? Though I don't plead myself, I've studied letters for domestic use. Don't imagine I have despised scholarship; why! I have two Libraries, one Greek, the other Latin. If you love me, then, let me know what the argument of your discourse was.'

Agamemnon had just begun, 'A poor man and a rich were at feud . . .,' when Trimalchio struck in with the question, 'What is a poor man!'

'Oh, capital!' cried Agamemnon; and went on to develop some dialectical problem or another.

Trimalchio summed up without an instant's hesitation as follows, 'If this is so, there's no question about it; if it's not so, why! there's an end of the matter.'

Whilst we were still acclaiming these and similar remarks with fulsome praise, he resumed, 'Pray, my dearest Agamemnon, do you recollect by any chance the twelve labours of Hercules, or the story of Ulysses, how the Cyclops twisted his thumb out of joint, after he was turned into a pig. I used to read these tales in Homer when I was a lad. Then the Sibyl! I saw her at Cumae with my own eyes hanging in a jar; and when the boys cried to her, "Sibyl, what would you?" she would answer, "I would die," – both of 'em speaking Greek.'

He was still in the middle of this nonsense when a tray supporting an enormous hog was set on the table. One and all we expressed our admiration at the expedition shown, and swore a mere ordinary fowl could not have been cooked in the time, – the more so as the hog appeared to be a much larger animal than the wild boar just before. Presently Trimalchio, staring harder and harder, exclaimed, 'What! what! isn't he gutted? No! by heaven! he's not. Call the cook in!'

The cook came and stood by the table, looking sadly crestfallen and saying he had clean forgotten. 'What! forgotten!' cried Trimalchio; 'to hear him, you would suppose he'd just omitted a pinch of pepper or a bit of cummin. Strip him!'

Instantly the cook was stripped, and standing between two tormentors, the picture of misery. But we all began to intercede for him, saying, 'Accidents will happen; do forgive him this once. If ever he does it again, not one of us will say a word in his favour.' For my own part I felt mercilessly indignant, and could not hold myself, but bending over to Agamemnon's ear, I whispered, 'Evidently he must be a villainous bad servant. To think of anybody forgetting to bowel a hog; by Gad! I would not let the fellow off, if he'd shown such carelessness about a fish.'

Not so Trimalchio, for with a smile breaking over his face, 'Well! well!' said he, 'as you have such a bad memory, bowel him now, where we can all see.'

Thereupon the cook resumed his tunic, seized his knife and with a trembling hand slashed open the animal's belly. In a moment, the apertures widening under the weight behind, out tumbled a lot of sausages and black-puddings.

At this all the servants applauded like one man, and chorussed, 'Gaius for ever!' Moreover the cook was gratified with a goblet of wine and a silver wreath, and received a drinking cup on a salver of Corinthian metal.

[From the episode of Eumolpus]

Enlivened by this discourse, I now began to question my companion, who was better informed on these points than myself, as to the dates of the different pictures and the subjects of some that baffled me. At the same time I asked him the reason of the supineness of the present day and the utter decay of the highest branches of art, and amongst the rest of painting, which now showed not the smallest vestige of its former excellence.

'It is greed of money,' he replied, 'has wrought the change. In early days, when plain worth was still esteemed, the liberal arts flourished, and the chief object of men's emulation was to ensure no discovery likely to benefit future ages long remaining undeveloped. To this end Democritus extracted the juices of every herb, and spent his life in experimenting, that no virtue of mineral or plant might escape detection. Similarly Eudoxus grew grey on the summit of a lofty mountain, observing the motions of the stars and firmament, while Chrysippus thrice purged his brain with hellebore, to stimulate its capacity and inventiveness. But to consider the sculptors only, – Lysippus was so absorbed in the modelling of a single figure that he actually perished from lack of food, and Myron,[10] who came near embodying the very souls of men and beasts in bronze, died too poor to find an heir. But we, engrossed with wine and women, have not the spirit to appreciate the arts already discovered; we can only criticize Antiquity, and devote all our energies, in precept and practice, to the faults of the old masters. What is become of Dialectic? of Astronomy? of Philosophy, that richly cultivated domain? Who nowadays has ever been known to enter a temple and engage to pay a vow, if only he may attain unto Eloquence, or find the fountain of wisdom? Not even do sound intellect and sound health any longer form the objects of men's prayers, but before ever they set food on the threshold of the Capitol, they promise lavish offerings, one if he may bury a wealthy relative, another if he may unearth a treasure, another if only he may live to reach his thirty million. The very Senate, the example of all that is right and good, is in the habit of promising a thousand pounds of gold to Capitoline Jove, and that no man may be ashamed of the lust of pelf, bribes the very God of Heaven. What wonder then if Painting is in decay, when all, gods and men alike, find a big lump of gold a fairer sight than anything those crack-brained Greek fellows, Apelles and Phidias,[11] ever wrought.'

[. . .]

It was quite dark and the woman had completed my orders for dinner when Eumolpus knocked at the door. I called out, 'How many of you are there?' and immediately proceeded to spy through a chink in the door to see whether Ascyltos had not come too. But seeing my guest was alone, I at once hastened to let him in. He threw himself on my pallet, and directly he observed Giton moving about in attendance he wagged his head and remarked, 'I like your Ganymede;[12] we shall have a good time to-day.' I was anything but pleased with this indiscreet beginning, and began to fear I had opened my doors to another Ascyltos. Eumolpus grew more and more pressing, and on the lad's serving him with wine, 'I like you better,' he said, 'than any of them at the Baths;' and draining his cup thirstily, added he had never been more vexed in his life. 'I tell you, at the Bath just now, I came very near getting a beating, merely because I tried to repeat a copy of verses to the bathers sitting around the basin. It was just like the Theatre – I was turned out of the place. Then I started to look for you in every corner of the building, shouting Encolpius! Encolpius! at the top of my voice. Not far off a naked youth, who had lost his clothes, and roaring with just the same clamorous indignation after Giton. For me, I was treated like a madman by the very slave lads, who mocked and mimicked me most insolently; he on the contrary was soon surrounded by a thronging multitude, clapping their hands and showing the most awe-struck admiration. The fact is, he possessed virile parts of such enormous mass and weight, the man really seemed only an appendage of his own member. Oh; an indefatigable worker! I warrant, the sort to begin yesterday, and finish tomorrow! Accordingly he soon found a way out of his difficulties; a bystander, a Roman knight, they said, of notorious character, wrapped his own cloak round the poor wanderer, and took him home with him, in order I imagine to have the sole enjoyment of so rich a windfall. But I should never have recovered so much as my own clothes from the Bathkeeper, had I not produced some one to vouch for me. So much better does it profit a man to train his member than his mind?'

During Eumolpus's narrative I changed countenance repeatedly, now jubilant at my hated rival's misfortunes, now saddened by his success. I held my tongue, however, pretending to know nothing of the matter, and set to work arranging the dinner table. I had hardly finished this, when our humble repast was brought in; the fare was homely, but succulent and substantial, and Eumolpus, our famished scholar, fell to with a will, extolling the simplicity of the viands in the following lines:

All things that may our simple wants assuage
Kind heaven bestows to ease our hunger's rage;
Wild herbs and berries from the woodland spray
Suffice the craving appetite to stay.
What man would thirst beside a stream, or stand
To front the wintry blast with fire at hand?
The law is armed to guard the marriage bed,
The chaste bride blameless yields her maidenhead.
Whate'er is needful, bounteous Nature gives;
Pride only in unbridled riot lives!

After satisfying his appetite, our philosopher began to moralize, indulging in many criticisms of such as despise familiar things and attach value only to what is rich and rare. To their perverted taste anything that is allowable is held cheap, while they display a morbid predilection for forbidden luxuries.

Facile success, a rose without a thorn,
An instant victory, are things I scorn.
The Phasian bird from distant Colchis[13] brought
And Afric fowl! are dainties ever sought,
For these are rarities; not so the goose
And bright-plumed duck, fit but for vulgar use.

The costly scar, choice fish from Syrtes's shore,
That cost poor fishers' lives, these all adore;
The mullet's out of date. The modern man
Deserts his wife to woo the courtesan;
The rose yields place to cinnamon. For naught
Is held of worth that is not dearly bought.

'Is this the way,' I cried, 'you keep your promise of making no more poetry to-day? On your conscience, spare us at least, who have never thrown a stone at you. Once let any one of the company drinking under the same roof with us scent out your poetship, he will rouse the whole neighbourhood and overwhelm us all in the same ruin. Have some pity on your friends, and remember the picture gallery and the baths.' But Giton, who was all gentleness, remonstrated with me for speaking so, and declared I was doing ill thus to jeer at my elders. He said I was forgetting my duty as a host, and after inviting a man to my table out of compassion, was nullifying the obligation by then insulting him. Other remarks follow, all equally imbued with moderation and good sense, and coming with added grace from so beautiful a mouth.

Anonymous translation, 1905, fraudulently attributed to Oscar Wilde

JUVENAL

From *The Sixth Satire*

In the days of Saturn,[14] I believe, Chastity still lingered on the earth, and was to be seen for a time – days when men were poorly housed in chilly caves, when one common shelter enclosed hearth and household gods, herds and their owners; when the hill-bred wife spread her silvan bed with leaves and straw and the skins of her neighbours the wild beasts – a wife not like to thee, O Cynthia, nor to thee, Lesbia,[15] whose bright eyes were clouded by a sparrow's death, but one whose breasts gave suck to lusty babes, often more unkempt herself than her acorn-belching spouse. For in those days, when the world was young, and the skies were new, men born of the riven oak, or formed of dust, lived differently from now, and had no parents of their own. Under Jove, perchance, some few traces of ancient modesty may have survived; but that was before he had grown his beard, before the Greeks had learned to swear by someone else's head, when men feared not thieves for their cabbages or apples, and lived with unwalled gardens. After that Astraea[16] withdrew by degrees to heaven, with Chastity as her comrade, the two sisters taking flight together.

To set your neighbour's bed a-shaking, Postumus, and to flout the Genius[17] of the sacred couch, is now an ancient and long-established practice. All other sins came later, the products of the age of iron; but it was the silver age that saw the first adulterers. Nevertheless, in these days of ours, you are preparing for a covenant, a marriage-contract and a betrothal; you are by now getting your hair cut by a master barber; you have also perhaps given a pledge to her finger. What! Postumus, are you, you who once had your wits, taking to yourself a wife? Tell me what Tisiphone,[18] what snakes are driving you mad? Can you submit to a she-tyrant when there is so much rope to be had, so many dizzy heights of windows standing open, and when the Aemilian bridge[19] offers itself to hand? Or if none of all these modes of exit hit your fancy, how much better to take some boy-bedfellow, who would never wrangle with you o' nights, never ask presents of you when in bed, and never complain that you took your ease and were indifferent to his solicitations!

But Ursidius approves of the Julian Law.[20] He purposes to bring up a dear little heir, though he will thereby have to do without the fine turtles, the bearded mullets, and all the legacy-hunting delicacies of the meat-market. What can you think impossible if Ursidius takes to himself a wife? if he, who has long been the most notorious of gallants, who has so often found safety in the corn-bin of the luckless Latinus,[21] puts his deluded head into the connubial noose? And what think you of his searching for a wife of the good old virtuous sort? O doctors, lance his over-blooded veins. A pretty fellow you! Why, if you have the good luck to find a modest spouse, you should prostrate yourself before the Tarpeian threshold, and sacrifice a heifer with gilded horns to Juno; so few are the wives worthy to handle the fillets of Ceres,[22] or from whose kisses their own father would not shrink! Weave a garland for thy doorposts, and set up wreaths of ivy over thy lintel! But will Hiberina be satisfied with one man? Sooner compel her to be satisfied with one eye! You tell me of the high repute of some maiden, who lives on her paternal farm: well, let her live at Gabii, at Fidenae, as she lived in her own country, and I will believe in your paternal farm. But will anyone tell me that nothing ever took place on a mountain side or in a cave? Have Jupiter and Mars become so senile?

Can our arcades show you one woman worthy of your vows? Do all the tiers in all our theatres hold one whom you may love without misgiving, and pick out thence? When the soft Bathyllus[23] dances the part of the gesticulating Leda, Tuccia cannot contain herself; your Apulian maiden heaves a sudden and longing cry of ecstasy, as though she were in a man's arms; the rustic Thymele is all attention, it is then that she learns her lesson.

Others again, when all the stage draperies have been put away; when the theatres are closed, and all is silent save in the courts, and the Megalesian games are far off from the Plebeian,[24] ease their dullness by taking to the mask, the thyrsus and the tights of Accius. Urbicus, in an Atellan interlude,[25] raises a laugh by the gestures of Autonoe; the penniless Aelia is in love with him. Other women pay great prices for the favours of a comedian; some will not allow Chrysogonus to sing. Hispulla has a fancy for tragedians; but do you suppose that any one will be found to love Quintilian?[26] If you marry a wife, it will be that the lyrist Echion or Glaphyrus, or the flute player Ambrosius, may become a father. Then up with a long dais in the narrow street! Adorn your doors and doorposts with wreaths of laurel, that your highborn son, O Lentulus, may exhibit, in his tortoiseshell cradle, the lineaments of Euryalus or of a murmillo![27]

When Eppia, the senator's wife, ran off with a gladiator to Pharos and the Nile and the ill-famed city of Alexandria, Canopus[28] itself cried shame upon the monstrous morals of our town. Forgetful of home, of husband and of sister, without thought of her country, she shamelessly abandoned her weeping children; and – more marvellous still – deserted Paris[29] and the games. Though born in wealth, though as a babe she had slept in a bedizened cradle on the paternal down, she made light of the sea, just as she had long made light of her good name – a loss but little accounted of among our soft litter-riding dames. And so with stout heart she endured the tossing and the roaring of the Tyrrhenian and Ionian Seas, and all the many seas she had to cross. For when danger comes in a right and honourable way, a woman's heart grows chill with fear; she cannot stand upon her trembling feet: but if she be doing a bold, bad thing, her courage fails not. For a husband to order his wife on board ship is cruelty: the bilge-water then sickens her, the heavens go round and round. But if she is running away with a lover, she feels no qualms: then she vomits over her husband; now she messes with the sailors, she roams about the deck, and delights in hauling at the hard ropes.

And what were the youthful charms which captivated Eppia? What did she see in him to allow herself to be called 'a she-Gladiator'? Her dear Sergius had already begun to shave; a wounded arm gave promise of a discharge, and there were sundry deformities in his face: a scar caused by the helmet, a huge wen upon his nose, a nasty humour always trickling from his eye. But then he was a gladiator! It is this that transforms these fellows into Hyacinths![30] it was this that she preferred to children and to country, to sister and to husband. What these women love is the sword: had this same Sergius received his discharge, he would have been no better than a Veiento.[31]

Do the concerns of a private household and the doings of Eppia affect you? Then look at those who rival the Gods, and hear what Claudius[32] endured. As soon as his wife perceived that her husband was asleep, this august harlot was shameless enough to prefer a common mat to the imperial couch. Assuming a night-cowl, and attended by a single maid, she issued forth; then, having concealed her raven locks under a blonde wig, she took her place in a brothel reeking with long-used coverlets. Entering an empty cell reserved for herself, she there took her stand, under the feigned name of Lycisca, her nipples bare and gilded, and exposed to view the womb that bore thee, O nobly-born Britannicus![33] Here she graciously received all comers, asking from each his fee; and when at length the keeper dismissed the rest, she remained to the very last before closing her cell, and with passion still raging hot within her went sorrowfully away. Then exhausted but unsatisfied, with soiled cheeks, and begrimed with the smoke of lamps, she took back to the imperial pillow all the odours of the stews.

[. . .]

But whence come these monstrosities? you ask; from what fountain do they flow? In days of old, the wives of Latium were kept chaste by their humble fortunes. It was toil and brief slumbers that kept vice from polluting their modest homes; hands chafed and hardened by Tuscan fleeces, Hannibal nearing the city, and husbands standing to arms at the Colline gate. We are now suffering the calamities of long peace. Luxury, more deadly than any foe, has laid her hand upon us, and avenges a conquered world. Since the day when Roman poverty perished, no deed of crime or lust has been wanting to us; from that moment Sybaris and Rhodes and Miletus have poured in upon our hills, with the begarlanded and drunken and unabashed Tarentum.[34] Filthy lucre first brought in amongst us foreign ways; wealth enervated and corrupted the ages with foul indulgences. What decency does Venus observe when she is drunken? when she cannot distinguish between head and groin, she eats giant oysters at midnight, pours foaming unguents into her unmixed Falernian, and drinks out of perfume-bowls, while the roof spins dizzily round, the table dances, and every light shows double!

Go to now and wonder what means the sneer with which Tullia snuffs the air, or what Maura whispers to her ill-famed foster-sister, when she passes by the ancient altar of Chastity? It is there that they set down their litters at night, and befoul the image of the Goddess, playing their filthy pranks for the morn to witness. Thence home they go; while you, when daylight comes, and you are on your way to salute your mighty friends, will tread upon the traces of your wife's abominations.

Well known to all are the mysteries of the Good Goddess,[35] when the flute stirs the loins and the Maenads of Priapus[36] sweep along, frenzied alike by the horn-blowing and the wine, whirling their locks and howling. What foul longings burn within their breasts! What cries they utter as the passion palpitates within! How drenched their limbs in torrents of old wine! Saufeia challenges the slave-girls to a contest. She wins the prize for wiggling her arse, but she has herself in turn to bow the knee to Medullina. And so the palm remains with the mistress, whose exploits match her birth! There is no pretence in the game; all is enacted to the life in a manner that would warm the cold blood of a Priam or a Nestor.[37] And now impatient nature can wait no longer: woman shows herself as she is, and the cry comes from every corner of the den, 'Let in the men!' If one favoured youth is asleep, another is bidden to put on his cowl and hurry along; if better cannot be got, a run is made upon the slaves; if they too fail, the water-carrier will be paid to come in. If they cannot find him, and there's a shortage of humans, in a trice she willingly offers her arse to be serviced by a donkey. O would that our ancient practices, or at least our public rites, were not polluted by scenes like these! But every Moor and every Indian knows about the 'lute-girl' who brought a penis larger than both of Caesar's anti-Cato speeches into the place which even a male mouse, all too conscious of his balls, avoids, the place where any picture showing a male form has to be covered up.[38]

Who ever sneered at the Gods in the days of old? Who would have dared to laugh at the earthenware bowls or black pots of Numa, or the brittle plates made out of Vatican clay? But nowadays at what altar will you not find a Clodius?

I hear all this time the advice of my old friends – keep your women at home, and put them under lock and key. Yes, but who will watch the warders? Wives are crafty and will begin with them. High or low their passions are all the same. She who wears out the black cobble-stones with her bare feet is no better than she who rides upon the necks of eight stalwart Syrians.

Ogulnia hires clothes to see the games; she hires attendants, a litter, cushions, female friends, a nurse, and a fair-haired girl to run her messages; yet she will give all that remains of the family plate, down to the last flagon, to some smooth-faced athlete. Many of these women are poor, but none of them pay any regard to their poverty, or measure themselves by the standard which that prescribes and lays down for them. Men, on the other hand, do sometimes have an eye to utility; the ant has at last taught some of them to dread cold and hunger. But your extravagant woman is never sensible of her dwindling means; and just as though money were for ever sprouting up afresh from her exhausted coffers, and she had always a full heap to draw from, she never gives a thought to what her pleasures cost her.

Whenever a fairy is admitted to a household he taints it. Folks let these fellows eat and drink with them, and merely have the vessels washed, not shivered to atoms as they should be when such lips have touched them. So even the gladiator school is better ordered than your establishment, for its trainer separates the vile from the decent, and sequesters the wearers of the ill-famed tunic even from their fellow trident-wielders; in the training-school, and even in jail, such creatures herd apart; but your wife condemns you to drink out of the same cup as these gentry, with whom the poorest streetwalker would refuse to sip the choicest wine. Them do women consult about marriage and divorce, with their society do they relieve boredom or business, from them do they learn lascivious motions and whatever else the teacher knows. But beware! that teacher is not always what he seems: true, he darkens his eyes and dresses like a woman, but adultery is his design. Mistrust him the more for his show of effeminacy; he is a valiant mattress-knight; there Triphallus drops the mask of Thais.[39] Whom are you fooling? not me; play this farce to those who cannot pierce the masquerade. I wager you are every inch a man; do you admit it, or must we wring the truth out of the maid-servants?

I know well the advice and warnings of my old friends: 'Put on a lock and keep your wife indoors.' Yes, and who will ward the warders? They get paid in kind for holding their tongues about their young lady's escapades; participation seals their lips. The wily wife arranges accordingly, and begins with them . . .

Translated by G. G. Ramsay, 1918
Some passages revised by Chris Baldick, 2011

SUETONIUS

From the *Lives of the Caesars*

[From the Life of Tiberius (Tiberius Claudius Nero Caesar, emperor 14–37 CE)]

Returning to the island of Capri, he became so negligent of government that he never filled vacancies arising among the equestrian order, the military staff, or the provincial administration, leaving Spain and Syria for several years without any consular governors. He allowed the Parthians to capture Armenia, the Dacians and Sarmatians to overrun Moesia, and the Germans to lay waste to Gaul, so humiliating and endangering the Empire in equal measure.

Shielded now by his private retreat, and secluded from the public gaze of Rome, he abandoned himself to all the perverted inclinations which he had previously tried to cover up, albeit without much success. Of these I shall here give a scrupulous account from the beginning. While still a young soldier, he had been such a heavy drinker that his nickname in camp was, instead of Tiberius Claudius Nero, *Biberius Caldius Mero*: 'Drinker of Neat Punch'. Once he had succeeded to the empire, and had undertaken the reform of public morality, he devoted two whole days and the night between to feasting and drinking with Pomponius Flaccus and Lucius Piso, whereupon he awarded the governership of Syria to the former, and the prefecture of Rome to the latter, endorsing them in their letters-patent as 'delightful companions at all hours of day or night'. When invited to dinner by Sestius Gallus, an extravagant old lecher who had been dismissed in disgrace from the Senate by Augustus and reprimanded by Tiberius himself only a few days previously, he accepted on condition that Gallus entertain him in exactly his usual style, so they would be waited on at table by naked girls. He promoted a virtually unknown candidate to the quaestorship ahead of the noblest contenders, simply because the man had downed a whole flagon of wine in one gulp at Tiberius's challenge. He lavished two hundred thousand sesterces upon Asellius Sabinus for composing a dialogue upon the quarrels of a mushroom, a fig-picker, an oyster, and a thrush. And he instituted a new office of Voluptuary-in-Chief, to which he appointed a knight of the realm, one Titus Caesonius Priscus.

In his retreat at Capri, he contrived a sodomy-lodge as a place in which to indulge his depravities privately: here, handpicked teams of girls and boy-prostitutes, artistes of perverted rutting known as his 'sphincter-gang', would writhe before him in threesomes to inflame his flagging lusts. He had a suite of rooms decorated with the lewdest pictures and statues, and provided with the writings of Elephantis,[40] so no visitor could be in any doubt as to what the emperor would require. He also set up bowers of debauchery among the woods and groves, where youngsters of both sexes posing as Pans and nymphs would prostitute themselves in caves and grottoes. So people openly referred to the place, by a pun on the island's name, as the 'old goatyard'.

But his outrages went even further, some being as unspeakable as they are incredible. For example, he would train little boys (whom he called his 'small-fry') to wriggle back and forth between his thighs while he was swimming and tickle him with licks and nibbles; and he would take sturdy but still unweaned babies and apply them to his penis as if to a teat. Such were the gratifications this man's nature inclined him to in his dotage. So when a painting by Parhasius, depicting Atalanta performing fellatio on Meleager,[41] was bequeathed to him with the proviso that if he found the subject offensive he could claim a million sesterces instead, he not only chose the picture but hung it up in his bedroom. Another story has it that during a sacrificial ceremony he became so excited by the attractions of the boy who was carrying the incense that, before the ritual was even finished, he hurried him and his brother, the flautist, outside and raped them both. When they joined one another in complaining at this violation, he promptly had their legs broken.

[From the Life of Caligula (Gaius Julius Caesar Germanicus, emperor 37–41 CE)]

He was strongly inclined to assume the crown, changing the nominally republican constitution to a monarchy; but, being told that he far exceeded the grandeur of kings and princes, he began to arrogate to himself a divine majesty. He ordered all the most beautiful and most revered images of the gods, including that of Jupiter Olympius, to be brought from Greece, so that he could have their heads removed and replaced with his own. Having continued part of the Palace as far as the Forum, and the temple of Castor and Pollux being converted into a kind of vestibule to his house, he often stationed himself between the twin brothers, and so presented himself to be worshipped by all votaries; some of whom saluted him by the name of *Jupiter Latialis.*[42] He also instituted a temple and priests, with choicest victims, in honour of his own divinity. In his temple stood a statue of gold, the exact image of himself, dressed every day in garments matching those he was wearing at the time. The wealthiest citizens offered to serve as his priests, paying immense bribes for the honour. The victims were flamingos, peacocks, bustards, guinea-fowls, and pheasant hens, each sacrificed on their respective days. On nights when the Moon was full, he was in the constant habit of inviting her to couple with him in his bed. In the daytime he talked in private to Jupiter Capitolinus, alternately whispering to him and turning his ear to him: sometimes he spoke aloud, and in railing language. For he was overheard to threaten the god thus: '*Raise thou me up, or I'll –*'. At last he claimed that the god had begged him to share his home, so he built a bridge over the temple of the Deified Augustus, by which he joined the Palace to the Capitol. Afterwards, he laid the foundations of a new palace in the very court of the Capitol, so as to be closer still.

[. . .]

He habitually committed incest with all his sisters;[43] and, at banquets attended by many guests, he placed each of them in order below him, whilst his wife reclined above him. It is believed that he deflowered one of them, Drusilla, before he had assumed the robe of manhood, and was even caught in the act by his grandmother Antonia, with whom they were staying together. When she was afterwards married to Cassius Longinus, a man of consular rank, he took her from him, and kept her constantly as if she were his lawful wife. Once when alarmed by an illness, he made a will appointing her heiress both of his estate and the Empire. After her death, he ordered a public mourning for her; during which it was a capital crime for any person to laugh, use the bath, or sup with his parents, wife, or children. Inconsolable with grief, he dashed by night from the City through Campania and on to Syracuse, then just as suddenly returned without shaving his beard, or trimming his hair. After that, whenever he had to swear a solemn oath, he always did so 'by the divinity of Drusilla', even in the assemblies of the people or before the soldiers. His remaining two sisters he did not treat with such fondness or regard; but frequently prostituted them to his catamites. So in the trial of Aemilius Lepidus,[44] he had no hesitation in condemning them as guilty of adultery, and of conniving in the conspiracy against him. Not only did he implicate them in the plot by publishing their own handwriting, procured by base and lewd means, but likewise he consecrated to Mars the Avenger three swords which, according to an inscription he attached to them, had been prepared by them to stab him.

It is difficult to say whether he acted more despicably to his wives by marrying them, by repudiating them, or by his conduct as a husband. Attending the wedding of Caius Piso with Livia Orestilla, he ordered the bride to be carried to his own house, but within a few days divorced her, and two years later banished her on suspicion of returning to the embraces of her former husband. Some say that he sent a messenger to Piso, who sat opposite to him at the wedding feast, with these words: 'Keep your hands off my wife', and that he immediately carried her off. Next day he published a proclamation announcing that he had taken a wife in the manner of Romulus and Augustus.[45] He suddenly summoned Lollia Paulina, who was in the province of her husband, a consular general, upon hearing that her grandmother was once very beautiful, and married her; but he soon afterwards discarded her, forbidding her further intimacy with any man. He loved with a most passionate and constant affection Caesonia, who was neither young nor beautiful (and was besides the mother of three daughters by another man) but a wanton of unbounded lasciviousness. When reviewing his troops, he would often have her ride beside him dressed in a military cloak, with shield and helmet. To his friends he even displayed her naked. After she had a child, he honoured her with the title of wife, declaring himself on the same day her husband and father of the child of which she was delivered. He named it Julia Drusilla, and after carrying it round the temples of all the goddesses, laid it on the lap of Minerva, to whom he entrusted her upbringing and schooling. He acknowledged her as his own child on account of her savage temper, which was such even in her infancy, that she would scratch her playmates' faces and eyes.

[. . .]

He never had the least regard either to the chastity of his own person, or that of others. He is said to have engaged in active and passive buggery with Marcus Lepidus, with Mnester the ballet-dancer, and with a number of foreign hostages. Valerius Catullus, a young man of a consular family, bawled aloud in public that he had sodomised the emperor, and had been quite exhausted by it. Besides his incest with his sisters, and his notorious passion for the prostitute Pyrallis, there was hardly any lady of distinction with whom he did not make free. He used commonly to invite them with their husbands to supper, and, as they passed by the couch on which he reclined at table, examine them very closely, like those who traffic in slaves, and would tilt up the face of any who cast her eyes down modestly. Then, whenever he was in the mood, he would quit the room, send for the woman he favoured, and in a short time return in a state of obvious dishevelment. He would then regale the company with a detailed critical assessment of her physical charms or defects and of her sexual performance. To some of these he granted divorces in the names of their absent husbands, and ordered these to be registered in the public records.

In the extent of his profuse expenditure, he surpassed all the prodigals that ever lived, inventing new ways of bathing, and unnatural meals and drinks: washing in precious unguents, both warm and cold, drinking pearls of immense value dissolved in vinegar, and serving up for his guests loaves and other foods modelled in gold; often saying that one should be either a thrifty type or an emperor. For several days at a time, he scattered prodigious amounts of money among the people, from the top of the Julian Basilica. He built two ships in Liburnian style, with ten banks of oars, poops ablaze with jewels, and multicoloured sails. These were fitted up with ample baths, galleries, and saloons, and supplied with a great variety of vines and other fruit-trees. In these he would sail by day along the coast of Campania, feasting amidst dancing and concerts of music. In building his palaces and villas, he was perversely devoted to achieving what was considered impossible. Accordingly, moles were formed in deep and inhospitable seas, rocks of the hardest stone cut away, plains raised to the height of mountains with a vast mass of earth, and the tops of mountains levelled by digging; and all these were to be executed with incredible speed, for the least remissness was a capital offence. Without dwelling on details, suffice to say that within less than a year he spent the entire fortune amassed by Tiberius, amounting to 2,700 millions of sesterces, and enormous sums beyond that.

[. . .]

In the fashion of his clothes, shoes, and all the rest of his dress, he scorned to wear what was proper for Romans, for men, or even for mere mortals. He often appeared in public wearing a short coat of stout cloth, richly embroidered and blazing with jewels, or a sleeved tunic with bracelets upon his arms; sometimes all in silk or in a woman's gown; at other times in slippers or buskins; sometimes shod like a soldier, sometimes like a woman. He commonly sported a golden beard fixed to his chin, and would brandish some divine symbol: a thunderbolt, a trident, or a serpent-entwined rod. Sometimes, too, he appeared dressed up as Venus. Even before a military campaign, he would festoon himself as a victorious general, sometimes wearing the breast-plate of Alexander the Great, stolen from his tomb.

[From the Life of Nero (Nero Claudius Caesar Augustus Germanicus, emperor 54–68 CE)]

As his vices gradually took a stronger hold on him, he laid aside his jocular pretence and broke out into heinous crimes, without the least attempt to conceal them. His revels were prolonged from midday to midnight, interspersed by warm baths, or in summer by snow-chilled dips. He often drained the artificial lakes of the Campus Martius and the Circus and held public dinners there, to which he invited common prostitutes of the town, and dancing-girls. Whenever he went down the Tiber to Ostia, or coasted through the gulf of Baiae, he had makeshift brothels erected along the shore and river banks; before which stood matrons posing as madams, beckoning him ashore. It was also his custom to invite himself to supper with his friends, one of whom spent no less than four million sesterces on floral garlands, while another spent even more on roses.

In addition to corrupting free-born boys and seducing married women, he raped Rubria, a Vestal Virgin. He nearly managed to marry Acte, his freedwoman, by suborning some men of consular rank to swear that she was of royal descent. He castrated the boy Sporus in an attempt to transform him into a woman. He even went so far as to marry him, with the full formalities of a dowry, a rose-coloured nuptial veil, and a numerous company at the wedding. When the ceremony was over, he had him conducted like a bride to his own house, and treated him as his wife. Somebody joked that Nero's father Domitius would have changed the world for the better by taking this sort of wife. Nero carried Sporus about with him in a litter, dressed in the rich attire of an empress, through all the solemn assemblies and fairs of Greece, and afterwards through the busiest streets of Rome, kissing him from time to time as they rode together. Everyone was convinced that he entertained an incestuous passion for his mother Agrippina, but her enemies prevented any consummation, fearing that it would put him entirely in the power of this ruthlessly ambitious woman; so he introduced amongst his concubines a whore who bore a striking resemblance to Agrippina. Even before this, it is said that whenever he rode in a litter with his mother, he would engage in incest with her, as the stains on his clothes showed.

He wallowed in every kind of filth, defiling every part of his body with some unclean perversion. Then he invented a new amusement, which was to be released from a den in the arena, covered with the skin of a wild beast, and then to attack the private parts of men and women who were were bound to stakes. Once he had whetted his appetites upon them, the finishing touch, shall we say, would be provided by his freedman Doryphorus. This man Nero married in the same way that Sporus had been married to himself, and he imitated the cries and shrieks of a young virgin when she is deflowered. I have been informed from numerous sources that he firmly believed no man in the world could stay chaste, or keep any part of his body undefiled, but that most men concealed their vices, and were cunning enough to keep them secret. To those, therefore, who openly confessed their unnatural lewdness, he forgave all other crimes.

He thought there was no other use of riches and money than to squander them away profusely; regarding all those who kept their expenses within due bounds as sordid wretches; and extolling those as truly noble and generous souls, who lavished away and wasted all they possessed. He praised and admired his uncle Caligula especially for squandering in a short time the vast fortune left him by Tiberius. Accordingly, he was himself extravagant beyond all bounds. He spent upon Tiridates[46] eight hundred thousand sesterces a day, a sum almost incredible, and, at his departure, presented him with upwards of a million. He likewise bestowed upon Menecrates the harper, and Spiculus the gladiator, estates and houses fit for men who have received the honour of a triumph. He enriched the usurer Cercopithecus Panerotes with estates both in town and country; later giving him a funeral of almost princely magnificence. He never wore the same garment twice. He was known to stake four hundred thousand sesterces on a throw of the dice. When fishing, he would use a golden net, strung with silken cords of purple and scarlet. It is said that he never travelled with fewer than a thousand baggage-carts, the mules being all shod with silver, the drivers dressed in scarlet jackets of the finest Canusian cloth, with a numerous train of footmen, and troops of Mauretanians, with bracelets on their arms mounted upon horses in splendid trappings.

In nothing was he more prodigal than in his buildings. He completed his palace by continuing it from the Palatine to the Esquiline hill, calling the building at first only 'The Passage', but, after it was burnt down and rebuilt, 'The Golden House'. Of its dimensions and furniture, it may be sufficient to say thus much: the porch was so high that there stood in it a colossal statue of himself a hundred and twenty feet in height; and the space included in it was so ample, that it had triple porticos a mile in length, and a lake like a sea, surrounded with buildings resembling a city. Within its area were corn-fields, vineyards, pastures, and woods, containing a vast number of animals of various kinds, both wild and tame. In other parts it was entirely overlaid with gold, and adorned with jewels and mother of pearl. The dining rooms were vaulted, and compartments of the ceilings, inlaid with ivory, were made to slide back, and scatter flowers; while they contained pipes which sprinkled perfumes upon the guests. The chief banqueting room was circular, and revolved perpetually, night, and day, in imitation of the motion of the celestial bodies. The baths were supplied with water from the sea and the Albula. Upon the dedication of this magnificent house after it was finished, all he said in approval of it was, that he had now a dwelling fit for a man.

[. . .]

When somebody in a conversation said 'When I am dead let fire devour the world', Nero said, 'No, let it be while I am living.' And he acted accordingly; for, pretending to be disgusted with the old buildings, and the narrow and winding streets, he set the city on fire so openly, that many of consular rank caught his own household servants on their property with tow and torches in their hands, but dared not meddle with them. Near his Golden House were some stone-built granaries, the site of which he greatly coveted, so he had them razed with siege-engines, and set them on fire. During six days and seven nights this terrible devastation continued, the people being obliged to fly to the tombs and monuments for lodging and shelter. Meanwhile, a vast number of stately buildings, the houses of generals celebrated in former times, and even then still decorated with the spoils of war, were reduced to ashes; as well as the temples of the gods, which had been vowed and dedicated by the kings of Rome, in the Punic and Gallic wars: in short, everything that was remarkable and worthy to be seen which time had spared. This fire he beheld from a tower in the house of Maecenas, and, greatly delighted, as he put it, 'with the beautiful effects of the conflagration', he sang a poem on the ruin of Troy, in the tragic dress he used on the stage. He promised to remove the bodies of those who had perished in the fire, and clear the rubble at his own expense; but he allowed no one to meddle with the remains of their own property, so that he could profit from this calamity by plunder and looting. But he not only received, but exacted contributions on account of the loss, until he had exhausted the means both of the provinces and private citizens.

To these terrible and shameful calamities brought upon the people by their emperor, were added some arising from misfortune. These included a plague, from which, within the space of one autumn, at least thirty thousand people died, as appeared from the registers in the temple of Libitina; a great disaster in Britain, where two of the Roman garrison towns were stormed, with dreadful casualties among our troops and allies; a shameful defeat of the army of the East, where, in Armenia, the legions were obliged to pass under the yoke, and we came close to losing Syria.

[. . .]

Arriving back at Rome, he made no appeal either to the Senate or people, but calling together some of the leading men at his own house, he held a hasty consultation upon the present state of affairs, and then, during the remainder of the day, led them about with him to view some newly invented musical instruments which were played by water. He exhibited all the parts, and spoke to them about the principles and difficulties of the contrivance, which, he told them, he intended to produce in the theatre, if Vindex[47] would give him leave.

Soon afterwards, he received intelligence that Galba and the Spaniards had declared against him; upon which, he fainted, and losing his reason, lay a long time speechless, and apparently dead. As soon as he recovered from this state of stupefaction, he tore his clothes, and beat his head, crying out, 'It is all over with me!' His nurse tried to comfort him, telling him that similar things had happened to other princes before him, but he replied, 'I am beyond all example wretched, for I have lost an empire whilst I am still living.' None the less, he did nothing but carry on with his usual luxury and indolence. Whenever he heard any good news from the provinces, he would throw another sumptuous entertainment and compose mocking ditties about the leaders of the revolt, singing these cheerfully while accompanying them with insulting gestures; these became public favourites. Once when he was smuggled into the theatre, he warned an actor he saw milking the audience's applause that he should not take such advantage of Nero's retirement from the stage.

At the first outbreak of the revolt, he is believed to have formed many monstrous but entirely typical plans. These were to employ assassins to butcher all the former provincial governors and army commanders, as men unanimously engaged in a conspiracy against him, and to replace them; to massacre the exiles in every quarter as potential insurrectionists, and all the Gaulish population in Rome as accomplices in their countrymen's rebellion; to abandon Gaul itself, to be laid waste and plundered by his armies; to poison the whole Senate at a feast; to set the city alight again, and then let wild beasts loose upon the people, so as to prevent them from containing the flames. But being deterred from the execution of these designs, not so much by remorse of conscience, as by despair of being able to effect them; and judging an expedition into Gaul necessary, he prematurely removed the consuls from their office; and in their place assumed the consulship himself without a colleague, saying the fates had decreed that Gaul could be conquered only by a consul. Upon assuming the insignia of office, after an entertainment at the palace, as he staggered out of the room on the arms of some of his friends, he declared that as soon as he arrived in the province he would make his appearance amongst the troops, unarmed, and do nothing but weep, which would bring the mutineers to repentance; and that the following day he would sing songs of triumph amid general rejoicing, which he really ought now to get down to composing.

In preparing for this expedition, his chief concern was to provide carriages for his musical instruments and stage props, to have the hair of the concubines he carried with him dressed in the fashion of men, and to supply them with battle-axes and Amazonian shields.

English version by Chris Baldick, after the 1796 Alexander Thomson translation as revised (1855) by Thomas Forester

ANONYMOUS

From the *Augustan History: The Life of Elagabalus*[48]

After he had spent the winter in Nicomedia, leading a depraved life of active and passive sodomy with men, the soldiers soon began to regret that they had conspired against Macrinus to make this man emperor, and they turned their thoughts toward his cousin Alexander, who on the murder of Macrinus had been hailed by the Senate as Caesar. For who could tolerate an emperor who would welcome lust into every bodily orifice, when not even a beast of this sort would be tolerated? Even at Rome he did nothing but send out agents to seek and bring back to the palace especially well-hung men so that he might enjoy their vigour. He also used to play the story of Paris in his house, with himself in the role of Venus, and would suddenly drop his clothing to the ground and fall naked on his knees, one hand on his breast, the other on his private parts, with his buttocks stuck out and thrust back in front of his fellow-pervert. Similarly, he would make up his face to resemble paintings of Venus, and he had his whole body depilated, regarding it as the principal enjoyment of his life to seem universally desirable.

He took money for honours and distinctions and positions of power, selling them in person or through his slaves and those who served his lusts. He made appointments to the Senate without regard to age, property, or rank, and solely for money, and he sold the positions of captain and tribune, legate and general, along with procuratorships and posts in palace. The charioteers Protogenes and Gordius, whom he had once raced with, he later made his associates in his daily life and actions. Many whose personal appearance pleased him he took from the stage, the circus, and the arena and brought to the palace. And he had such a passion for Hierocles that he kissed him in the groin, a place which it is indecent even to mention, declaring that he was celebrating the festival of Flora.

[. . .]

All sorts of filthy anecdotes about his life have been put into writing, but since those are not worth recording, I have seen fit to relate only such deeds as illustrate his extravagance. Some of these were reportedly done before he ascended the throne, others after he was made emperor; as he himself declared, his models were Apicius among commoners and, among emperors, Otho and Vitellius.[49] For example, he was the first commoner to cover his couches with golden coverlets – for this was lawful then by authorisation of Marcus Antoninus, who had sold at public auction all the imperial trappings. Also, he gave summer banquets in various colours, one day a green banquet, another day an iridescent one, and a blue one after that, varying them continually every day of the summer. Moreover, he was the first to use silver urns and casseroles, and vessels of chased silver – one hundred pounds in weight, some of them defiled by the lewdest designs. He was also the first to concoct wine seasoned with mastic and with pennyroyal and all such luxuries found in our own times. He did not invent rose wine, but he used to make it more fragrant by adding pulverized pine-cone. In fact, none of those kinds of drink is to be found in books before the time of Elagabalus. For him, indeed, life was nothing but a quest for pleasures. He was the first to make force-meat of fish, or of oysters of various kinds or similar shell-fish, or of lobsters, crayfish, and squills. He used to strew roses and all manner of flowers, such as lilies, violets, hyacinths, and narcissus, over his banqueting-rooms, his couches and his porticoes, and then stroll about in them. He would refuse to swim in a pool unless it were perfumed with saffron or some other prized essence. And he could not rest easily on cushions unless these were stuffed with rabbit-fur or feathers from under the wings of partridges, and he used to change the pillows frequently.

He often showed contempt for the Senate, calling them slaves in togas, while he treated the Roman people as peasants and the equestrian order as nonentities. He frequently invited the city-prefect to a drinking-bout after a banquet and also summoned the prefects of the guard, sending a master of ceremonies, in case they declined, to compel them to come. And he intended to create a city-prefect for each district of Rome, thus making fourteen for the city; and he would have done it, too, had he lived, for he was always ready to promote men of the basest character and the lowest calling.

He had couches made of solid silver for use in his banqueting-rooms and his bed-chambers. In imitation of Apicius he frequently ate camels' heels and also cocks' combs taken from the living birds, and the tongues of peacocks and nightingales, because he was told that those who ate them were immune from the plague. He also served to the palace attendants huge platters heaped up with the innards of mullets, and flamingo brains, partridge eggs, thrush brains, and the heads of parrots, pheasants, and peacocks. And the beards of the mullets that he served were so large that they were brought on, in place of cress or parsley or pickled beans or fenugreek, in well-filled bowls and dishes – a particularly amazing performance.

He fed his dogs on goose-livers. Among his pets he had lions and leopards, which had been rendered harmless and trained by tamers, and these he would suddenly order during the dessert and the after-dessert to get up on the couches, thereby causing an amusing panic, for none knew that the beasts were harmless. He sent grapes from Apamea to his stables for his horses, and he fed parrots and pheasants to his lions and other wild animals. For ten successive days, too, he served wild sows' udders with the wombs, at the rate of thirty a day, also serving peas with gold-pieces, lentils with onyx, beans with amber, and rice with pearls; and he also sprinkled pearls instead of pepper on fish and mushrooms. In a banqueting-room with a reversible ceiling he once overwhelmed his hangers-on with violets and other flowers, so that some were actually smothered to death, being unable to crawl up to the surface. He flavoured his swimming-pools and bath-tubs with essence of spices or of roses or wormwood. And once he invited the common mob to a drinking-bout, and himself drank with the populace, imbibing so much that, on seeing what he alone consumed, people supposed he had drained one of his swimming-pools. As banquet-favours, he gave eunuchs, or four-horse chariots, or saddled horses, or mules, or litters, or carriages, or a thousand gold pieces or a hundred pounds of silver.

At his banquets he would also distribute lucky chances inscribed on spoons, the chance of one person reading 'ten camels', of another 'ten flies', of another 'ten pounds of gold', of another 'ten pounds of lead', of another 'ten ostriches', of another 'ten hen's eggs', so that they were lucky chances indeed and men tried their luck. These he also gave at his games, distributing chances for ten bears or ten dormice, ten lettuces or ten pounds of gold. Indeed he was the first to introduce this practice of giving chances, which we still maintain. And the performers too he invited to what really were chances, giving as prizes a dead dog or a pound of beef, or else a hundred gold pieces, or a hundred pieces of silver, or a hundred coppers, and so on. All this so pleased the populace that on each occasion they rejoiced that he was emperor.

He gave a naval spectacle, it is said, on the circus-canals, which had been filled with wine, and he sprinkled the people's cloaks with perfume made from the wild grape; also he drove a chariot drawn by four elephants on the Vatican Hill, destroying the tombs which obstructed the way, and he harnessed four camels to a chariot at a private spectacle in the circus. He is also said to have collected serpents with the aid of priests of the Marsian nation and suddenly let them loose before dawn, when the populace usually assembled for the better-attended games; and many people were injured by bites as well as in the general panic. He would wear a tunic made wholly of cloth of gold, or one made of purple, or a Persian one studded with jewels, and at such times he would say that he felt oppressed by the weight of his pleasures. He even wore jewels on his shoes, sometimes engraved ones – a practice which aroused the derision of all, as if, indeed, the engraving of famous artists could be seen on jewels attached to his feet. He wished to wear also a jewelled diadem to enhance his beauty and make his face look more like a woman's; and in his own house he did wear one. He promised a phoenix to some guests, it is said, or in lieu of the bird a thousand pounds of gold, and this sum he handed out in the imperial residence. He constructed swimming-pools filled with sea-water in places especially far inland, and would hand them over to individual friends who swam in them; or at another time he would fill them with fish. One summer he made a mountain of snow in the pleasure-garden attached to his house, having snow carried there for the purpose. When on the sea-coast he never ate fish, but in places furthest inland he regularly served all kinds of sea-food, and the country folk in the interior he regularly fed with the semen of lampreys and pikes.

The fish he ate were cooked in a bluish sauce that preserved their natural colour, as though they were still in the sea-water. He supplied the swimming-pools that he used with essence of roses and with the flowers themselves, and when he bathed with all his courtiers he would provide oil of nard for the hot-rooms; he also furnished balsam-oil for the lamps. He never, except with his wife, had intercourse with the same woman twice, and he set up brothels in his house for his friends, his clients, and his slaves. He never spent less on a banquet than one hundred thousand sesterces, that is, thirty pounds of silver; and sometimes he even spent as much as three million, all told. In fact, he even outdid the banquets of Vittelius and Apicius. He would take fish from his ponds by the ox-load, and then, as he passed through the market, bewail the public poverty. He used to bind his hangers-on to a water-wheel and, by a turn of the wheel, plunge them into the water and then bring them back to the surface again, while calling them river-Ixions.[50] He used Laconian marble and porphyry to pave the courtyards of his 'Antonine' Palace; this pavement lasted down to within our own memory but was recently torn up and destroyed. And he planned to erect a single column of enormous size, which could be ascended inside, and to place on its summit the god Elagabalus, but although he planned to bring it from the district of Thebes, he could not obtain enough stone.

When his friends became drunk he would often shut them up, and suddenly during the night let in his lions and leopards and bears – all of them harmless – so that his friends on awakening at dawn, or worse, during the night, would find lions and leopards and bears sharing their room; and some even died as a result. Some of his humbler friends he would seat on air-pillows instead of on cushions and let out the air while they were dining, so that often the diners were suddenly found under the table. Finally, he was the first to think of placing a semi-circular group of guests on the ground instead of on couches, so that the air-pillows could be loosened by slave-boys stationed at their feet, letting the air out.

When adultery was represented on the stage, he would order what was usually simulated to be done authentically. He often purchased prostitutes from all the pimps and then set them free. Once during a private conversation the question arose as to how many men in Rome had hernias, at which he issued an order that all of them should be identified and brought to his baths, and then he bathed with them, some of them being men of distinction. Before a banquet he would frequently watch gladiatorial fights and boxing matches, from a couch spread for himself in an upper gallery; and during luncheon he would exhibit criminals in wild-beast hunts. His hangers-on would often be served during dessert with food made of wax or wood or ivory, sometimes of earthenware, or at times even of marble or stone; so that everything he ate himself would be served to them too, but in different materials just for show, so all the while they would merely drink with each course and wash their hands, just as if they had really eaten.

He is reputed to have been the first Roman to wear clothing wholly of silk, although garments partly of silk were in use before his time. Linen that had been washed he would never touch, saying that washed linen was worn only by beggars.

[. . .]

He gathered together in a public building all the whores from the circus, the theatre, the stadium and every other place of amusement, and from the public baths, and then harangued them in military fashion, addressing them as 'comrades' and lecturing them on a variety of perversions and sexual positions. Afterwards he invited to a similar assembly pimps, catamites gathered from far and wide, and lewd boys and youths. And whereas he had appeared before the whores in a woman's costume with protruding breasts, he met the catamites dressed as a boy-prostitute. After his speech he announced a bounty of three gold pieces each, just as if they were soldiers, and asked them to pray the gods that they might find others to recommend to him.

He also used to play tricks on his slaves, even ordering them to bring him a thousand pounds of spider-webs and offering them a prize; and he is said to have collected ten thousand pounds of the webs, then remarking that one could see from that how extensive a city was Rome. He also used to send to his hangers-on as their yearly allowance of provisions jars of frogs, scorpions, snakes, and suchlike reptiles, and he would shut up a vast number of flies in jars of this sort and call them tamed bees.

He often brought four-horse chariots from the circus into his banqueting-rooms or porticoes while he lunched or dined, compelling his guests to drive, even though they were old men and some of them had held public office. Even when he had become emperor, he would give an order to bring in to him ten thousand mice, a thousand weasels, or a thousand shrew-mice. So skilful were his confectioners and dairymen, that all the various kinds of food that were served by his meat-cooks or fruit-cooks, they would also serve up, making them now out of confectionery or again out of dairy products. His hangers-on he would serve with dinners made of glass, and at times he would send to their table only embroidered napkins with pictures of the food that was set before himself, as many in number as the courses which he was to have, so that they were served only with representations made by the needle or the loom. Sometimes, however, paintings too were displayed to them, so that they were served with the whole dinner, as it were, but were all the while tormented by hunger. He would also mix jewels with apples and flowers, and he would throw out of the window quite as much food as he served to his friends. He gave an order, too, that an amount of public grain equal to one year's tribute should be given to all the whores, pimps, and catamites who were within the city walls, and promised an equal amount to those beyond, for, thanks to the foresight of his predecessors, there was in Rome at that time a store of grain equal to seven years' tribute.

He would harness four huge dogs to a chariot and drive about within the royal residence, and he did the same thing, before he was made emperor, on his country estates. He even appeared in public driving four enormous stags. Once he harnessed lions to his chariot and called himself the Great Mother, and on another occasion, tigers, and called himself Bacchus; and he always appeared in the particular costume in which the deity he was representing was usually depicted. He kept at Rome tiny Egyptian snakes, called by the natives 'good genii', besides hippopotami, a crocodile, and a rhinoceros, and, in fact, everything Egyptian that was available. And sometimes at his banquets he served ostriches, saying that the Jews had been commanded to eat them.

Something he is said to have done certainly seems most odd: he invited men of the highest rank to a luncheon and covered a semi-circular couch with saffron-flowers, and then said that he was providing them with the kind of hay that their rank demanded. The occupations of the day he performed at night, and those of the night in the daytime, and he considered it a mark of luxury to wait until a late hour before rising from sleep and beginning to hold his levee, and also to remain awake until morning. He received his courtiers every day, and he seldom let any go without a gift, save those he found to be thrifty, for he regarded these as worthless.

His chariots were jewelled and golden, for he scorned those that were merely of silver or ivory or bronze. He would harness women of exceptional beauty to a one-wheeled cart in fours, in twos, in threes or even more, and would drive them about, usually naked himself, as too were the women pulling him.

He had the custom, too, of asking to dinner eight bald men, or else eight one-eyed men, or eight gouty men, or eight deaf men, or eight dark men, or eight tall men, or, again, eight fat men, his purpose being, in the case of these last, since they could not be accommodated on one couch, to call forth general laughter. He would present to his guests all the silver plate that he had in the banqueting-room and the entire supply of goblets, and he did it very often too. He was the first Roman emperor to serve at a public banquet diluted fish-pickle, for previously this had been only a soldier's dish – a usage which later was promptly restored by Alexander. He would propose to his guests, as well, by way of a challenge, that they should invent new sauces to add flavour to the food, and he would offer a very large prize for the man whose invention should please him, even presenting him with a silk garment – then regarded as a rarity and a mark of honour. On the other hand, if the sauce did not please him, the inventor was ordered to continue eating it until he invented a better one. Of course he always sat among costly flowers or perfumes, and he loved to hear the prices of the food served at his table exaggerated, declaring it to be an appetizer for the banquet.

He dressed himself up as a confectioner, a perfumer, a cook, a shop-keeper, or a pimp, and he even practised all these occupations in his own house continually. At one dinner where there were many tables he brought in the heads of six hundred ostriches, for the brains to be eaten. Occasionally he gave a banquet in which he would serve twenty-two courses of lavish dishes, and between each course he and his guests would bathe and fornicate with women, all taking an oath that they were enjoying themselves. And once he gave a banquet in which one course was served in the house of each guest, and although one lived on the Capitol, one on the Palatine, one beyond the Rampart, one on the Caelian, and one across the Tiber, still each course was served in one of their houses in turn, and they went about to the homes of all. So it was hardly possible to finish the banquet within a whole day, especially as between the courses they bathed and fornicated with women. He always served a course of Sybariticum, consisting of oil and fish-pickle, which the Sybarites invented in the year in which they all perished. It is also said that he constructed baths in many places, bathed in them once, and immediately demolished them, merely in order that he might not derive any advantage from them. And he is said to have done the same with houses, military headquarters and summer-houses. However, these and some other things that beggar belief were, I believe, fabricated by those who wished to vilify Elagabalus in order to curry favour with Alexander.

He is said to have purchased a very famous and beautiful prostitute for one hundred thousand sesterces and then kept her untouched like a virgin. When someone asked him, before he became emperor, 'Are you not afraid of becoming poor?' he is said to have answered 'What could be better than that I should be my own heir, and my wife's too?' He had abundant means, besides, bequeathed to him by many out of regard for his father. He said, too, that he did not wish to have sons, in case one of them turned out to be thrifty. He used to order perfumes from India to be burned without coals, to fill his houses with the fumes. Even when a commoner he never made a journey with fewer than sixty wagons, though his grandmother Varia used to protest that he would squander all his wealth; but as emperor he would take with him, it is said, as many as six hundred, asserting that the king of the Persians travelled with ten thousand camels and Nero with five hundred carriages. The reason for all these vehicles was the vast number of his pimps, madams, whores, catamites, and well-hung fellow-perverts. In the public baths, he always bathed with the women, and he even treated them himself with a depilatory ointment, applying it also to his own beard and – shameful to relate – in the same place where the women were treated and at the same hour. He shaved his minions' groins, using the razor with his own hand, with which he would then shave his beard. He would strew gold and silver dust about a portico and then lament that he could not strew amber dust too; and he often did this when he proceeded on foot to his horse or his carriage, as they do today with golden sand.

He never put on the same shoes twice, and is said never to have worn the same ring a second time. He often tore up costly garments. Once he took a whale and weighed it and then sent his friends its weight in fish. He sank some heavily laden ships in the harbour and then said that this indicated greatness of soul. He would empty his bowels in golden vessels, and his urinals were made of murra or onyx. And he is said to have remarked: 'If I ever have an heir, I shall appoint a guardian for him, to make him do what I have myself done and intend to do.' He was accustomed as well to have dinners served to him of a special kind: one day he would eat nothing but pheasant, serving only pheasant-meat at every course; another day he would serve only chicken; on another, one kind of fish, and then another kind; on another day pork; on another ostrich, or greens, or fruits, or sweets, or dairy products. He would often shut up his friends in hostels overnight with old Ethiopian hags and compel them to stay there until morning, saying that the most beautiful women were kept in these places. He did this same thing with boys, too – for then, before the time of Philip,[51] that is, such a thing was lawful. Sometimes he laughed so loud in the theatre that no one else could be heard by the audience. He could sing and dance, play the pipes, the horn and the mandolin, and he performed on the organ. He is also said to have visited in a single day every prostitute of the circus, the theatre, the amphitheatre, and all the public places of Rome, covering his head with a muleteer's cap so as to go unrecognised; but without satisfying his lusts, he gave each prostitute a gold coin, saying as he did so: 'Tell no-one, but this is a gift from Antoninus.' He invented certain new perversions, surpassing even the sphincter-specialists retained by earlier emperors, and he was well-acquainted with all the arrangements of Tiberius, Caligula, and Nero.

A prophecy had been made to him by some Syrian priests that he would die a violent death. And so he had prepared ropes woven with purple and scarlet silk, so that if the need arose he could put an end to his life by the noose. He had golden swords prepared too, with which to stab himself if violence encroached. He also had poisons ready, concealed in onyxes and sapphires and emeralds, with which to kill himself if destruction threatened. And he also built himself a very high tower with gilded and jewelled boards laid before him, for him to hurl himself down upon; for even his death, he declared, should be costly and luxurious, so that it might be said that no one had ever died in this fashion. But all these preparations availed him nothing, for, as we have said, he was killed by common soldiers, dragged through the streets, shoved degradingly into sewers, and finally slung into the Tiber.

Translation by David Magie (1924), extensively revised by Chris Baldick

DÉSIRÉ NISARD

From 'Lucan, or The Decadence', *Cultural-Critical Studies of the Poets of the Latin Decadence*, chapter 7

Poets of lesser ages compose works of art in which we find choice passages; but poets of the decadence write beautiful lines. This does not mean that we cannot find choice passages in their works: we do encounter really beautiful examples, especially in Juvenal and in Lucan, although their poetry is inferior to that of their predecessors. It does mean, though, that the kind of beauty that matters most in decadent poetry lies in isolated lines, or what in critical jargon we may call flourishes [*traits*].

XVII Flourishes as the Basis of Beauty in Periods of Decadence

In periods of decadence, then, beauty appears in the form of the flourish. In decadent poetry there is none, or scarcely any, of that magnificent expansiveness that Virgil gives us, in which every element is imbued with the same intensity, every image comes naturally without seeming elaborate or contrived, where nothing is sacrificed for the sake of striking effects, and where language conjures no mirages beyond the grasp of thought.

The flourish offers us a stimulating but questionable kind of beauty, the kind that wakes the reader up amid an otherwise lifeless passage. There is something in the flourish that pleases and provokes us, but whether this is the idea or the turn of phrase is hard to say. You may ponder over this special effect, assess it, analyse the pleasure it gives (undeniable as that is), but I defy you to justify it in terms of your feelings or by the light of reason. Now compare it with the pleasure given you by the poetic beauty to be found in the ancient epics or in the great ages of literature. In these cases we feel that we have gained an enlarged moral or philosophical perspective, a kind of truth that is felt as well as understood, whose light reveals to us our own hearts. But with decadent poetry, what do we feel, apart from the pleasure of surprise prompted by some unusual juxtaposition, some happy combination of words, some neatly finished phrase or quip? In lesser periods, the poet composes the poem for the sake of the choice passage; but the decadent poet writes his choice passage for the sake of the flourish. And at the cost of so much carelessness and so much effort leading up to it! It seems practically as though the poet knows that he has nothing better to offer us than his final flourish, so he sacrifices all the rest to it: he tires you out with mundane details and leaden verses so you will find his flourish more appetizing. In rhyming poems, the flourish is brought about by artificial padding; and we find more or less the same process wherever poetry has fallen into a state of decadence.

When all is said and done, the flourish, such as it is, and despite the dubious admiration it invites and the easy target it offers to criticism, can produce an effect that is pleasant enough (especially coming after tediously prolonged padding), so long as it is not used too frequently. But in decadent poetry it turns up all the time, rounding off every stanza and every speech, like the refrain of a popular song. The more imaginative and ingenious the poet is, the more flourishes he will scatter about; so, if we take these effects as embellishments, then there are some poems that are so strongly spiced with them that we could fault them for being rather too beautiful. Beauty is a word more applicable to simplicity than to self-consciousness, but I have often heard it applied to certain contemporary poets who are so prolific with this kind of flourish that we should reproach them gently for repeatedly courting admiration. Indeed, while we may be full of admiration for the first flourishes we come across in a book of verse, this admiration will cool if they proliferate, so we will carry on reading only from reluctance to contradict ourselves. If the whole book is full of them, we will put it aside instantly, having found it too beautified. The truth of the matter is that any beauty we grow tired of is not real beauty, our admiration for it not surviving beyond our initial surprise. On the other hand, our admiration for genuine beauty is like a gentle flame that never goes out so long as we live. Such feelings are more self-interested than one might think: we admire only what benefits us, whatever enhances the treasures of our minds, and poetry that offers us no such genuine profit will be admired only out of consideration for the author or, often enough, as a matter of fashion.

XVIII The Flourish, as the Kind of Beauty Appreciated Most by Youthful Tastes

The flourish is a kind of beauty greatly appreciated by the young, at a time when their admiration is untroubled by any consideration of intellectual attainments. There is a certain phase of vacancy in the years between adolescence and early manhood when the mind feasts upon colours and surface appearances, not suspecting that there is anything beyond these. In this phase, the mind's extremely restless curiosity, stimulated by all the restrictions and constraints of its upbringing, urges it to see everything there is to see, while preventing it from seeing anything in depth. These are the years that belong to the poet of a decadent period. We savour his doubtful beauties all the more when we give no thought to any benefit we could derive from them; when what we ask for is impressions rather than knowledge. This explains why paltry poems sprinkled with flourishes are preferred to those masterpieces whose sole inspiration is the eloquent voice of reason. At that age, the mind skims so rapidly and lightly over everything that you would need to wave a red rag in front of it to hold its attention; as for more profound contemplative poems, it will flit past them without any inkling of the depths they conceal.

I have noticed that even among young people brought up on the study of such poetry, what strikes them the most are a few flourishes that have slipped in on account of a failure of inspiration or a lapse in taste, these being either derivative sound-effects or bombastic phrases. They are charmed by sumptuous lines, by academic styles of beauty, finding in them an alloy of golden-age writings with baser metals. I once assumed that the resources of a good classical education would protect them adequately from the seductions of such verse; but when decadent poetry is put before them, not only do they lap it up eagerly, they invest this new-found admiration with the ardour of emancipated spirits who are shaking off a taste that has been prescribed for them, permitted at last not to take its merits on trust any longer.

Nothing could be simpler and more natural. Questionable kinds of beauty are bound to suit an uncertain time of life. Audacity of style is more to a young man's liking than the truths of experience clothed in a subdued style. The poetical beauties of great periods are usually no more than fine public expressions of universal truths and of experience. We can only take these at our teacher's word, at least until we reach the age at which we can compare our knowledge with our experience. People say 'comparison is not the same thing as reason', but it is also true to say that reason is always comparative. So, those who have had nothing with which to make comparisons cannot be brought unprompted to appreciate poetical beauty, which is precisely the expression of things that they have not yet encountered. There is something rather inconsistent, surely, in asking a young man to judge portrayals of the human heart when he has not yet listened to his own heart, in expecting him to appreciate the higher truths of experience when he is still only a pupil, or in discussing life with someone who hasn't yet lived.

We come back to the great poets only once we have been the heroes of their poems, each in our own little sphere and according to our sensibility; that is, once we have loved and hated and suffered just like those individually named but universal characters of theirs, who act out in their poems the drama of human life. After we have left school, we are sometimes cut off from these masters, either by following another path in life or because we are led astray by literary fashions that throw up doubtful talents. But after some years devoted to gathering all kinds of impressions, good or bad, when at last we have steadied ourselves, we unwittingly come across a thousand delicate links between these first experiments with life and recollections of poetry learnt at school; these surprise us, stimulate us, interest us, and end up leading us back to those poets whose mastery of beauty also teaches us what is good.

Only then do our literary ideas take shape and establish themselves. We bid farewell to the poets of decadent periods and their purple passages, and we reserve our hours of leisure for the earliest poets, for the poets of the golden ages, for those of the highest genius who have uttered in immortal words the truths essential to the preservation of man's moral grandeur, whenever and wherever it is found, individually, in family life, or in the service of the State.

If I were asked what purpose may be served by decadent poetry and its doubtful attractions, I would say (once the critics have compiled their historical notes on it all) 'To make us love poetry of greater periods'. For a healthy mind, occasional admiration for the beauties of decadent writers provides a certain elasticity to the imagination, encourages a comparative disposition, and leads eventually to a sensible and natural reaction in favour of the finer kinds of poetry that had been abandoned upon leaving school. As for unhealthy minds, dragging themselves through the poetry of the golden ages for a lifetime would not set them to rights.

1834; translated by Jane Desmarais and Chris Baldick, 2011

THÉOPHILE GAUTIER

From 'Charles Baudelaire'

While he granted the old masters the full admiration their historic merits deserved, he felt no obligation to adopt them as models. They had had the good fortune to have arrived in the world's younger days: at the dawning, so to speak, of humanity, when nothing had yet been expressed, when each form, each image, and each feeling had a charm still virginal in its novelty. The great commonplaces which form the basis for all human thought were then in full bloom, and were quite sufficient for these simple minds in addressing a rather infantile public. Yet these broad poetical themes became worn out by repetition, as coins lose their relief when kept too long in circulation. And besides, life having since become more complicated and increasingly burdened with thoughts and ideas, it could no longer be represented artificially in the spirit of a former age. Much as genuine innocence charms us, a contrived pretence of innocence will exasperate us unpleasantly. The defining quality of the nineteenth century is hardly its naivety: in portraying its thoughts, dreams, and speculations it needs a rather more intricate idiom than what we might call classical language. Literature is like the day, with a morning, noon, evening, and night. Instead of vain discussions of whether dawn should be preferred to dusk, we must paint our allotted hour, and with a palette laden with all the colours needed to portray the effects this hour brings us. Has the sunset not its own beauty, just like dawn? These coppery reds, these greenish golds, these turquoise shades melting into sapphire, all these tints blending and fading in the great final conflagration, these monstrously strange shapes of clouds shot through by beams of light, akin to some huge toppling Babel of the skies: are these not just as poetical as rosy-fingered Dawn? – not that we would disparage her either. Yet the Hours running before the Day's chariot in Guido's ceiling[52] have long since flown.

The poet of *Les Fleurs du mal* loved what is mistakenly called the style of 'the decadence', which is nothing other than art attaining that final maturity to which ageing civilisations give rise as the sun sets on them: an ingenious, complex, erudite style full of subtler shades and refinements, constantly pushing back the boundaries of language, borrowing from every kind of technical vocabulary, taking its colours from every palette, its notes from every keyboard, forcing itself to articulate thought at its most inexpressible and form in its most uncertain and fugitive contours; a style attuned to, and thereby capable of conveying, the subtle secrets of neurosis, the outpourings of ageing passion turning to depravity, and the strange hallucinations of obsession inclining to madness. This decadent style is the last word of the Word itself, called upon to express everything and pushed to the furthest extremity. In this connection, we may be reminded of the language of the later Roman Empire, already mottled with the green hues of decomposition and a little gamy, and of the intricate refinements of the Byzantine school, that final form of Greek art fallen into deliquescence. But truly such is the necessary and destined idiom of peoples and civilisations for whom an artificial life has replaced a natural one, giving rise to hitherto unknown human needs. And this style condemned by pedants is no easy thing, for it expresses new ideas in new forms and with words as yet unheard. By contrast with the classical style, it allows for shading; and in such shadows the spectres of superstition and the haggard ghosts of insomnia swirl in confusion: nocturnal terrors, remorse shuddering and cowering at the slightest sound, monstrous dreams that only the impotent could resist, obscure fantasies that would astonish the daylight hours, indeed everything gloomy, misshapen and indistinctly horrible that the soul hides away in its furthest and deepest recesses.

It is not hard to see that the fourteen hundred words of Racine's dialect are insufficient for an author who has set himself the hard task of rendering modern people and modern things in their infinite complexity and variegated colours. And so Baudelaire, a good latinist despite his poor showing in the *baccalauréat* examinations, preferred Apuleius, Petronius, Juvenal, St Augustine, and Tertullian, whose style has the black sheen of ebony, above Virgil or Cicero.[53] He ventured even as far as Church Latin, both for its prose writings and for those rhyming hymns that replace the forgotten rhythms of antiquity. Under the title *Franciscae meae laudes*,[54] he also addressed 'to a learned and devout milliner' (such is the wording of the dedication) an exercise in Latin verse rhymed in the pattern Brizeux calls ternary, comprising three rhymes in succession rather than interwoven alternately as in Dante's *terza rima*. Appended to this strange poem is a note, no less peculiar, which we transcribe here, because it confirms and explains what we have just said about the idioms of the decadence:

1868; translated by Chris Baldick, 2011

CHARLES BAUDELAIRE

Note to *Franciscae meae laudes*

I trust that the reader shares my impression that the language of the later Latin decadence – that final sigh of a sturdy physique already transfigured in preparation for the life of the spirit – is particularly suited to the expression of the kinds of emotional intensity felt and understood in the sphere of modern poetry. Its mysticism is the polar opposite of that sensuality which alone was recognised by Catullus and his followers at the other end of the magnet, those being poets whose bluntness was purely fleshly. In this marvellous language, blemishes and irregularities of style seem to me to express the compulsive carelessness of passion flouting the rules in self-forgetfulness. Words adapted to new senses display the charming awkwardness of the Northern barbarian kneeling before Roman beauty. As for the punning that is heard among its pedantic lispings, does this not exhibit the wild, fantastical grace of infancy?

1857; translated by Chris Baldick, 2011

STEFAN GEORGE

'Eastward stands the lofty shrine' ('Gegen osten ragt der bau')

Eastward stands the lofty shrine,
Savage, wondrous, looming greatly,
Lavishing on Zeus divine
Rites bizarre yet grave and stately:

Here, enticingly half-nude
Dancers lead the moving column
Through a sun-parched solitude.
Blessed by sacrifice most solemn,
Boys, prepare for priestly tread
Unctuous palm leaves' soothing powers;
Then on silvered sand strew dead
Lilies and narcissus flowers!

On the threshold take your rest,
Where the icon is presented
Solely to the frequent guest
Whose devotion, long unstinted,
Yields from babbling lips a prayer.
Brother-guests debarred from pressing,
Godhead's riddling image there
Still pronounces constant blessing.

Youthful voices echo long.
Scent of soothing balm comes weaving
Through a smoky vapour strong,
Kiss of sweetest myrrh receiving.

1892; translated by Frank Krause and Chris Baldick, 2011

'Dashed is the goblet' ('Becher am boden')

Dashed is the goblet,
Scattered the pearls:
Each wearied harlot,
Slender in curls,
Sinks to the carpet;
Candle-smoke swirls.
Thighs disentangled,
Breast freed from limb;
Petalled heads languid,
Fume-drowsed and dim.
Lord of *le vin*, quit!
Death, end the banquet!

Roses raining,
Crimson-staining,
Come caressing?
Pallid blooming
For consuming?
Pinkish-red ones,
Yellow dead ones'
Ghostly kissing
Here as blessing?

Nets of plunder
Rent asunder:
Gushing petals.
Rain of roses
Buries under.[55]

1892; translated by Frank Krause and Chris Baldick, 2011

Notes

1 An aphrodisiac made from ragwort.
2 An expensive white wine from the slopes of Mount Falernus.
3 A god of fertility, adopted by the Romans light-heartedly as a god of gardens, where statues representing him with an enormously swollen phallus were supposed to scare off birds and thieves.
4 From the Greek island of Delos, birthplace of the god Apollo. The translator has taken some liberties at this point, implying misleadingly that Delos was, like Lesbos, associated with a particular sexual vice. In fact Petronius's obscure joke here alludes to 'the Delian' (i.e. Apollo) in his role as god of medicine supposedly serving in person as castrator of eunuchs.

5 More exactly, singers and musicians accompanying a dancer (the *pantomimus*) in a form of mythological ballet that bears no relation to the modern pantomime.
6 A small song-bird, still eaten as a delicacy in Italy.
7 A herbal purgative.
8 In Greek mythology, a satyr skilled as a flautist, who challenged the god Apollo to a musical contest. He lost, Apollo's reward being to flay him alive. He became a popular figure in Roman decorative art.
9 Team or company. Slaves in larger households or estates were commonly organised into groups of ten.
10 The first three named were early Greek philosophers, Eudoxus being notable for his astronomical researches; the latter two were famous Greek sculptors.
11 The most celebrated ancient Greek painter and sculptor, respectively.
12 Giton is a character in Petronius's story, a sexually alluring boy pursued and fought over by the narrator Encolpius and his companions. The mythological Ganymede was a beautiful boy abducted by Jove (Zeus) to serve as his cup-bearer; but his name (which in its Latin form, Catamitus, gives us our word 'catamite') was widely applied to rent-boys and young boyfriends.
13 Colchis: Ancient kingdom in the Caucasus. The Phasian bird is the pheasant. Fisher's lives: The Syrtes were gulfs on the Libyan coast, of which the shallow sandbars were hazardous to shipping.
14 The fabled Golden Age of peace and plenty, before Jove (Zeus) overthrew Saturn (Cronos) as chief of the gods, ushering in successive inferior ages of silver, bronze, and iron.
15 Names given by the earlier Roman poets Propertius and Catullus respectively to the mistresses addressed in their love poems. It is significant here that Catullus's 'Lesbia' was a married woman.
16 A daughter of Zeus, and the last goddess to leave this world at the close of the Golden Age, later retiring to the heavens as the constellation Virgo.
17 The guardian spirit of a married man's fertility, commonly represented by a bronze ornament at the head of the marriage-bed.
18 One of the snake-haired crones known as the Erinnyes (Furies), charged with the tormenting of mortal wrongdoers.
19 The oldest stone bridge across the Tiber at Rome, renovated by Augustus but much later (in 1598) destroyed by flooding.
20 A law enacted by Augustus in 9 CE, restricting the inheritance rights of childless people while granting privileges to parents of three or more children.
21 An actor in the comic role of a wife's hastily concealed lover.
22 The annual festival of the corn-goddess Ceres featured a procession of white-robed women, who were required to have abstained from sex for at least the previous nine days.
23 A noted ballet-dancer (*pantomimus*) of the time.
24 The Megalesian games were held in early April; the Plebeian in early November.
25 A form of low-life comedy or farce, usually presented as an afterpiece to a tragic play, rather than as an interlude.
26 The famous rhetorician, author of the standard guide to oratorical arts.

27 Euryalus was a celebrated gladiator. A *murmillo* was a kind of gladiator dressed in heavy Gaulish armour with a fish design on his crest.
28 An ancient port town just to the east of Alexandria, here used as a metonym for the Nile delta region.
29 An actor.
30 Hyacinthus was a beautiful young man in Greek myth.
31 Presumed to be Eppia's husband.
32 Roman emperor 41–54 CE, believed by contemporaries to be slow-witted. The following passage concerns his notoriously promiscuous wife Messalina, who was 34 years his junior.
33 The short-lived (41–55 CE) son of Claudius by Messalina.
34 The Sybarites, Greek colonists whose city was destroyed by rival powers in 510 BCE, are still a byword for effetely luxurious self-indulgence. To a lesser degree, the wealthy Greek cities of Miletus and Rhodes attracted similar suspicions in the eyes of Romans. Citizens of the Italian port of Tarentum had, during a festival in 281 BCE in which they wore garlands, drunkenly insulted an ambassador from Rome.
35 The fertility cult of the *Bona Dea* (Good Goddess) was practised in supposedly orgiastic rites conducted by women only, led by the incumbent magistrate's wife and by the Vestal Virgins.
36 See note 3 above.
37 Elderly heroes of the legendary Trojan War, both too old and wise to be swayed by youthful passions.
38 Publius Clodius, a maverick Roman patrician who profaned the strictly women-only rites of the *Bona Dea* in 62 BCE by slipping in disguised as a lute-girl. He was also the lover of Julius Caesar's second wife Pompeia, in whose house the festival was held that year; this incident led Caesar to divorce her. Clodius escaped punishment by bribing jurors at his trial.
39 Triphallus is another name for the over-endowed fertility god Priapus, not because his distinctive member was triplicated but because it was at least three times larger than normal. Thais was a legendary Greek courtesan, mistress of Alexander the Great; she incited him, after a drunken party, to burn down the royal palace of Persepolis.
40 An author of pornographic stories, thought to have been a woman.
41 In Greek myth, Atalanta was a princess who took up the masculine activities of boar-hunting and foot-racing. Meleager was a hero who fell in love with Atalanta, inviting her to join him and others on the legendary Calydonian boar-hunt, in which she drew first blood. The pair were favourite figures in Roman decorative art.
42 The Jupiter of Latium, i.e. of Rome.
43 Caligula had three sisters Julia Livilla, Drusilla, and Agrippina.
44 The husband of Caligula's sister Drusilla, and at one time named by the emperor as his heir; but in 39 CE Caligula produced forged letters implicating him both in adultery with his other two sisters and in a treacherous plot. He was executed and, by order of the Senate, denied a burial.
45 In Roman legend, Romulus, the city's founder, had peopled his settlement

by capturing the womenfolk of the neighbouring Sabine tribe. The emperor Augustus had acquired his wife Livia (Caligula's great-grandmother) by obliging her husband to divorce her.

46 The king of Armenia, whose visit to Rome is recounted earlier in Suetonius's narrative.

47 The leader of a major Gallic revolt against Nero.

48 Elagabalus (sometimes spelt Heliogabalus) was born Varius Avitus Bassianus, probably in 203. Following the example of his cousin and predecessor Caracalla, he adopted the politically reassuring name Marcus Aurelius Antoninus (after the revered second-century emperor) upon his accession as emperor in 218 following the Battle of Antioch, at which time he was only fourteen years of age. His short reign (he was deposed at the age of eighteen, in 222) was marked by growing resentment in Rome at his flagrant violations of Roman religious and sexual norms.

49 Apicius was a famous gourmet of the period of Tiberius's reign. Otho was a friend of Nero, and briefly succeeded that emperor in 68–9 before being overthrown by forces loyal to Vitellius, a notorious glutton who reigned as emperor for a few months in 69.

50 In mythology, Ixion was a king who, for the crime of propositioning Zeus's wife Hera, was fixed forever to a revolving wheel of fire in the underworld.

51 Marcus Julius Philippus, sometimes known as Philippus Arabs (Philip the Arab), emperor from 244 to 249. His attempts to outlaw homosexuality are mentioned by some other ancient sources.

52 The frescoed ceiling of the Casino dell' Aurora in the grounds of the Roman Palazzo Pallavicini-Rospigliosi, completed in 1616 by the Bolognese artist Guido Reni (1575–1642), representing *Apollo in His Chariot Preceded by Aurora Bringing Light to the World.*

53 The poet Virgil (70–19 BCE) and the prose writer Cicero (106–43 BCE) belong to the 'Golden' age (*c.* 80 BCE–14 CE) of Latin literature favoured by nineteenth-century schoolmasters, whereas Baudelaire's favoured authors belong to the so-called 'decadence' of Latin writing that succeeded it: Petronius wrote in about 60 CE, Apuleius, Juvenal, and the Christian author Tertullian in the second century; Augustine in the early fifth.

54 'Praises for my Francisca', the only poem of *Les Fleurs du mal* not written in French. The dedication, and Baudelaire's note, which follows below, appeared only in the first edition.

55 The second and third parts of the poem are based, like much in George's *Algabal* collection, on legends of the third-century Roman emperor Elagabalus. Specifically, the allusion here is to a passage in the *Augustan History* (see above, p. 69) in which the emperor is said to have deluged his dinner-guests with violets dropped from a reversible ceiling in such numbers that some banqueters suffocated. George here adapts the episode to imagine a torrent of roses dropped from suspended fishing nets.

3

DECADENT VERSE

Decadent verse shows no formal or technical features that distinguish it from the mainstream of non-decadent poetry in the second half of the nineteenth century. With the exception of only a few experiments in free verse and prose poetry, it follows the technical conservatism of its age in favouring fixed rhyming forms in both lyric (especially the sonnet) and narrative verse (especially the ballad). Its truly distinctive features lie in subject matter and in figurative treatment: a determined avoidance of positive natural imagery and a contrary preference for recurrent tropes of decline, decrepitude and disease, often interwoven with an eroticism in which artificiality, cruelty, and sterility are emphasised. Its typical imagery adopts certain favoured flora (lilies, orchids), fauna (snakes), shades (pallor), moods (languor) and female figures (the harlot or dancer as *femme fatale*), eventually with such mannered regularity as to invite parody. In its rhetorical performance, it shows a significant preference for the mock prayer or invocation, often a blasphemous inversion of devotional verse in the Christian tradition: Baudelaire's 'Les Litanies de Satan' and 'La Prière d'un païen' set the pattern adopted by Swinburne in 'Hymn to Proserpine' and 'Dolores', which is in turn developed by Ernest Dowson in 'Libera Me' and again in Lionel Johnson's 'The Dark Angel'.

Although it draws partly upon a melancholic strain of Romanticism of the 1820s and 1830s (Keats, Poe, Lamartine, early Tennyson), the Decadent tradition in nineteenth-century poetry was launched by Charles Baudelaire (1821–67) in his collection *Les Fleurs du mal* (1857, revised 1861). In the world of Baudelaire's verse, Nature is firmly shut out, as it had been in his hero Poe's work, and we occupy a hallucinatory realm of urban squalor populated by beggars, criminals, lesbians, gamblers, and prostitutes, while the poet's voice veers unpredictably among moods of depressive world-weariness (*spleen*), perverse desire, horror, boredom (*ennui*), exotic escapism, and Satanic cruelty. For a number of reasons *Les Fleurs du mal* has come to be seen as a founding work of modern literature, its strange new tones of symbolic suggestion reverberating well beyond the narrowly Decadent tradition that a small number of its poems inaugurate. The same applies to Baudelaire's major 'Symbolist' followers, Paul Verlaine (1844–96) and the more technically innovative Stéphane Mallarmé (1842–98). Both these French poets laid the foundations of modern poetry by subordinating description and didactic argument to the subtler suggestion of mood, so that the few poems in which they employ directly 'decadent' motifs remain significant but still incidental to their larger achievements.

With Baudelaire's first and most gifted English disciple, Algernon Charles Swinburne (1837–1909), the case is different. In terms of French poetic schools, Swinburne is less a Symbolist than a Parnassian: that is to say, his work aspires to a 'classical' purity that shuns the contemporary metropolitan world in favour of ancient Lesbos. His strong personal interest in flagellant masochism (*le vice Anglais*) attracted him to one strand in Baudelaire's work, namely its perverse eroticism; and this he developed relentlessly in his notorious collection *Poems and Ballads* (1866). At this early point in his career, before he was persuaded to pursue less controversial subjects, Swinburne appeared as the first consistently Decadent poet, in that he repeatedly invoked the pagan sensuality and cruelty of imperial Rome in protest against the Christian morality of his time, most clearly in the nostalgic monologue 'Hymn to Proserpine', and again in the references to Nero in his masochist prayer 'Dolores'. It is often said of Swinburne that his extraordinary facility in adapting Greek metrical patterns into English, along with his gift for alliteration and assonance, result in a kind of verse that is all sound-effect at the expense of memorable sense; and indeed there is a soporific repetitiousness to his style, as with the rhyming of 'Gods' with 'rods' three times in the same poem. Yet to the many horrified readers of *Poems and Ballads*, his sense was all too clear, and in its celebration of 'Roman' sexual abnormalities all too clearly decadent.

The foundations of this tradition having been laid in the 1860s, a second wave of Decadent verse emerged in the 1880s (the intervening decade having been a barren one), among poets who had been born in the 1850s, like Oscar Wilde (1854–1900) and the French writer Jean Lorrain (1855–1906), or in the 1860s. An important feature of this revival is its international scope, as the influences of Baudelaire, the French Symbolists and Swinburne were felt by poets from Ireland (Wilde), Italy (Gabriele d'Annunzio (1863–1938)), and Belgium (Maurice Maeterlinck (1862–1949)) before being picked up in the early 1890s by the emigrant Scottish poet John Davidson (1857–1909) and by Stefan George (1868–1933), the German lyric poet who translated verse by Baudelaire, Verlaine, Mallarmé, and Swinburne.[1]

The second burst of Decadent poetry among English poets of that generation arrived slightly later, in the early 1890s, which is partly why literary Decadence is often misrepresented in the English-speaking world as a fleeting 'Nineties' phenomenon. The London branch of what had become an international poetic Decadence can be divided into writers who touch upon decadent themes intermittently, and those who identify themselves almost entirely with the movement. In the first group belong the sonneteers Eugene Lee-Hamilton (1845–1907) and John Barlas (1860–1914), along with Davidson and Lionel Johnson (1867–1902); in the second group of confirmed Decadents we would place Wilde with Ernest Dowson (1867–1900), John Gray (1866–1934), the poet-critic Arthur Symons (1865–1945), and the slightly younger Theodore Wratislaw (1871–1933). Of these, the short-lived alcoholic Dowson was the most talented poet, two or three of his works having outlasted those of his contemporaries in modern memory.

It was Arthur Symons, none the less, who established himself as the dominant figure in English Decadent verse, and not only on account of his editorship of the *Savoy* (1896), his championing and occasional translation of the French Symbolists, or his critical reflections on the Decadent movement itself. As a poet, Symons created in his third collection *London Nights* (1895; revd 1897) a carefully circumscribed and thus consistent world of eroticised artifice, an enclosed 'hothouse' world of music-hall footlights, orchids, cosmetics, dancing girls, prostitutes, and scented 'Sin', to which he returned repeatedly (although he wrote verse on other subjects) in later collections, even after his delicate talent was wrecked by a major nervous breakdown in 1908–9. Symons's erotic imagination, like the practical connoisseurship upon which it was based, is clearly much tamer than those of Baudelaire or of Swinburne, all of its desired objects being white heterosexual women without whips. Whether that be regarded as a disappointment or not, the best of his poems exhibit a precision and integrity that foreshadow the Imagist poets of the next generation. We have, incidentally, referred to Symons here as 'English', which is justified by his conviction that he was essentially Cornish by heritage, despite the migratory accident of his having been born in Wales.

Two final notes are in order here, on Yeats and on dates. Although W. B. Yeats (1865–1939) enjoyed a close artistic association with his contemporary Symons and was well acquainted with several other Decadent poets, his own verse is unusually resistant to specifically decadent themes. As an Irish cultural nationalist of his time, he was more interested poetically in the renewal of civilisations than in their exhaustion, so we have not chosen any of his poems for this section. As for the order in which these poets are presented below, we have placed them not by date of birth but according to the publication date of the first poem by which each is represented. This arrangement, we hope, brings out more clearly the evolution of this tradition from Baudelaire all the way through to the Edwardian latecomer James Elroy Flecker (1884–1915); but it does give rise to one apparent oddity, in that the two chosen sonnets of John Barlas were first published twenty-one years after his death, although these were almost certainly composed in the early 1890s or late 1880s. On the subject of Barlas, we are especially pleased to present below the first reliable text of 'Beauty's Anadems' to have appeared in any modern anthology, all previous reprintings having been flawed by mistranscription.

CHARLES BAUDELAIRE

Poison (Le Poison)

Booze can redecorate the most awful kip
  With a luxurious glaze
And make miraculous porticoes rise up
  In a crimson haze
Like the sun setting behind cloudy skies.

Dope expands the sphere of the infinite,
  The limits of the known,
Arrests the moment and exhausts delight,
  Flooding the brain
With more dark pleasure than it can contain.

These pale beside the green poison that drips
  From your green eyes,
Lakes where my soul confronts itself and gulps
  Where hot reveries
Come crowding in to drink the bitter depths.

These things are nothing to the wild sensation
  Of your slavering mouth
Which chews my harsh soul to distraction
  And, giddy with intoxication,
Transports me swooning to the shores of death.

1857; translated by Derek Mahon, 2011

Spleen (Spleen III)

I am like the King of a land of rains and ditches,
Young and yet old, impotent among my riches,
Who, scorning the bows of his tutors and of his Priests,
Endures the weariness of his savage Beasts.
Neither his hawks nor his game can ever divert him
Nor can his people who die before him hurt him.
He says of a woman: 'Who can ever test her?'

He is unmoved by the ballads of his jester;
His bed is like a tomb one finds in Cadiz,
Nor can this fine Prince in his wanton Ladies
Excite their passions, nor when his wine smells musty,
Admire to excess their dresses lewd and lusty.
The wise men who make gold for him never could
Extirpate the corrupt element in his blood.
For these baths of blood the Romans used, remember
Who can, his sins from July to December,
Have never warmed this cold corpse stupefied,
Where instead of blood the green waters of Lethe[2] glide.

1857; translated by Arthur Symons, 1925

La Destruction

The Devil stirs about me without rest,
And round me floats like noxious air and thin:
I breathe this poison-air which scalds my breast,
And fills me with desires of monstrous sin.

Knowing my love of Art, he sometimes takes
The shape of supple girls supremely fair;
And with a wily, canting lie he makes
My heated lips his shameful potions share.

Then far he leads me from the sight of God,
Crushed with fatigue, to where no man has trod –
To the vague, barren plains where silence sounds,

And hurls into my face his foul construction
Of slimy clothes, and gaping, putrid wounds,
And all the bleeding harness of Destruction!

1857; translated by Vincent O'Sullivan, 1896

Lesbos

Mother of Latin games and Grecian graces,
Lesbos, whose kisses are magnificent,
Hot as the nights and fresh as foreign faces,
These have the passions of girls malevolent,
– Mother of Latin games and Grecian graces,

Lesbos, where the kisses are profoundly throbbing,
As seas in storms that furiously are forming
Into huge waves, the hearts of virgins sobbing

Deeper than love and in their bosoms swarming:
Lesbos, where the kisses are profoundly throbbing.

Lesbos, where the Phrynes[3] in their superb acting
Give voice to all the winds that fly between us,
The Paphian[4] stars in envy are contracting
A love for Sappho, jealous of no Venus!
– Lesbos, where the Phrynes in their acting,

Lesbos, land of nights hot and languorous,
That make at their mirrors, in their sterility,
Hollow-eyed girls, of their bodies amorous,
Caress the ripe fruits of their nubility –
Lesbos, land of nights hot and languorous,

Let Plato frown who had no sense of virtue;
You draw your pardon from your own excesses
Of amorous kisses, nothing now can hurt you,
Unexhausted in your Lesbian caresses.
Let Plato frown who had no sense of virtue.

Eternity around you seemed to harden
All of respite that keeps you all from pity
In the immensity of an expected pardon
From an unknown and very distant City.
Eternity around you seemed to harden.

Who of the Gods will dare to judge you ever
And give you up to certain hard conditions
Whose balances are simply one's endeavour
To save oneself from self and self's perditions?
Who of the Gods will dare to judge you ever?

Just or unjust, which do you want for reason,
Virgins sublime? What shall we have hereafter
In matters of love and in matters of treason
When heaven and hell shall echo back our laughter?
– Just or unjust, which do you want for reason?

For Lesbos has chosen me as the least ruinous
Of Poets to sing of the Virgins, lovely, idle,
For from a child I was admitted to the mysterious
Frantic laughter that has nor bit nor bridle;
For Lesbos has chosen me as the least ruinous

Of Poets who without the least confusion
Keep watch over the passions of these daughters

Of fruitful Lesbos women, into the illusion
Of all that wanders between the winds and waters.
A Poet who without the least confusion

Knows the sea's passions, how the storm-waves harden
And that around the rock for all its sobbing
The sea one night shall give Lesbos back for pardon
The adored dead body of Sappho,[5] lifeless, throbbing,
For the sea's passion, where the storm-waves harden!

Of the male Sappho, the Poet and the Lover,
Fairer than Venus in her pallid pleasures!
– Azure is vanquished by the spots that cover
The tenebrous circle traced by the mad measures
Of male Sappho, the Poet and the Lover!

Fairer than Venus on the world arising
And pouring the treasures of her charms unwonted
And her youth's beauty for the sun's surprising
On the old Ocean of her daughter enchanted:
Fairer than Venus on the world arising!

– Of Sappho who died of too much passionate dreaming,
When, insulting the Rite and the Cult invented,
She had given her body to her loved Phaon,[6] scheming
More than all body's pride: genius demented
Of Sappho who died of too much passionate dreaming.

And since this time Lesbos is self-lamented,
And, despite the cries of the Universe perverted,
Intoxicates herself, herself tormented,
Whose cries are heard along her shores deserted.
And since this time Lesbos is self-lamented!

1857; translated by Arthur Symons, 1925

Femmes Damnées

Like moody beasts they lie along the sands;
Look where the sky against the sea-rim clings:
Foot stretches out to foot, and groping hands
Have languors soft and bitter shudderings.

Some, smitten hearts with the long secrecies,
On velvet moss, deep in their bowers' ease,
Prattling the love of timid infancies,
Are tearing the green bark from the young trees.

Others, like sisters, slowly walk and grave;
By rocks that swarm with ghostly legions,
Where Anthony saw surging on the waves
The purple breasts of his temptations.

Some, by the light of crumbling, resinous gums,
In the still hollows of old pagan dens,
Call thee in aid to their deliriums
O Bacchus! cajoler of ancient pains.

And those whose breasts for scapulars are fain
Nurse under their long robes the cruel thong!
These, in dim woods, where huddling shadows throng,
Mix with the foam of pleasure tears of pain.

1857; translated by John Gray, 1893

Les Métamorphoses du vampire

And yet the woman, who all things remembers,
Writhing her limbs as serpents on the embers,
Beating her breasts, as if herself she hated,
Utters these words by her musk impregnated:
– 'I, my lips are moist, and I know the science
Of losing in a bed's depths my defiance;
I dry all tears of all that have the passion
For these my breasts, my laughter is their fashion.
I replace, for those men who see me naked,
The sun, the moon, the stars, so must you take it!
I have, dear learned man, the power to rifle
Flesh in my velveted arms, the strength to stifle
Certain, when I am naked, such igniting
To furnace-heat, as they my flesh are biting,
Who on this mattress swoon, these to enslave me:
The impotent angels would be damned to save me!'

When out of all my bones she had sucked the marrow,
And as I turned to her, in the act to harrow
My senses in one kiss, to end her chatter,
I saw a gourd that was filled full with foul matter!
I closed mine eyes, all my body shivering,
And when I opened them, in the dawn's quivering,
I saw at my side a puppet of derision,
Who had made of its blood too much provision,
Then fragments of a skeleton in confusion

That of themselves made a mere mist of illusion
Or of a sign-board at the end of a batten
The winter wind swung, as it seemed, in Latin.

1857; translated by Arthur Symons, 1925

Litany to Satan (Les Litanies de Satan)

O grandest of the Angels, and most wise,
O fallen God, fate-driven from the skies,
Satan, at last take pity on our pain.

O first of exiles who endurest wrong,
Yet growest, in thy hatred, still more strong,
Satan, at last take pity on our pain!

O subterranean King, omniscient,
Healer of man's immortal discontent,
Satan, at last take pity on our pain.

To lepers and to outcasts thou dost show
That Passion is the Paradise below.
Satan, at last take pity on our pain.

Thou, by thy mistress Death, hast given to man
Hope, the imperishable courtesan.
Satan, at last take pity on our pain.

Thou givest to the Guilty their calm mien
Which damns the crowd around the guillotine.
Satan, at last take pity on our pain.

Thou knowest the corners of the jealous Earth
Where God has hidden jewels of great worth.
Satan, at last take pity on our pain.

Thou stretchest forth a saving hand to keep
Such men as roam upon the roofs in sleep.
Satan, at last take pity on our pain.

Thy power can make the halting Drunkard's feet
Avoid the peril of the surging street.
Satan, at last take pity on our pain.

Thou, to console our helplessness, didst plot
The cunning use of powder and of shot.
Satan, at last take pity on our pain.

Thy awful name is written as with pitch
On the unrelenting foreheads of the rich.
Satan, at last take pity on our pain.

In strange and hidden places thou dost move
Where women cry for torture in their love.
Satan, at last take pity on our pain.

Father of those whom God's tempestuous ire
Has flung from Paradise with sword and fire,
Satan, at last take pity on our pain.

Prayer
Satan, to thee be praise upon the Height
Where thou wast king of old, and in the night
Of Hell, where thou dost dream on silently.
Grant that one day beneath the Knowledge-tree,
When it shoots forth to grace thy royal brow,
My soul may sit, that cries upon thee now.

1857; translated by James Elroy Flecker, 1907

Afternoon Song (Chanson d'après-midi)

Although your wicked brows
Give you a strange look
So far from angelic,
Witch with enticing eyes

Frivolous and skittish,
I love you in slow motion
With the fierce adoration
Of a priest for his fetish.

Desert and forest scent
The thick, swinging hair
You shake out with an air
Mysterious and intent.

Nymph tenebrous and warm,
Your wild limbs dispense
An odour like incense
Rich with a vespral charm.

No potion, however strong,
Equals the given head

When you raise the dead
Under your cunning tongue.

Delirious with self-hunger
For your own breasts and back,
You ravish the hot sack
In a delicious languor.

At times, as if to subdue
Some peculiar spite,
You concentrate on the bite
And on the serious screw,

Tearing at hip and thigh
With a primaeval giggle;
And then my frantic goggle
Rests in your lunar eye.

Beneath your satin heel
And silken toe I set
My genius, my delight,
My fate and my dark soul –

A soul given new light
And colour by this bright
Explosion of white heat
In my Siberian night!

1861; translated by Derek Mahon, 2011

A Pagan's Prayer (La Prière d'un païen)

O still not the might of thy fire,
  Quicken my dulled desire,
Pleasure, torture of souls!
  Hear when I cry to thee!
    O'er my heart a numbness rolls;
Stay not the flames of thine ire,
    Diva, supplicem exaudi![7]

Goddess, shed forth in the air,
  Flame in the depths of our being,
Pity a spirit laid bare,
  A stricken heart that is fleeing
    To thee from its slumber's wrong;
That sings to thine eyes with a sacrifice
    Before thee of brazen song.

Pleasure, be thou my queen!
  For ever I'll kiss thy feet.
    Put on a siren's form,
A form of velvet sheen
    And flesh that is soft and sweet,
      To take my senses by storm.

Or pour thou upon my face
    The perfume of thy slumber
      Drugged by the magic of wine,
Deep as the mystic of space,
    O shapeless, of shapes without number,
      Pleasure, shadow divine!

1868; translated by Edward H. Lascelles, 1920

Epilogue

With heart at rest I climbed the citadel's
Steep height, and saw the city as from a tower,
Hospital, brothel, prison, and such hells,

Where evil comes up softly like a flower.
Thou knowest, O Satan, patron of my pain,
Not for vain tears I went up at that hour;

But, like an old sad faithful lecher, fain
To drink delight of that enormous trull
Whose hellish beauty makes me young again.

Whether thou sleep, with heavy vapours full,
Sodden with day, or, new apparelled, stand
In gold-laced veils of evening beautiful,

I love thee, infamous city! Harlots and
Hunted have pleasures of their own to give,
The vulgar herd can never understand.

1869; translated by Arthur Symons, 1905

STÉPHANE MALLARMÉ

Autumn Blues (Plainte d'automne)

Ever since Maria left for another star – Orion perhaps; Altair; or you, green Venus? – I've been savouring my solitude. What long days I've spent alone with my cat. By 'alone' I mean, of course, 'without another material being', for a cat is a *mystical* presence, a spirit. So I can honestly say that I've spent long days alone with my cat, and alone too with one of the last authors of the Roman decadence; for, now that the fair creature is no more, I've been strangely enamoured of everything contained in the phrase 'decline and fall'. By the same token, my favourite time of year is the drawn-out end of summer immediately preceding autumn, and my favourite time of day, the time I set aside for my walk, that moment when the sun, before disappearing, throws a yellow copper light on the grey walls, a red copper light on the window-panes. Similarly, the sort of literature I now read for pleasure is that exquisite poetry from the last days of Rome – only, however, in so far as it breathes no hint of the barbarians' thrilling approach, much less starts babbling the early Christian authors' baby Latin.

So there I was, reading one of those touching poems whose cosmetic finish is so much more pleasing than any youthful glow, one hand plunged in the fur of an innocent beast, when a barbarous barrel-organ started up slowly and mournfully under the window, playing to a long avenue of poplars whose leaves struck me as cheerless even in spring – ever since, in fact, Maria walked there last with her candelabrum. A music for the lonely, yes indeed. A piano twinkles, a fiddle-bow draws light from the riven strings; but the barrel-organ, in this reminiscential dusk, set me desperately dreaming. And while it murmured a hackneyed, cheerfully popular tune, introducing some sort of gaiety to the neighbourhood, I asked myself why this trite refrain should touch me so to the quick, like a romantic ballad, and bring tears to my eyes. I listened carefully but flung no coin from the window – not wishing to change position, reluctant to notice that the instrument was not the only singer.

1864; translated by Derek Mahon, 2011

Anguish (Angoisse)

Tonight I do not come to conquer thee,
O Beast that dost the sins of the whole world bear,
Nor with my kisses' weary misery
Wake a sad tempest in thy wanton hair;
It is that heavy and that dreamless sleep
I ask of the close curtains of thy bed,
Which, after all thy treacheries, folds thee deep,
Who knowest oblivion better than the dead.
For Vice, that gnaws with keener tooth than Time,
Brands me as thee, of barren conquest proud;
But while thou guardest in thy breast of stone
A heart that fears no fang of any crime,

I wander palely, haunted by my shroud,
Fearing to die if I but sleep alone.

1866; translated by Arthur Symons, 1900; revised 1902

Sigh (Soupir)

My soul, calm sister, towards thy brow, whereon scarce grieves
An autumn strewn already with its russet leaves,
And towards the wandering sky of thine angelic eyes,
Mounts, as in melancholy gardens may arise
Some faithful fountain sighing whitely towards the blue!
Towards the blue pale and pure that sad October knew,
When, in those depths, it mirrored languors infinite,
And agonising leaves upon the waters white,
Windily, drifting, traced a furrow cold and dun,
Where, in one long last ray, lingered the yellow sun.

1866; translated by Arthur Symons, 1898

The Tomb of Charles Baudelaire (Le Tombeau de Charles Baudelaire)

The buried temple through the sewer's
sepulchral mouth dribbling mud and rubies
abominably reveals some idol of Anubis[8]
its whole muzzle flaring in a savage bark

or should the new gas twist the warped wick
wiping we know opprobrium suffered
haggard lighting of a deathless pubis
whose nocturnal flight shadows the lamp in the street

What votive leaves dried in cities without evening
can ever bless like her sit back against
the marble vainly of Baudelaire

wrapped shimmering absent in a veil
she his Shade a guardian poison
ever to be breathed though we die of it.

1895; translated by Martin Sorrell, 2011

A. C. SWINBURNE

Hymn to Proserpine
(After the proclamation in Rome of the Christian faith)[9]

Vicisti, Galileae.[10]

I have lived long enough, having seen one thing, that love hath an end;
Goddess and maiden and queen, be near me now and befriend.
Thou art more than the day or the morrow, the seasons that laugh or
that weep;
For these give joy and sorrow; but thou, Proserpina, sleep.
Sweet is the treading of wine, and sweet the feet of the dove;
But a goodlier gift is thine than foam of the grapes or love.
Yea, is not even Apollo, with hair and harpstring of gold,
A bitter God to follow, a beautiful God to behold?
I am sick of singing: the bays burn deep and chafe: I am fain
To rest a little from praise and grievous pleasure and pain.
For the Gods we know not of, who give us our daily breath,
We know they are cruel as love or life, and lovely as death.
O Gods dethroned and deceased, cast forth, wiped out in a day!
From your wrath is the world released, redeemed from your chains,
men say.
New Gods are crowned in the city; their flowers have broken your rods;
They are merciful, clothed with pity, the young compassionate Gods.
But for me their new device is barren, the days are bare;
Things long past over suffice, and men forgotten that were.
Time and the Gods are at strife; ye dwell in the midst thereof,
Draining a little life from the barren breasts of love.
I say to you, cease, take rest; yea, I say to you all, be at peace,
Till the bitter milk of her breast and the barren bosom shall cease.
Wilt thou yet take all, Galilean? but these thou shalt not take,
The laurel, the palms and the paean, the breasts of the nymphs in
the brake;
Breasts more soft than a dove's, that tremble with tenderer breath;
And all the wings of the Loves, and all the joy before death;
All the feet of the hours that sound as a single lyre,
Dropped and deep in the flowers, with strings that flicker like fire.
More than these wilt thou give, things fairer than all these things?
Nay, for a little we live, and life hath mutable wings.
A little while and we die; shall life not thrive as it may?
For no man under the sky lives twice, outliving his day.
And grief is a grievous thing, and a man hath enough of his tears:

Why should he labour, and bring fresh grief to blacken his years?
Thou hast conquered, O pale Galilean; the world has grown grey from
thy breath;
We have drunken of things Lethean, and fed on the fullness of death.
Laurel is green for a season, and love is sweet for a day;
But love grows bitter with treason, and laurel outlives not May.
Sleep, shall we sleep after all? for the world is not sweet in the end;
For the old faiths loosen and fall, the new years ruin and rend.
Fate is a sea without shore, and the soul is a rock that abides;
But her ears are vexed with the roar and her face with the foam of
the tides.
O lips that the live blood faints in, the leavings of racks and rods!
O ghastly glories of saints, dead limbs of gibbeted Gods!
Though all men abase them before you in spirit, and all knees bend,
I kneel not neither adore you, but standing, look to the end.
All delicate days and pleasant, all spirits and sorrows are cast
Far out with the foam of the present that sweeps to the surf of the past:
Where beyond the extreme sea-wall, and between the remote sea-gates,
Waste water washes, and tall ships founder, and deep death waits:
Where, mighty with deepening sides, clad about with the seas as
with wings,
And impelled of invisible tides, and fulfilled of unspeakable things,
White-eyed and poisonous-finned, shark-toothed and serpentine-curled,
Rolls, under the whitening wind of the future, the wave of the world.
The depths stand naked in sunder behind it, the storms flee away;
In the hollow before it the thunder is taken and snared as a prey;
In its sides is the north-wind bound; and its salt is of all men's tears;
With light of ruin, and sound of changes, and pulse of years:
With travail of day after day, and with trouble of hour upon hour;
And bitter as blood is the spray; and the crests are as fangs that devour:
And its vapour and storm of its steam as the sighing of spirits to be;
And its noise as the noise in a dream; and its depth as the roots of the sea:
And the height of its heads as the height of the utmost stars of the air:
And the ends of the earth at the might thereof tremble, and time is
made bare.
Will ye bridle the deep sea with reins, will ye chasten the high sea
with rods?
Will ye take her to chain her with chains, who is older than all ye Gods?
All ye as a wind shall go by, as a fire shall ye pass and be past;
Ye are Gods, and behold, ye shall die, and the waves be upon you at last.
In the darkness of time, in the deeps of the years, in the changes of things,
Ye shall sleep as a slain man sleeps, and the world shall forget you
for kings.

Though the feet of thine high priests tread where thy lords and our
forefathers trod,
Though these that were Gods are dead, and thou being dead art a God,
Though before thee the throned Cytherean[11] be fallen, and hidden
her head,
Yet thy kingdom shall pass, Galilean, thy dead shall go down to thee dead.
Of the maiden thy mother men sing as a goddess with grace clad around;
Thou art throned where another was king; where another was queen
she is crowned.
Yea, once we had sight of another: but now she is queen, say these.
Not as thine, not as thine was our mother, a blossom of flowering seas,
Clothed round with the world's desire as with raiment, and fair as
the foam,
And fleeter than kindled fire, and a goddess, and mother of Rome.
For thine came pale and a maiden, and sister to sorrow; but ours,
Her deep hair heavily laden with odour and colour of flowers,
White rose of the rose-white water, a silver splendour, a flame,
Bent down unto us that besought her, and earth grew sweet with
her name.
For thine came weeping, a slave among slaves, and rejected; but she
Came flushed from the full-flushed wave, and imperial, her foot
on the sea.
And the wonderful waters knew her, the winds and the viewless ways,
And the roses grew rosier, and bluer the sea-blue stream of the bays.
Ye are fallen, our lords, by what token? we wist that ye should not fall.
Ye were all so fair that are broken; and one more fair than ye all.
But I turn to her still, having seen she shall surely abide in the end;
Goddess and maiden and queen, be near me now and befriend.
O daughter of earth, of my mother, her crown and blossom of birth,
I am also, I also, thy brother; I go as I came unto earth.
In the night where thine eyes are as moons are in heaven, the night where
thou art,
Where the silence is more than all tunes, where sleep overflows from
the heart,
Where the poppies are sweet as the rose in our world, and the red rose
is white,
And the wind falls faint as it blows with the fume of the flowers of
the night,
And the murmur of spirits that sleep in the shadow of Gods from afar
Grows dim in thine ears and deep as the deep dim soul of a star,
In the sweet low light of thy face, under heavens untrod by the sun,
Let my soul with their souls find place, and forget what is done and
undone.

Thou art more than the Gods who number the days of our temporal breath;
For these give labour and slumber; but thou, Proserpina, death.
Therefore now at thy feet I abide for a season in silence. I know
I shall die as my fathers died, and sleep as they sleep; even so.
For the glass of the years is brittle wherein we gaze for a span;
A little soul for a little bears up this corpse which is man.
So long I endure, no longer; and laugh not again, neither weep.
For there is no God found stronger than death; and death is a sleep.

1866

Satia Te Sanguine[12]

If you loved me ever so little,
  I could bear the bonds that gall,
I could dream the bonds were brittle;
  You do not love me at all.

O beautiful lips, O bosom
  More white than the moon's and warm,
A sterile, a ruinous blossom
  Is blown your way in a storm.

As the lost white feverish limbs
  Of the Lesbian Sappho, adrift
In foam where the sea-weed swims,
  Swam loose for the streams to lift,

My heart swims blind in a sea
  That stuns me; swims to and fro,
And gathers to windward and lee
  Lamentation, and mourning, and woe.

A broken, an emptied boat,
  Sea saps it, winds blow apart,
Sick and adrift and afloat,
  The barren waif of a heart.

Where, when the gods would be cruel,
  Do they go for a torture? where
Plant thorns, set pain like a jewel?
  Ah, not in the flesh, not there!

The racks of earth and the rods
  Are weak as foam on the sands;
In the heart is the prey for gods,
  Who crucify hearts, not hands.

Mere pangs corrode and consume,
   Dead when life dies in the brain;
In the infinite spirit is room
   For the pulse of an infinite pain.

I wish you were dead, my dear;
   I would give you, had I to give,
Some death too bitter to fear;
   It is better to die than live.

I wish you were stricken of thunder
   And burnt with a bright flame through,
Consumed and cloven in sunder,
   I dead at your feet like you.

If I could but know after all,
   I might cease to hunger and ache,
Though your heart were ever so small,
   If it were not a stone or a snake.

You are crueller, you that we love,
   Than hatred, hunger, or death;
You have eyes and breasts like a dove,
   And you kill men's hearts with a breath.

As plague in a poisonous city
   Insults and exults on her dead,
So you, when pallid for pity
   Comes love, and fawns to be fed.

As a tame beast writhes and wheedles,
   He fawns to be fed with wiles;
You carve him a cross of needles,
   And whet them sharp as your smiles.

He is patient of thorn and whip,
   He is dumb under axe or dart;
You suck with a sleepy red lip
   The wet red wounds in his heart.

You thrill as his pulses dwindle,
   You brighten and warm as he bleeds,
With insatiable eyes that kindle
   And insatiable mouth that feeds.

Your hands nailed love to the tree,
   You stript him, scourged him with rods,

And drowned him deep in the sea
  That hides the dead and their gods.

And for all this, die will he not;
  There is no man sees him but I;
You came and went and forgot;
  I hope he will some day die.

1866

Dolores
(Notre-Dame des Sept Douleurs)[13]

Cold eyelids that hide like a jewel
  Hard eyes that grow soft for an hour;
The heavy white limbs, and the cruel
  Red mouth like a venomous flower;
When these are gone by with their glories,
  What shall rest of thee then, what remain,
O mystic and sombre Dolores,
  Our Lady of Pain?

Seven sorrows the priests give their Virgin;
  But thy sins, which are seventy times seven,
Seven ages would fail thee to purge in,
  And then they would haunt thee in heaven:
Fierce midnights and famishing morrows,
  And the loves that complete and control
All the joys of the flesh, all the sorrows
  That wear out the soul.

O garment not golden but gilded,
  O garden where all men may dwell,
O tower not of ivory, but builded
  By hands that reach heaven from hell;
O mystical rose of the mire,
  O house not of gold but of gain,
O house of unquenchable fire,
  Our Lady of Pain!

O lips full of lust and of laughter,
  Curled snakes that are fed from my breast,
Bite hard, lest remembrance come after
  And press with new lips where you pressed.
For my heart too springs up at the pressure,
  Mine eyelids too moisten and burn;

Ah, feed me and fill me with pleasure,
Ere pain come in turn.

In yesterday's reach and to-morrow's,
Out of sight though they lie of to-day,
There have been and there yet shall be sorrows
That smite not and bite not in play.
The life and the love thou despisest,
These hurt us indeed, and in vain,
O wise among women, and wisest,
Our Lady of Pain.

Who gave thee thy wisdom? what stories
That stung thee, what visions that smote?
Wert thou pure and a maiden, Dolores,
When desire took thee first by the throat?
What bud was the shell of a blossom
That all men may smell to and pluck?
What milk fed thee first at what bosom?
What sins gave thee suck?

We shift and bedeck and bedrape us,
Thou art noble and nude and antique;
Libitina thy mother, Priapus[14]
Thy father, a Tuscan and Greek.
We play with light loves in the portal,
And wince and relent and refrain;
Loves die, and we know thee immortal,
Our Lady of Pain.

Fruits fail and love dies and time ranges;
Thou art fed with perpetual breath,
And alive after infinite changes,
And fresh from the kisses of death;
Of languors rekindled and rallied,
Of barren delights and unclean,
Things monstrous and fruitless, a pallid
And poisonous queen.

Could you hurt me, sweet lips, though I hurt you?
Men touch them, and change in a trice
The lilies and languors of virtue
For the raptures and roses of vice;
Those lie where thy foot on the floor is,
These crown and caress thee and chain,

O splendid and sterile Dolores,
   Our Lady of Pain.

There are sins it may be to discover,
   There are deeds it may be to delight.
What new work wilt thou find for thy lover,
   What new passions for daytime or night?
What spells that they know not a word of
   Whose lives are as leaves overblown?
What tortures undreamt of, unheard of,
   Unwritten, unknown?

Ah beautiful passionate body
   That never has ached with a heart!
On thy mouth though the kisses are bloody,
   Though they sting till it shudder and smart,
More kind than the love we adore is,
   They hurt not the heart or the brain,
O bitter and tender Dolores,
   Our Lady of Pain.

As our kisses relax and redouble,
   From the lips and the foam and the fangs
Shall no new sin be born for men's trouble,
   No dream of impossible pangs?
With the sweet of the sins of old ages
   Wilt thou satiate thy soul as of yore?
Too sweet is the rind, say the sages,
   Too bitter the core.

Hast thou told all thy secrets the last time,
   And bared all thy beauties to one?
Ah, where shall we go then for pastime,
   If the worst that can be has been done?
But sweet as the rind was the core is;
   We are fain of thee still, we are fain,
O sanguine and subtle Dolores,
   Our Lady of Pain.

By the hunger of change and emotion,
   By the thirst of unbearable things,
By despair, the twin-born of devotion,
   By the pleasure that winces and stings,
The delight that consumes the desire,
   The desire that outruns the delight,

By the cruelty deaf as a fire
   And blind as the night,

By the ravenous teeth that have smitten
   Through the kisses that blossom and bud,
By the lips intertwisted and bitten
   Till the foam has a savour of blood,
By the pulse as it rises and falters,
   By the hands as they slacken and strain,
I adjure thee, respond from thine altars,
   Our Lady of Pain.

Wilt thou smile as a woman disdaining
   The light fire in the veins of a boy?
But he comes to thee sad, without feigning,
   Who has wearied of sorrow and joy;
Less careful of labour and glory
   Than the elders whose hair has uncurled;
And young, but with fancies as hoary
   And grey as the world.

I have passed from the outermost portal
   To the shrine where a sin is a prayer;
What care though the service be mortal?
   O our Lady of Torture, what care?
All thine the last wine that I pour is,
   The last in the chalice we drain,
O fierce and luxurious Dolores,
   Our Lady of Pain.

All thine the new wine of desire,
   The fruit of four lips as they clung
Till the hair and the eyelids took fire,
   The foam of a serpentine tongue,
The froth of the serpents of pleasure,
   More salt than the foam of the sea,
Now felt as a flame, now at leisure
   As wine shed for me.

Ah thy people, thy children, thy chosen,
   Marked cross from the womb and perverse!
They have found out the secret to cozen
   The gods that constrain us and curse;
They alone, they are wise, and none other;
   Give me place, even me, in their train,

O my sister, my spouse, and my mother,
   Our Lady of Pain.

For the crown of our life as it closes
   Is darkness, the fruit thereof dust;
No thorns go as deep as a rose's,
   And love is more cruel than lust.
Time turns the old days to derision,
   Our loves into corpses or wives;
And marriage and death and division
   Make barren our lives.

And pale from the past we draw nigh thee,
   And satiate with comfortless hours;
And we know thee, how all men belie thee,
   And we gather the fruit of thy flowers;
The passion that slays and recovers,
   The pangs and the kisses that rain
On the lips and the limbs of thy lovers,
   Our Lady of Pain.

The desire of thy furious embraces
   Is more than the wisdom of years,
On the blossom though blood lie in traces,
   Though the foliage be sodden with tears.
For the lords in whose keeping the door is
   That opens on all who draw breath
Gave the cypress to love, my Dolores,
   The myrtle to death.

And they laughed, changing hands in the measure,
   And they mixed and made peace after strife;
Pain melted in tears, and was pleasure;
   Death tingled with blood, and was life.
Like lovers they melted and tingled,
   In the dusk of thine innermost fane;
In the darkness they murmured and mingled,
   Our Lady of Pain.

In a twilight where virtues are vices,
   In thy chapels, unknown of the sun,
To a tune that enthralls and entices,
   They were wed, and the twain were as one.
For the tune from thine altar hath sounded
   Since God bade the world's work begin,

And the fume of thine incense abounded,
  To sweeten the sin.

Love listens, and paler than ashes,
  Through his curls as the crown on them slips,
Lifts languid wet eyelids and lashes,
  And laughs with insatiable lips.
Thou shalt hush him with heavy caresses,
  With music that scares the profane;
Thou shalt darken his eyes with thy tresses,
  Our Lady of Pain.

Thou shalt blind his bright eyes though he wrestle,
  Thou shalt chain his light limbs though he strive;
In his lips all thy serpents shall nestle,
  In his hands all thy cruelties thrive.
In the daytime thy voice shall go through him,
  In his dreams he shall feel thee and ache;
Thou shalt kindle by night and subdue him
  Asleep and awake.

Thou shalt touch and make redder his roses
  With juice not of fruit nor of bud;
When the sense in the spirit reposes,
  Thou shalt quicken the soul through the blood.
Thine, thine the one grace we implore is,
  Who would live and not languish or feign,
O sleepless and deadly Dolores,
  Our Lady of Pain.

Dost thou dream, in a respite of slumber,
  In a lull of the fires of thy life,
Of the days without name, without number,
  When thy will stung the world into strife;
When, a goddess, the pulse of thy passion
  Smote kings as they revelled in Rome;
And they hailed thee re-risen, O Thalassian,[15]
  Foam-white, from the foam?

When thy lips had such lovers to flatter;
  When the city lay red from thy rods,
And thine hands were as arrows to scatter
  The children of change and their gods;
When the blood of thy foemen made fervent
  A sand never moist from the main,

As one smote them, their lord and thy servant,
  Our Lady of Pain.

On sands by the storm never shaken,
  Nor wet from the washing of tides;
Nor by foam of the waves overtaken,
  Nor winds that the thunder bestrides;
But red from the print of thy paces,
  Made smooth for the world and its lords,
Ringed round with a flame of fair faces,
  And splendid with swords.

There the gladiator, pale for thy pleasure,
  Drew bitter and perilous breath;
There torments laid hold on the treasure
  Of limbs too delicious for death;
When thy gardens were lit with live torches;
  When the world was a steed for thy rein;
When the nations lay prone in thy porches,
  Our Lady of Pain.

When, with flame all around him aspirant,
  Stood flushed, as a harp-player stands,
The implacable beautiful tyrant,
  Rose-crowned, having death in his hands;
And a sound as the sound of loud water
  Smote far through the flight of the fires,
And mixed with the lightning of slaughter
  A thunder of lyres.[16]

Dost thou dream of what was and no more is,
  The old kingdoms of earth and the kings?
Dost thou hunger for these things, Dolores,
  For these, in a world of new things?
But thy bosom no fasts could emaciate,
  No hunger compel to complain
Those lips that no bloodshed could satiate,
  Our Lady of Pain.

As of old when the world's heart was lighter,
  Through thy garments the grace of thee glows,
The white wealth of thy body made whiter
  By the blushes of amorous blows,
And seamed with sharp lips and fierce fingers,
  And branded by kisses that bruise;

When all shall be gone that now lingers,
  Ah, what shall we lose?

Thou wert fair in the fearless old fashion,
  And thy limbs are as melodies yet,
And move to the music of passion
  With lithe and lascivious regret.
What ailed us, O gods, to desert you
  For creeds that refuse and restrain?
Come down and redeem us from virtue,
  Our Lady of Pain.

All shrines that were Vestal are flameless,
  But the flame has not fallen from this;
Though obscure be the god, and though nameless
  The eyes and the hair that we kiss;
Low fires that love sits by and forges
  Fresh heads for his arrows and thine;
Hair loosened and soiled in mid orgies
  With kisses and wine.

Thy skin changes country and colour,
  And shrivels or swells to a snake's.
Let it brighten and bloat and grow duller,
  We know it, the flames and the flakes,
Red brands on it smitten and bitten,
  Round skies where a star is a stain,
And the leaves with thy litanies written,
  Our Lady of Pain.

On thy bosom though many a kiss be,
  There are none such as knew it of old.
Was it Alciphron once or Arisbe,[17]
  Male ringlets or feminine gold,
That thy lips met with under the statue,
  Whence a look shot out sharp after thieves
From the eyes of the garden-god[18] at you
  Across the fig-leaves?

Then still, through dry seasons and moister,
  One god had a wreath to his shrine;
Then love was the pearl of his oyster,
  And Venus rose red out of wine.
We have all done amiss, choosing rather
  Such loves as the wise gods disdain;

Intercede for us thou with thy father,
  Our Lady of Pain.

In spring he had crowns of his garden,
  Red corn in the heat of the year,
Then hoary green olives that harden
  When the grape-blossom freezes with fear;
And milk-budded myrtles with Venus
  And vine-leaves with Bacchus he trod;
And ye said, 'We have seen, he hath seen us,
  A visible God.'

What broke off the garlands that girt you?
  What sundered you spirit and clay?
Weak sins yet alive are as virtue
  To the strength of the sins of that day.
For dried is the blood of thy lover,
  Ipsithilla,[19] contracted the vein;
Cry aloud, 'Will he rise and recover,
  Our Lady of Pain?'

Cry aloud; for the old world is broken;
  Cry out; for the Phrygian[20] is priest,
And rears not the bountiful token
  And spreads not the fatherly feast.
From the midmost of Ida,[21] from shady
  Recesses that murmur at morn,
They have brought and baptized her, Our Lady,
  A goddess new-born.

And the chaplets of old are above us,
  And the oyster-bed teems out of reach;
Old poets outsing and outlove us,
  And Catullus[22] makes mouths at our speech.
Who shall kiss, in thy father's own city,
  With such lips as he sang with, again?
Intercede for us all of thy pity,
  Our Lady of Pain.

Out of Dindymus[23] heavily laden
  Her lions draw bound and unfed
A mother, a mortal, a maiden,
  A queen over death and the dead.
She is cold, and her habit is lowly,
  Her temple of branches and sods;

Most fruitful and virginal, holy,
   A mother of gods.

She hath wasted with fire thine high places,
   She hath hidden and marred and made sad
The fair limbs of the Loves, the fair faces
   Of gods that were goodly and glad.
She slays, and her hands are not bloody;
   She moves as a moon in the wane,
White-robed, and thy raiment is ruddy,
   Our Lady of Pain.

They shall pass and their places be taken,
   The gods and the priests that are pure.
They shall pass, and shalt thou not be shaken?
   They shall perish, and shalt thou endure?
Death laughs, breathing close and relentless
   In the nostrils and eyelids of lust,
With a pinch in his fingers of scentless
   And delicate dust.

But the worm shall revive thee with kisses;
   Thou shalt change and transmute as a god,
As the rod to a serpent that hisses,
   As the serpent again to a rod.
Thy life shall not cease though thou doff it;
   Thou shalt live until evil be slain,
And good shall die first, said thy prophet,[24]
   Our Lady of Pain.

Did he lie? did he laugh? does he know it,
   Now he lies out of reach, out of breath,
Thy prophet, thy preacher, thy poet,
   Sin's child by incestuous Death?
Did he find out in fire at his waking,
   Or discern as his eyelids lost light,
When the bands of the body were breaking
   And all came in sight?

Who has known all the evil before us,
   Or the tyrannous secrets of time?
Though we match not the dead men that bore us
   At a song, at a kiss, at a crime –
Though the heathen outface and outlive us,
   And our lives and our longings are twain –

Ah, forgive us our virtues, forgive us,
  Our Lady of Pain.

Who are we that embalm and embrace thee
  With spices and savours of song?
What is time, that his children should face thee?
  What am I, that my lips do thee wrong?
I could hurt thee – but pain would delight thee;
  Or caress thee – but love would repel;
And the lovers whose lips would excite thee
  Are serpents in hell.

Who now shall content thee as they did,
  Thy lovers, when temples were built
And the hair of the sacrifice braided
  And the blood of the sacrifice spilt,
In Lampsacus fervent with faces,
  In Aphaca[25] red from thy reign,
Who embraced thee with awful embraces,
  Our Lady of Pain?

Where are they, Cotytto or Venus,
  Astarte or Ashtaroth,[26] where?
Do their hands as we touch come between us?
  Is the breath of them hot in thy hair?
From their lips have thy lips taken fever,
  With the blood of their bodies grown red?
Hast thou left upon earth a believer
  If these men are dead?

They were purple of raiment and golden,
  Filled full of thee, fiery with wine,
Thy lovers, in haunts unbeholden,
  In marvellous chambers of thine.
They are fled, and their footprints escape us,
  Who appraise thee, adore, and abstain,
O daughter of Death and Priapus,
  Our Lady of Pain.

What ails us to fear overmeasure,
  To praise thee with timorous breath,
O mistress and mother of pleasure,
  The one thing as certain as death?
We shall change as the things that we cherish,
  Shall fade as they faded before,

As foam upon water shall perish,
  As sand upon shore.

We shall know what the darkness discovers,
  If the grave-pit be shallow or deep;
And our fathers of old, and our lovers,
  We shall know if they sleep not or sleep.
We shall see whether hell be not heaven,
  Find out whether tares be not grain,
And the joys of thee seventy times seven,
  Our Lady of Pain.

1866

PAUL VERLAINE

Mystic Evening Light (Crépuscule du soir mystique)

Memory and Setting Sun
Redden and tremble on the blazing horizon
Of Hope receding and spreading
Wide, like a mysterious screen
Painted with copious blossoms
– Dahlia, lily, buttercup and tulip –
Which leap up round a trellis
And twine among the sickly exhalations
Of hothouse perfumes whose poison,
– Dahlia, lily, buttercup and tulip –
Drowning my senses, my soul, my reason,
In one vast and swooning faint fuses
Memory and Setting Sun.

1866; translated by Martin Sorrell, 2011

L'Allée

As in the age of shepherd king and queen,
Painted and frail amid her nodding bows,
Under the sombre branches and between
The green and mossy garden-ways she goes,
With little mincing airs one keeps to pet
A darling and provoking perroquet.
Her long-trained robe is blue, the fan she holds

With fluent fingers girt with heavy rings,
So vaguely hints of vague erotic things
That her eye smiles, musing among its folds.
– Blonde too, a tiny nose, a rosy mouth,
Artful as that sly patch that makes more sly,
In her divine unconscious pride of youth,
The slightly simpering sparkle of the eye.

1869; translated by Arthur Symons, 1896

Languor (Langueur)

To Georges Courteline

I am the Empire in its decadence, where one
By one they pass, the great Barbarians white, –
Composing, in an idle mood, acrostics light,
In style of gold where dance the languors of the sun.

My lonely soul's heart-sick with weariness alone.
Yonder they say is waged the long drawn bloody fight.
O weak of will, and full of this corroding blight!
Unable to enjoy life's flower – no triumphs won –

To seek calm death, life's final blessing, no desire!
All's drunk! Bathyllus,[27] have you quit your laughter gay?
Ah, all is drunk, – all eaten! Nothing more to say!

Only a silly poem you scatter in the fire;
Only a sullen slave neglected of all men;
Only a sad disgust, for reasons past my ken!

1884; translated by Bergen Applegate, 1916

On the Balcony (Sur le balcon)

Two forms watching the swallows in their flight.
One pale, with jet black hair; the other blonde
And pink – their flowing garments of old blond
Like vague serpents twining, cloudlike and light.

Both languorous as asphodels where bright
The sky glows with a full moon, soft and round,
Whose rays throb with emotion, deep, profound.

Thus, with arms pressing their bodies supple,
Strange couple pitying every other couple,
They dream upon the moonlit balcony.

Behind them in the room's rich somber shade,
Enthroned in stately pomp, as in a play,
And full of perfumes, stands the Bed, unmade.

1889; translated by Bergen Applegate, 1916

GABRIELE D'ANNUNZIO

Prelude

As from corrupted flesh the over-bold
Young vines in dense luxuriance rankly grow,
And strange weird plants their horrid buds unfold
O'er the foul rotting of a corpse below;

As spreading crimson flowers with centred gold
Like the fresh blood of recent wounds o'erflow,
Where vile enormous chrysalids are rolled
In the young leaves, and cruel blossoms blow:

E'en so within my heart malignant flowers
Of verse swell forth: the leaves in fearful gloom
Exhale a sinister scent of human breath.

Lured by the radiance of the blood-red bowers,
The unconscious hand is stretched to pluck the bloom,
And the sharp poison fills the veins with death.

1882; translated by G. A. Greene, 1893

OSCAR WILDE

The Harlot's House

We caught the tread of dancing feet,
We loitered down the moonlit street,
And stopped beneath the Harlot's House.

Inside, above the din and fray,
We heard the loud musicians play
The *Treues Liebes Herz* of Strauss.[28]

Like strange mechanical grotesques,
Making fantastic arabesques,
The shadows raced across the blind.

We watched the ghostly dancers spin,
To sound of horn and violin,
Like black leaves wheeling in the wind.

Like wire-pulled Automatons,
Slim silhouetted skeletons
Went sidling through the slow quadrille,

Then took each other by the hand,
And danced a stately saraband;
Their laughter echoed thin and shrill.

Sometimes a clock-work puppet pressed
A phantom lover to her breast,
Sometimes they seemed to try and sing.

Sometimes a horrible Marionette
Came out and smoked its cigarette
Upon the steps like a live thing.

Then turning to my love I said,
'The dead are dancing with the dead,
The dust is whirling with the dust.'

But she, she heard the violin,
And left my side and entered in:
Love passed into the House of Lust.

Then suddenly the tune went false,
The dancers wearied of the waltz,
The shadows ceased to wheel and whirl,

And down the long and silent street,
The dawn with silver-sandalled feet,
Crept like a frightened girl.

1885

JEAN LORRAIN

Decadence (Décadence)

Like water-lilies, fat and deathly pale
Is fair-haired Sapphus with his eyes perverse.
His poems smell of rouge, and something worse:
This bard of Lesbos gives off odours stale

From lurking among washrooms. Without fail,
He gilds the stinking waters that immerse
His haunts, and sprinkles on his tasteless verse
Some fruity flavour that will speed its sale.

Oh such a suave, obliging soul is he,
As pretty as a boy past puberty.
Putrescently he gleams, and cannily
Scorning the newer poets, all unread,
He joins the worship of the honoured dead
Whose lines he knows just how to steal instead.

1885; translated by Chris Baldick, 2011

Narcissus (Retour de Lesbos I: Narcisse)

Nor sweetest languid strains of flutes and strings,
In cadence wafting through an evening's calm,
Nor swooning odours hazy incense brings,
Nor knowing smiles, nor youth's bare arm
Restore my heart to hope's imaginings.
Envied by harlots for its virgin charm,
My body now to blackest lilies clings,
Trembling, and weary of love's false alarm.

Their gloomy petals open to my lips,
Those darkest lilies, blooms of sombre night
Have told me all my shame and chaste disgrace . . .
Alas, I peer into my loathsome deeps
And taste the strangely sweet delight
Such knowledge grants my self-adoring face!

1887; translated by Chris Baldick, 2011

MAURICE MAETERLINCK

Temptations (Tentations)

Green as the sea, temptations creep
  Through the shadows of the mind,
  Where with flaming flowers entwined
Dark ejaculations leap –

Stems obscure that coil and thrust
  In the moon's unhallowed glow,

And the autumnal shadows throw
Of their auguries of lust.

And the moon may hardly shine
Through their fevered fast embrace:
Limb and slimy limb enlace,
Emerald and serpentine.

Sacrilegiously they grow,
And their secret will reveal,
Dismal as regrets that steal
O'er men dying in the snow;

And their mournful shadows hide
Tangled wounds that mark the thrust
Of the azure swords of lust
In the crimson flesh of pride.

When will the dreams of earth, alas,
Find in my heart their final tomb?
O let Thy glory, Lord, illume
This dark and evil house of glass,

And that oblivion nought may win!
The dead leaves of their fevers fall,
The stars between their lips, and all
The viscerae of woe and sin!

1889; translated by Bernard Miall, 1915

JOHN DAVIDSON

A Ballad of a Nun

From Eastertide to Eastertide
For ten long years her patient knees
Engraved the stones – the fittest bride
Of Christ in all the diocese.

She conquered every earthly lust;
The abbess loved her more and more;
And, as a mark of perfect trust,
Made her the keeper of the door.

High on a hill the convent hung,
Across a duchy looking down,

Where everlasting mountains flung
  Their shadows over tower and town.

The jewels of their lofty snows
  In constellations flashed at night;
Above their crests the moon arose;
  The deep earth shuddered with delight.

Long ere she left her cloudy bed,
  Still dreaming in the orient land,
On many a mountain's happy head
  Dawn lightly laid her rosy hand.

The adventurous sun took Heaven by storm;
  Clouds scattered largesses of rain;
The sounding cities, rich and warm,
  Smouldered and glittered in the plain.

Sometimes it was a wandering wind,
  Sometimes the fragrance of the pine,
Sometimes the thought how others sinned,
  That turned her sweet blood into wine.

Sometimes she heard a serenade
  Complaining sweetly far away:
She said, 'A young man woos a maid';
  And dreamt of love till break of day.

Then would she ply her knotted scourge
  Until she swooned; but evermore
She had the same red sin to purge,
  Poor, passionate keeper of the door!

For still night's starry scroll unfurled,
  And still the day came like a flood:
It was the greatness of the world
  That made her long to use her blood.

In winter-time when Lent drew nigh,
  And hill and plain were wrapped in snow,
She watched beneath the frosty sky
  The nearest city nightly glow.

Like peals of airy bells outworn
  Faint laughter died above her head
In gusts of broken music borne:
  'They keep the Carnival,' she said.

Her hungry heart devoured the town:
  'Heaven save me by a miracle!
Unless God sends an angel down,
  Thither I go though it were Hell.'

She dug her nails deep in her breast,
  Sobbed, shrieked, and straight withdrew the bar:
A fledgling flying from the nest,
  A pale moth rushing to a star.

Fillet and veil in strips she tore;
  Her golden tresses floated wide;
The ring and bracelet that she wore
  As Christ's betrothed, she cast aside.

'Life's dearest meaning I shall probe;
  Lo! I shall taste of love at last!
Away!' She doffed her outer robe,
  And sent it sailing down the blast.

Her body seemed to warm the wind;
  With bleeding feet o'er ice she ran:
'I leave the righteous God behind;
  I go to worship sinful man.'

She reached the sounding city's gate;
  No question did the warder ask:
He passed her in: 'Welcome, wild mate!'
  He thought her some fantastic mask.

Half-naked through the town she went;
  Each footstep left a bloody mark;
Crowds followed her with looks intent;
  Her bright eyes made the torches dark.

Alone and watching in the street
  There stood a grave youth nobly dressed;
To him she knelt and kissed his feet;
  Her face her great desire confessed.

Straight to his house the nun he led:
  'Strange lady, what would you with me?'
'Your love, your love, sweet lord,' she said;
  'I bring you my virginity.'

He healed her bosom with a kiss;
  She gave him all her passion's hoard;

And sobbed and murmured ever, 'This
  Is life's great meaning, dear, my lord.

'I care not for my broken vow;
  Though God should come in thunder soon,
I am sister to the mountains now,
  And sister to the sun and moon.'

Through all the towns of Belmarie[29]
  She made a progress like a queen.
'She is,' they said, 'whate'er she be,
  The strangest woman ever seen.

'From fairyland she must have come,
  Or else she is a mermaiden.'
Some said she was a ghoul, and some
  A heathen goddess born again.

But soon her fire to ashes burned;
  Her beauty changed to haggardness;
Her golden hair to silver turned;
  The hour came of her last caress.

  At midnight from her lonely bed
  She rose, and said, 'I have had my will.'
The old ragged robe she donned, and fled
  Back to the convent on the hill.

Half-naked as she went before,
  She hurried to the city wall,
Unnoticed in the rush and roar
  And splendour of the carnival.

No question did the warder ask:
  Her ragged robe, her shrunken limb,
Her dreadful eyes! 'It is no mask;
  It is a she-wolf, gaunt and grim!'

She ran across the icy plain;
  Her worn blood curdled in the blast;
Each footstep left a crimson stain;
  The white-faced moon looked on aghast.

She said between her chattering jaws,
  'Deep peace is mine, I cease to strive;
Oh, comfortable convent laws,
  That bury foolish nuns alive!

'A trowel for my passing-bell,
  A little bed within the wall,
A coverlet of stones; how well
  I there shall keep the Carnival!'

Like tired bells chiming in their sleep,
  The wind faint peals of laughter bore;
She stopped her ears and climbed the steep,
  And thundered at the convent door.

It opened straight: she entered in,
  And at the wardress' feet fell prone:
'I come to purge away my sin;
  Bury me, close me up in stone.'

The wardress raised her tenderly;
  She touched her wet and fast-shut eyes:
'Look, sister; sister, look at me;
  Look; can you see through my disguise?'

She looked and saw her own sad face,
  And trembled, wondering, 'Who art thou?'
'God sent me down to fill your place:
  I am the Virgin Mary now.'

And with the word, God's mother shone:
  The wanderer whispered, 'Mary, hail!'
The vision helped her to put on
  Bracelet and fillet, ring and veil.

'You are sister to the mountains now,
  And sister to the day and night;
Sister to God.' And on the brow
  She kissed her thrice, and left her sight.

While dreaming in her cloudy bed,
  Far in the crimson orient land
On many a mountain's happy head
  Dawn lightly laid her rosy hand.

1894

ERNEST DOWSON

Non sum qualis eram bonae sub regno Cynarae[30]

Last night, ah, yesternight, betwixt her lips and mine
There fell thy shadow, Cynara! thy breath was shed
Upon my soul between the kisses and the wine;
And I was desolate and sick of an old passion,
Yea, I was desolate and bowed my head:
I have been faithful to thee, Cynara! in my fashion.

All night upon mine heart I felt her warm heart beat,
Night-long within mine arms in love and sleep she lay;
Surely the kisses of her bought red mouth were sweet;
But I was desolate and sick of an old passion,
When I awoke and found the dawn was gray:
I have been faithful to thee, Cynara! in my fashion.

I have forgot much, Cynara! gone with the wind,
Flung roses, roses riotously with the throng,
Dancing, to put thy pale, lost lilies out of mind;
But I was desolate and sick of an old passion,
Yea, all the time, because the dance was long:
I have been faithful to thee, Cynara! in my fashion.

I cried for madder music and for stronger wine,
But when the feast is finished and the lamps expire,
Then falls thy shadow, Cynara! the night is thine;
And I am desolate and sick of an old passion,
Yea, hungry for the lips of my desire:
I have been faithful to thee, Cynara! in my fashion.

1891

Transition

A little while to walk with thee, dear child;
  To lean on thee my weak and weary head;
Then evening comes: the winter sky is wild,
  The leafless trees are black, the leaves long dead.

A little while to hold thee and to stand,
  By harvest-fields of bending golden corn;
Then the predestined silence, and thine hand,
  Lost in the night, long and weary and forlorn.

A little while to love thee, scarcely time
  To love thee well enough; then time to part,
To fare through wintry fields alone and climb
  The frozen hills, not knowing where thou art.

Short summer-time and then, my heart's desire,
  The winter and the darkness: one by one
The roses fall, the pale roses expire
  Beneath the slow decadence of the sun.

1899

Rondeau

Ah, Manon, say, why is it we
Are one and all so fain of thee?
Thy rich red beauty debonnaire
In very truth is not more fair,
Than the shy grace and purity
That clothe the maiden maidenly;
Her gray eyes shine more tenderly
And not less bright than thine her hair,
  Ah, Manon, say!
Expound, I pray, the mystery
Why wine-stained lip and languid eye,
And most unsaintly Maenad air,
Should move us more than all the rare
White roses of virginity?
  Ah, Manon, say!

1899

Libera Me[31]

Goddess the laughter-loving, Aphrodite, befriend!
Long have I served thine altars, serve me now at the end,
Let me have peace of thee, truce of thee, golden one, send.

Heart of my heart have I offered thee, pain of my pain,
Yielding my life for the love of thee into thy chain;
Lady and goddess be merciful, loose me again.

All things I had that were fairest, my dearest and best,
Fed the fierce flames on thine altar: ah, surely, my breast
Shrined thee alone among goddesses, spurning the rest.

Blossom of youth thou hast plucked of me, flower of my days;
Stinted I nought in thine honouring, walked in thy ways,
Song of my soul pouring out to thee, all in thy praise.

Fierce was the flame while it lasted, and strong was thy wine,
Meet for immortals that die not, for throats such as thine,
Too fierce for bodies of mortals, too potent for mine.

Blossom and bloom hast thou taken, now render to me
Ashes of life that remain to me, few though they be,
Truce of the love of thee, Cyprian,[32] let me go free.

Goddess the laughter-loving, Aphrodite, restore
Life to the limbs of me, liberty, hold me no more
Having the first-fruits and flower of me, cast me the core.

1899

A Last Word

Let us go hence: the night is now at hand;
   The day is overworn, the birds all flown;
   And we have reaped the crops the gods have sown;
Despair and death; deep darkness o'er the land,
Broods like an owl; we cannot understand
   Laughter or tears, for we have only known
   Surpassing vanity: vain things alone
Have driven our perverse and aimless band.

Let us go hence, somewhither strange and cold,
   To Hollow Lands where just men and unjust
   Find end of labour, where's rest for the old,
Freedom to all from love and fear and lust.
Twine our torn hands! O pray the earth enfold
Our life-sick hearts and turn them into dust.

1899

JOHN GRAY

The Barber

1

I dreamed I was a barber; and there went
Beneath my hand, oh! manes extravagant.

Beneath my trembling fingers, many a mask
Of many a pleasant girl. It was my task
To gild their hair, carefully, strand by strand;
To paint their eyebrows with a timid hand;
To draw a bodkin, from a vase of kohl,
Through the closed lashes; pencils from a bowl
Of sepia to paint them underneath;
To blow upon their eyes with a soft breath.
They lay them back and watched the leaping bands.

2

The dream grew vague. I moulded with my hands
The mobile breasts, the valley; and the waist
I touched; and pigments reverently placed
Upon their thighs in sapient spots and stains,
Beryls and crysolites and diaphanes,
And gems whose hot harsh names are never said.
I was a masseur; and my fingers bled
With wonder as I touched their awful limbs.

3

Suddenly, in the marble trough, there seems
O, last of my pale mistresses, Sweetness!
A twylipped[33] scarlet pansie. My caress
Tinges thy steelgray eyes to violet.
Adown thy body skips the pit-a-pat
Of treatment once heard in a hospital
For plagues that fascinate, but half appal.

4

So, at the sound, the blood of me stood cold.
Thy chaste hair ripened into sullen gold.
The throat, the shoulders, swelled and were uncouth.
The breasts rose up and offered each a mouth.
And on the belly pallid blushes crept,
That maddened me, until I laughed and wept.

1893

LIONEL JOHNSON

The Dark Angel

Dark Angel, with thine aching lust
To rid the world of penitence:
Malicious Angel, who still dost
My soul such subtile violence!

Because of thee, no thought, no thing,
Abides for me undesecrate:
Dark Angel, ever on the wing,
Who never reachest me too late!

When music sounds, then changest thou
Its silvery to a sultry fire:
Nor will thine envious heart allow
Delight untortured by desire.

Through thee, the gracious Muses turn
To Furies, O mine Enemy!
And all the things of beauty burn
With flames of evil ecstasy.

Because of thee, the land of dreams
Becomes a gathering place of fears:
Until tormented slumber seems
One vehemence of useless tears.

When sunlight glows upon the flowers,
Or ripples down the dancing sea:
Thou, with thy troop of passionate powers,
Beleaguerest, bewilderest, me.

Within the breath of autumn woods,
Within the winter silences:
Thy venomous spirit stirs and broods,
O Master of impieties!

The ardour of red flame is thine,
And thine the steely soul of ice:
Thou poisonest the fair design
Of nature, with unfair device.

Apples of ashes, golden bright;
Waters of bitterness, how sweet!

O banquet of a foul delight,
Prepared by thee, dark Paraclete![34]

Thou art the whisper in the gloom,
The hinting tone, the haunting laugh:
Thou art the adorner of my tomb,
The minstrel of mine epitaph.

1894

EUGENE LEE-HAMILTON

Baudelaire

A Paris gutter of the good old times,
Black and putrescent in its stagnant bed,
Save where the shamble oozings fringe it red,
Or scaffold trickles, or nocturnal crimes.

It holds dropped gold; dead flowers from tropic climes;
Gems true and false, by midnight maskers shed;
Old pots of rouge; old broken phials that spread
Vague fumes of musk, with fumes from slums and slimes.

And everywhere, as glows the set of day,
There floats upon the winding fetid mire
The gorgeous iridescence of decay:

A wavy film of colour, gold and fire,
Trembles all through it as you pick your way,
And streaks of purple that are straight from Tyre.[35]

1894

ARTHUR SYMONS

Lilian I: Proem

This was a sweet white wildwood violet
I found among the painted slips that grow
Where, under hot-house glass, the flowers forget
How the sun shines, and how the cool winds blow.

The violet took the orchid's colouring,
Tricked out its dainty fairness like the rest;

Yet still its breath was as the breath of Spring,
   And the wood's heart was wild within its breast.

The orchid mostly is the flower I love,
   And violets, the mere violets of the wood,
For all their sweetness, have not power to move
   The curiosity that rules my blood.

Yet here, in this spice-laden atmosphere,
   Where only nature is a thing unreal,
I found in just a violet, planted here,
   The artificial flower of my ideal.

1895

White Heliotrope

The feverish room and that white bed,
   The tumbled skirts upon a chair,
   The novel flung half-open, where
Hat, hair-pins, puffs, and paints, are spread;

The mirror that has sucked your face
   Into its secret deep of deeps,
   And there mysteriously keeps
Forgotten memories of grace;

And you, half dressed and half awake,
   Your slant eyes strangely watching me,
   And I, who watch you drowsily,
With eyes that, having slept not, ache;

This (need one dread? nay, dare one hope?)
   Will rise, a ghost of memory, if
   Ever again my handkerchief
Is scented with White Heliotrope.

1895

Bianca IX: Wine of Circe

Circe,[36] the wine of Circe! Sorceress, I
Have lived, but can your magic bid me die?
I would die exquisitely, of the bliss
Of one intense, intolerable kiss.
Cease these caresses brimming at my lips,
While, fluttering, your magnetic finger-tips

Race in a maze of circles up my arm.
Silently, let your eyes begin their charm.
You lean above me, and you strain me close,
Pantingly close, against your breast: the rose
Of your lips reddens to a rose of fire,
That sinks and wavers, odorously, nigher.
And your breast beats upon me like a sea
Of warmth and perfume, ah! engulphing me
Into the softness of its waves that cover
My drowning senses amorously over.
Your eyes intoxicate me: deeper yet
Pour me oblivion! I shall soon forget
Earth holds another woman: let me drain,
Circe, the wine of Circe, once again!
The rose of fire descends, the stars of fire
Bend from the night of heaven to my desire.
And your eyes burn on mine, and your lips burn
Like living fire through all my veins that yearn,
As, with one throb of rapt, surrendering breath,
Life dies into the ecstasy of Death.

1895

Bianca X: Liber Amoris

What's virtue, Bianca? Have we not
Agreed the word should be forgot,
That ours be every dear device
And all the subtleties of vice,
And, in diverse imaginings,
The savour of forbidden things,
So only that the obvious be
Too obvious for you and me,
And the one vulgar final act
Remain an unadmitted fact?

And, surely, we were wise to waive
A gift we do not lose, but save.
What moment's reeling blaze of sense
Were rationally recompense
For all the ecstasies and all
The ardours demi-virginal?
Bianca, I tell you, no delights
Of long, free, unforbidden nights,

Have richlier filled and satisfied
The eager moments as they died,
Than your voluptuous pretence
Of unacquainted innocence,
Your clinging hands and closing lips
And eyes slow sinking to eclipse
And cool throat flushing to my kiss;
That sterile and mysterious bliss,
Mysterious, and yet to me
Deeper for that dubiety.

Once, but that time was long ago,
I loved good women, and to know
That lips my lips dared never touch
Could speak, in one warm smile, so much.
And it seemed infinitely sweet
To worship at a woman's feet,
And live on heavenly thoughts of her,
Till earth itself grew heavenlier.
But that rapt mood, being fed on air,
Turned at the last to a despair,
And, for a body and soul like mine,
I found the angels' food too fine.
So the mood changed, and I began
To find that man was merely man,
Though women might be angels; so,
I let the aspirations go,
And for a space I held it wise
To follow after certainties.
My heart forgot the ways of love,
No longer now my fancy wove
Into admitted ornament
Its spider's web of sentiment.
What my hands seized, that my hands held,
I followed as the blood compelled,
And finding that my brain found rest
On some unanalytic breast,
I was contented to discover
How easy 'tis to be a lover.
No sophistries to ravel out,
No devious martyrdoms of doubt,
Only the good firm flesh to hold,
The love well worth its weight in gold,

Love, sinking from the infinite,
Now just enough to last one night.
So the simplicity of flesh
Held me a moment in its mesh,
Till that too palled, and I began
To find that man is mostly man
In that, his will being sated, he
Wills ever new variety.
And then I found you, Bianca! Then
I found in you, I found again
That chance or will or fate had brought
The curiosity I sought.
Ambiguous child, whose life retires
Into the pulse of those desires
Of whose endured possession speaks
The passionate pallor of your cheeks;
Child, in whom neither good nor ill
Can sway your sick and swaying will,
Only the aching sense of sex
Wholly controls, and does perplex,
With dubious drifts scarce understood,
The shaken currents of your blood;
It is your ambiguity
That speaks to me and conquers me,
Your swooning heats of captive bliss,
Under my hands, under my kiss,
And your strange reticences, strange
Concessions, your illusive change,
The strangeness of your smile, the faint
Corruption of your gaze, a saint
Such as Luini[37] loved to paint.

What's virtue, Bianca? nay, indeed,
What's vice? for I at last am freed,
With you, of virtue and of vice:
I have discovered Paradise.
And Paradise is neither heaven,
Where the spirits of God are seven,
And the spirits of men burn pure,
Nor is it hell, where souls endure
An equal ecstasy of fire,
In like repletion of desire;
Nay, but a subtlier intense

Unsatisfied appeal of sense,
Ever desiring, ever near
The goal of all its hope and fear,
Ever a hair's-breadth from the goal.

So Bianca satisfies my soul.

1895

Hallucination

I

One petal of a blood-red tulip pressed
Between the pages of a Baudelaire:
No more; and I was suddenly aware
Of the white fragrant apple of a breast
On which my lips were pastured; and I knew
That dreaming I remembered an old dream.
Sweeter than any fruit that fruit did seem,
Which, as my hungry teeth devoured it, grew
Ever again, and tantalised my taste.
So, vainly hungering, I seemed to see
Eve and the serpent and the apple-tree,
And Adam in the garden, and God laying waste
Innocent Eden, because man's desire,
Godlike before, now for a woman's sake
Descended through the woman to the snake.
Then as my mouth grew parched, stung as with fire
By that white fragrant apple, once so fair,
That seemed to shrink and spire into a flame,
I cried, and wakened, crying on your name:
One blood-red petal stained the Baudelaire.

II

Is it your face, is it a dream?
Your face I dream in such a mist
Of rosy gold and amethyst?
Is it your eyes that flicker and gleam
Like mocking stars beneath the shade
Of leafy hair that seems to have curled
Its tendrils to blot out the world?
Dreams are the truth: let the world fade!

And these warm spires of heat that rise
Out of my heart into my brain
Are they not flames lighted in vain
At the enchantment of your eyes?
I shudder with the fear of hope,
Giddy expectancy consumes
My senses; but what breath perfumes
The air with scents of heliotrope?
I sicken with a wild desire,
I drown in sweetness, till it seems
As if the after-taste of dreams
Came back into my mouth like fire.

1902

London

The sun, a fiery orange in the air,
Thins and discolours to a disc of tin,
Until the breathing mist's mouth sucks it in;
And now there is no colour anywhere,
Only the ghost of greyness; vapour fills
The hollows of the streets, and seems to shroud
Gulfs where a noise of multitude is loud
As unseen water falling among hills.
Now the light withers, stricken at the root,
And, in the evil glimpses of the light,
Men as trees walking loom through lanes of night
Hung from the globes of some unnatural fruit.
To live, and to die daily, deaths like these,
Is it to live, while there are winds and seas?

1906

The Andante of Snakes

They weave a slow andante as in sleep,
Scaled yellow, swampy black, plague-spotted white;
With blue and lidless eyes at watch they keep
A treachery of silence; infinite

Ancestral angers brood in these dull eyes
Where the long-lineaged venom of the snake
Meditates evil; woven intricacies
Of Oriental arabesque awake,

Unfold, expand, contract, and raise and sway
Swoln heart-shaped heads, flattened as by a heel,
Erect to suck the sunlight from the day,
And stealthily and gradually reveal

Dim cabalistic signs of spots and rings
Among their folds of faded tapestry;
Then these fat, foul, unbreathing, moving things
Droop back to stagnant immobility.

1906

Song of the Sirens

Our breasts are cold, salt are our kisses,
Your blood shall whiten in our sea-blisses;
A man's desire is a flame of fire,
But chill as water is our desire,
Chill as water that sucks in
A drowning man's despairing chin
With a little kissing noise;
And like the water's voice our voice.

Our hands are colder than your lovers',
Colder than pearls that the sea covers;
Are a girl's hands as white as pearls?
Take the hands of the sea-girls,
And come with us to the under-sands;
We will hold in our cold hands
Flaming heart and burning head,
And put thought and love to bed.

We are the last desires; we have waited,
Till, by all things mortal sated,
And by dreams deceived, the scorn
Of every foolish virgin morn,
You, awakening at last,
Drunken, beggared of the past,
In the last lust of despair
Tangle your souls into our hair.

1906

Nini Patte-en-l'Air[38]

(*Casino de Paris*)

The gold Casino's Spring parterre
Flowers with the Spring, this golden week;
Glady, Toloche, Valtesse,[39] are there;
But all eyes turn as one to seek
The drawers of Nini Patte-en-l'air.

Surprising, sunset-coloured lace,
In billowy clouds of gold and red,
They whirl and flash before one's face;
The little heel above her head
Points an ironical grimace.

And mark the experimental eyes,
The naughty eloquence of feet,
The appeal of subtly quivering thighs,
The insinuations indiscreet
Of pirouetting draperies.

What exquisite indecency,
Select, supreme, severe, an art!
The art of knowing how to be
Part lewd, aesthetical in part,
And *fin-de-siècle* essentially.

The Maenad[40] of the Decadence,
Collectedly extravagant,
Her learned fury wakes the sense
That, fainting, needs for excitant
This science of concupiscence.

(Paris, May 14, 1892)

1920

The Woman in the Moon

A naked youth adores the mocking Sun,
With a woman's sidelong eyes and lips,
Before unto the stormless Sea he dips.
The dark girl has the weariness of one
Who, after being satiated, is not won;
He, with some fever in his finger-tips,
Urges the fever in the girl who strips

Her body naked. Sinister, alone,
The dishevelled seaweed shifts under their feet;
Upon the margin of the moonless sea
What shall the end be of their agony?
He to Salome:[41] 'It is the moon we see,
And not the Sun. O moon's maiden, O cheat,
The globe of the Earth, fruit from a fruitless Tree!'

1923

THEODORE WRATISLAW

Orchids

Orange and purple, shot with white and mauve,
Such in a greenhouse wet with tropic heat
One sees these delicate flowers whose parents throve
In some Pacific island's hot retreat.

Their ardent colours that betray the rank
Fierce hotbed of corruption whence they rose
Please eyes that long for stranger sweets than prank
Wild meadow-blooms and what the garden shows.

Exotic flowers! How great is my delight
To watch your petals curiously wrought,
To lie among your splendours day and night
Lost in a subtle dream of subtler thought.

Bathed in your clamorous orchestra of hues,
The palette of your perfumes, let me sleep
While your mesmeric presences diffuse
Weird dreams: and then bizarre sweet rhymes shall creep

Forth from my brain and slowly form and make
Sweet poems as a weaving spider spins,
A shrine of loves that laugh and swoon and ache,
A temple of coloured sorrows and perfumed sins!

1896

White Lilies

Flowers rare and sweet I sent, whose delicate white
Should, grouping at her corsage, interlace

Their purity with her corrupted grace,
With the full throat and mouth of my delight.

Evil design! To see the pale flowers slight
The beauty of the worn and powdered face,
Mingling their costly virtue with the trace
Of ancient loves that live in time's despite.

How soon they died, poor blossoms! at her throat
Ere of the last valse died the last sad note:
No more than love of her meant to endure,

For all the savour of her lips, the spice
Of her frail spirit steeped in cultured vice,
Gracefully bad and delicately impure!

1896

Etchings: At the Empire[42]

The low and soft luxurious promenade,
Electric-light, pile-carpet, the device
Of gilded mirrors that repeat you thrice;
The crowd that lounges, strolls from yard to yard;

The calm and brilliant Circes[43] who retard
Your passage with the skirts and rouge that spice
The changeless programme of insipid vice,
And stun you with a languid strange regard;

Ah! what are these, the perfume and the glow,
The ballet that coruscates down below,
The glittering songstress and the comic stars,

Ah! what are these, although we sit withdrawn
Above our sparkling tumblers and cigars,
To us so like to perish with a yawn?

1896

Sonnet Macabre

I love you for the grief that lurks within
Your languid spirit, and because you wear
Corruption with a vague and childish air,
And with your beauty know the depths of sin;

Because shame cuts and holds you like a gin,
And virtue dies in you slain by despair,
Since evil has you tangled in its snare
And triumphs on the soul good cannot win.

I love you since you know remorse and tears,
And in your troubled loveliness appears
The spot of ancient crimes that writhe and hiss:

I love you for your hands that calm and bless,
The perfume of your sad and slow caress,
The avid poison of your subtle kiss.

1896

Hothouse Flowers

I hate the flower of wood or common field.
I cannot love the primrose nor regret
The death of any shrinking violet,
Nor even the cultured garden's banal yield.

The silver lips of lilies virginal,
The full deep bosom of the enchanted rose
Please less than flowers glass-hid from frosts and snows
For whom an alien heat makes festival.

I love those flowers reared by man's careful art,
Of heady scents and colours: strong of heart
Or weak that die beneath the touch or knife,

Some rich as sin and some as virtue pale,
And some as subtly infamous and frail
As she whose love still eats my soul and life.

1896

JAMES ELROY FLECKER

Narcissus

O thou with whom I dallied
   Through all the hours of noon –
Sweet water-boy, more pallid
   Than any watery moon;
Above thy body turning

White lily-buds were strewn:
Alas, the silver morning,
Alas, the golden noon!

Alas, the clouds of sorrow,
The waters of despair!
I sought thee on the morrow,
And never found thee there.
Since first I saw thee splendid,
Since last I called thee fair,
My happy ways have ended
By waters of despair.

The pool that was thy dwelling
I hardly knew again,
So black it was, and swelling
With bitter wind and rain.
Amid the reeds I lingered
Between desire and pain
Till evening, rosy-fingered,
Beckoned to night again.

Yet once when sudden quiet
Had visited the skies,
And stilled the stormy riot,
I looked upon thine eyes.
I saw they wept and trembled
With glittering mysteries,
But yellow clouds assembled
Redarkening the skies.

O listless thou art lying
In waters cool and sweet,
While I, dumb brother, dying,
Faint in the desert heat.
Though thou dost love another,
Still let my lips entreat:
Men call me fair, O brother,
And women honey-sweet.

1907

Envoy

The young men leap, and toss their golden hair,
Run round the land, or sail across the seas:

But one was stricken with a sore disease –
The lean and swarthy poet of despair.

Know me, the slave of fear and death and shame,
A sad Comedian, a most tragic Fool,
Shallow, imperfect, fashioned without rule,
The doubtful shadow of a demon flame.

1907

JOHN BARLAS

Beauty's Anadems[44]

A dagger-hilt crusted with flaming gems:
A queen's rich girdle clasped with tiger's claws;
A lady's glove or a cat's velvet paws;
The whisper of a judge when he condemns;
Fierce night-shade berries purple on their stems
Among the rose's healthsome scarlet haws;
A rainbow-sheathed snake with jagged jaws:
Such are queen Beauty's sovran anadems.
For she caresses with a poisoned hand,
And venom hangs about her moistened lips,
And plots of murder lurk within her eyes
She loves lewd girls dancing a saraband
The murderer stabbing till all his body drips,
And thee, my gentle lady, and thy soft sighs.

1935 (probably written c. 1890)

Terrible Love

The marriage of two murderers in the gloom
Of a dark fane to hymns of blackest night;
Before a priest who keeps his hands from sight
Hidden away beneath his robe of doom,
Lest any see the flowers of blood that bloom
For gems upon the fingers, red on white;
The while far up in domes of dizzy height
The trumpets of the organ peal and boom:
Such is our love. Oh sweet delicious lips
From which I fancy all the world's blood drips!
Oh supple waist, pale cheek, and eyes of fire,

Hard little breasts and white gigantic hips,
And blue-black hair with serpent coils that slips
Out of my hand in hours of red desire.

1935 (probably written c. 1890)

Notes

1 See pp. 81–2 above for examples of George's own decadent verse.
2 River of oblivion in the Graeco-Roman underworld.
3 Courtesans, after Phryne, a celebrated courtesan of fourth-century Athens.
4 Of Paphos, a centre of the Aphrodite cult in Cyprus.
5 The poet Sappho is supposed to have committed suicide by throwing herself off a cliff into the sea. She is referred to as 'male' in the next lines on account of her masculine pursuits: poetry and making love to women.
6 A boatman with whom Sappho fell in love. The Greek legend attributes her suicide to Phaon's rejection of her, but here Baudelaire changes her motive to shame at violating the all-female code of her cult by taking Phaon as her lover.
7 Latin: 'Goddess, heed my prayer!'
8 The dog-headed Egyptian god of tombs.
9 Proserpina or Persephone was queen of the underworld, and daughter of the Earth-goddess Demeter. The first Christian emperor of Rome, Constantine I, decreed legal toleration of Christians by his Edict of Milan in 313, but did not overtly establish his faith as the official religion. The Proserpine/Proserpina variation is Swinburne's, for metrical reasons.
10 Latin: 'Thou hast conquered, Galilean'. These were believed to be the dying words of the emperor Julian (361–3), known by Christians as 'the Apostate' for his eventually futile attempts to reverse the Christianisation of Rome begun by his uncle Constantine.
11 One of the common titles of the love-goddess Aphrodite, known in Rome as Venus, after her birthplace, Cythera.
12 Latin: 'glut thyself with blood'. The phrase comes from Latin renditions of a story told by the Greek historian Herodotus about the death of the Persian king Cyrus: a tribal queen (Tomyris of the Massagetai people) whose son had been killed by Cyrus immersed the king's severed head in a bowl of blood, calling on him to drink his fill of the blood he had always craved.
13 French: 'Our Lady of the Seven Sorrows', the first of several titles and phrases applied to the Virgin Mary that Swinburne here perverts in the service of his own alternative Madonna-figure, who emerges as a masochistic version of Aphrodite/Venus.
14 Libitina was the goddess of burials, Priapus the phallic fertility god of gardens.
15 A title given to Aphrodite, who was born from the sea (Greek, *thalassa*).
16 This stanza refers to the emperor Nero and his obsession with music at the time of the great fire in Rome.
17 Common Greek masculine and feminine names, here indicating standard types of Greek youth rather than particular mythological characters.

18 Priapus again, who is also the 'One god' mentioned in the next stanza.
19 Ipsitilla is a girl addressed by Catullus (see note 22 below) in one of his love poems.
20 Phrygia was an ancient kingdom in Asia Minor (now Turkey), and home to the cult of the goddess Cybele, whose priests castrated themselves in devotion to her; which is why they cannot rear 'the bountiful token'. Swinburne here uses Cybele as an ancient anti-sexual counterpart to the Virgin Mary, a parallel antagonist to his Lady.
21 A mountain in Crete, sacred to Zeus.
22 Roman poet of the first century BCE, noted for erotic and satirical verse.
23 Mountain in Phrygia, sacred to Cybele.
24 The 'prophet' here and in the next stanza is almost certainly the Marquis de Sade.
25 Lampsacus was a centre of the worship of Priapus, Aphaca of the cult of Aphrodite.
26 Cotyto, more often called Cotys, was a goddess worshipped in the northern Greek region of Thrace. Astarte and Ashtaroth are Greek and Biblical names respectively for Ishtar, the goddess of love and war in Mesopotamia (now Iraq).
27 A celebrated ballet dancer (*pantomimus*) in Rome at the time of Juvenal, who mentions him in his Sixth Satire. Born a slave in Alexandria, he was famed for his comical performances.
28 The German title means 'Faithful Dear Heart'; but the attribution to Strauss (presumably the so-called 'Waltz-King' Johann Strauss the Younger (1825–99)) is bogus: there is no composition of this name by him or by his father.
29 An imaginary land of marvels. The place-name appears in the General Prologue to Chaucer's *Canterbury Tales*. Chaucerian editors have conjectured that this may refer to 'Benamarin', an old North-African kingdom, but Davidson clearly intends a setting that is not to be found on any map.
30 Latin: 'I am not the man I was under the good Cynara's reign'. The quotation is from Horace's *Odes* (bk 4, ode 1), where the name refers to a former mistress.
31 'Free me'.
32 Another title for Aphrodite/Venus, after her homeland of Cyprus.
33 Twin-lipped (Gray's coinage).
34 The Paraclete is in most contexts the Holy Spirit, but in this 'dark' version is the unholy spirit of Satan.
35 Ancient Phoenician port city in what is now Lebanon, famed in ancient times for its extensive trade and especially for its production of expensive purple dyes.
36 In Greek mythology, especially in Homer's *Odyssey*, Kirke or Circe is a minor goddess and sorceress with the power to change men into animals with her magic potions: she transforms Odysseus's companions into pigs, but is persuaded to change them back again.
37 Bernardino Luini (*c.* 1480–1532), Italian painter.
38 A noted music-hall artiste, nicknamed 'foot-in-the-air' for her distinctive high-kicking action.
39 All celebrated music-hall artistes of the time.

40 Maenads were female devotees of Bacchus (Dionysus), famed for their ecstatic dances.

41 The name, if not the character here, is that of the stepdaughter of Herod Antipas, who, at the prompting of her mother Herodias, demanded the head of John the Baptist (and thus his execution) from Herod after he had promised her whatever she wished, her dancing having pleased him. The Biblical accounts of Mark (6) and Matthew (14) do not name her, but the historian Josephus does. She became a favoured figure of deadly feminine power in Decadent writing and art, notably in Oscar Wilde's French play *Salome* (1893).

42 The Empire Theatre in London's Leicester Square, a music-hall that had become notorious as a resort for up-market prostitutes who exhibited themselves in its 'promenade' (an open area at the back of the dress circle). In 1894 the anti-vice campaigners of the National Vigilance Association persuaded the municipal authorities, amid much public controversy, to require the closure of the promenade as a condition of the theatre's licence. This stipulation was revoked a year later, the prostitutes having simply decamped to rival music-halls.

43 Prostitutes, here indicated ungallantly through the rhetorical device of *antonomasia* by the name of the Homeric sorceress (cf. note 36 above) who transforms men into pigs.

44 Garlands worn on the head.

❧ 4 ❧

DECADENT FICTION

In the category of prose fiction are found some of the defining works of the Decadent literary tradition, including its most celebrated book, J.-K. Huysmans's novel *A Rebours* (1884), from which we provide some translated extracts in this part of the anthology. Along with that novel, one other prose work represented here is essential to the understanding of literary Decadence: Aubrey Beardsley's highly original but incomplete erotic narrative *The Story of Venus and Tannhäuser*. Once we look beyond those central Decadent texts, though, we find the fiction of this tradition on the whole less distinctive than its verse or its manifestos, in that it overlaps with and clearly derives from broader currents of nineteenth-century writing.

One way of clarifying this point is to indicate the multiple influences exerted by the American poet, critic, and storyteller Edgar Allan Poe (1809–49). Some of Poe's stories founded the modern line of detective fiction; others redefined the tradition of the Gothic tale of terror. Meanwhile his influence upon one of the founders of the Decadent poetic tradition, Charles Baudelaire, was profound, too: Poe's work in effect showed Baudelaire and his successors how to transmute the Romantic inheritance into a new realm of self-contained psychological obsessions.

When Decadent fiction in the proper sense emerged in France with the *Contes cruels* (1883) of Philippe-Auguste Villiers de l'Isle-Adam (1838–89), it was clearly a product of Poe's macabre sensationalism in the short-story form, although adapted to a more sophisticated readership. Arthur Symons discovered Villiers's stories in the late 1880s: 'I know nothing in any language more perfect, more delicate in touch, more subtle in texture, more exquisite in charm', he wrote to Remy de Gourmont of the *Contes cruels.*[1] What possibly appealed to Symons in such a story as 'The Eleventh-Hour Guest', reprinted below, was that Villiers had succeeded in weaving the morbid obsessions typical of Poe's tales into a fictional world of languid Parisian elegance, of idle debauchees supping flirtatiously with courtesans, that chimed with the new Decadent sensibility. While Decadent fiction inherited its narrative compulsions from the Gothic or macabre tale, then, it folded these into the fictional evocation of a certain refined way of life, more fully developed in the early novels of Gabriele d'Annunzio (1863–1938) – here illustrated with a sample chapter from his *Il Piacere* – in which the modern Roman aristocratic heroes exhibit their expensive tastes in furnishings and in women.

The indebtedness of Decadent fiction to Poe's Gothic formula appears frequently in the form of such motifs as deadly curses and contagions, which echo from Poe's own 'The Masque of the Red Death' through to Rachilde's 'The Grape-Harvest of Sodom'. A similar curse-like motif recurs as the secret vice, which is narcotic in Jean Lorrain's 'Funeral Oration'. In general, the newly distinctive element that the Decadent writers bring to prose fiction is their emphasis upon sexual perversity. Whereas in the detective and Gothic traditions deriving from Poe, the dark secret of the narrative tends to be murder or insanity, in Decadent fiction it is more often revealed to be an 'abnormality' of the erotic life: nymphomania in Jean Moréas's 'La Faënza', and male homosexuality both in Rachilde's 'The Grape-Harvest of Sodom' and in the episode we extract from Marcel Proust's *Le Temps retrouvé.*

Decadent fiction may be understood in general terms, then, as an unstable compound of Gothic or horror-story ingredients with elements of lurid eroticism and of glamorous 'high-society' setting and characterisation. In any individual work, the balance of these elements will of course vary, but the instabilities of the hybrid form will tend to assert themselves. We have not selected here any extract from Oscar Wilde's prose romance *The Picture of Dorian Gray* (1890), because the book is very well-known and available in cheap editions everywhere; but it illustrates the same point, in the way that its macabre melodramatic plot sits so uneasily both with its attempts to announce a new 'way of life' in the aphorisms and aesthetic doctrines of Lord Henry Wotton, and with its coded homoerotic implications. (We have reprinted the Preface to this work in Chapter 1, pp. 32–3.)

Two outstanding works of Decadent fiction appear to exempt themselves from such problems by adopting more purified purposes and literary modes. Beardsley's *Story of Venus and Tannhäuser* is entirely untroubled by the ghost of Poe, being a most unusual exercise in purely playful erotic pastiche, one in which elaborately artificial style is cultivated at the expense of polymorphously perverse content. It is almost certainly the unique example of a genre that only Beardsley could have devised, namely mock-rococo pornographic romance. Huysmans's more celebrated *A Rebours* is a novel only in name, having no plot, macabre or otherwise. It is rather an extended case-study of a single character, the wealthy eccentric Jean Floressas Des Esseintes, the account of whose private world is designed to explore the possibilities of a consistently artificial – and thus decadent – individual way of life; and it is elaborated at times into digressively arcane inventories of its protagonist's tastes in flowers, food, furnishings, jewels, books, and much more. Our selections below comprise the first chapter's account of Des Esseintes's house and its interior décor, then extracts from the twelfth chapter, in its description of his taste in books.

The plotless design of *A Rebours* is one of the features of Decadent fiction that connects it with the experiments in the next century of such modernist writers as Proust, Woolf, Joyce, and Musil. Our last extract here comes from the final instalment of Marcel Proust's novel-sequence *A la recherche du temps perdu* (1913–27), which features the eccentric homosexual aristocrat Charlus, a character who was based in part upon one of the models earlier used by Huysmans for his portrait of Des Esseintes: the minor poet and critic Count Robert de Montesquiou (1855–1921). The fictional Charlus in Paris during the First World War here unfolds a lavish parallel between the threatened destruction of Paris and the fate of Pompeii. In so doing, he recapitulates those endlessly tempting analogies between modern France and ancient Rome with which the Decadent tradition had begun.

A further distinctive feature of the Decadent line in fiction may be noted. In contrast with the minor canons of Decadent verse and criticism, it allowed some room for the efforts of women writers, in the first place Rachilde (Marguerite Eymery, 1860–1953), whose first novel, *Monsieur Vénus* (1884), had appeared in the same year as *A Rebours*. Along with a story from her, we include a shorter piece by Kate Chopin (1851–1904), one of the few American writers attuned to the languorous moods of Decadent writing.

Many of the items in this part of the book are complete short stories, but others are passages excerpted from longer works: Chapter 1 and passages from a later chapter of *A Rebours* itself; a chapter slightly abridged from d'Annunzio's *Il Piacere*; and the short episode from Proust. In the case of Beardsley's unfinished *Venus and Tannhäuser*, we have included the whole of the surviving story, but have omitted Beardsley's facetious footnotes along with his prefatory mock dedication. The textual history of Beardsley's tale is complicated, as it appeared during his brief lifetime only in a heavily bowdlerised serial version as 'Under the Hill' (in the *Savoy*, 1896), then after his death in a bowdlerised book version under the same title (1904), and then in a pirated but unexpurgated version as *The Story of Venus and Tannhäuser* (1907). Modern editions of the story are necessarily collations of these three imperfect editions. We have followed the textual collation proposed by Stephen Calloway and David Colvin in their edition, retitled 'Under the Hill'.[2] However, our text departs from theirs in some minor corrections, in some aspects of punctuation and hyphenation, and in more frequent italicisation of French words and phrases. We offer also the first fully annotated text of this story. In the process of annotation we have found many of Beardsley's historical, biographical, and literary allusions to be mischievously bogus.

EDGAR ALLAN POE

The Masque of the Red Death

The 'Red Death' had long devastated the country. No pestilence had ever been so fatal, or so hideous. Blood was its Avatar and its seal – the redness of horror of blood. There were sharp pains, and sudden dizziness, and then profuse bleeding at the pores, with dissolution. The scarlet stains upon the body and especially upon the face of the victim, were the pest ban which shut him out from the aid and from the sympathy of his fellow-men. And the whole seizure, progress, and termination of the disease, were the incidents of half an hour.

But the Prince Prospero was happy and dauntless and sagacious. When his dominions were half-depopulated, he summoned to his presence a thousand hale and light-hearted friends from among the knights and dames of his court, and with these retired to the deep seclusion of one of his castellated abbeys. This was an extensive and magnificent structure, the creation of the prince's own eccentric yet august taste. A strong and lofty wall girdled it in. This wall had gates of iron. The courtiers, having entered, brought furnaces and massy hammers and welded the bolts. They resolved to leave means neither of ingress nor egress to the sudden impulses of despair or of frenzy from within. The abbey was amply provisioned. With such precautions the courtiers might bid defiance to contagion. The external world could take care of itself. In the meantime it was folly to grieve, or to think. The prince had provided all the appliances of pleasure. There were buffoons, there were improvisatori, there were ballet-dancers, there were musicians, there was Beauty, there was wine. All these and security were within. Without was the 'Red Death'.

It was towards the close of the fifth or sixth month of his seclusion, and while the pestilence raged most furiously abroad, that the Prince Prospero entertained his thousand friends at a masked ball of the most unusual magnificence.

It was a voluptuous scene, that masquerade. But first let me tell of the rooms in which it was held. These were seven – an imperial suite. In many palaces, however, such suites form a long and straight vista, while the folding doors slide back nearly to the walls on either hand, so that the view of the whole extent is scarcely impeded. Here the case was very different, as might have been expected from the duke's love of the *bizarre*. The apartments were so irregularly disposed that the vision embraced but little more than one at a time. There was a sharp turn at every twenty or thirty yards, and at each turn a novel effect. To the right and left, in the middle of each wall, a tall and narrow Gothic window looked out upon a closed corridor which pursued the windings of the suite. These windows were of stained glass whose colour varied in accordance with the prevailing hue of the decorations of the chamber into which it opened. That at the eastern extremity was hung, for example, in blue – and vividly blue were its windows. The second chamber was purple in its ornaments and tapestries, and here the panes were purple. The third was green throughout, and so were the casements. The fourth was furnished and lighted with orange – the fifth with white – the sixth with violet. The seventh apartment was closely shrouded in black velvet tapestries that hung all over the ceiling and down the walls, falling in heavy folds upon a carpet of the same material and hue. But in this chamber only, the colour of the windows failed to correspond with the decorations. The panes here were scarlet – a deep blood colour. Now in no one of the seven apartments was there any lamp or candelabrum, amid the profusion of golden ornaments that lay scattered to and fro or depended from the roof. There was no light of any kind emanating from lamp or candle within the suite of chambers. But in the corridors that followed the suite there stood, opposite to each window, a heavy tripod, bearing a brazier of fire, that projected its rays through the tinted glass and so glaringly illumined the room. And thus were produced a multitude of gaudy and fantastic appearances. But in the western or black chamber the effect of the fire-light that streamed upon the dark hangings through the blood-tinted panes was ghastly in the extreme, and produced so wild a look upon the countenances of those who entered, that there were few of the company bold enough to set foot within its precincts at all.

It was in this apartment, also, that there stood against the western wall, a gigantic clock of ebony. Its pendulum swung to and fro with a dull, heavy, monotonous clang; and when the minute-hand made the circuit of the face, and the hour was to be stricken, there came from the brazen lungs of the clock a sound which was clear and loud and deep and exceedingly musical, but of so peculiar a note and emphasis that, at each lapse of an hour, the musicians of the orchestra were constrained to pause, momentarily, in their performance, to harken to the sound; and thus the waltzers perforce ceased their evolutions; and there was a brief disconcert of the whole gay company; and, while the chimes of the clock yet rang, it was observed that the giddiest grew pale, and the more aged and sedate passed their hands over their brows as if in confused reverie or meditation. But when the echoes had fully ceased, a light laughter at once pervaded the assembly; the musicians looked at each other and smiled as if at their own nervousness and folly, and made whispering vows, each to the other, that the next chiming of the clock should produce in them no similar emotion; and then, after the lapse of sixty minutes (which embrace three thousand and six hundred seconds of the Time that flies), there came yet another chiming of the clock, and then were the same disconcert and tremulousness and meditation as before.

But, in spite of these things, it was a gay and magnificent revel. The tastes of the duke were peculiar. He had a fine eye for colours and effects. He disregarded the *decora* of mere fashion. His plans were bold and fiery, and his conceptions glowed with barbaric lustre. There are some who would have thought him mad. His followers felt that he was not. It was necessary to hear and see and touch him to be *sure* that he was not.

He had directed, in great part, the movable embellishments of the seven chambers, upon occasion of this great *fête;* and it was his own guiding taste which had given character to the masqueraders. Be sure they were grotesque. There were much glare and glitter and piquancy and phantasm – much of what has been since seen in *Hernani*.[3] There were arabesque figures with unsuited limbs and appointments. There were delirious fancies such as the madman fashions. There were much of the beautiful, much of the wanton, much of the *bizarre*, something of the terrible, and not a little of that which might have excited disgust. To and fro in the seven chambers there stalked, in fact, a multitude of dreams. And these – the dreams – writhed in and about, taking hue from the rooms, and causing the wild music of the orchestra to seem as the echo of their steps. And, anon, there strikes the ebony clock which stands in the hall of the velvet. And then, for a moment, all is still, and all is silent save the voice of the clock. The dreams are stiff-frozen as they stand. But the echoes of the chime die away – they have endured but an instant – and a light, half-subdued laughter floats after them as they depart. And now again the music swells, and the dreams live, and writhe to and fro more merrily than ever, taking hue from the many-tinted windows through which stream the rays from the tripods. But to the chamber which lies most westwardly of the seven there are now none of the maskers who venture; for the night is waning away; and there flows a ruddier light through the blood-coloured panes; and the blackness of the sable drapery appals; and to him whose foot falls upon the sable carpet, there comes from the near clock of ebony a muffled peal more solemnly emphatic than any which reaches *their* ears who indulged in the more remote gaieties of the other apartments.

But these other apartments were densely crowded, and in them beat feverishly the heart of life. And the revel went whirlingly on, until at length there commenced the sounding of midnight upon the clock. And then the music ceased, as I have told; and the evolutions of the waltzers were quieted; and there was an uneasy cessation of all things as before. But now there were twelve strokes to be sounded by the bell of the clock; and thus it happened, perhaps, that more of thought crept, with more of time, into the meditations of the thoughtful among those who revelled. And thus too, it happened, perhaps, that before the last echoes of the last chime had utterly sunk into silence, there were many individuals in the crowd who had found leisure to become aware of the presence of a masked figure which had arrested the attention of no single individual before. And the rumour of this new presence having spread itself whisperingly around, there arose at length from the whole company a buzz, or murmur, expressive of disapprobation and surprise – then, finally, of terror, of horror, and of disgust.

In an assembly of phantasms such as I have painted, it may well be supposed that no ordinary appearance could have excited such sensation. In truth the masquerade licence of the night was nearly unlimited; but the figure in question had out-Heroded Herod, and gone beyond the bounds of even the prince's indefinite decorum. There are chords in the hearts of the most reckless which cannot be touched without emotion. Even with the utterly lost, to whom life and death are equally jests, there are matters of which no jest can be made. The whole company, indeed, seemed now deeply to feel that in the costume and bearing of the stranger neither wit nor propriety existed. The figure was tall and gaunt, and shrouded from head to foot in the habiliments of the grave. The mask which concealed the visage was made so nearly to resemble the countenance of a stiffened corpse that the closest scrutiny must have had difficulty in detecting the cheat. And yet all this might have been endured, if not approved, by the mad revellers around. But the mummer had gone so far as to assume the type of the Red Death. His vesture was dabbled in *blood* – and his broad brow, with all the features of the face, was besprinkled with the scarlet horror.

When the eyes of Prince Prospero fell upon this spectral image (which, with a slow and solemn movement, as if more fully to sustain its *rôle*, stalked to and fro among the waltzers) he was seen to be convulsed in the first moment with a strong shudder either of terror or distaste; but, in the next, his brow reddened with rage.

'Who dares,' – he demanded hoarsely of the courtiers who stood near him – 'who dares insult us with this blasphemous mockery? Seize him and unmask him – that we may know whom we have to hang, at sunrise, from the battlements!'

It was in the eastern or blue chamber in which stood the Prince Prospero as he uttered these words. They rang throughout the seven rooms loudly and clearly, for the prince was a bold and robust man, and the music had become hushed at the waving of his hand.

It was in the blue room where stood the prince, with a group of pale courtiers by his side. At first, as he spoke, there was a slight rushing movement of this group in the direction of the intruder, who at the moment was also near at hand, and now, with deliberate and stately step, made closer approach to the speaker. But from a certain nameless awe with which the mad assumptions of the mummer had inspired the whole party, there were found none who put forth hand to seize him; so that, unimpeded, he passed within a yard of the prince's person; and, while the vast assembly, as if with one impulse, shrank from the centres of the rooms to the walls, he made his way uninterruptedly, but with the same solemn and measured step which had distinguished him from the first, through the blue chamber to the purple – through the purple to the green – through the green to the orange – through this again to the white – and even thence to the violet, ere a decided movement had been made to arrest him. It was then, however, that the Prince Prospero, maddening with rage and the shame of his own momentary cowardice, rushed hurriedly through the six chambers, while none followed him on account of a deadly terror that had seized upon all. He bore aloft a drawn dagger, and had approached, in rapid impetuosity, to within three or four feet of the retreating figure, when the latter, having attained the extremity of the velvet apartment, turned suddenly and confronted his pursuer. There was a sharp cry – and the dagger dropped gleaming upon the sable carpet, upon which, instantly afterwards, fell prostrate in death the Prince Prospero. Then, summoning the wild courage of despair, a throng of the revellers at once threw themselves into the black apartment, and, seizing the mummer, whose tall figure stood erect and motionless within the shadow of the ebony clock, gasped in unutterable horror at finding the grave cerements and corpse-like mask, which they handled with so violent a rudeness, untenanted by any tangible form.

And now was acknowledged the presence of the Red Death. He had come like a thief in the night. And one by one dropped the revellers in the blood-bedewed halls of their revel, and died each in the despairing posture of his fall. And the life of the ebony clock went out with that of the last of the gay. And the flames of the tripods expired. And Darkness and Decay and the Red Death held illimitable dominion over all.

1842

PHILIPPE-AUGUSTE VILLIERS DE L'ISLE-ADAM

The Eleventh-Hour Guest (Le Convive des dernières fêtes)

For Madame Nina de Villard

The unknown is the lion's share.

– François Arago[4]

The statue of the Commander[5] can come and have supper with us; he can give us his hand. We will still take it. And perhaps he will be the one to feel cold.

One evening during the Carnival of 186–, C——, a friend of mine, and

I, as the result of circumstances entirely due to the hazards of a 'vague and ardent' boredom, were alone in a stage-box at the Opera Ball.

For a few minutes we had been admiring, through the dust, the tumultuous mosaic of the mummers shouting under the chandeliers and dancing to Strauss's magic bow.

All of a sudden the door of the box opened; three ladies, with a rustle of silk, came forward between the heavy chairs, and, after taking off their masks, said: 'Good evening!' to us.

They were three young women of exceptional wit and beauty. We had met them occasionally in the artistic world of Paris. Their names were Clio the Blonde, Antonie Chantilly, and Susannah Jackson.

'Have you come here to play truant, ladies?' inquired C——, offering them seats.

'Oh, we were going to have supper on our own,' said Clio the Blonde, 'because the men here are as horrible as they are boring, and they were beginning to make us feel gloomy.'

'Yes, we were just leaving when we caught sight of you', said Antonie Chantilly.

'So come along with us, if you've nothing better to do', concluded Susannah Jackson.

'Splendid!' C—— replied calmly.

'Would you object strongly to the Maison Dorée?'

'Heaven forbid!' said the dazzling Susannah Jackson, opening out her fan.

'Then take your notebook, my dear fellow,' C—— went on, turning to me, 'reserve the red room, and send the note off by Miss Jackson's footman. That, I think, is the way to set about it, unless you have any objections.'

'Monsieur,' Miss Jackson said to me, 'if you go to the trouble of bestirring yourself for our sakes, you will find the individual in question strutting about the foyer, dressed as a phoenix or a fly. He answers to the transparent pseudonym of Baptiste or Lapierre. Do us this favour – and come back quickly to love us perpetually.'

For the last few moments I had not been listening to anybody. I was looking at a stranger in a box opposite us, a man of thirty-five or thirty-six, with a face of Oriental pallor; he was holding a pair of opera-glasses and gave me a bow.

'Why, it's my stranger from Wiesbaden!' I muttered to myself, after searching my memory.

As this gentleman had rendered me, in Germany, one of those little services which custom allows travellers to exchange – a matter of some cigars, I believe, whose merits he had indicated to me in the smoking-room – I returned his bow.

A minute later, in the foyer, while I was looking around for the phoenix in question, I saw the stranger coming towards me. Since his greeting had been extremely friendly, it seemed to me a matter of courtesy to invite him to join us if he felt too lonely in this crowd.

'And whom shall I have the honour to introduce to our gracious company?' I asked with a smile, when he had accepted.

'Baron von H——', he told me. 'But in view of the carefree appearance of those ladies, the difficulties of pronunciation, and this splendid carnival evening, permit me to adopt another name for an hour. Any name will do', he added. 'I know!' (and he began to laugh): 'Call me Baron Saturn, if you like.'

This caprice surprised me slightly, but as the atmosphere was one of general madness, I coldly presented him to our ladies of fashion under the mythological name to which he had chosen to be reduced.

His whim told in his favour: the ladies decided that he must be some Arabian Nights monarch travelling incognito. Clio the Blonde, clasping her hands together, went so far as to murmur the name of a certain Jud who was notorious at that time, a sort of criminal who was still at large and to whom various murders had apparently brought exceptional fame and fortune.[6]

Once the usual courtesies had been exchanged, the ever considerate Susannah Jackson asked, between two irresistible yawns:

'Supposing the baron did us the favour of having supper with us, to achieve the desirable symmetry?'

He started to decline the invitation.

'Susannah said that to us like Don Juan speaking to the Commander's statue', I replied jokingly. 'These Scots are so solemn!'

'Monsieur Saturn should have been asked to come and kill Time with us', said C——, who, in his cold way, wanted the invitation to be issued 'in a regular fashion'.

'I am very sorry to have to decline', the baron replied. 'But an event of absolutely *capital* interest calls for my presence quite early this morning.'

'A mock duel?' asked Clio the Blonde, pulling a face.

'No, Madame: a serious encounter,' said the baron, 'since you deign to inquire about the matter.'

'Oh, I'll wager it's just some remark made at the Opera!' exclaimed the beautiful Susannah Jackson. 'Your tailor, infatuated with a cavalry uniform, has probably called you an artist or a demagogue. My good sir, that sort of remark isn't worth fighting over: anybody can see that you are a foreigner.'

'I am something of a foreigner everywhere, Madame', replied Baron Saturn with a bow.

'Come now! Do you always wait to be asked twice?'

'Rarely, I assure you!' the strange individual murmured in the most gallant and most ambiguous manner.

C—— and I exchanged glances: we were out of our depth: what did the man mean? His answer, however, struck us as quite amusing.

But, like a child taking a fancy to what it is denied, Antonie exclaimed:

'You belong to us till dawn, and I'm taking your arm!'

He gave in; and we left the theatre.

So that string of irrelevancies had been necessary to produce this final result: we were going to find ourselves in relatively close contact with a man about whom we knew nothing, except that he had gambled at the Wiesbaden casino and that he had studied the various flavours of Havana cigars.

But what did it matter? Is not the simplest thing nowadays to shake hands with everybody?

On the boulevard Clio the Blonde lolled laughingly in the back of the barouche, and told her half-breed groom, who was waiting slavishly:

'To the Maison Dorée!'

Then, leaning towards me, she said:

'I don't know your friend: what sort of a man is he? He intrigues me tremendously. He has such an *odd* look in his eyes!'

'Our *friend*?' I answered. 'Why, I've met him twice at the very most, last season in Germany.'

She looked at me in astonishment.

'Well, and what about you?' I went on. 'He comes to our box to pay his respects and you invite him to supper on the strength of an introduction at a masked ball! Granting that you have been guilty of an imprudence worthy of a thousand deaths, it's a little late to get alarmed about our guest. If tomorrow we don't feel like continuing our acquaintance, we shall greet each other as we did today: that's all. A supper-party doesn't mean anything.'

There is nothing more amusing than pretending to understand certain artificial susceptibilities.

'What! you don't know better than that who people are? And what if he were a . . .'

'Haven't I given you his name – Baron Saturn? Are you afraid of compromising yourself, Mademoiselle?' I added in a stern voice.

'You're insufferable, you know!'

'He doesn't look like a Greek,[7] so our little adventure is simplicity itself. An amusing millionaire – isn't that the ideal?'

'He strikes me as a decent fellow, that Monsieur Saturn', said C——.

'And a rich man is always entitled to respect, at least at carnival time', concluded the lovely Susannah in a calm voice.

The horses set off; the stranger's heavy carriage followed us. Antonie Chantilly, better known by the somewhat affected *nom de guerre* of Yseult, had accepted his mysterious company in it.

Once we had settled down in the red room, we instructed Joseph not to allow any living creature near us, with the exception of the oysters, Joseph himself, and our illustrious friend the fantastic little Doctor Florian Les Eglisottes, if by any chance he came along to suck his proverbial crayfish.

A burning log was crumbling in the fireplace. All around us floated insipid smells of dress materials, warm furs, and winter flowers. The glow from the candelabra enveloped a small console on which the sad wine of Aï was freezing in silver pails. Bunches of camellias, swelling out at the end of their binding wires, filled the crystal vases on the table.

Outside, a thin, dull drizzle was falling, mingled with snow; it was a bitterly cold night; we could hear the sound of carriages and the shouting of mummers coming away from the Opera. It was like a hallucination of Gavarni, Deveria, and Gustave Doré.[8]

To muffle these noises, the windows were closed and the curtains carefully draped across them.

The guests, then, were the Saxon Baron Von H——, the fair-haired Smynthian[9] C——, and myself; then Susannah Jackson, the Blonde, and Antonie.

During the supper, which was enlivened by sparkling follies, I idly gave way to my innocent mania for observation; and I must say that I soon realized that my companion was indeed deserving of attention.

No, he was not a gay fellow, this guest of passage! True, his features and his bearing had all the conventional distinction which makes people acceptable, and his accent was not irritating like that of some foreigners; only now and then his pallor took on a singularly pale, even ghastly hue; his lips were thinner than a pencil line; and his forehead always remained a little furrowed, even when he smiled.

Having noticed these details and a few others, with that unconscious attention with which certain writers are necessarily endowed, I began to regret having introduced him, without due consideration, into our company – and I resolved that at dawn I would strike him off our list of acquaintances. I am speaking here, of course, of C—— and myself; for the happy chance which had granted us, that evening, our feminine guests, was sure to carry them away again, like visions, at the end of the night.

And then, before long, the stranger attracted our attention with a special peculiarity. Without being remarkable for the intrinsic value of its ideas, his conversation kept us on the alert by virtue of the vague implication which the sound of his voice seemed to slip into it on purpose.

This detail surprised us all the more in that we found it impossible, when we examined what he said, to discover any meaning in it other than that of a polite phrase. And two or three times he gave us a start, C—— and myself, with the way in which he emphasized his words and with the impression of some imprecise hidden meaning which they left with us.

All of a sudden, in the middle of a fit of laughing due to one of Clio the Blonde's facetious remarks – which were really most amusing – I had a vague idea that I had seen the baron in circumstances entirely different from those at Wiesbaden.

His face was, in fact, unforgettable, the features were so strongly marked, and the glow in his eyes when he blinked created the impression of an inner torch.

What were those circumstances? I tried in vain to clarify them in my mind. Shall I go so far as to reveal the obscure ideas which they aroused in me?

They were those of an event such as one sees in a dream.

Where could it have been? How was I to reconcile my usual memories with these intense, remote ideas of murder, of profound silence, of mist, of frightened faces, of torches and blood, which rose to the surface of my consciousness, with an unbearable feeling of actuality, at the sight of this individual?

'Come!' I muttered to myself. 'Am I dreaming things tonight?'

I drank a glass of champagne.

The sound waves of the nervous system have mysterious vibrations of this sort. They deaden, so to speak, with their multiple echoes, the analysis of the initial blow which produced them. The memory makes out the atmosphere surrounding the object, but the object itself is lost in this general sensation and remains stubbornly indistinguishable.

It is like those once familiar faces which, seen again unexpectedly, disturb the mind by evoking a host of impressions which are still asleep and which *at the time* it is impossible to define.

But the stranger's distinguished manners, playful reserve, and bizarre dignity – veils, as it were, hung across the undoubtedly sombre reality of his character – led me, for the moment at least, to treat this comparison as a freak of the imagination, a sort of visual perversion born of the feverish excitement of the night.

I therefore resolved to put a good face on for the party, in accordance with my duty and pleasure.

We left the table in order of juniority, and ripples of laughter mingled with harmonious sallies played at random on the piano by delicate fingers.

I consequently forgot all my preoccupations. Soon the air was full of sparkling conceits, light-hearted confessions, vague kisses (sounding like those leaves which frivolous girls slap on the backs of their hands), and dazzling smiles and diamonds: the magic of the deep mirrors silently reflected, in long bluish lines stretching to infinity, lights and gestures.

C—— and I gave ourselves up to our dreams in the midst of the conversation.

Objects are transfigured according to the magnetism of the human beings who approach them, things having no significance for people other than that which the latter are *able* to give them.

Thus the modern character of the crude gilt, the heavy furniture, and the plain glasses, was redeemed by my gaze and that of my lyrical friend C——.

For us, the candelabra were necessarily made of pure gold, and the carvings were undoubtedly the work of an authentic Quinze-Vingt[10] craftsman, a born goldsmith. It was clear that the furniture could only emanate from a Lutheran upholsterer who had gone mad as a result of the religious persecutions under Louis XIII. Who could have been responsible for the crystals but a Prague glassmaker, depraved by some Penthesilean[11] passion? The damask draperies were assuredly none other than those ancient robes which had finally been discovered at Herculaneum, in the chest containing the sacred *velaria* of the temples of Asclepius or Pallas.[12] The truly remarkable coarseness of the material could be explained, at a pinch, by the corrosive action of the earth and lava, and this precious flaw made it unique.

As for the tablecloth, we retained some doubts about its origin. There was every reason to regard it as a sample of lacustrian homespun. At the very least we did not despair of finding, in the symbols embroidered on it, signs of an accadian or troglodyte provenance. Perhaps we were faced with the countless lengths of the shroud of Xisouthros,[13] which had been bleached and retailed as tablecloths. On examination, however, we had to be content with finding on it what we took to be the cuneiform inscription of a menu recorded under Nimrod; and already we began imagining Monsieur Oppert's surprise and joy when he learnt of what was at least a recent discovery.[14]

Then, too, Night was casting its shadows, half-tints, and strange effects over everything, reinforcing our fancies and convictions.

The coffee was steaming in the transparent cups; C—— was drawing voluptuously on a Havana and enveloping himself in wisps of white smoke, like a demi-god in a cloud.

Baron von H——, his eyes half-closed, was stretched out on a sofa, looking rather commonplace, with a glass of champagne in one pale hand which was hanging down towards the carpet. He seemed to be listening attentively to the wonderful nocturnal duet from Wagner's *Tristan and Isolde*, which Susannah was playing on the piano, giving full value to the incestuous modulations. Antonie and Clio the Blonde, radiant and folded in each other's arms, sat in silence during that able musician's slow resolution of the chords.

For my part, charmed to the point of insomnia, I was listening too, next to the piano.

Each of our pale, fickle beauties had chosen to wear velvet that evening.

The touching Antonie, with her violet eyes, was in black, without a single piece of lace. But since the velvet line of her dress was not hemmed, her neck and shoulders, like real Carrara marble, stood out sharply against the material.

She wore a thin gold ring on her little finger, and three sapphire cornflowers shone in her chestnut hair, which hung far below her waist in two curly plaits.

As for her moral character, an august person asked her one evening whether she was 'a decent woman'.

'Yes, Your Royal Highness,' Antonie replied, 'seeing that decent nowadays means nothing more than good-natured.'

Clio the Blonde, an exquisite creature with black eyes – as befitted the goddess of Impertinence – and a disillusioned young woman whom Prince Solt—— had baptized in the Russian fashion by pouring foaming Roederer[15] over her hair, was in a close-fitting green velvet dress, and a river of rubies covered her breast.

This young creole of twenty was cited as a model of all the reprehensible virtues. She would have intoxicated the most austere of Greek philosophers and the most profound of German metaphysicians. Countless dandies had fallen in love with her to the point of exchanging sword thrusts, signing bills of exchange, and sending bunches of violets.

She had just returned from Baden, where she had lost between eighty and a hundred thousand francs at the gaming tables, laughing like a child.

As for her moral character, a repulsive old Teutonic lady, shocked at this sight, had said to her at the Casino:

'Mademoiselle, take care! One has to eat a little bread sometimes, and you appear to be forgetting it.'

'Madame,' the beautiful Clio had replied, blushing scarlet, 'thank you for your advice. In return, allow me to inform you that, for some people, bread has never been anything but an old-fashioned fad.'

Susannah Jackson, the Scottish Circe, with her hair as black as night, her spear-like eyes, and her acid phrases, was sparkling nonchalantly in red velvet.

Try to avoid that woman, young stranger! Let me warn you that she is like quicksands: she swallows up the nervous system. She exudes desire. A prolonged attack of enervating folly would be your lot. She numbers several deaths among her memories. Her type of beauty, in which she has complete confidence, drives mere mortals to frenzy.

Her body is like a dark lily, virginal in spite of everything. It justifies her name which, I believe, is the ancient Hebrew for that flower.

However sophisticated you believe yourself to be, young stranger (perhaps at what is still a tender age), if your evil star allows you to encounter Susannah Jackson, we have only to imagine a young man exclusively nourished on eggs and milk for twenty years and suddenly, without any warning, submitted to an exasperating, continuous diet of pungent spices and condiments whose sharp, burning flavour convulses, shatters, and maddens him, to have a speaking likeness of you during the next two weeks.

The skilful charmer has amused herself sometimes by reducing blasé old lords to tears, for it is only through pleasure that she can be seduced. Her dream, according to odd remarks she has made, is to go and bury herself in a millionaire residence, on the banks of the Clyde, with a handsome boy whom she would while away the time by killing at her leisure.

As for her moral character, the sculptor C.B. was teasing her one day about the terrible little black mark which she has near one of her eyes.

'The unknown artist who carved you out of marble', he said, 'overlooked that little stone.'

'Don't say anything against that little stone', replied Susannah; 'it's the one that trips men up.'

She was the womanly equivalent of a panther.

Each of these women of the night wore at her belt a velvet mask in green, red or black, with twin favours in steel.

As for myself (if it is absolutely necessary to talk about that guest), I too wore a mask; the only difference was that mine was less obvious.

Just as at the theatre, sitting in a centre stall, you listen, so as not to disturb your neighbours – out of courtesy, in other words – to some play written in a tedious style and dealing with a subject which you dislike, so I lived out of politeness.

Not that this prevented me from gaily sporting a flower in my buttonhole, as a true knight of the Order of Springtime.

Finally Susannah left the piano. I took a bunch of flowers from the table and offered it to her with a mocking look in my eyes.

'You are a *diva*!' I said. 'Wear one of these flowers for the love of your unknown lovers.'

She picked a sprig of hortensia which she amiably fastened to her bodice.

'I don't read anonymous letters!' she replied, replacing the rest of my bouquet on the piano.

The dazzling and profane creature joined her hands on the shoulder of one of us – no doubt in order to return to her seat.

'Oh, cold Susannah,' C—— said to her with a laugh, 'I do believe you came into this world simply to remind us that snow can burn.'

This, to my mind, was one of those subtle compliments such as the end of a supper-party often inspires, and whose meaning – if they have a meaning – is as tenuous as a hair. Nothing comes closer to being a stupid remark and sometimes the difference is absolutely imperceptible. When I heard this compliment I realized that the wick of the company's brains was in danger of smoking and that swift action was called for.

Since a mere spark is sometimes enough to rekindle a flame, I decided to strike it, at all costs, from our silent guest.

At that moment Joseph came in, bringing us a peculiar potion – iced punch – for we had resolved to get as drunk as lords.

For the last minute I had been watching Baron Saturn. He looked anxious and impatient. I saw him take his watch out, give Antonie a diamond, and stand up.

'Great heavens, lord of distant lands,' I exclaimed, sitting astride a chair between two wisps of cigar smoke, 'you aren't thinking of leaving us yet, are you? You would be giving the impression of some mystery or other, and that is bad form, you know!'

'My apologies,' he replied, 'but it is a matter of a duty which cannot be postponed and which brooks no further delay. Please accept my gratitude for the pleasant hours which I have just spent with you.'

'Then it really is a duel?' Antonie asked with a show of anxiety.

'Nonsense!' I cried, imagining that it was in fact some carnival quarrel. 'I am sure you are exaggerating the importance of this affair. Your man is probably under a table somewhere. Before creating a pendant to Gérôme's picture, in which you would play the victor, Harlequin,[16] send the footman to the duelling-ground in your place, to find out if they are waiting for you; if they are, your horses will easily make up the lost time.'

'Yes, indeed!' C—— said quietly, backing me up. 'Pay court instead to the beautiful Susannah, who is dying of love for you. You'll save yourself a cold – and console yourself by spending a million or two. Look, listen, and decide.'

'Gentlemen,' said Baron Saturn, 'I must admit that *I am blind and deaf as often as God permits.*'

He uttered this unintelligible remark with such solemnity that it plunged us into the most ridiculous conjectures; and I even forgot the spark in question. We were looking at one another with embarrassed smiles, not knowing what to think of this 'pleasantry', when all of a sudden I gave an involuntary exclamation: I had just remembered *where* I had first seen that man!

And it suddenly seemed to me that the glasses, the faces, the curtains, the whole nocturnal banquet was lit up by an evil glow, a red glow matching the exit of our guest, like certain theatrical effects.

'Monsieur,' I whispered in his ear, 'forgive me if I am making a mistake . . . but it seems to me that I had the *pleasure* of meeting you five or six years ago, in a big city in the South – Lyons, I suppose – about four o'clock in the morning, on a public square.'

Saturn slowly raised his head and, gazing at me closely, said:

'Ah! That's possible.'

'Yes!' I went on, returning his gaze. 'Wait a moment! On that square there was a melancholy object which two student friends of mine had taken me to see – and which I resolved never to set eyes on again.'

'Really?' said Monsieur Saturn. 'And what was that object, if it is not indiscreet to ask?'

'Something like a scaffold – a guillotine, Monsieur, if I remember rightly. . . . Yes it was a guillotine . . . I'm sure of that now!'

These few words had been exchanged in an undertone between the baron and myself. C—— and the ladies were chatting in the shadows, a few feet away, near the piano.

'That's it! I remember!' I added, raising my voice. 'Well, what do you think of that, Monsieur, for a memory? Although you passed me very quickly, your carriage was held up by mine for a moment, and allowed me to catch a glimpse of you in the light of the torches. The circumstances engraved your face on my mind. It wore the expression which I can see on your features now.'

'That's right!' replied Monsieur Saturn with a laugh. 'I must admit that your memory is surprisingly accurate.'

The man's shrill laugh gave me the impression of a pair of scissors slicing through a lock of hair.

'One detail', I went on, 'particularly struck me. I saw you, from a distance, get out of your carriage near the place where the guillotine was standing and, unless I was misled by a resemblance. . . .'

'You were not misled, my *dear* sir,' he replied, 'it was I.'

At this answer I felt that the conversation had become icy, and that perhaps I was failing in the courtesy which an executioner of such a peculiar stamp was entitled to expect from us. I was accordingly looking for some commonplace remark to change the course of the thoughts which were occupying the two of us, when the beautiful Antonie turned away from the piano and said casually:

'By the way, ladies and gentlemen, did you know that there's an execution this morning?'

'Ah!' I exclaimed, strangely disturbed by these few words.

'It's that poor Doctor de la P——', Antonie continued sadly. 'He used to be my doctor. For my part, all I hold against him is the fact that he defended himself before the judges; I thought he had more pluck. When your fate is already sealed, it seems to me that at the very most you should laugh in the faces of those lawyers. Monsieur de la P—— has forgotten himself.'

'What! Is it today? Are you sure?' I asked, trying to assume an indifferent tone of voice.

'At six o'clock, ladies and gentlemen, the fatal hour!' replied Antonie. 'Ossian, the handsome lawyer, the darling of the Faubourg Saint-Germain, came to tell me last night, as his way of paying court. I had forgotten all about it. It seems that they have sent for a foreigner to help Monsieur de

Paris;[17] in view of the serious nature of the case and the eminence of the condemned man.'

Without realizing the absurdity of these last words, I turned towards Monsieur Saturn. He was standing at the door, wrapped in a long black cloak, with his hat in his hand, and an official air about him.

The punch had turned my head a little: to be quite honest, I felt in a quarrelsome mood. As I was afraid that, by inviting him, I had committed what I believe is commonly called a 'bloomer', the face of this intruder (whoever he might be) was getting on my nerves, and I was hard put to it to refrain from telling him so.

'Baron,' I said to him with a smile, 'judging by your peculiar insinuations, we should be almost entitled to ask you if it is like the Law that you are "deaf and blind as often as God permits".'

He came up to me, bent forward smilingly, and answered in an undertone: 'Be quiet: there are ladies present!'

He bowed all round and went out, leaving me silent, trembling slightly, and unable to believe my ears.

A word by the way, reader. When Stendhal wanted to write a somewhat sentimental love story, it is known that he was in the habit of re-reading half a dozen pages of the Penal Code, in order – so he said – to obtain the right tone. For my part, having taken it into my head to write certain stories, I had found it more practical, after due reflection, to go in the evenings to a café in the Passage de Choiseul where the late Monsieur X——, the former executioner of Paris, used to come, *almost* every day, to play his little game of cards incognito. He seemed to me to be as well-bred as any other man; he spoke in a very deep but clear voice, with a kindly smile. I used to sit at a table near by, and it amused me slightly when he called out: 'My turn to cut!' without meaning any harm. It was there, I remember, that I had my most *poetic* inspirations, to use a bourgeois expression. So I was proof against that gross feeling of conventional horror which gentlemen of his profession arouse in passers-by.

It was therefore odd that I should feel, at that moment, in the grip of such an intense emotion, because our chance guest had just declared that he was one of them.

C——, who had joined us during the last words of our conversation, tapped me on the shoulder.

'Are you out of your mind?' he asked me.

'He may have inherited a fortune and just be carrying on his work until they appoint a successor', I murmured, upset by the fumes from the punch.

'I see', said C——. 'So you think he is really connected with the ceremony in question?'

'Then you grasped the meaning of our little chat, my dear fellow?' I whispered to him. 'It was short but instructive. The fellow is a common executioner! Probably a Belgian. He's the foreigner Antonie was talking about just now. But for his presence of mind, I would have been the cause of his frightening those young women.'

'Come now!' exclaimed C——. 'An executioner with a carriage costing thirty thousand francs, who gives diamonds to his neighbour at table, and who has supper at the Maison Dorée on the eve of attending to a customer? Since you started going to the Café de Choiseul you have been seeing executioners everywhere. Have a glass of punch! Your Monsieur Saturn is a practical joker, you know?'

At these words it seemed to me that logic and cold reason were on the side of my friend the poet. Feeling extremely annoyed, I hurriedly picked up my hat and gloves, and made for the door, muttering:

'Very well.'

'You are right', said C——.

'I don't like heavy sarcasm', I added, opening the door. 'And if I catch up with that gloomy joker, I swear that . . .'

'Wait a minute: let's play at *Who goes first?*' said C——.

I was going to make a suitable reply and then disappear when, behind my shoulder, a cheerful, familiar voice exclaimed under the raised curtain.

'No need for that! Stay here, my dear fellow.'

Our illustrious friend, little Doctor Florian Les Eglisottes, had come in during our last words: he was standing before me, hopping up and down, in his snow-covered cloak.

'My dear doctor,' I said to him, 'I shall be at your service in a moment, but . . .'

He stopped me.

'When I have told you the story of the man who was leaving this room when I arrived,' he went on, 'I wager that you won't feel like calling him to account for his remarks any more. In any case, it's too late: his carriage has already taken him a long way from here.'

He said this in such a strange tone of voice that he decided me to stay.

'Let us hear your story, doctor', I said, sitting down after a moment. 'But remember, Les Eglisottes, you are responsible for my inaction and take it on your learned head.'

The great physician placed his gold-knobbed stick in a corner, gallantly brushed the fingers of our three beautiful prodigals with his lips, poured himself a little Madeira, and in the middle of the impressive silence caused by this incident and his own arrival, began in these terms.

'I understand the whole of this evening's adventure. I feel sure that I know what has happened as well as if I had been here with you. What has occurred here, without being exactly alarming, is none the less something which could have become so.'

'What's that?' said C——.

'The gentleman in question is indeed Baron von H——; he comes from a great German family; and he is rich to the tune of several millions; but . . .'

The doctor looked at us all.

'But the remarkable mental disease with which he is afflicted, and which has been diagnosed by the medical Faculties of Munich and Berlin, is the most extraordinary and chronic of all the monomanias recorded to this day!' concluded the doctor, in the same tone of voice as if he had been giving one of his lectures in comparative physiology.

'A lunatic! What does that mean, Florian?' murmured C——, going to push home the slender bolt on the door.

The ladies themselves had changed their smiles at this revelation.

For my part, I really felt as if I had been dreaming for the last few minutes.

'A lunatic!' exclaimed Antonic. 'But surely people like that are locked up?'

'I thought I had pointed out that the baron was a millionaire several times over', Les Eglisottes replied solemnly. 'So it is he who has other people locked up, if you please.'

'And what is his type of mania?' asked Susannah. 'Speaking for myself, I warn you that I consider the gentleman perfectly charming.'

'You may not be of that opinion in a few minutes, Madame!' the doctor went on, lighting a cigarette.

The pale light of dawn was tinging the window-panes, the candles were turning yellow, and the fire was burning low; what we were hearing gave us the feeling of a nightmare. The doctor was not a man given to joking; we could be sure that what he was saying was as coldly real as the apparatus standing over there on the square.

'It would appear', he continued, between two sips of Madeira, 'that as soon as he came of age, that silent young man set sail for the East Indies; he travelled a great deal in the countries of Asia. There begins the dense mystery which conceals the origin of his insanity. During certain rebellions in the Far East he witnessed the harsh punishments which the laws in force in those parts inflict on rebels and criminals. To begin with, he probably watched them simply out of traveller's curiosity. But, at the sight of these tortures, it would seem that instincts of inconceivable cruelty awoke in him, troubled his brain, poisoned his blood, and finally turned him into the bizarre creature he has become. Just imagine, he bought his way into the old prisons in the principal cities of Persia, Indo-China, and Tibet, and on several occasions persuaded the governors to allow him to carry out the horrible duties of justiciary in place of the Oriental executioners. You know the incident of the forty pounds of human eyes which were brought on two gold plates to Shah Nasser-Edin,[18] the day he made his ceremonial entry into a rebel city? The baron, dressed as a native of the country, was one of the most fanatical perpetrators of that atrocity. The execution of the two leaders of the rebellion was more formal in its horror. They were sentenced, first to have all their teeth pulled out with pincers, and then to have those same teeth hammered into their heads, which were shaved for the occasion – and this in such a way as to form the Persian initials of the glorious name of Feth-Ali-Shah's successor. Again it was our enthusiast who, in return for a sack of rupees, obtained permission to execute them himself, with the consummate awkwardness which marks him out . . . Incidentally, which do you consider the more insane – the man who orders tortures like that, or the man who carries them out? The question shocks you? Bah! If the first of those two men deigned to come to Paris, we should be only too honoured to put on firework displays for him and order our armies' flags to be dipped in salute as he passes – even saying that this was in the name of the "immortal principles of 1789". So let us go on . . . If we are to believe the reports of Captain Hobbs and Captain Egginson, the refinements which his growing monomania suggested to him on these occasions surpassed, in their sublime absurdity, those of Tiberius and Heliogabalus – and all those mentioned in the annals of humanity. For nobody can match the perfection of a madman in the sphere in which he is insane.'

Doctor Les Eglisottes stopped and looked at each of us in turn with mocking eyes.

We had been listening so attentively that we had let our cigars go out while he was talking.

'Once he had returned to Europe,' the doctor went on, 'Baron von H——, who was so surfeited as to give reason to hope that he was cured, was soon afflicted once more with his fever. He had only one dream, more morbid and bloodchilling than all the abject reveries of the Marquis de Sade; and that was, quite simply, to obtain letters patent as Chief Executioner of all the capitals of Europe. He maintained that skill and tradition were on the decline in this artistic branch of civilization and that there was danger in delay; and, conscious of the services which he had rendered in the East, he wrote, in the applications he kept sending off, that if the sovereigns deigned to honour him with their confidence, he hoped to wring from the criminals the most tuneful howls which any magistrate had ever heard in the precincts of a cell. Incidentally, when anybody mentions Louis XVI in his presence, his eyes light up with the most extraordinary posthumous hatred; for Louis XVI was the sovereign who thought fit to abolish the preliminary torture, and that monarch is probably the only man Baron von H—— has ever hated.

'He always failed in his applications, as you can imagine, and it was thanks to the efforts of his heirs that he was not locked up as he deserved. There are in fact certain clauses in the will left by his father, the late Baron von H——, forcing the family to safeguard his civic rights on account of the huge financial losses which his civic death would involve for the man's relatives. He accordingly travels about at liberty. He is on the best of terms with all the gentlemen who dispense capital punishment. In every town he passes through, his first call is on them. He has often offered them considerable sums to let him operate in their place – and between ourselves,' the doctor added with a wink, 'I believe that in Europe he has succeeded in corrupting a few of them.

'Apart from these escapades, one can say that his insanity is inoffensive, since it is practised only on people marked out by the Law. Outside his mental disease, Baron von H—— has the reputation of a man of peaceful and even engaging ways. Now and then, perhaps, his ambiguous charm sends a shiver down the spine of friends who know about his dreadful obsession, but that is all.

'None the less, he often speaks of the East with a certain regret, and he is due to return there very soon.

'His failure to obtain the diploma of Chief Torturer of the globe has plunged him into dire melancholy. Imagine the dreams of Torquemada or Arbuez, of the Duke of Alba or the Duke of York.[19] His monomania grows worse from day to day. Thus, every time an execution is arranged, he is informed by secret messengers – before the gentlemen of the axe themselves! He runs, he flies, he eats up the miles, and a place is reserved for him at the foot of the guillotine. He is there at this very moment: he would not sleep easy if he had not obtained the last glance of the condemned man.

'That, ladies and gentlemen, is the man with whom you have had the good fortune to spend the night. I should add that, when he has emerged from his madness, and in his social relations, he is a man of irreproachable manners and a conversationalist of the greatest charm, gaiety, and . . .'

'Enough, doctor, please!' cried Antonie and Clio the Blonde, whom Florian's shrill, sardonic badinage had affected to an extraordinary degree.

'But he's the sweetheart of the Guillotine!' murmured Susannah. 'He's the dilettante of Torture!'

'Really,' stammered C——, 'if I didn't know you, doctor . . .'

'You wouldn't believe it?' broke in Les Eglisottes. 'I didn't believe it myself for a long time; but if you like, we can go over there now. I happen to have my card with me; we shall be able to get to him, in spite of the line of cavalry. All I ask of you is to watch his face while the sentence is being carried out. After that you will have no more doubts.'

'Thank you very much for the invitation!' exclaimed C——. 'I prefer to believe you, however mysterious and absurd the thing may seem.'

'Oh, your baron is quite a fellow!' the doctor went on, attacking a pile of crayfish which had miraculously remained intact.

Then, seeing that we had all turned gloomy, he said:

'You mustn't be unduly surprised or upset by my confidences on this subject. What makes the thing so hideous is the particular nature of the man's monomania. As for the rest, a lunatic is a lunatic, and nothing more. Read the works of the mental specialists: you will find there cases of well-nigh astonishing strangeness; and I assure you that we rub shoulders with such cases in broad daylight, at every moment of our lives, without suspecting anything.'

'My dear friends,' C—— concluded, after a moment of general stupor, 'I confess I would not feel any definite revulsion at clinking my glass against a glass held out to me by a secular arm, as people used to say when executioners' arms could be religious. I would not seek out the occasion, but if it occurred, I can say without boasting – and Les Eglisottes above all will understand me – that the sight or even the company of somebody who dispenses capital punishment would not affect me in the least. I have never really understood the *effect* of melodramas on that subject.

'But the sight of a man who has gone out of his mind because he cannot *legally* occupy that post – there you have something which really does affect me. And I don't hesitate to say this: if, among Mankind, there are some souls which have escaped from a Hell, our guest of this evening is one of the worst one could meet. It is no use calling him mad: that doesn't explain his original nature. A real executioner would leave me indifferent; our dreadful maniac gives me a shiver which I can't define!'

The silence which greeted C——'s words was as solemn as if Death had suddenly shown its skull between the candelabra.

'I feel slightly unwell', said Clio the Blonde in a voice broken by nervous strain and the chill of the dawn. 'Don't leave me on my own. Come to the villa. Let us try to forget this adventure, gentlemen; come along: there are baths, horses, and beds to sleep in.' (She scarcely knew what she was saying.) 'It is in the middle of the Bois, and we shall be there in twenty minutes. Please understand me. The thought of that man almost makes me ill, and if I were alone I should be afraid of seeing him suddenly come in with a lamp in his hand lighting up his thin, frightening smile.'

'We have certainly had a strange night!' said Susannah Jackson.

Les Eglisottes had finished his crayfish and wiped his mouth with a satisfied expression.

We rang: Joseph appeared. While we were settling with him, the Scottish woman, touching her cheeks with a little puff of swansdown, quietly murmured to Antonie:

'Haven't you something to say to Joseph, little Yseult?'

'Yes,' the pale, pretty creature replied, 'and you have guessed what it is.'

Then, turning to the head waiter, she went on:

'Joseph, take this ring: the ruby is a little dark for me. Don't you think so, Suzanne? All these diamonds look as if they were weeping around this drop of blood. You will have it sold today and give the sum it fetches to the beggars who pass the house.'

Joseph took the ring, gave that sleepwalker's bow which only he knew how to make, and went out to call up the carriages while the ladies finished adjusting their dresses, wrapped themselves in their long black satin dominoes, and put on their masks again.

Six o'clock struck.

'One moment', I said, pointing to the clock: 'this is an hour which makes us all to some degree accessories to that man's madness. So let us be more indulgent towards it. Aren't we all, at this very moment, implicitly guilty of a barbarity almost as grim as his?'

At these words everybody stood still, in a profound silence.

Susannah looked at me from behind her mask: I had the impression of a gleam of steel. She turned her head away and hurriedly opened the window.

The hour was striking in the distance, in all the belfries of Paris.

At the sixth stroke everybody gave a violent shudder – and I looked thoughtfully at the head of a brass demon with contorted features, who was holding in a hook the bloody waves of the red curtains.

1874; revised 1883; translated by Robert Baldick, 1963

J.-K. HUYSMANS

From *Against Nature (A Rebours)*

[Chapter 1]

Over two months elapsed before Des Esseintes could immerse himself in the peaceful silence of his house at Fontenay,[20] for purchases of all sorts still kept him perambulating the streets and ransacking the shops from one end of Paris to the other. And this was in spite of the fact that he had already made endless inquiries and given considerable thought to the matter before entrusting his new home to the decorators.

He had long been a connoisseur of colours both simple and subtle. In former years, when he had been in the habit of inviting women to his house, he had fitted out a boudoir with delicate carved furniture in pale Japanese camphor-wood under a sort of canopy of pink Indian satin, so that their flesh borrowed soft warm tints from the light which hidden lamps filtered through the awning.

This room, where mirror echoed mirror, and every wall reflected an endless succession of pink boudoirs, had been the talk of all his mistresses, who loved steeping their nakedness in this warm bath of rosy light and breathing in the aromatic odours given off by the camphor-wood. But quite apart from the beneficial effect which this tinted atmosphere had in bringing a ruddy flush to complexions worn and discoloured by the habitual use of cosmetics and the habitual abuse of the night hours, he himself enjoyed, in this voluptuous setting, peculiar satisfactions – pleasures which were in a way heightened and intensified by the recollection of past afflictions and bygone troubles.

Thus, in hateful and contemptuous memory of his childhood, he had suspended from the ceiling of this room a little silver cage containing a cricket which chirped as other crickets had once chirped among the embers in the fireplaces at the Château de Lourps. Whenever he heard this familiar sound, all the silent evenings of constraint he had spent in his mother's company and all the misery he had endured in the course of a lonely, unhappy childhood came back to haunt him. And when the movements of the woman he was mechanically caressing suddenly dispelled these memories and her words or laughter brought him back to the present reality of the boudoir, then his soul was swept by tumultuous emotions: a longing to take vengeance for the boredom inflicted on him in the past, a craving to sully what memories he retained of his family with acts of sensual depravity, a furious desire to expend his lustful frenzy on cushions of soft flesh and to drain the cup of sensuality to its last and bitterest dregs.

At other times, when he was weighed down by splenetic boredom, and the rainy autumn weather brought on an aversion for the streets, for his house, for the dirty yellow sky and the tarmacadam clouds, then he took refuge in this room, set the cage swinging gently to and fro and watched its movements reflected *ad infinitum* in the mirrors on the walls, until it seemed to his dazed eyes that the cage itself was not moving but that the boudoir was tossing and turning, waltzing round the house in a dizzy whirl of pink.

Then, in the days when he had thought it necessary to advertise his individuality, he had decorated and furnished the public rooms of his house with ostentatious oddity. The drawing-room, for example, had been partitioned off into a series of niches, which were styled to harmonize vaguely, by means of subtly analogous colours that were gay or sombre, delicate or barbarous, with the character of his favourite works in Latin and French. He would then settle down to read in whichever of these niches seemed to correspond most exactly to the peculiar essence of the book which had taken his fancy.

His final caprice had been to fit up a lofty hall in which to receive his tradesmen. They used to troop in and take their places side by side in a row of church stalls; then he would ascend an imposing pulpit and preach them a sermon on dandyism, adjuring his bootmakers and tailors to conform strictly to his encyclicals on matters of cut, and threatening them with pecuniary excommunication if they did not follow to the letter the instructions contained in his monitories and bulls.

By these means he won a considerable reputation as an eccentric – a reputation which he crowned by wearing suits of white velvet with gold-laced waistcoats, by sticking a bunch of Parma violets in his shirt-front in lieu of a cravat, and by entertaining men of letters to dinners which were greatly talked about. One of these meals, modelled on an eighteenth-century original, had been a funeral feast to mark the most ludicrous of personal misfortunes. The dining-room, draped in black, opened out on to a garden metamorphosed for the occasion, the paths being strewn with charcoal, the ornamental pond edged with black basalt and filled with ink, and the shrubberies replanted with cypresses and pines. The dinner itself was served on a black cloth adorned with baskets of violets and scabious;[21] candelabra shed an eerie green light over the table and tapers flickered in the chandeliers.

While a hidden orchestra played funeral marches, the guests were waited on by naked negresses wearing only slippers and stockings in cloth of silver embroidered with tears.

Dining off black-bordered plates, the company had enjoyed turtle soup, Russian rye bread, ripe olives from Turkey, caviare, mullet botargo, black puddings from Frankfurt, game served in sauces the colour of liquorice and boot-polish, truffle jellies, chocolate creams, plum-puddings, nectarines, pears in grape-juice syrup, mulberries, and black heart-cherries. From dark-tinted glasses they had drunk the wines of Limagne and Roussillon, of Tenedos, Valdepeñas, and Oporto. And after coffee and walnut cordial, they had rounded off the evening with kvass, porter, and stout.

On the invitations, which were similar to those sent out before more solemn obsequies, this dinner was described as a funeral banquet in memory of the host's virility, lately but only temporarily deceased.

In time, however, his taste for these extravagant caprices, of which he had once been so proud, died a natural death; and nowadays he shrugged his shoulders in contempt whenever he recalled the puerile displays of eccentricity he had given, the extraordinary clothes he had worn, and the bizarre furnishing schemes he had devised. The new home he was now planning, this time for his own personal pleasure and not to astonish other people, was going to be comfortably though curiously appointed: a peaceful and unique abode specially designed to meet the needs of the solitary life he intended to lead.

When the architect had fitted up the house at Fontenay in accordance with his wishes, and when all that remained was to settle the question of furniture and decoration, Des Esseintes once again gave long and careful consideration to the entire series of available colours.

What he wanted was colours which would appear stronger and clearer in artificial light. He did not particularly care if they looked crude or insipid in daylight, for he lived most of his life at night, holding that night afforded greater intimacy and isolation and that the mind was truly roused and stimulated only by awareness of the dark; moreover he derived a peculiar pleasure from being in a well lighted room when all the surrounding houses were wrapped in sleep and darkness, a sort of enjoyment in which vanity may have played some small part, a very special feeling of satisfaction familiar to those who sometimes work late at night and draw aside the curtains to find that all around them the world is dark, silent, and dead.

Slowly, one by one, he went through the various colours.

Blue, he remembered, takes on an artificial green tint by candlelight; if a dark blue like indigo or cobalt, it becomes black; if pale, it turns to grey; and if soft and true like turquoise, it goes dull and cold. There could, therefore, be no question of making it the keynote of a room, though it might be used to help out another colour.

On the other hand, under the same conditions the iron greys grow sullen and heavy; the pearl greys lose their blue sheen and are metamorphosed into a dirty white; the browns become cold and sleepy; and as for the dark greens such as emperor green and myrtle green, they react like the dark blues and turn quite black. Only the pale greens remained – peacock green, for instance, or the cinnabar and lacquer greens – but then artificial light kills the blue in them and leaves only the yellow, which for its part lacks clarity and consistency.

Nor was there any point in thinking of such delicate tints as salmon pink, maize, and rose; for their very effeminacy would run counter to his ideas of complete isolation. Nor again was it any use considering the various shades of purple, which with one exception lose their lustre in candlelight. That exception is plum, which somehow survives intact, but then what a muddy reddish hue it is, unpleasantly like lees of wine! Besides, it struck him as utterly futile to resort to this range of tints, in so far as it is possible to see purple by ingesting a specified amount of santonin,[22] and thus it becomes a simple matter for anyone to change the colour of his walls without laying a finger on them.

Having rejected all these colours, he was left with only three: red, orange, and yellow.

Of the three, he preferred orange, so confirming by his own example the truth of a theory to which he attributed almost mathematical validity: to wit, that there exists a close correspondence between the sensual make-up of a person with a truly artistic temperament and whatever colour that person reacts to most strongly and sympathetically.

In fact, leaving out of account the majority of men, whose coarse retinas perceive neither the cadences peculiar to different colours nor the mysterious charm of their gradation; leaving out also those bourgeois optics that are insensible to the pomp and glory of the clear, bright colours; and considering only those people with delicate eyes that have undergone the education of libraries and art-galleries, it seemed to him an undeniable fact that anyone who dreams of the ideal, prefers illusion to reality, and calls for veils to clothe the naked truth, is almost certain to appreciate the soothing caress of blue and its cognates, such as mauve, lilac, and pearl grey, always provided they retain their delicacy and do not pass the point where they change their personalities and turn into pure violets and stark greys.

The hearty, blustering type on the other hand, the handsome, full-blooded sort, the strapping he-men who scorn the formalities of life and rush straight for their goal, losing their heads completely, these generally delight in the vivid glare of the reds and yellows, in the percussion effect of the vermilions and chromes, which blind their eyes and intoxicate their senses.

As for those gaunt, febrile creatures of feeble constitution and nervous disposition whose sensual appetite craves dishes that are smoked and seasoned, their eyes almost always prefer that most morbid and irritating of colours, with its acid glow and unnatural splendour – orange.

There could therefore be no doubt whatever as to Des Esseintes's final choice; but indubitable difficulties still remained to be solved. If red and yellow become more pronounced in artificial light, the same is not true of their compound, orange, which often flares up into a fiery nasturtium red.

He carefully studied all its different shades by candlelight and finally discovered one which he considered likely to keep its balance and answer his requirements.

Once these preliminaries were over, he made every effort to avoid, in his study at any rate, the use of Oriental rugs and fabrics, which had become so commonplace and vulgar now that upstart tradesmen could buy them in the bargain basement of any department-store.

The walls he eventually decided to bind like books in large-grained crushed morocco: skins from the Cape glazed by means of strong steel plates under a powerful press.

When the lining of the walls had been completed, he had the mouldings and the tall plinths lacquered a deep indigo, similar to the colour coachbuilders use for the panels of carriage bodies. The ceiling, which was slightly coved, was also covered in morocco; and set in the middle of the orange leather, like a huge circular window open to the sky, there was a piece of royal-blue silk from an ancient cope on which silver seraphim had been depicted in angelic flight by the weavers' guild of Cologne.

After everything had been arranged according to plan, these various colours came to a quiet understanding with each other at nightfall: the blue of the woodwork was stabilized and, so to speak, warmed up by the surrounding orange tints, which for their part glowed with undiminished brilliance, maintained and in a way intensified by the close proximity of the blue.

As to furniture, Des Esseintes did not have to undertake any laborious treasure-hunts, in so far as the only luxuries he intended to have in this room were rare books and flowers. Leaving himself free to adorn any bare walls later on with a few drawings and paintings, he confined himself for the present to fitting up ebony bookshelves and bookcases round the greater part of the room, strewing tiger skins and blue fox furs about the floor, and installing beside a massive moneychanger's table of the fifteenth century, several deep-seated wing-armchairs and an old church lectern of wrought iron, one of those antique singing-desks on which deacons of old used to place the antiphonary and which now supported one of the weighty folios of Du Cange's *Glossarium mediae et infimae Latinatis*.[23]

The windows, with panes of bluish crackle-glass or gilded bottle-punts which shut out the view and admitted only a very dim light, were dressed with curtains cut out of old ecclesiastical stoles, whose faded gold threads were almost invisible against the dull red material.

As a finishing touch, in the centre of the chimney-piece, which was likewise dressed in sumptuous silk from a Florentine dalmatic, and flanked by two Byzantine monstrances of gilded copper which had originally come from the Abbaye-au-Bois at Bièvre, there stood a magnificent triptych whose separate panels had been fashioned to resemble lace-work. This now contained, framed under glass, copied on real vellum in exquisite missal lettering and marvellously illuminated, three pieces by Baudelaire: on the right and left, the sonnets *La Mort des amants* and *L'Ennemi*, and in the middle, the prose poem bearing the English title *Anywhere out of the World*.

[Opening pages of Chapter 12]

During the days that followed his return home, Des Esseintes browsed through the books in his library, and at the thought that he might have been parted from them for a long time he was filled with the same heartfelt satisfaction he would have enjoyed if he had come back to them after a genuine separation. Under the impulse of this feeling, he saw them in a new light, discovering beauties in them he had forgotten ever since he had bought and read them for the first time.

Everything indeed – books, bric-à-brac, and furniture – acquired a peculiar charm in his eyes. His bed seemed softer in comparison with the pallet he would have occupied in London; the discreet and silent service he got at home delighted him, exhausted as he was by the very thought of the noisy garrulity of hotel waiters; the methodical organization of his daily life appeared more admirable than ever, now that the hazard of travelling was a possibility.

He steeped himself once more in this refreshing bath of settled habits, to which artificial regrets added a more bracing and more tonic quality.

But it was his books that chiefly engaged his attention. He took them all down from their shelves and examined them before putting them back, to see whether, since his coming to Fontenay, the heat and damp had not damaged their bindings or spotted their precious papers.

He began by going through the whole of his Latin library; then he rearranged the specialist works by Archelaus, Albertus Magnus, Raymond Lully, and Arnaud de Villanova[24] dealing with the cabbala and the occult sciences; and lastly he checked all his modern books one by one. To his delight he discovered that they had one and all kept dry and were in good condition.

This collection had cost him considerable sums of money, for the truth was that he could not bear to have his favourite authors printed on rag-paper, as they were in other people's libraries, with characters like hobnails in a peasant's boots.

In Paris in former days, he had had certain volumes set up just for himself and printed on hand-presses by specially hired workmen. Sometimes he would commission Perrin of Lyons, whose slim, clear types were well adapted for archaic reimpressions of old texts; sometimes he would send to England or America for new characters to print works of the present century; sometimes he would apply to a house at Lille which for hundreds of years had possessed a complete fount of Gothic letters; sometimes again he would commandeer the fine old Enschedé printing-works at Haarlem, whose foundry has preserved the stamps and matrices of the so-called *lettres de civilité*.[25]

He had done the same with the paper for his books. Deciding one fine day that he was tired of the ordinary expensive papers – silver from China, pearly gold from Japan, white from Whatman's, greyish brown from Holland, buff from Turkey and the Seychal mills – and disgusted with the machine-made varieties, he had ordered special hand-made papers from the old mills at Vire where they still use pestles once employed to crush hempseed. To introduce a little variety into his collection, he had at various times imported certain dressed fabrics from London – flock papers and rep papers – while to help mark his contempt for other bibliophiles, a Lübeck manufacturer supplied him with a glorified candle-paper, bluish in colour, noisy and brittle to the touch, in which the straw fibres were replaced by flakes of gold such as you find floating in Danzig brandy.

In this way he had got together some unique volumes, always choosing unusual formats and having them clothed by Lortic, by Trautz-Bauzonnet, by Chambolle, by Capé's successors, in irreproachable bindings of old silk, of embossed ox-hide, of Cape goat-skin – all full bindings, patterned and inlaid, lined with tabby or watered silk, adorned in ecclesiastic fashion with metal clasps and corners, sometimes even decorated by Gruel-Engelmann in oxidized silver and shining enamel.

Thus he had had Baudelaire's works printed with the admirable episcopal type of the old house of Le Clere, in a large format similar to that of a mass-book, on a very light Japanese felt, a bibulous paper as soft as elder-pith, its milky whiteness faintly tinged with pink. This edition, limited to a single copy and printed in a velvety China-ink black, had been dressed outside and lined inside with a mirific and authentic flesh-coloured pig-skin, one in a thousand, dotted all over where the bristles had been and blind-tooled in black with designs of marvellous aptness chosen by a great artist.

On this particular day, Des Esseintes took this incomparable volume down from his shelves and fondled it reverently, rereading certain pieces which in this simple but priceless setting seemed to him deeper and subtler than ever.

His admiration for this author knew no bounds. In his opinion, writers had hitherto confined themselves to exploring the surface of the soul, or such underground passages as were easily accessible and well lit, measuring here and there the deposits of the seven deadly sins, studying the lie of the lodes and their development, recording for instance, as Balzac did, the stratification of a soul possessed by some monomaniacal passion – ambition or avarice, paternal love or senile lust.

Literature, in fact, had been concerned with virtues and vices of a perfectly healthy sort, the regular functioning of brains of a normal conformation, the practical reality of current ideas, with never a thought for morbid depravities and other-worldly aspirations; in short, the discoveries of these analysts of human nature stopped short at the speculations, good or bad, classified by the Church; their efforts amounted to no more than the humdrum researches of a botanist who watches closely the expected development of ordinary flora planted in common or garden soil.

Baudelaire had gone further; he had descended to the bottom of the inexhaustible mine, had picked his way along abandoned or unexplored galleries, and had finally reached those districts of the soul where the monstrous vegetations of the sick mind flourish.

There, near the breeding-ground of intellectual aberrations and diseases of the mind – the mystical tetanus, the burning fever of lust, the typhoids and yellow fevers of crime – he had found, hatching in the dismal forcing-house of *ennui*, the frightening climacteric of thoughts and emotions.

He had laid bare the morbid psychology of the mind that has reached the October of its sensations, and had listed the symptoms of souls visited by sorrow, singled out by spleen; he had shown how blight affects the emotions at a time when the enthusiasms and beliefs of youth have drained away, and nothing remains but the barren memory of hardships, tyrannies, and slights, suffered at the behest of a despotic and freakish fate.

He had followed every phase of this lamentable autumn, watching the human creature, skilled in self-torment and adept in self-deception, forcing its thoughts to cheat one another in order to suffer more acutely, and ruining in advance, thanks to its powers of analysis and observation, any chance of happiness it might have.

Then, out of this irritable sensitivity of soul, out of this bitterness of mind that savagely repulses the embarrassing attentions of friendship, the benevolent insults of charity, he witnessed the gradual and horrifying development of those middle-aged passions, those mature love-affairs where one partner goes on blowing hot when the other has already started blowing cold, where lassitude forces the amorous pair to indulge in filial caresses whose apparent juvenility seems something new, and in motherly embraces whose tenderness is not only restful but also gives rise, so to speak, to interesting feelings of remorse about a vague sort of incest.

In a succession of magnificent pages he had exposed these hybrid passions, exacerbated by the impossibility of obtaining complete satisfaction, as well as the dangerous subterfuges of narcotic and toxic drugs, taken in the hope of deadening pain and conquering boredom. In a period when literature attributed man's unhappiness almost exclusively to the misfortunes of unrequited love or the jealousies engendered by adulterous love, he had ignored these childish ailments and sounded instead those deeper, deadlier, longer-lasting wounds that are inflicted by satiety, disillusion, and contempt upon souls tortured by the present, disgusted by the past, terrified and dismayed by the future.

The more Des Esseintes re-read his Baudelaire, the more he appreciated the indescribable charm of this writer who, at a time when verse no longer served any purpose except to depict the external appearance of creatures and things, had succeeded in expressing the inexpressible – thanks to a solid, sinewy style which, more than any other, possessed that remarkable quality, the power to define in curiously healthy terms the most fugitive and ephemeral of the unhealthy conditions of weary spirits and melancholy souls.

After Baudelaire, the number of French books that had found their way on to his shelves was very limited. Without a doubt he was utterly insensible to the merits of those works it is good form to enthuse over. The 'side-splitting mirth' of Rabelais and the 'common-sense humour' of Molière had never brought so much as a smile to his lips; and the antipathy he felt to these buffooneries was so great that he did not hesitate to liken them, from the artistic point of view, to the knockabout turns given by the clowns at any country fair.

[Closing pages of Chapter 12: on Barbey d'Aurevilly]

Admittedly this latter writer[26] was far too compromising, far too independent a son of the Church. In the long run, the others would always eat humble pie and fall back into line, but he was the *enfant terrible* the party refused to own, who went whoring through literature and brought his women half-naked into the sanctuary. It was only because of the boundless contempt Catholicism has for all creative talent that an excommunication in due and proper form had not outlawed this strange servant who, under the pretext of doing honour to his masters, broke the chapel windows, juggled with the sacred vessels, and performed step-dances round the tabernacle.

Two of Barbey d'Aurevilly's works Des Esseintes found particularly enthralling: *Un Prêtre marié* and *Les Diaboliques*. Others, such as *L'Ensorcelée, Le Chevalier des Touches* and *Une Vieille Maîtresse,* were doubtless better balanced and more complete works, but they did not appeal so strongly to Des Esseintes, who was really interested only in sickly books, undermined and inflamed by fever.

In these comparatively healthy volumes Barbey d'Aurevilly was constantly tacking to and fro between those two channels of Catholic belief which eventually run into one: mysticism and sadism. But in the two books which Des Esseintes was now glancing through, Barbey had thrown caution to the winds, had given rein to his steed, and had ridden full tilt down one road after another, as far as he could go.

All the horrific mystery of the Middle Ages brooded over that improbable book *Un Prêtre marié*; magic was mixed up with religion, sorcery with prayer; while the God of original sin, more pitiless, more cruel than the Devil, submitted his innocent victim Calixte to uninterrupted torments, branding her with a red cross on the forehead, just as in olden times he had one of his angels mark the houses of the unbelievers he meant to kill.

These scenes, like the fantasies of a fasting monk affected with delirium, were unfolded in the disjointed language of a fever patient. But unfortunately, among all the characters galvanized into an unbalanced life like so many Hoffmann Coppelias,[27] there were some, the Néel de Néhou for instance, who seemed to have been imagined in one of those periods of prostration that always follow crises; and they were out of keeping in this atmosphere of melancholy madness, into which they introduced the same note of unintentional humour as is sounded by the little zinc lordling in hunting-boots who stands blowing his horn on the pedestal of so many mantelpiece clocks.

After these mystical divagations, Barbey had enjoyed a period of comparative calm, but then a frightening relapse had occurred.

The belief that man is an irresolute creature pulled this way and that by two forces of equal strength, alternately winning and losing the battle for his soul; the conviction that human life is nothing more than an uncertain struggle between heaven and hell; the faith in two opposed entities, Satan and Christ – all this was bound to engender those internal discords in which the soul, excited by the incessant fighting, stimulated as it were by the constant promises and threats, ends up by giving in and prostitutes itself to whichever of the two combatants has been the more obstinate in its pursuit.

In *Un Prêtre marié*, it was Christ whose temptations had been successful and whose praises were sung by Barbey d'Aurevilly; but in *Les Diaboliques*, the author had surrendered to the Devil, and it was Satan he extolled. At this point there appeared on the scene that bastard child of Catholicism which for centuries the Church has pursued with its exorcisms and its *autos-da-fé*–sadism.[28]

This strange and ill-defined condition cannot in fact arise in the mind of an unbeliever. It does not consist simply in riotous indulgence of the flesh, stimulated by bloody acts of cruelty, for in that case it would be nothing more than a deviation of the genetic instincts, a case of satyriasis developed to its fullest extent; it consists first and foremost in a sacrilegious manifestation, in a moral rebellion, in a spiritual debauch, in a wholly idealistic, wholly Christian aberration. There is also something in it of joy tempered by fear, a joy analogous to the wicked delight of disobedient children playing with forbidden things for no other reason than that their parents have expressly forbidden them to go near them.

The truth of the matter is that if it did not involve sacrilege, sadism would have no *raison d'être;* on the other hand, since sacrilege depends on the existence of a religion, it cannot be deliberately and effectively committed except by a believer, for a man would derive no satisfaction whatever from profaning a faith that was unimportant or unknown to him.

The strength of sadism then, the attraction it offers, lies entirely in the forbidden pleasure of transferring to Satan the homage and the prayers that should go to God; it lies in the flouting of the precepts of Catholicism, which the sadist actually observes in topsy-turvy fashion when, in order to offend Christ the more grievously, he commits the sins Christ most expressly proscribed – profanation of holy things and carnal debauch.

In point of fact, this vice to which the Marquis de Sade had given his name was as old as the Church itself; the eighteenth century, when it was particularly rife, had simply revived, by an ordinary atavistic process, the impious practices of the witches' sabbath of medieval times – to go no further back in history.

Des Esseintes had done no more than dip into the *Malleus Maleficorum*, that terrible code of procedure of Jacob Sprenger's[29] which permitted the Church to send thousands of necromancers and sorcerers to the stake; but that was enough to enable him to recognize in the witches' sabbath all the obscenities and blasphemies of sadism. Besides the filthy orgies dear to the Evil One – nights devoted alternately to lawful and unnatural copulation, nights befouled by the bestialities of bloody debauch – he found the same parodies of religious processions, the same ritual threats and insults hurled at God, the same devotion to his Rival – as when the Black Mass was celebrated over a woman on all fours whose naked rump, repeatedly soiled, served as the altar, with the priest cursing the bread and wine, and the congregation derisively taking communion in the shape of a black host stamped with a picture of a he-goat.

This same outpouring of foul-mouthed jests and degrading insults was to be seen in the works of the Marquis de Sade, who spiced his frightful sensualities with sacrilegious profanities. He would rail at Heaven, invoke Lucifer, call God an abject scoundrel, a crazy idiot, spit on the sacrament of communion, do his best in fact to besmirch with vile obscenities a Divinity he hoped would damn him, at the same time declaring, as a further act of defiance, that that Divinity did not exist.

This psychic condition Barbey d'Aurevilly came close to sharing. If he did not go as far as Sade in shouting atrocious curses at the Saviour; if, out of greater caution or greater fear, he always professed to honour the Church, he none the less addressed his prayers to the Devil in true medieval fashion, and in his desire to defy the Deity, likewise slipped into demonic erotomania, coining new sensual monstrosities, or even borrowing from *La Philosophie dans le boudoir* a certain episode which he seasoned with fresh condiments to make the story *Le Dîner d'un athée*.[30]

The extraordinary book that contained this tale was Des Esseintes's delight; he had therefore had printed for him in bishop's-purple ink, within a border of cardinal red, on a genuine parchment blessed by the Auditors of the Rota,[31] a copy of *Les Diaboliques* set up in those *lettres de civilité* whose peculiar hooks and flourishes, curling up or down, assume a satanic appearance.

Not counting certain poems of Baudelaire's which, in imitation of the prayers chanted on the nights of the witches' sabbath, took the form of infernal litanies, this book, among all the works of contemporary apostolic literature, was the only one to reveal that state of mind, at once devout and impious, towards which nostalgic memories of Catholicism, stimulated by fits of neurosis, had often impelled Des Esseintes.

With Barbey d'Aurevilly, the series of religious writers came to an end. To tell the truth, this pariah belonged more, from every point of view, to secular literature than to that other literature in which he claimed a place that was denied him. His wild romantic style, for instance, full of twisted expressions, outlandish turns of phrase, and far-fetched similes, whipped up his sentences as they galloped across the page, farting and jangling their bells. In short, Barbey looked like a stallion among the geldings that filled the ultramontane stables.

Such were Des Esseintes's reflections as he dipped into the book, re-reading a passage here and there; and then, comparing the author's vigorous and varied style with the lymphatic, stereotyped style of his fellow writers, he was led to consider that evolution of language so accurately described by Darwin.

Closely associated with the secular writers of his time, brought up in the Romantic school, familiar with the latest books and accustomed to reading modern publications, Barbey inevitably found himself in possession of an idiom which had undergone many profound modifications, and which had been largely renovated since the seventeenth century.

The very opposite had been the case with the ecclesiastical writers; confined to their own territory, imprisoned within an identical, traditional range of reading, knowing nothing of the literary evolution of more recent times and absolutely determined, if need be, to pluck their eyes out rather than recognize it, they necessarily employed an unaltered and unalterable language, like that eighteenth-century language which the descendants of the French settlers in Canada normally speak and write to this day, no variation in vocabulary or phraseology having ever been possible in their idiom, cut off as it is from the old country and surrounded on all sides by the English tongue.

Des Esseintes's musings had reached this point when the silvery sound of a bell tinkling a little angelus told him that breakfast was ready. He left his books where they were, wiped his forehead and made for the dining-room, telling himself that of all the volumes he had been rearranging, the works of Barbey d'Aurevilly were still the only ones whose thought and style offered those gamy flavours and unhealthy spots, that bruised skin and sleepy taste which he so loved to savour in the decadent writers, both Latin and monastic, of olden times.

1884; translated by Robert Baldick, 1959

JEAN MORÉAS

La Faënza

I

Among the fashionable party-going set, she went by the Italianate name of La Faënza,[32] because of her skin, which seemed to have been bronzed by the Neapolitan sun, and her big black eyes – eyes that could knock you dead at the crossroads, like blunderbusses in the woods of Abruzzi. But she was a French country girl, born near Tours, and at barely sixteen she had married an honest lawyer in his fifties, named Verdal, who after only fourteen months of marriage had left her a widow, with a young boy on her hands and in financial straits. After a while she had become tired of the dull monotony of country life, and dreamed of luxury and easy pleasures; so she had allowed a disgraced sub-prefect to take her up to Paris, where he soon abandoned her so that he could marry the daughter of a wealthy tradesman in the rue du Sentier.

As she was just into her twenties, and her wide appealing eyes could melt anybody's heart, and her hair hung down, not to her feet but at least down to her well-rounded dancer's hips, she was not without opportunities to cast off the last shreds of her respectability by haunting the fashionable bars. In the marketplace of seduction, her stock was high, and some of those respectable madams who engage so profitably in the white-slave trade right under the noses of the police offered her lucrative business. It was not long before every bail-jumping playboy, every spendthrift heir of the gentry, every gaucho adventurer, and every semi-reformed roulette-player was vying for the honour of placing fistfuls of gold on the pink marble mantelpiece of her bedchamber. She maintained a town-house just like a highly paid actress, with flunkeys in short breeches and implausibly rotund coachmen.

Then began for the lovely La Faënza a splendid reign that lasted more than ten years. It was the usual story of the pretty girl who fishes up on the streets of Paris with few scruples and plenty of bosom. She dressed in ruinously expensive style, with extravagant hats. Oriental fabrics that a shah would envy adorned her drawing room, while her boudoir was hung with Venetian jewel-bordered mirrors, to show off the majestic curves of her waist. She even had wit, or what passes in Paris as wit, the kind you pick up from sucking prawns in the stale atmosphere of private dining rooms. Flashy young men keen to win their spurs, and ageing pleasure-seekers anxious to keep up their renowned exploits, contended for the glory of settling her dressmakers' bills or the rent for her holiday villas in Nice and Normandy. To cut a long story short, amid all the exhilaration of her success, she overlooked the fact that she was turning the corner into that sorry age of stubborn wrinkles, loose teeth, and autumnally fading hair. In fact she had every right to overlook it: although she was thirty-four years old, her skin was still silken and marble-smooth, her teeth perkily white, and from her charming head, like that of Giorgione's Virgin, hung a cascade of hair that could defy the deadliest comb.

We should recall that La Faënza had a son from her marriage. The child was brought up by an elderly aunt. His mother saw him once when he was eight years old, but after that paid him no attention apart from sending money and a few letters full of that false sentimentality common to her profession. The elderly aunt, in the hope of concealing his mother's conduct from him, had got him enlisted in one of the African regiments. At the age of nineteen he was serving as a non-commissioned officer when he distinguished himself during the latest uprising and earned a military decoration, but unfortunately his injuries obliged him to leave the army. On hearing this news, La Faënza was suddenly overcome by boundless maternal tenderness, and she resolved to forsake the sweet indulgences of hired love to devote the remainder of her days to the welfare of her abandoned child. She sold up her town-house, her jewels, and her horses, and retired to a property in Touraine that a right-wing politician had given her some while before. And this is how the lovely La Faënza became Madame Verdal again, the honest lawyer's widow, the exemplary mother, the pious and charitable lady.

II

Philippe was a handsome young man of nineteen or twenty with a neat moustache, a girlish figure, and dovelike eyes. He had hardly the slightest suspicion about his mother's past, as she came up with countless clever lies to account for their prolonged separation. He began to adore her with all the ardour of a heart that had been shut off until now from familial affections. La Faënza, on her side, became literally crazy about her son, her handsome Philippe.

The property in which the retired courtesan resolved to expiate her sweet sins was a charming villa with green shutters around which morning glory and nasturtiums with blood-red calyxes wound themselves in serpentine motions. A small grove that had grown up freely around it wrapped the house in the exquisite mystery of flickering shadows. In its shadiest corner, under the parasol made by a giant polonia, the chattering of woodpeckers mingled with the babbling of water that flowed from a nymph's urn into a little marble pond fringed with moss and yellow lichen.

Mother and son led a gently tranquil life there for several months. They made so much fuss over each other that it often verged on the ridiculous, their excessive fondness interspersed with feigned sulks. La Faënza had completely forgotten her former life: grandstand seats at the racecourse, boxes at the theatre, horse-riding in the Pyrenees and yachting parties at Trouville, dinner parties at her splendid house at Parc Monceau, supping late in the best restaurants, where carafes of champagne and glasses of Chartreuse in various colours made those incorrigible young dandies seem more ridiculous than ever . . . She had even ended up believing quite sincerely that she had been a saintly woman all her life.

But despite all their fondness for one another, they did not settle into intimacy: that open and carefree kind of intimacy that grows between the mother who has spanked her child and the child who has grown up clinging to his mother's skirts. And this was only to be expected. As we have mentioned, La Faënza had seen her son only the once since her elopement with the sub-prefect, at a time when he had been only a youngster. She was now seeing him suddenly grown up as a young man with a fearsome moustache and a proper soldier's scar on his brow. For the son's part, his mother was a stranger, so it was like seeing her for the first time. All this explains readily why they sometimes found themselves addressing each other with the formal *vous*, their relationship marked by a curious reserve and by unnecessary courtesy.

Madame Verdal had cast aside La Faënza, and the courtesan was completely dead within her. She dressed austerely in black silk dresses trimmed with jade, with very few rings, while her earrings were fetchingly modest. She wore her hair in a plain headband, and wore no make-up beyond simple face-powder. With such comportment, and with a considerable income from rents, it is little surprise that her neighbours held her in esteem.

Among those with whom the ex-courtesan was on good terms, we should accord the highest rank to the Mouflet family, of which the father, Evariste Mouflet, was a retired notary, a dull provincial afflicted with an incurable mania for feeble jokes. The mother, Olympe, was a solidly respectable woman who had taken no lovers, apart from three or four of her husband's clerks. Their three girls were really quite attractive, as notary's daughters go. The slender figure of the eldest daughter, Mademoiselle Clémentine, might have been especially appealing, had it not been for those appalling guano-coloured dresses made from vicuña wool, bought from a Monsieur Worth in some local shop. She had wide, startled eyes under her rather comely brown hair, and better still she had a seventeen-year-old bosom, which looked most promising.

The ex-courtesan and the notary's family would often visit each other to take tea, to play harmless parlour-games, and to mangle a number of operatic arias on their poorly tuned pianos. Philippe, whose horse-riding days at Kroumir had hardly taught him an exacting dress-sense, found Mademoiselle Clémentine's vicuña dresses entirely to his taste, although he preferred the treasures that they concealed. Mademoiselle Clémentine, for her part, felt no unconquerable aversion from the brown moustache. And needless to say, her parents found new qualities to admire every day in the sole heir of a lady who enjoyed an income of fifty thousand pounds. And so the young ones courted each other without concealment, right in front of La Faënza, who did not even notice a thing.

One evening in July, the whole Mouflet family was gathered in the ex-courtesan's dining-room. After a few polkas banged out by the youngest of the girls, and a little idle chat, the lawyer proposed that in this stifling heat, a stroll in the shade of the garden would be refreshing; and they all eagerly agreed.

It was a glorious evening. The full moon shone like a fabulous gold coin in the cloudless sky. They all took different directions along the paths, which were lit intermittently by glow-worms among the moss.

La Faënza had been looking for her son for a few minutes, when she thought she could discern, on a stone bench in the shadiest nook of the garden, two shadowy figures entwined. On the alert, she could have sworn she heard the sound of kisses intermingled with the lapping of the water that flowed into the marble ponds. Holding her breath, she made her way towards the stone bench, from behind a hedge of rose-bushes. Her son Philippe was in the midst of whispering sweet nothings into the ear of Mademoiselle Clémentine.

At this, the ex-courtesan's heart was overwhelmed by unfamiliar sensations: she felt giddy for a moment, then her eyes dilated. Choking with rage, she drew herself up to her full height before the poor dumbstruck lovers, and addressed Mademoiselle Mouflet in no uncertain terms:

'How stupid of me not to recognise all this time that you have been coming round here to steal my son. As if I would hand over all my money to feed a crooked lawyer and his young sluts. And as for your mother, well, she's no better, sleeping with the servants! Everyone for miles around knows about it. Don't ever set foot here again, the stinking lot of you, or I'll clear you out with my broom . . .'

Forgetting herself utterly in her fit of temper, Madame Verdal had reverted to her former rowdy self. When the rest of the Mouflets hastened to the noise of the dispute, she floored them with even more foul-mouthed insults. M. Mouflet responded with an indignant tirade, and then led away his terrified wife and daughters.

Philippe just stood there looking distraught, unable to understand any of this. La Faënza went back into her house in an indescribable state of exasperation. She wept and sobbed, and writhed on the carpet, foaming at the mouth. Then she suddenly got up and kissed her son full on the lips, cackling like a madwoman.

III

After a few days of sulking, mother and son were reconciled, and their fondness revived. Every day they took long walks across the fields, from which they returned like lovers in olden days, holding wisps of broom in their hands. In the mornings, they would go out riding in the woods for hours at a time, while in the evenings they would go and ripple the calm waters of a nearby pool in a dinghy, under the romantic moonlight. Curiously, a remarkable change had come over La Faënza's habits since the incident in the garden. Breaking with the austere style she had adopted since her conversion, she divested herself of the sober matron's uncomely outfit, and had begun once more to sport the expensive brightly coloured fabrics, the ostrich-feathered hats, and the long doeskin gloves. The jewels that she had not wanted to part with were reclaimed from their red velvet cases to adorn her long, slender hands and her queenly neck. Face-powder no longer sufficed to beautify her, so she had rediscovered the subtle cosmetics and rare perfumes that restored her youthfulness. She paid special attention to her underwear, expert as she was in its fascinations: she put on silk chemises bordered with antique lace, and pale pink stockings with ribbon rosettes glinting with fiery diamonds. The modest furnishings of her bedchamber were transformed beyond recognition. Recalling the provocative luxuries of her courtesan's boudoir, she now surrounded herself with low, soft furnishings which enclosed her like voluptuous arms, with Syrian fabrics, rugs from Karaman, and mottled tiger-skins in which bare feet could wriggle and offer themselves for quivering kisses. Perfumes burned continually in richly wrought incense-burners, and armfuls of white roses mingled their last breaths with the warmth of the wood crackling in the lofty fireplace.

She busied herself a great deal with her son's clothing, telling him 'this isn't stylish', or 'that suits you well', or 'that coat is creased at the back', or 'this jacket fits you neatly'. She would part his hair for him, and wax his moustache, just as she had done with her lovers in the days when she had been the kept woman of fat bankers.

Sometimes in the evenings, at some ungodly hour she would call him into her bedroom, and there, in the unsteady light of the pink candles, her statuesque body barely contained by her brazenly revealing cambric chemise, she would flaunt herself before the long wardrobe mirror to show off her stunning breasts and the impudent curve of her hips, and would say to her son, with an inviting glance,

'I'm still beautiful, aren't I? You would be madly in love with me if I weren't your mother, wouldn't you?'

Then she would laugh loudly, flashing the ivory splendour of her teeth like an animal. Feline in her sinuous nonchalance, she would move enticingly over to Philippe and sit on his lap. The blushing Philippe, his eyes alight with unconscious lechery, could hardly dare to look at her. After a few moments spent twirling her son's moustache and kissing his pallid lips and carefully curled hair, she would roll on to her tiger-skin rug, munch a few biscuits, drain a glass of port in one gulp, then skip like a gazelle in between her expensively embroidered sheets, close her gorgeously smooth eyelids with their long curling lashes, and say between half-closed lips,

'To bed with you, sir. It's late, and I'm feeling sleepy.'

As for Philippe's poor little heart and his agitated nerves, they had been shattered beyond repair. Often he would set out before dawn on restive horses across the plains, scarcely aware of the reason for his reckless speed; or he would go out shooting wild ducks for whole days at a time in typhoidal swamps. He was restless, moody, and irritable, often seeking absurd excuses to pick quarrels with his mother, saying he was finally fed up with this idle existence, that it was shameful for a young man at his age, that he would *most assuredly* return to his regiment. Then there would be touching scenes with tearful appeals for forgiveness and protestations of filial love, followed by prolonged caresses and rapturous kisses on the lips.

IV

That day, they had dined, as La Faënza's whim would have it, in the little boudoir draped with mauve satin. Wan twilight filtered mournfully through the panes of the narrow window. La Faënza had said 'Let's not light the candles, this half-light is so pleasant'. He had kept his silence, frowning slightly. A scent of magnolia hung in the heavy air. She lit a cigarette, while he lit up his soldier's pipe. Nearly ten minutes passed in embarrassed silence. Looking straight at her son, La Faënza said,

'Anything wrong?'

'No.'

A few more minutes passed in silence. Suddenly, bracing her limbs in a supreme effort, she threw herself at her son's feet, clasped him desperately, and said, as if with her last breath:

'Philippe, you don't love me!'

He hung his head in silence. At that, she sprang quickly to her feet and walked around feverishly. Coming to a sudden halt, she said, in a hollow voice:

'My God, this is so awful! It must come to an end. Listen to me, Philippe. You know it, you can feel it: I love you. And it's not a mother's love I feel for you, but the longing of a lovesick woman, a mistress, do you understand? Oh yes, I want you, and you shall be mine!'

She let out the mocking laugh of a lunatic, then continued:

'I am your mother; but what do I care for that? It's not as if I know you. I met you once when you were seven. You're a stranger, a lovely boy who turned my head . . . And you don't even desire me! But take a look at me: I'm as beautiful as if I were still twenty! But then there's the morality of it. Oh, morals! I couldn't give a damn for them! Anyway, you don't know, your aunt hid it all from you . . . I was . . . a kept woman . . . what they call a tart. All my wealth, and yours too, comes from that . . . so you're not entitled to put on any scrupulous airs. We're both in the gutter, Philippe, so let's stay there.'

He looked at her, stunned. Becoming ever more frantic, she continued:

'You've seen me in my chemise, and you know I have a marvellous bosom; princes would pay its weight in gold for it . . . My Philippe, we shall be happy together. Wouldn't you like that? Oh, I do love you so, and we shall die together . . . in love . . .'

She leapt upon her son like a maenad. Sweeping him up in her lithe arms, she rolled him onto the couch, puffing her heady breath into his face. He felt lost in a voluptuous swoon. Then, with a desperate effort of will, he suddenly broke free of this embrace and stood up. He tensed his legs, then looked around him with a wild expression.

La Faënza was now completely beside herself, and she threw herself on to her son once more. Then, with his face hardened and his mouth dreadfully contorted, Philippe seized a Japanese dagger whose sharp blade was glinting on a weirdly patterned bedside table, and stabbed her violently in the neck.

She fell on to the carpet without a cry, the blood gushing from her.

1886; translated by Chris Baldick, 2011

GABRIELE D'ANNUNZIO

From *The Child of Pleasure* (*Il Piacere*): from Book III, Chapter 1

After a brief stay at Naples, Andrea reached Rome on the 24th of October, a Sunday, in the first heavy morning rain of the Autumn season. He experienced an extraordinary pleasure in returning to his apartments in the Casa Zuccari, his tasteful and charming *buen retiro*.[33] There he seemed to find again some portion of himself, something he had missed. Nothing was altered; everything about him retained, in his eyes, that indescribable look of life which material objects assume, amongst which one has lived and loved and suffered. His old servants, Jenny and Terenzio, had taken the utmost care of everything, and Stephen had attended to every detail likely to conduce to his master's comfort.

It was raining. Andrea went to the window and stood for some time looking out upon his beloved Rome. The piazza of the Trinità de' Monti was solitary and deserted, left to the guardianship of its obelisk. The trees along the wall that joins the church to the Villa Medici, already half stripped of their leaves, rustled mournfully in the wind and the rain. The Pincio alone still shone green, like an island in a lake of mist.[34]

And as he gazed, one sentiment dominated all the others in his heart; the sudden and lively re-awakening of his old love for Rome – fairest Rome – that city of cities, immense, imperial, unique – like the sea, for ever young, for ever new, for ever mysterious.

'What time is it?' Andrea asked of Stephen.

It was about nine o'clock. Feeling somewhat tired, he determined to have a sleep: also, that he would see no one that day and spend the evening quietly at home. Seeing that he was about to re-enter the life of the great world of Rome, he wished, before taking up the old round of activity, to indulge in a little meditation, a slight preparation; to lay down certain rules, to discuss with himself his future line of conduct.

'If any one calls,' he said to Stephen, 'say that I have not yet returned; and let the porter know it too. Tell James I shall not want him to-day, but he can come round for orders this evening. Bring me lunch at three – something very light – and dinner at nine. That is all.'

He fell asleep almost immediately. The servants woke him at two and informed him that, just before twelve o'clock, the Duke of Grimiti had called, having heard from the Marchesa d'Atelata that he had returned to town.

'Well?'

'Il Signor Duca left word that he would call again in the afternoon.'

'Is it still raining? Open the shutters wide.'

The rain had stopped, the sky was lighter. A band of pale sunshine streamed into the room and spread over the tapestry representing *The Virgin with the Holy Child and Stefano Sperelli*, a work of art brought by Giusto Sperelli from Flanders in 1508. Andrea's eyes wandered slowly over the walls, rejoicing in the beautiful hangings, the harmonious tints; and all these things so familiar and so dear to him seemed to offer him a welcome. The sight of them afforded him intense pleasure, and then the image of Maria Ferrès rose up before him.

He raised himself a little on the pillows, lit a cigarette and abandoned himself luxuriously to his meditations. An unwonted sense of comfort and well-being filled his body, while his mind was in its happiest vein. His thoughts mingled with the rings of smoke in the subdued light in which all forms and colours assume a pleasing vagueness.

Instead of reverting to the days that were past, his thoughts carried him forward into the future. – He would see Donna Maria again in two or three months – perhaps much sooner; there was no saying. Then he would resume the broken thread of that love which held for him so many obscure promises, so many secret attractions. To a man of culture, Donna Maria Ferrès was the Ideal Woman, Baudelaire's *Amie avec des hanches*,[35] the perfect *Consolatrix*, the friend who can hold out both comfort and pardon. Though she had marked those sorrowful lines in the volume of Shelley, she had, most assuredly, said very different words in her heart. 'I can never be thine!'[36] Why *never*? Ah, there had been too much passionate intensity for that in the voice in which she answered him that day in the wood at Vicomile – 'I love you! I love you! I love you!'

He could hear her voice now, that never-to-be-forgotten voice!

Stephen knocked at the door. 'May I remind the Signor Conte that it is three o'clock?'

Andrea rose and passed into the octagonal room to dress. The sun shone through the lace window screens and sparkled on the Hispano-Mauresque tiles, the innumerable toilet articles of crystal and silver, the bas-reliefs on the antique sarcophagus; its dancing reflections imparting a delightful sense of movement to the air. He felt in the best of spirits, completely cured, full of the joy and the vivacity of life. He was inexpressibly happy to be back in his home once more. All that was most frivolous, most capricious, most worldly in him awoke with a bound. It was as if the surrounding objects had the power to evoke in him the man of former days. His sensual curiosity, his elasticity, his ubiquity of mind reappeared. He already began to feel the necessity of expansion, of mixing in the world of pleasure and with his friends.

He discovered that he was very hungry, and ordered the servant to bring the lunch at once. He rarely dined at home, but for special occasions – some *recherché* lunch or private little supper – he had a dining-room decorated with eighteenth-century Neapolitan tapestries which Carlo Sperelli had ordered of Pietro Duranti in 1766 from designs by Storace. The seven wall panels represented episodes of Bacchic love, the portières and the draperies above the doors and windows having groups of fruit and flowers. Shades of gold – pale or tawny – predominated, and mingling with the warm, pearly flesh-tints and sombre blues, formed a harmony of colour that was both delicate and sumptuous.

'When the Duke of Grimiti comes back, show him up,' he said to the servant.

Into this room, too, the sun, sinking towards the Monte Mario, shot his dazzling rays. You could hear the rumble of the carriages in the piazza of the Trinità de' Monti. The rain over, it looked as if all the luminous gold of the Roman October were spread out over the city.

'Open the window,' he said to the servant.

The noise of the carriage wheels was louder now, a soft damp breeze stirred the curtains lightly.

'Divine Rome!' he thought as he looked at the sky between the wide curtains.

An irresistible curiosity drew him to the open window.

Rome appeared, all pearly gray, spread out before him, its lines a little blurred like a faded picture, under a Claude Lorraine[37] sky, sprinkled with ethereal clouds, their noble grouping lending to the clear spaces between an indescribable delicacy, as flowers lend a new grace to the verdure which surrounds them. On the distant heights the gray deepened gradually to amethyst. Long trailing vapours slid through the cypresses of the Monte Mario like waving locks through a comb of bronze. Close by, the pines of the Monte Pincio spread their sun-gilded canopies, Below, on the piazza, the obelisk of Pius VI looked like a pillar of agate. Under this rich autumnal light everything took on a sumptuous air.

Divine Rome!

He feasted his eyes on the prospect before him. Looking down, he saw a group of red-robed clerics pass along by the church; then the black coach of a prelate with its two black, long-tailed horses; then other open carriages containing ladies and children. He recognised the Princess of Ferentino with Barbarella Viti, followed by the Countess of Lucoli driving a pair of ponies and accompanied by her great Danish hound. A perturbing breath of the old life passed over his spirit, awakening indeterminate desires in his heart.

He left the window and returned to his lunch. The sun shone on the wall and lit up a dance of satyrs round a Silenus.[38]

'The Duke of Grimiti and two other gentlemen,' announced the servant.

The Duke entered with Ludovico Barbarisi and Giulio Musellaro. Andrea hastened forward to meet them and they greeted him warmly.

'You, Giulio!' exclaimed Sperelli, who had not seen his friend for more than two years. 'How long have you been in Rome?'

'Only a week. I was going to write to you to Schifanoja, but thought I would rather wait till you came back. And how are you? You are looking a little thin, but very well. It was only when I got back to Rome that I heard of your affair; otherwise I would certainly have come from India to offer you my services. At the beginning of May, I was at Padmavati in the Bahara. What a heap of things I have to tell you!'

'And so have I!'

They shook hands heartily a second time. Sperelli seemed overjoyed. None of his friends were so dear to him as Musellaro, for his noble character, his keen and penetrating mind and rare culture.

'Ruggiero – Ludovico – sit down. Giulio, will you sit here?'

He offered them tea, cigarettes, liqueurs. The conversation grew very lively. Grimiti and Barbarisi gave the news of Rome, especially the more spicy items of society gossip. The aroma of the tea mingled with that of the tobacco.

'I have brought you a chest of tea,' said Musellaro to Sperelli, 'and much better tea too than your famous Kien Loung used to drink.'

'Ah, do you remember, in London, how he used to make tea after the poetical method of the Great Emperor?'

'I say,' said Grimiti, 'do you know that the fair Clara Green is in Rome? I saw her on Sunday at the Villa Borghese. She recognised me and stopped her carriage to speak to me. She is as lovely as ever. You remember her passion for you, and how she went on when she thought you were in love with Constance Landbrooke? She instantly asked for news of you.'

'I should be very pleased to see her again. Does she still dress in green and wear sunflowers in her hat?'

'Oh no. She has apparently abandoned the aesthetic for good and all. She goes in for feathers now. On Sunday, she was wearing an enormous hat à la Montpensier with a perfectly fabulous feather in it.'

'The season is in full swing, I suppose?'

'Earlier than usual this year, both as to saints and sinners.'

'Which of the saints are already in Rome?'

'Almost all – Giulia Moceto, Barbarella Viti, the Princess of Micigliano, Laura Miano, the Marchesa Massa d'Alba, the Countess Lucoli –'

'I saw her just now from the window, driving. And I saw your cousin too, with Barbarella Viti.'

'My cousin is only here till tomorrow, then she goes back to Frascati. On Wednesday, she gives a kind of garden party at the villa in the style of the Princess of Sagan. Costume is not absolutely *de rigueur*, but the ladies will all wear Louis XV or Directoire hats. We are going.'

'You are not leaving Rome again so soon, I hope?' Grimiti asked of Sperelli.

'I shall stay till the beginning of November. Then I am going to France for a fortnight to see about some horses. I shall be back in Rome about the end of the month.'

'Talking of horses,' said Ludovico, 'Leonetto Lanza wants to sell *Campomorto*. You know it – a magnificent animal, a first-rate jumper. That would be something for you.'

'How much does he want for it?'

'Fifteen thousand lire, I think.'

'Well, we might see –'

'Leonetto is going to be married directly. He got engaged this summer at Aix-les-Bains.'

'I forgot to tell you,' said Musellaro, 'that Galleazo Secinaro sends you his remembrances. We travelled back from India together. If you only knew of all Galleazo's doughty deeds on the journey! He is at Palermo now, but he will be in Rome in January.'

'And Gino Bomminaco begs to be remembered to you,' added Barbarisi.

'Ah, ha!' exclaimed the duke with a burst of laughter, 'you should get Gino to tell you the story of his adventure with Donna Giulia Moceto. You are, I fancy, in a position to give us some details on the subject of Donna Giulia.'

Ludovico, too, began to laugh.

'Oh, I know,' broke in Musellaro, 'you have made the most tremendous conquests in Rome. *Gratulator tibi!*'[39]

'But tell me – do tell me about this adventure,' asked Andrea with impatient curiosity.

These subjects excited him. Encouraged by his friends, he launched forth into a discourse on female beauty, displaying the profound knowledge and fervour of a connoisseur, taking a pleasure in using the most highly-coloured expressions, with the subtle distinctions of an artist and a libertine. Indeed, had any one taken the trouble to write down the conversation of the four young men within these walls, hung with the voluptuous scenes of the Bacchic tapestries, it might well have formed the *Breviarum arcanum*[40] of upper-class corruption at the end of the nineteenth century.

The shades of evening were falling, but the air was still permeated with light as a sponge absorbs the water. Through the windows, one caught a glimpse of the horizon and a band of orange against which the cypresses of the Monte Mario stood out sharply like the teeth of a great ebony rake. Ever and anon, came the cawing of the rooks, assembling in groups on the roof of the Villa Medici before descending on the Villa Borghese and into the narrow Valley of Sleep.

'What are you going to do this evening?' Barbarisi asked Andrea.

'I really don't know.'

'Well, then, come with us – dinner at eight, at Doney's, to inaugurate his new restaurant at the Teatro Nazionale.'

'Yes, come with us, do come with us!' entreated Giulio Musellaro.

'Besides the three of us,' continued the duke, 'there will be Giulia Arici, Bébé Silva and Maria Fortuna – That reminds me – capital idea! – you bring Clara Green.'

'A capital idea!' echoed Ludovico Barbarisi.

'And where shall I find Clara Green?'

'At the Hotel de l'Europe, close by, in the Piazza di Spagna. A note from you would put her in the seventh heaven. She is certain to give up any other engagement she may have.'

Andrea was quite agreeable to the plan.

'But it would be better if I called on her,' he said. 'She is pretty sure to be in now. Don't you think so, Ruggiero?'

'Well, dress quick and come out with us now.'

Clara Green had just come in. She received Andrea with childish delight. No doubt she would have preferred to dine alone with him, but she accepted the invitation without hesitating, wrote a note to excuse herself from a previous engagement, and sent the key of her box at the theatre to a lady friend. She seemed overjoyed. She told him a string of sentimental stories, and vowed that she had never been able to forget him; holding Andrea's hands in hers while she talked.

'I love you more than words can say, Andrew.'

She was still young. With her pure and regular profile, her pale gold hair parted and knotted very low on her neck, she looked like a beauty in a Keepsake. A certain affectation of aestheticism clung to her since her liaison with the poet-painter Adolphus Jeckyll, a disciple in poetry of Keats, in painting of Holman Hunt; a composer of obscure sonnets, a painter of subjects from the *Vita Nuova*. She had sat to him for a *Sibylla Palmifera* and a *Madonna with the Lily*. She had also sat to Andrea for a study of the head of Isabella in Boccaccio's story.[41] Art therefore had conferred upon her the stamp of nobility. But, at bottom, she possessed no spiritual qualities whatsoever; she even became tiresome in the long-run by reason of that sentimental romanticism so often affected by English *demi-mondaines* which contrasts so strangely with the depravity of their licentiousness.

'Who would have thought that we should ever be together again, Andrew?'

An hour later, Andrea left her and returned to the Palazzo Zuccari by the little flight of steps leading from the Piazza Mignanelli to the Trinità. The murmur of the city floated up the solitary little stairway through the mild air of the October evening. The stars twinkled in a cool pure sky. Down below, at the Palazza Casteldelfino, the shrubs inside the little gate cast vague uncertain shadows in the mysterious light, like marine plants waving at the bottom of an aquarium. From the palace, through a lighted window with red curtains, came the tinkle of a piano. The church bells were ringing. Andrea felt his heart suddenly grow heavy. The recollection of Donna Maria came back to him with a rush, filling him with a dim sense of regret, almost of remorse. What was she doing at this moment? Thinking? Suffering? Deep sadness fell upon him. He felt as if something in the depths of his heart had taken flight – he could not define what it was, but it affected him as some irreparable loss.

He thought of his plan of the morning – an evening of solitude in the rooms to which some day perhaps she might come, an evening sad yet sweet, in company with remembrances and dreams, in company with her spirit, an evening of meditation and self-communings. In truth, he had kept well to his promises! He was on his way to a dinner with friends and *demi-mondaines* and, doubtless, would go home with Clara Green afterwards.

His regret was so poignant, so intolerable, that he dressed with unwonted rapidity, jumped into his brougham and arrived at the hotel before the appointed time. He found Clara ready and waiting, and offered her a drive round the streets of Rome to pass the time till eight o'clock.

They drove throught the Via del Babuino, round the obelisk in the Piazza del Popolo, along the Corso and to the right down the Via della Fontanella di Borghese, returning by the Montecitorio to the Corso which they followed as far as the Piazza di Venezia and so to the Teatro Nazionale. Clara kept up an incessant chatter, bending, every other minute, towards her companion to press a kiss on the corner of his mouth, screening the furtive caress behind a fan of white feathers which gave out a delicate odour of 'white rose'. But Andrea appeared not to hear her, and even her caress only drew from him a slight smile.

'*Che pensi?*' she asked, pronouncing the Italian words with a certain hesitation that was very taking.

'Nothing,' returned Andrea, taking up one of her ungloved hands and examining the rings.

'*Chi lo sa!*' she sighed, throwing a vast amount of expression into these three words, which foreign women pick up at once, because they imagine that they contain all the pensive melancholy of Italian love. '*Chi lo sa!*'[42]

With a sudden change of humour, Andrea kissed her on the ear, slipped an arm round her waist and proceeded to say a host of foolish things to her. The Corso was very lively, the shop windows resplendent, newspaper-vendors yelled, public and private vehicles crossed the path of their carriage; all the stir and animation of Roman evening life was in full swing from the Piazza Colonna to the Piazza di Venezia.

It was ten minutes past eight by the time they reached Doney's. The other guests were already there. Andrea Sperelli greeted the assembled company, and taking Clara Green by the hand –

'This,' he said, 'is Miss Clara Green, *ancilla Domini, Sibylla palmifera, candida puella*,'

'*Ora pro nobis*'[43] replied Musellaro, Barbarisi, and Grimiti in chorus.

The women laughed though they did not understand. Clara smiled, and slipping out of her cloak appeared in a white dress, quite simple and short, with a V-shaped opening back and front, a knot of sea-green ribbon on her left shoulder, and emeralds in her ears, perfectly unabashed by the triple scrutiny of Giulia Arici, Bébé Silva and Maria Fortuna.

Musellaro and Grimiti were old acquaintances; Barbarisi was introduced.

Andrea proceeded – 'Mercedes Silva, nicknamed Bébé – *chica pero guapa*.'[44]

'Maria Fortuna, a veritable *Fortuna publica* for our Rome which has the good fortune to possess her.'[45]

Then, turning to Barbarisi – 'Do us the honour to present us to this lady who is, if I am not mistaken, the divine Giulia Farnese.'

'No – Arici,' Giulia broke in.

'Oh, I beg your pardon, but really, to believe that, I should have to call upon all my powers of credulity and to consult Pinturicchio in the Fifth Room.'

He uttered these absurdities with a grave smile, amusing himself by bewildering and teasing these pretty fools. In the *demi-monde* he adopted a manner and style entirely his own, using grotesque phrases, launching the most ridiculous paradoxes or atrocious impertinences under cover of the ambiguity of his words; and all this in most original language, rich in a thousand different flavours, like a Rabelaisian *olla podrida*,[46] full of strong spices and succulent morsels.

'Pinturicchio,' asked Giulia turning to Barbarisi; 'who's that?'

'Pinturicchio,' exclaimed Andrea, 'oh, a sort of feeble house-painter who once took it into his head to paint your picture on a door in the Pope's apartments. Never mind him – he is dead.'

'Dead? How?'

'In a most appalling manner! His wife's lover was a soldier from Perugia in garrison at Siena – ask Ludovico – he knows all about it, but has never liked to tell you, for fear of hurting your feelings. Allow me to inform you, Bébé, that the Prince of Wales does not begin to smoke till between the second and third courses – never sooner. You are anticipating.'

Bébé Silva had lighted a cigarette and was eating oysters, while she let the smoke curl through her nostrils. She was like a restless schoolboy, a little depraved hermaphrodite; pale and thin, the brightness of her eyes heightened by fever and kohl, with lips that were too red, and short and rather woolly hair that covered her head like an astrachan cap. Fixed tightly in her left eye was a single eyeglass; she wore a high stiff collar, a white necktie, an open waistcoat, a little black coat of masculine cut and a gardenia in her button-hole. She affected the manners of a dandy and spoke in a deep husky voice. And just therein lay the secret of her attraction – in this imprint of vice, of depravity, of abnormality, in her appearance, her attitudes and her words.

1889; translated with some abridgement by Georgina Harding, 1898

JEAN LORRAIN

Funeral Oration (Oraison funèbre)

I have just buried my friend Jacques. We had been friends since childhood; and we were as close at thirty-four as we had been growing up in the little coastal village, scarcely touched by the torpor and numbing calm of the province, and with our eyes fixed on the eternal dream of the shifting horizons of the moaning seas.

Even here, in Paris, I am haunted by the image of the burial in the village graveyard, all the more desolate in the calm, white, winter landscape; this image pursues me like some obsessive nightmare.

Here, as there, the snowflakes descend like a blanket from a low and leaden sky, and my enduring impression is of nothing more sleep-inducing than this graveyard of quilted corpses, swaddled in white, as though buried in swan's-down.

I see the delicate fretwork of the tomb gates and the dark foliage of the evergreen shrubs, their edges outlined by fine frost. The town is close by but there is no sound, either from workshops, or factory bells; all the spaces between buildings, all the shouts and murmurs, are stifled by the layers of snow, extinguished by its slow and gentle fall. It is like the cascade of large petals, immaculate and white on the ink-black sea between the high cliffs, immaculately white against the despair of the gloomy sky.

The ceremony is over, and there is a rush of great winter overcoats, dusted with hoar frost, across the cemetery. At the entrance the family stand in line, dressed in black, bare-headed, shivering, while they shake the hands of each guest, puffed up by the condolences; the very image of self-importance.

Jacques's brother has a sickly pallor, intensified by the sickly colour of the sky; it brings to mind the pale faces of the Napoleon's frozen troops as they suffered atrocities during the retreat from Moscow.

A moiré silk hat, glossy among the shabby head-gear of the locals, signals the presence of a Parisian out of place at this pauper's funeral. I recognise de Saunis, a member at Jacques's club, whose path I already crossed on arrival at the railway station.

I go up to him, and we shake hands.

'Have you come from Paris just to attend the ceremony?' I ask.

'Yes, I have,' he replied, and then, ironically, from the depths of his furs, 'I never take the trouble for a wedding, but for a funeral, always.' After a pause, he continued, 'Poor Armenjean, snuffed out, but he was only thirty-three, wasn't he? What did he die of? Anaemia, perhaps, but more like he was ruined by life – first of all by the parties, and then by ether – that dreadful ether! A pretty habit he acquired from that Suzanne!'

And on that note, the swaggering idiot slips away down a side turning, his back bowed beneath the falling snow, and is off, totally delighted at having spoilt the kindly gesture that brought him here with some silly boulevard gossip: but there are others walking behind us, and he must impress the provincials, and maintain his reputation as a *fin-de-siècle* Parisian!!! to be a kind of Gaudissart[47] figure by speaking ill of the dead, pursuing his stupid trade as a commercial traveller to the grave.

At the gates of the cemetery, there is another surprise. The door of a coupé bangs open, and Madame ****, a relative of Jacques's – a pretty woman in her thirties, who has been more or less, I believe, his mistress – falls into my arms with stifled sobs, and a histrionic and glamorous show of sorrow, set off by her fresh, rosy complexion, blonde hair, and elegant mourning-dress.

'Such a tragedy, my friend.' (She calls me her friend twice, as if she has known me all her life, and it is the end of the world!) 'I knew he was ill, of course, but how could I foresee this? I have come from Rouen this very morning: I did not receive the telegram until yesterday, I had twenty-five people coming to dinner, and it was impossible to put them off: it was an official dinner! After the soirée, I went to pieces. I felt like an actress who had just lost her mother.'

I look into her eyes, which are very beautiful, dark blue and pearly with tears: she is more of an actress than she believes, this pretty relative, for she did not allow her grief to interfere with one of the few balls of winter. Rouen is thirty leagues away from this provincial hole and her black dress suits her very well: she looks like the actress, Madame Réjane.[48]

But Madame pulls me up into her coupé, all the while dabbing at her eyes with a fine lace handkerchief. 'He loved her so much, that girl, he couldn't live without her, and he died for her as she died.' And clasping me nervously, she said in the unmistakable tones of a jealous woman: 'Was she at least pretty, this Suzanne . . . brunette or blonde . . . because, you know, he has died like her, an etheromaniac, poisoned . . .?' In telling her what I knew, the secret drama of Jacques's last years suddenly came clear to me. From the few words I had earlier exchanged with de Saunis, and the conversation I was now having with Madame ****, I began to see a pattern emerge. I saw the disturbing figure of Suzanne Evrard; as a ghoul, or kind of vampire, a phantasmal and tragic being that stands before me a pretty girl, perhaps a little too tall and a little too broad, but with such a shapely figure that she seems like a great, delicious flower, drooping and heavy. I find myself sinisterly dreaming of the peculiar brilliance of her black eyes, the feverish eyes of an etheromaniac, glaring and open against her dull complexion.

Two scenes from the recesses of my memory, which I had hitherto refused to recognise, parade themselves before me, synthesising for me the image of an evil and deadly spirit.

The first occasion was two years ago. It was the night of the Opera Ball, and Jacques, Suzanne, myself, and a motley crew of male and female partygoers, had ended up at the Maison d'Or, until three in the morning . . .

I recall it with the lucidity of a sleepwalker, the remains of the supper, half-finished desserts scattered on the stained tablecloth, the marquise's crystal champagne-glasses still half-full, the women standing before the mirrors, readjusting the hoods of their dominoes upon their foreheads.

Jacques was very drunk, and had fallen asleep, his forehead resting on his crossed his arms on the table. The poor chap was very pale, but he was, nevertheless, very handsome by the light of the flickering candles, which were on the point of burning through to the candlesticks: he was pale, like a corpse, and handsome, but his handsomeness was that of one exhausted by depravity; his thin, red moustache, twisted up at the ends, gave him the look of a swashbuckler.

Suzanne had got up and stood behind him, her full, satin domino making her appear taller than she was. She rested a gloved hand on the sleeper's shoulder in order to rouse him and tell him that it was time to go. 'He's as drunk as a lord!', one of the others giggled; and indeed, Jacques was so drunk that he slumped further forward on the table and made no attempt to get up.

Suzanne took off her gloves then, and laid her bare fingers gently on the nape of his neck, stroking him amorously, and then, scratching him with the tip of her fingernail, she pretended to purr like a cat. Jacques still did not move; desperate times, desperate measures: Suzanne pulled from her domino a gilded bottle stopped with emery, poured some of its contents into a champagne-glass, and brought it to the lips of the sleeper. Jacques awoke with a sudden start. Suzanne, smiling as ever, put the glass into his hand, whereupon he, suddenly sober, drained it, got up, staggering all the while, put on his fur-trimmed coat, and excused himself. Then we left!

The restorative that Suzanne had administered was none other than ether, that ether which never lets go, and which, six months later – by which time she had earned the reputation of an etheromaniac – was the cause of her death! I see her now, standing majestically in her black domino, pouring poison into her lover with one hand, a hideous and tragic mockery of the gesture just made with her other, which had adjusted her green, satin mask: Suzanne was a woman in a dream that night, masked in pale satin, the colour of which matched her sleeves and the ribbons of her domino.

The second scene from my memory is more recent. Suzanne was already dead, and had been for at least ten months. I am with a crowd of partying night-birds that had ended up at Les Halles, at the Soulas or some similar all-night restaurant.

At the counter were market-gardeners, their scarves tied around their heads, drinking punch or hot toddies, talking in raucous, throaty voices. From a spiral staircase draped in green baize came the strains of a waltz picked out by the finger of a drunk.

In the next room, separated from the counter by a partition, an amusing scene was taking place. An angry customer, assisted by a policeman and the owner of the establishment, was pulling at the silk sleeves of a young woman.

This creature, an habitué of the all-night restaurant, had come upon the customer in the booth where he was dining; in order to get rid of the sponger, the man – a wholesaler from the provinces – had rummaged in his breast-pocket, and given her twenty sous. Then, when it came for him to pay his bill, he could not find the money; suddenly sobering up, he realised that he was missing twenty francs, and that instead of giving the girl a franc he must have given her a louis.

Incandescent with rage, the man had immediately rushed down to the room below, where the girl was still to be found, stretched out in a dead sleep on a bench. Now, while she doltishly and stubbornly denied the charge, all the while swearing at the owner and laughing at the policeman, she was being stripped and searched.

I can still see the woman's large frame laid out on the bench, with her bare legs dangling from her faded dress, her bonnet over her ear, and her happy, boozy smile (the search had revealed that she had nothing hidden in her black stockings). I can still see her supposed victim, drunk, with staring eyes and ruffled hair, long strands down over his forehead, his manner desperate but resolute, with a murderous look in his eye. I recall also the shrug of the owner's shoulders as he returned to the counter, and the slouching gait of the policeman as he took up his position once more at the street corner, shrugging like the owner, tired and uncaring.

But that which I remember most of all in the corner of this dive is a very elegant black suit, white cravat, and a sprig of heather in the buttonhole. The man was sat with a bottle of whisky, which he was mixing with ether.

He took a large swig of pure ether, a measure which would have scorched the guts of someone like you and me . . . That etheromaniac, that exhausted night-prowler, that gallivanting party animal, that neurotic who never went to bed before eight o'clock in the morning and never got up until seven in the evening, when the lights came on, that was him, Jacques, my friend from childhood, yesterday's deceased! Four years ago, one of the most celebrated young daddies' boys, had gone from bon viveur to waster . . . What is there to say, he went all out to forget, and he forgot . . .

I saw again the depressed, mute, taciturn figure in the dark corner of Les Halles, his face prematurely aged and sickly, a twenty-nine-year-old man who looked fifty, claimed by ether in the same way as morphine had claimed so many others: Jacques, the lover of that poor Suzanne. Jacques – my friend, Jacques – had become in ten months one of the most charming drunks of our *fin de siècle.*

I find myself now weaving a legend around Jacques's habit, which I would have liked to believe: that he tried to poison the memories of a mistress he worshipped, who had died in the full flush of their relationship, only months into their affair, full of love and sensual intoxication.

But the truth – a sinister and terrifying truth – must be known. Suzanne was an etheromaniac, and they poisoned each other together; killed by her own vice, the woman had bequeathed the same terrible fate to her lover beyond the grave. Jacques had outlived her, but they were complicit in their crime, and so the dead reclaimed the living, and now they are together, forever.

I have just buried my friend Jacques. We had been friends since childhood; and we were as close at thirty-four as we had been growing up in the little coastal village, scarcely touched by the torpor and numbing calm of the province, and with our eyes fixed on the eternal dream of the shifting horizons of the moaning seas.

1891; translated by Jane Desmarais, 2011

KATE CHOPIN

An Egyptian Cigarette

My friend, the Architect, who is something of a traveller, was showing us various curios which he had gathered during a visit to the Orient.

'Here is something for you,' he said, picking up a small box and turning it over in his hand. 'You are a cigarette-smoker; take this home with you. It was given to me in Cairo by a species of fakir, who fancied I had done him a good turn.'

The box was covered with glazed, yellow paper, so skilfully gummed as to appear to be all one piece. It bore no label, no stamp – nothing to indicate its contents.

'How do you know they are cigarettes?' I asked, taking the box and turning it stupidly around as one turns a sealed letter and speculates before opening it.

'I only know what he told me,' replied the Architect, 'but it is easy enough to determine the question of his integrity.' He handed me a sharp, pointed paper-cutter, and with it I opened the lid as carefully as possible.

The box contained six cigarettes, evidently hand-made. The wrappers were of pale-yellow paper, and the tobacco was almost the same colour. It was of finer cut than the Turkish or ordinary Egyptian, and threads of it stuck out at either end.

'Will you try one now, Madam?' asked the Architect, offering to strike a match.

'Not now and not here,' I replied, 'after the coffee, if you will permit me to slip into your smoking-den. Some of the women here detest the odour of cigarettes.'

The smoking-room lay at the end of a short, curved passage. Its appointments were exclusively oriental. A broad, low window opened out upon a balcony that overhung the garden. From the divan upon which I reclined, only the swaying treetops could be seen. The maple leaves glistened in the afternoon sun. Beside the divan was a low stand which contained the complete paraphernalia of a smoker. I was feeling quite comfortable, and congratulated myself upon having escaped for a while the incessant chatter of the women that reached me faintly.

I took a cigarette and lit it, placing the box upon the stand just as the tiny clock, which was there, chimed in silvery strokes the hour of five.

I took one long inspiration of the Egyptian cigarette. The grey-green smoke arose in a small puffy column that spread and broadened, that seemed to fill the room. I could see the maple leaves dimly, as if they were veiled in a shimmer of moonlight. A subtle, disturbing current passed through my whole body and went to my head like the fumes of disturbing wine. I took another deep inhalation of the cigarette.

'Ah! the sand has blistered my cheek! I have lain here all day with my face in the sand. Tonight, when the everlasting stars are burning, I shall drag myself to the river.'

He will never come back.

Thus far I followed him; with flying feet; with stumbling feet; with hands and knees, crawling; and outstretched arms, and here I have fallen in the sand.

The sand has blistered my cheek; it has blistered all my body, and the sun is crushing me with hot torture. There is shade beneath yonder cluster of palms.

I shall stay here in the sand till the hour and the night comes.

I laughed at the oracles and scoffed at the stars when they told that after the rapture of life I would open my arms inviting death, and the waters would envelop me.

Oh! how the sand blisters my cheek! and I have no tears to quench the fire. The river is cool and the night is not far distant.

I turned from the gods and said: 'There is but one; Bardja is my god.' That was when I decked myself with lilies and wove flowers into a garland and held him close in the frail, sweet fetters.

He will never come back. He turned upon his camel as he rode away. He turned and looked at me crouching here and laughed, showing his gleaming white teeth.

Whenever he kissed me and went away he always came back again. Whenever he flamed with fierce anger and left me with stinging words, he always came back. But to-day he neither kissed me nor was he angry. He only said:

'Oh! I am tired of fetters, and kisses, and you. I am going away. You will never see me again. I am going to the great city where men swarm like bees. I am going beyond, where the monster stones are rising heavenward in a monument for the unborn ages. Oh! I am tired. You will see me no more.'

And he rode away on his camel. He smiled and showed his cruel white teeth as he turned to look at me crouching here.

How slow the hours drag! It seems to me that I have lain here for days in the sand, feeding upon despair. Despair is bitter and it nourishes resolve.

I hear the wings of a bird flapping above my head, flying low, in circles.

The sun is gone.

The sand has crept between my lips and teeth and under my parched tongue.

If I raise my head, perhaps I shall see the evening star.

Oh! the pain in my arms and legs! My body is sore and bruised as if broken. Why can I not rise and run as I did this morning? Why must I drag myself thus like a wounded serpent, twisting and writhing?

The river is near at hand. I hear it – I see it – Oh! the sand! Oh! the shine! How cool! how cold!

The water! the water! In my eyes, my ears, my throat! It strangles me! Help! will the gods not help me?

Oh! the sweet rapture of rest! There is music in the Temple. And here is fruit to taste. Bardja came with the music – The moon shines and the breeze is soft – A garland of flowers – let us go into the King's garden and look at the blue lily, Bardja.

The maple leaves looked as if a silvery shimmer enveloped them. The grey-green smoke no longer filled the room. I could hardly lift the lids of my eyes. The weight of centuries seemed to suffocate my soul that struggled to escape, to free itself and breathe.

I had tasted the depths of human despair.

The little clock upon the stand pointed to a quarter past five. The cigarettes still reposed in the yellow box. Only the stub of the one I had smoked remained. I had laid it in the ash tray.

As I looked at the cigarettes in their pale wrappers, I wondered what other visions they might hold for me; what might I not find in their mystic fumes? Perhaps a vision of celestial peace; a dream of hopes fulfilled; a taste of rapture, such as had not entered into my mind to conceive.

I took the cigarettes and crumpled them between my hands. I walked to the window and spread my palms wide. The light breeze caught up the golden threads and bore them writhing and dancing far out among the maple leaves.

My friend, the Architect, lifted the curtain and entered, bringing me a second cup of coffee.

'How pale you are!' he exclaimed, solicitously. 'Are you not feeling well?'

'A little the worse for a dream,' I told him.

1900

RACHILDE

The Grape-Harvest of Sodom (Les Vendanges de Sodome)

To Maurice Maeterlinck

At daybreak the earth was fuming like an infernally musty cellar, and the vineyard at the heart of the vast plain gleamed in the fierce early sunlight whose crimson-fringed heat was already fermenting the huge grapes in which gigantic pips showed like dark eyes bulging from their sockets. As if thrust up from the depths of some abyss of boiling pitch, this vineyard flaunted its wealth of ruddy-golden foliage in monstrous abundance: its straggling branches writhed like molten metal around their grapes, which swarmed over the soft golden clay as the russet earth like a living body exhaled scents of fresh sap mingled with warm pestilential vapours. Unbridled as a prolific animal in the pangs of its multiple births, it sprawled in frightful convulsions, furiously throwing out garlands straining for the sun like the imploring arms of those who seem tormented yet are revelling in heavenly sins. Meanwhile its overheated juices brimmed over, flooding it with a dew heavy as tears. Wantonly it spawned its prodigious dark fruits, smooth and glossy like the dubious offspring of some organic tar in their hints of soot and of devilish sweetness distilled from volcanic turbulence. And from some of the half-rotten grapes, leaking from scarlet labial slits, there oozed an unspeakably sweet liquor which maddened the bees to their deaths.

Between the heavens, so red that they seemed inflamed, and the plain, so yellow as to look dusted with saffron, not a single bird was singing, and nothing was moving; the vineyard was stirred only by a muffled boiling drone of hungry insects. Amidst that forest of golden boughs within the land's crude wine-press (a colossal trough of pure granite hollowed out as if for human sacrifice), could be seen a fabulous lizard, decked in shimmering green scales and with darting eyes of hyacinth-blue, basking impassively, his silvery belly heaving every so often with hard breath: he, too, felt the almost deadly intoxication.

Little by little, the clouds shed their smoky glow and faded to opalescent white as they cleared and dissolved. Then the sun alone dominated the sky whose blue assumed a metallic dazzle and burned silently as it poured down torrents of transparent heat. As far as the eye could see, the land of Judaea spread out, its spindly fig-trees unable to provide the feeblest veil of shade. A few of these stunted trees, with their hairy finger-shaped leaves, were warped as if in protest against their lot, their tangled branches shining with the clear oozings of sap that ringed them like amber bracelets. And saplings bent over by the double fire from above and below stooped limply like innocent men condemned.

At the far horizon, beyond the remotest shrubbery, overlooking the dim outline of a city wall, there loomed a stone tower, ivory-white and bone-pale, a tower that soared giddying towards the deep blue heavens like a path to infinity, and that scattered a circling flock of great white birds seeking atop it a perch.

From that distant tower the men of Sodom set out, making their way to the vineyard.

They were led by an old man of two-hundred years or so, a gloomy giant distinguished by his bald, bony, toothless and crazily lolling head, over which flopped the end of a linen robe. This loose garment clung to his stiff limbs like a shroud. The father, the chieftain and the patriarch, he towered above his retinue of descendants, his head resembling a rectangular star gleaming with lunar brilliance. Having been dumb for countless years, he gave signals with a rod. Beside him crowded his eldest sons, sturdy men with great black beards. One of these, called Horeb, wore a leather belt from which he hung some shining cups which jangled melodiously.

Next came a younger group headed by Phaleg, a near-naked giant with flesh as smooth as pink-veined marble and a rough red beard. He carried on his head a pile of wicker baskets containing wheat cakes.

At a respectful distance behind these pranced the adolescents, clad in short robes and in belts decorated with curious embroidery. They flung their thick blond tresses behind them as women do. The most beautiful among them, a child with lips like purple plums of a shade plucked from mysterious sunsets, was called Sineus. In his innocence he had festooned his tight-fitting goatskin tunic with flowers, so that when he reached the vineyard, the bees forsook the grapes and sought his virginal flesh, buzzing at his shoulders harmlessly: they mistook him for a honeycomb, so blond was he.

Once they had sung a joyous hymn, the grape-pickers began to fill up their baskets. The elders plucked the heaviest grapes at a slow and steady pace, while the youngsters flung themselves about greedily and noisily. After a while, the patriarch, who had seated himself at the edge of the granite trough, stood up and lifted his rod, and everyone crowded round to empty their heaped baskets. Then the old man sat down again, nodded, and the gang returned to work with their baskets emptied. Some of them unwittingly spattered their legs with bright red juice; others knowingly smeared it across their breasts. Sineus threw himself passionately into the task of treading the grapes, mixing in handfuls of wild roses the while. As midday approached they had all become tired, so they lay down to sleep side by side around the feet of their aged patriarch, who stayed seated at the vat's edge. Inflexible in his statuesque posture before all those lusty fellows dripping with wine, he looked like the supreme image of eternal death.

Then, treading stealthily from the nearest grove of fig-trees, there emerged a truly outlandish creature: a woman. She was pale, slender, naked, her limbs covered in a hair so fair and downy that she seemed to be wrapped in fine linen threaded with gold filaments. Her brow stood out against the sky's azure, smooth and flawless as the dazzling blade of a sword. Her hair reached to the ground, sweeping up a few rustling yellowed leaves. Her heels, rounded like peaches, hardly seemed to touch the ground as she skipped along with the carefree gait of an animal. But the twin points of her breasts were fearfully dark, as if scorched to blackness.

She approached the sleeping Sineus, and first ate up all the grapes that he had carelessly left in his basket, devouring them like a wild beast. Then she slid over to him like a serpent and lay down beside him. Soon the boy awoke, sensing that his flesh was in the grip of impure hands. He whimpered as he roused himself and pushed the woman from him, his tearful cries now echoed by all his brothers roaring furiously.

The old man rose up and lifted his rod against the intruder, fixing her in a deathly glare. As they all surrounded the woman, they knew her as one of those seductresses whom the elders of Sodom had cast out of their city. Stern in their righteous wrath, the men of God had resolved to rid themselves of these madwomen, whose insatiable lusts seemed never to abate from dusk until dawn. For several years now, the menfolk had resolutely maintained their own chastity lest the strength they needed at harvest-time be drained into those sinks of debauchery, the girls of Sodom. They had cast out even their own wives and sisters, sparing only the old women and those in childbirth. The rest had been cleared out of the marketplace and swept off the streets, beaten black and blue, their breasts lacerated as all their clothing was ripped from them, and had been chased away as bitches. Driven out into the desert, they had staggered away across the burning sands towards Gomorrha. Many had died in the open, overcome by the furnace-like heat, but some had survived by raiding the vineyards.

Not one of these accursed women, however, had repented her ways: their bodies, still racked by frenzied lust, thrilled to the rays of the sun while the fire of their wombs burned on like the earth's mysterious core. And here was one of those bitches showing her hunger for the male by preying upon a child as tender as she was.

'Who are you?' asked Horeb.

'I am Sarai!'

Sineus hid his face in the crook of his elbow.

'What do you want?' said Phaleg.

'I am thirsty.'

Thirsty, indeed! They all looked at one another until their father grimly lifted up his rod, at which sign each stooped to pick up a stone. The woman, her golden skin glowing like the sun, stretched out her arms like twin rays. In a voice so shrill that they all flinched, she cried out:

'A curse upon you all!'

'Yes, I recognise you now,' said Horeb. 'One night you stole my finest metal cups.'

'So do I,' said Phaleg. 'You tempted me into sin on the Sabbath day.'

'As for me,' groaned Sineus with tears in his eyes, 'I know nothing of you, and never wished to.'

The old man lowered his rod.

'She should be stoned!' they all roared.

The woman had no time to flee. Thirty stones were flung at her. Her breasts were burst to scarlet shreds, her brow wreathed with red lacings. Panting and squirming, her tangled hair snagging on vine-leaves, she shrank and crawled like a grovelling snake, then slid into the vat of fermenting juice. She clutched at the heaps of crushed grapes, then went quite still, flavouring the blood of the grapes with the exquisite wine of her veins. Before her final agonies were even over, the men climbed down into the trough and began to trample her with their feet. But as they did so, those gigantic pips resembling rolling eyes welled up with a look that sealed the supreme curse.

In the evening, their duty righteously fulfilled, the harvesters shared out their wheat cakes and filled up their cups. They had not bothered to recover the corpse, and were all drunk by now, groggier from the killing than from their wine. Hurling blasphemies against the woman, they drank up that horrible love-poisoned liquor. It was on that same night, as a howling of unknown beasts echoed in the distance, as the air thickened with the smell of sulphur, as the huge tower assumed a skeletal pallor in the dreary moonlight, that the Sodomites first perpetrated their sin against nature in the embrace of their young brother Sineus, whose soft shoulders tasted to them of honey.

1900; translated by Chris Baldick, 2011

AUBREY BEARDSLEY

The Story of Venus and Tannhäuser

Chapter I How the Chevalier Tannhäuser entered into the Hill of Venus

The Chevalier Tannhäuser,[49] having lighted off his horse, stood doubtfully for a moment beneath the ombre gateway of the Venusberg, troubled with an exquisite fear lest a day's travel should have too cruelly undone the laboured niceness of his dress. His hand, slim and gracious as La Marquise du Deffand's in the drawing by Carmontelle,[50] played nervously about the gold hair that fell upon his shoulders like a finely-curled peruke, and from point to point of a precise toilet the fingers wandered, quelling the little mutinies of cravat and ruffle.

It was taper-time; when the tired earth puts on its cloak of mists and shadows, when the enchanted woods are stirred with light footfalls and slender voices of the fairies, when all the air is full of delicate influences, and even the beaux, seated at their dressing-tables, dream a little.

A delicious moment, thought Tannhäuser, to slip into exile.

The place where he stood waved drowsily with strange flowers, heavy with perfume, dripping with odours. Gloomy and nameless weeds not to be found in Mentzelius.[51] Huge moths, so richly winged they must have banqueted upon tapestries and royal stuffs, slept on the pillars that flanked either side of the gateway, and the eyes of all the moths remained open, and were burning and bursting with a mesh of veins. The pillars were fashioned in some pale stone, and rose up like hymns in the praise of pleasure, for, from cap to base, each one was carved with loving sculptures, showing such a cunning invention and such a curious knowledge that Tannhäuser lingered not a little in reviewing them. They surpassed all that Japan has ever pictured from her *maisons vertes*,[52] all that was ever painted in the cool bathrooms of Cardinal La Motte, and even outdid the astonishing illustration to Jones's *Nursery Numbers.*

'A pretty portal,' murmured the Chevalier, correcting his sash.

As he spoke, a faint sound of singing was breathed out from the mountain, faint music as strange and distant as sea-legends that are heard in shells.

'The Vespers of Venus, I take it,' said Tannhäuser, and struck a few chords of accompaniment ever so lightly upon his little lute. Softly across the spell-bound threshold the song floated and wreathed itself about the subtle columns till the moths were touched with passion, and moved quaintly in their sleep. One of them was awakened by the intenser notes of the Chevalier's lute strings, and fluttered into the cave. Tannhäuser felt it was his cue for entry.

'Adieu,' he exclaimed, with an inclusive gesture, and 'Goodbye, Madonna' as the cold circle of the moon began to show, beautiful and full of enchantments. There was a shadow of sentiment in his voice as he spoke the words.

'Would to heaven,' he sighed, 'I might receive the assurance of a looking-glass before I make my debut! However, as she is a goddess, I doubt not her eyes are a little sated with perfection, and may not be displeased to see it crowned with a tiny fault.'

A wild rose had caught upon the trimmings of his ruff, and in the first flush of displeasure he would have struck it brusquely away, and most severely punished the offending flower. But the ruffled mood lasted only a moment, for there was something so deliciously incongruous in the hardy petal's invasion of so delicate a thing, that Tannhäuser withheld the finger of resentment, and vowed that the wild rose should stay where it had clung – a passport, as it were, from the upper to the lower world.

'The very excess and violence of the fault,' he said, 'will be its excuse;' and, undoing a tangle in the tassel of his stick, stepped into the shadowy corridor that ran into the bosom of the wan hill, stepped with the admirable aplomb and unwrinkled suavity of Don John.[53]

Chapter II Of the manner in which Venus was coiffed and prepared for supper

Before a toilet that shone like the altar of Nôtre Dame des Victoires, Venus was seated in a little dressing-gown of black and heliotrope. The coiffeur Cosmé was caring for her scented *chevelure*, and with tiny silver tongs, warm from the caresses of the flame, made delicious intelligent curls that fell as lightly as a breath about her forehead and over her eyebrows, and clustered like tendrils round her neck. Her three favourite girls, Pappelarde, Blanchemains, and Loreyne, waited immediately upon her with perfume and powder in delicate *flaçons* and frail cassolettes, and held in porcelain jars the ravishing paints prepared by Chateline for those cheeks and lips that had grown a little pale with anguish of exile. Her three favourite boys, Claude, Clair, and Sarrasine, stood amorously about with salver, fan and napkin. Millamant held a slight tray of slippers, Minette some tender gloves, La Popelinière – mistress of the robes – was ready with a frock of yellow and yellow. La Zambellina bore the jewels, Florizel some flowers, Amadour a box of various pins, and Vadius a box of sweets. Her doves, ever in attendance, walked about the room that was panelled with the gallant paintings of Jean Baptiste Dorat,[54] and some dwarfs and doubtful creatures sat here and there, lolling out their tongues, pinching each other, and behaving oddly enough. Sometimes Venus gave them little smiles.

As the toilet was in progress, Priapusa, the fat manicure and *fardeuse*,[55] strode in and seated herself by the side of the dressing-table, greeting Venus with an intimate nod. She wore a gown of white watered silk with gold lace trimmings, and a velvet necklet of false vermilion. Her hair hung in bandeaux over her ears, passing into a huge chignon at the back of her head, and the hat, wide-brimmed and hung with a valance of pink muslin, was floral with red roses.

Priapusa's voice was full of salacious unction; she had terrible little gestures with the hands, strange movements with the shoulders, a short respiration that made surprising wrinkles in her bodice, a corrupt skin, large horny eyes, a parrot's nose, a small loose mouth, great flaccid cheeks, and chin after chin. She was a wise person, and Venus loved her more than any of her servants, and had a hundred pet names for her, such as, Dear Toad, Pretty Pol, Cock-robin, Dearest Lip, Touchstone, Little Cough-drop, Bijou, Buttons, Dear Heart, Dick-dock, Mrs Manly, Little Nipper, Cochon-de-lait, Naughty-naughty, Blessèd Thing, and Trump.

The talk that passed between Priapusa and her mistress was of that excellent kind that passes between old friends, a perfect understanding giving to scraps of phrases their full meaning, and to the merest reference a point. Naturally Tannhäuser, the newcomer, was discussed a little. Venus had not seen him yet, and asked a score of questions on his account that were delightfully to the point.

Priapusa told the story of his arrival, his curious wandering in the gardens, and calm satisfaction with all he saw there, his impromptu affection for a slender girl upon the first terrace, of the crowd of frocks that gathered round and pelted him with roses, of the graceful way he defended himself with his mask, and of the queer reverence he made to the God of all gardens, kissing that deity with a pilgrim's devotion. Just now Tannhäuser was at the baths, and was creating a favourable impression.

The report and the coiffing were completed at the same moment.

'Cosmé,' said Venus, 'you have been quite sweet and quite brilliant. You have surpassed yourself tonight.'

'Madam flatters me,' replied the antique old thing, with a girlish giggle under his black satin mask. ''Gad, Madam; sometimes I believe I have no talent in the world, but tonight I must confess to a touch of the vain mood.'

It would pain me horribly to tell you about the painting of her face; suffice it that the sorrowful work was accomplished frankly, magnificently, and without a shadow of deception.

Venus slipped away the dressing-gown, and rose before the mirror in a flutter of frilled things. She was adorably tall and slender. Her neck and shoulders were wonderfully drawn, and the little malicious breasts were full of the irritation of loveliness that can never be entirely comprehended, or ever enjoyed to the utmost. Her arms and hands were loosely but delicately articulated, and her legs were divinely long. From the hip to the knee, twenty-two inches; from the knee to the heel, twenty-two inches, as befitted a Goddess.

I should like to speak more particularly about her, for generalities are not of the slightest service in a description. But I am afraid that an enforced silence here and there would leave such numerous gaps in the picture that it had better not be begun at all than left unfinished.

Priapusa grew quite lyric over the dear little person, and pecked at her arms with kisses.

'Dear Tongue, you must really behave yourself,' said Venus, and called Millamant to bring her the slippers.

The tray was freighted with the most exquisite and shapely *pantoufles*, sufficient to make Cluny[56] a place of naught. There were shoes of grey and black and brown suède, of white silk and rose satin, and velvet and sarcenet; there were some of sea-green sewn with cherry blossoms, some of red with willow branches, and some of grey with bright-winged birds. There were heels of silver, of ivory, and of gilt; there were buckles of very precious stones set in most strange and esoteric devices; there were ribands tied and twisted into cunning forms; there were buttons so beautiful that the buttonholes might have no pleasure till they closed upon them; there were soles of delicate leathers scented with maréchale, and linings of soft stuffs scented with the juice of July flowers. But Venus, finding none of them to her mind, called for a discarded pair of blood-red maroquine, diapered with pearls. They looked very distinguished over her white silk stockings.

As the tray was being carried away, the capricious Florizel snatched as usual a slipper from it, and fitted the foot over his penis, and made the necessary movements. That was Florizel's little caprice. Meantime, La Popelinière stepped forward with the frock.

'I shan't wear one tonight,' said Venus. Then she slipped on her gloves.

When the toilet was at an end all her doves clustered round her feet, loving to *frôler* her ankles with their plumes, and the dwarfs clapped their hands, and put their fingers between their lips and whistled. Never before had Venus been so radiant and compelling. Spiridion, in the corner, looked up from his game of Spellicans and trembled. Claude and Clair, pale with pleasure, stroked and touched her with their delicate hands, and wrinkled her stockings with their nervous lips, and smoothed them with their thin fingers; and Sarrasine undid her garters and kissed them inside and put them on again, pressing her thighs with his mouth. The dwarfs grew very daring, I can tell you. There was almost a mêlée. They illustrated pages 72 and 73 of Delvau's Dictionary.[57]

In the middle of it all, Pranzmungel announced that supper was ready upon the fifth terrace. 'Ah!' cried Venus, 'I'm famished!'

Chapter III How Venus supped and thereafter was mightily amused by the curious pranks of her entourage

She was quite delighted with Tannhäuser, and, of course, he sat next her at supper.

The terrace, made beautiful with a thousand vain and fantastical devices, and set with a hundred tables and four hundred couches, presented a truly splendid appearance. In the middle was a huge bronze fountain with three basins. From the first rose a many-breasted dragon, and four little Loves mounted upon swans, and each Love was furnished with a bow and arrow. Two of them that faced the monster seemed to recoil in fear, two that were behind made bold enough to aim their shafts at him. From the verge of the second sprang a circle of slim golden columns that supported silver doves with tails and wings spread out. The third, held by a group of grotesquely attenuated satyrs, was centred with a thin pipe hung with masks and roses, and capped with children's heads.

From the mouths of the dragon and the Loves, from the swans' eyes, from the breasts of the doves, from the satyrs' horns and lips, from the masks at many points, and from the children's curls, the water played profusely, cutting strange arabesques and subtle figures.

The terrace was lit entirely by candles. There were four thousand of them, not numbering those upon the tables. The candlesticks were of a countless variety, and smiled with moulded *cochônneries*.[58] Some were twenty feet high, and bore single candles that flared like fragrant torches over the feast, and guttered till the wax stood round the tops in tall lances. Some, hung with dainty petticoats of shining lustres, had a whole bevy of tapers upon them, devised in circles, in pyramids, in squares, in cuneiforms, in single lines regimentally and in crescents.

Then on quaint pedestals and Terminal Gods and gracious pilasters of every sort, were shell-like vases of excessive fruits and flowers that hung about and burst over the edges and could never be restrained. The orange-trees and myrtles, looped with vermilion sashes, stood in frail porcelain pots, and the rose-trees were wound and twisted with superb invention over trellis and standard. Upon one side of the terrace, a long gilded stage for the comedians was curtained off with Pagonian tapestries, and in front of it the music-stands were placed. The tables arranged between the fountain and the flight of steps to the sixth terrace were all circular, covered with white damask, and strewn with irises, roses, kingcups, colombines, daffodils, carnations and lilies; and the couches, high with soft cushions and spread with more stuffs than could be named, had fans thrown upon them, and little amorous surprise packets.

Beyond the escalier stretched the gardens, which were designed so elaborately and with so much splendour that the architect of the Fêtes d'Armailhacq[59] could have found in them no matter for cavil, and the still lakes strewn with profuse barges full of gay flowers and wax marionettes, the alleys of tall trees, the arcades and cascades, the pavilions, the grottoes, and the garden-gods – all took a strange tinge of revelry from the glare of the light that fell upon them from the feast.

The frockless Venus and Tannhäuser, with Priapusa and Claude and Clair, and Farcy, the chief comedian, sat at the same table. Tannhäuser, who had doffed his travelling suit, wore long black silk stockings, a pair of pretty garters, a very elegant ruffled shirt, slippers and a wonderful dressing gown. Claude and Clair wore nothing at all, delicious privilege of immaturity, and Farcy was in ordinary evening clothes. As for the rest of the company, it boasted some very noticeable dresses, and whole tables of quite delightful coiffures. There were spotted veils that seemed to stain the skin with some exquisite and august disease, fans with eye-slits in them, through which their bearers peeped and peered; fans painted with figures and covered with the sonnets of Sporion and the short stories of Scaramouche; and fans of big living moths stuck upon mounts of silver sticks. There were masks of green velvet that make the face look trebly powdered; masks of the heads of birds, of apes, of serpents, of dolphins, of men and women, of little embryons and of cats; masks like the faces of gods; masks of coloured glass, and masks of thin talc and of india-rubber. There were wigs of black and scarlet wools, of peacocks' feathers, of gold and silver threads, of swansdown, of the tendrils of the vine, and of human hairs; huge collars of stiff muslin rising high above the head; whole dresses of ostrich feathers curling inwards; tunics of panthers' skins that looked beautiful over pink tights; capotes of crimson satin trimmed with the wings of owls; sleeves cut into the shapes of apocryphal animals; drawers flounced down to the ankles, and flecked with tiny, red roses; stockings clocked with *fêtes galantes*,[60] and curious designs; and petticoats cut like artificial flowers. Some of the women had put on delightful little moustaches dyed in purples and bright greens, twisted and waxed with absolute skill; and some wore great white beards after the manner of Saint Wilgeforte.[61] Then Dorat had painted extraordinary grotesques and vignettes over their bodies, here and there. Upon a cheek, an old man scratching his horned head; upon a forehead, an old woman teased by an impudent amor; upon a shoulder, an amorous *singerie*;[62] round a breast, a circlet of satyrs; about a wrist, a wreath of pale, unconscious babes; upon an elbow, a bouquet of spring flowers; across a back, some surprising scenes of adventure; at the corners of a mouth, tiny red spots; and upon a neck, a flight of birds, a caged parrot, a branch of fruit, a butterfly, a spider, a drunken dwarf, or, simply, some initials. But most wonderful of all were the black silhouettes painted upon the legs, and which showed through a white silk stocking like a sumptuous bruise.

The supper provided by the ingenious Rambouillet was quite beyond parallel. Never had he created a more exquisite menu. The consommé impromptu alone would have been sufficient to establish the immortal reputation of any chef. What, then, can I say of the *Dorade bouillie sauce maréchale*, the *ragôut aux langues de carpes*, the *ramereaux à la charnière*, the *ciboulette de gibier à l'espagnole*, the *pâté de cuisses d'oie aux pois de Monsalvie*, the *queues d'agneau au clair de lune*, the *artichauts à la Grecque*, the *charlotte de pommes à la Lucy Waters*, the *bombes à la marée*, and the *glaces aux rayons d'or*? A veritable *tour de cuisine* that surpassed even the famous little suppers given by the Marquis de Réchale at Passy, and which the Abbé Mirliton pronounced 'impeccable, and too good to be eaten'.[63]

Ah! Pierre Antoine Berquin de Rambouillet; you are worthy of your divine mistress!

Mere hunger quickly gave place to those finer instincts of the pure gourmet, and the strange wines, cooled in buckets of snow, unloosed all the *décolleté* spirits of astonishing conversation and atrocious laughter.

Chapter IV How the court of Venus behaved strangely at her supper

At first there was the fun with the surprise packets that contained myriads of amusing things, then a general criticism of the decorations, everyone finding a different meaning in the fall of festoon, turn of twig, and twist of branch. Pulex, as usual, bore the palm for insight and invention, and tonight he was more brilliant than ever. He leant across the table and explained to the young page, Macfils de Martaga, what thing was intended by a certain arrangement of roses. The young page smiled and hummed the refrain of

'La petite balette'. Sporion, too, had delicate perceptions, and was vastly entertained by the disposition of the candelabra.

As the courses advanced, the conversation grew bustling and more personal. Pulex and Cyril and Marisca and Cathelin opened a fire of raillery. The infidelities of Cerise, the difficulties of Brancas, Sarmean's caprices that morning in the lily garden, Thorilliere's declining strength, Astarte's affection for Roseola, Felix's impossible member, Cathelin's passion for Sulpilia's poodle, Sola's passion for herself, the nasty bite that Marisca gave Chloe, the *épilatière*[64] of Pulex, Cyril's diseases, Butor's illness, Maryx's tiny cemetery, Lesbia's profound fourth letter, and a thousand amatory follies of the day were discussed.

From harsh and shrill and clamant, the voices grew blurred and inarticulate. Bad sentences were helped out by worse gestures, and at one table Scabius could only express himself with his napkin, after the manner of Sir Jolly Jumble in the first part of the *Soldier's Fortune* of Otway.[65] Basalissa and Lysistrata tried to pronounce each other's names, and became very affectionate in the attempt; and Tala, the tragedian, robed in roomy purple, and wearing plume and buskin, rose to his feet, and with swaying gestures began to recite one of his favourite parts. He got no further than the first line, but repeated it again and again, with fresh accents and intonations each time, and was only silenced by the approach of the asparagus that was being served by satyrs dressed in white muslin.

Clitor and Sodon had a violent struggle over the beautiful Pella, and nearly upset a chandelier. Sophie became very intimate with an empty champagne bottle, swore it had made her *enceinte*,[66] and ended by having a mock accouchement on the top of the table; and Belamour pretended to be a dog, and pranced from couch to couch on all fours, biting and barking and licking. Mellefont crept about dropping love philtres into glasses. Juventus and Ruella stripped and put on each other's things, Spelto offered a prize for whoever should come first, and Spelto won it! Tannhäuser, just a little *grisé*,[67] lay down on the cushions and let Julia do whatever she liked.

I wish I could be allowed to tell you what occurred round table 15 just at this moment. It would amuse you very much, and would give you a capital idea of the habits of Venus's retinue. Indeed, for deplorable reasons, by far the greater part of what was said and done at this supper must remain unrecorded and even unsuggested.

Venus allowed most of the dishes to pass untasted, she was so engaged with the beauty of Tannhäuser. She laid her head many times on his robe, kissing him passionately; and his skin, at once firm and yielding, seemed to those exquisite little teeth of hers, the most incomparable pasture. Her upper lip curled and trembled with excitement, showing the gums. Tannhäuser, on his side, was no less devoted. He adored her all over and all the things she had on, and buried his face in the folds and flounces of her linen, and ravished away a score of frills in his excess. He found her exasperating, and crushed her in his arms, and slaked his parched lips at her mouth. He caressed her eyelids softly with his finger tips, and pushed aside the curls from her forehead, and did a thousand gracious things, tuning her body as a violinist tunes his instrument before he plays upon it.

Priapusa snorted like an old war horse at the sniff of powder, and tickled Tannhäuser and Venus by turns, and slipped her tongue down their throats, and refused to be quiet at all until she had had a mouthful of the Chevalier. Claude, seizing his chance, dived under the table and came up on the other side just under the queen's couch, and before she could say 'One!' he was taking his coffee *aux deux colonnes*.[68] Clair was furious at his friend's success, and sulked for the rest of the evening.

Chapter V Of the ballet danced by the servants of Venus

After the fruits and fresh wines had been brought in by a troop of woodland creatures, decked with green leaves and all sorts of Spring flowers, the candles in the orchestra were lit, and in another moment the musicians bustled into their places. The wonderful Titurel de Schentefleur was the *chef d'orchestre*, and the most insidious of conductors. His bâton dived into a phrase and brought out the most magical and magnificent things, and seemed rather to play every instrument than to lead it. He could add a grace even to Scarlatti and a wonder to Beethoven. A delicate, thin, little man with thick lips and a *nez retroussé*, with long black hair and curled moustache, in the manner of Molière. What were his amatory tastes, no one in the Venusberg could tell. He generally passed for a virgin, and Cathos had nicknamed him 'The Solitaire'.

Tonight he appeared in a court suit of white silk, brilliant with decorations. His hair was curled in resplendent ringlets that trembled like springs at the merest gesture of his arm, and in his ears swung the diamonds given him by Venus.

The orchestra was, as usual, in its uniform of red vest and breeches trimmed with gold lace, white stockings and red shoes. Titurel had written a ballet for the evening *divertissement*, founded upon De Bergerac's comedy of *Les Bacchanales de Sporion*,[69] in which the action and dances were designed by him as well as the music.

I

The curtain rose upon a scene of rare beauty, a remote Arcadian valley, a delicious scrap of Tempe, gracious with cool woods and watered with a little river. It was early morning, and the re-arisen sun, like the prince in the 'Sleeping Beauty', woke all the earth with his lips. In that golden embrace the night dews were caught up and made splendid, the trees were awakened from their obscure dreams, the slumber of the birds was broken, and all the flowers of the valley rejoiced, forgetting their fear of the darkness.

Suddenly, to the music of pipe and horn, a troop of satyrs stepped out from the recesses of the woods, bearing in their hands nuts and green boughs and flowers and roots and whatsoever the forest yielded, to heap upon the altar of the mysterious Pan that stood in the middle of the stage; and from the hills came down the shepherds and shepherdesses, leading their flocks and carrying garlands upon their crooks. Then a rustic priest, white-robed and venerable, came slowly across the valley followed by a choir of radiant children.

The scene was admirably stage-managed, and nothing could have been more varied yet harmonious than this Arcadian group. The service was quaint and simple, but with sufficient ritual to give the *corps-de-ballet* an opportunity of showing its dainty skill. The dancing of the satyrs was received with huge favour, and when the priest raised his hand in final blessing, the whole troop of worshippers made such an intricate and elegant exit that it was generally agreed that Titurel had never before shown so fine an invention.

Scarcely had the stage been empty for a moment, when Sporion entered, followed by a brilliant rout of dandies and smart women. Sporion was a tall, slim, depraved young man with a slight stoop, a troubled walk, an oval impassable face, with its olive skin drawn tightly over the bone, strong scarlet lips, long Japanese eyes, and a great gilt toupet. Round his shoulders hung a high-collared satin cape of salmon pink, with long black ribands untied and floating about his body. His coat of sea-green spotted muslin was caught in at the waist by a scarlet sash with scalloped edges, and frilled out over the hips for about six inches. His trousers, loose and wrinkled, reached to the end of the calf, and were brocaded down the sides, and ruched magnificently at the ankles. The stockings were of white kid, with stalls for the toes, and had delicate red sandals strapped over them. But his little hands, peeping out from their frills, seemed quite the most insinuating things, such supple fingers tapering to the point, with tiny nails stained pink, such unquenchable palms, lined and mounted like Lord Fanny's in *Love at all Hazards*,[70] and such blue-veined, hairless backs! In his left hand he carried a small lace handkerchief broidered with a coronet.

As for his friends and followers, they made the most superb and insolent crowd imaginable, but to catalogue the clothes they had on would require a chapter as long as the famous tenth in Pénillière's history of underlinen.[71] On the whole they looked a very distinguished chorus.

Sporion stepped forward and explained with swift and various gesture that he and his friends were tired of the amusements, wearied with the poor pleasures offered by the civil world, and had invaded the Arcadian valley hoping to experience a new frisson in the destruction of some shepherd's or some satyr's naïveté, and the infusion of their venom among the dwellers of the woods.

The chorus assented with languid but expressive movements.

Curious, and not a little frightened at the arrival of the worldly company, the sylvans began to peep nervously at those subtle souls through the branches of the trees, and one or two fauns and a shepherd or so crept out warily. Sporion and all the ladies and gentlemen made enticing sounds and invited the rustic creatures with all the grace in the world to come and join them. By little batches they came, lured by the strange looks, by the scents and the doings, and by the brilliant clothes, and some ventured quite near, timorously fingering the delicious textures of the stuffs. Then Sporion and each of his friends took a satyr or a shepherdess or something by the hand, and made the preliminary steps of a courtly measure, for which the most admirable combinations had been invented, and the most charming music written.

The pastoral folk were entirely bewildered when they saw such restrained and graceful movements, and made the most grotesque and futile efforts to imitate them. *Dio mio*, a pretty sight! A charming effect too was obtained by the intermixture of stockinged calf and hairy leg, of rich brocaded bodice and plain blouse, of tortured head-dress and loose untutored locks. When the dance was ended, the servants of Sporion brought on champagne, and, with many pirouettes, poured it magnificently into slender glasses, and tripped about plying those Arcadian mouths that had never before tasted such a royal drink.

* * *

Then the curtain fell with a pudic rapidity.

II

'Twas not long before the invaders began to enjoy the first fruits of their expedition, plucking them in the most seductive manner with their smooth fingers, and feasting lip and tongue and tooth, whilst the shepherds and satyrs and shepherdesses fairly gasped under the new joys, for the pleasure they experienced was almost too keen for their simple and untilled natures. Sporion and the rest of the rips and ladies tingled with excitement and frolicked like young lambs in a fresh meadow. Again and again the wine was danced round, and the valley grew as busy as a market day. Attracted by the noise and the merrymaking, all those sweet infants I told you of skipped suddenly on to the stage, and began clapping their hands and laughing immoderately at the passion and disorder and commotion, and mimicking the nervous staccato movements they saw in their pretty childish way.

In a flash, Sporion disentangled himself and sprang to his feet, gesticulating as if he would say, 'Ah, the little dears!' 'Ah, the rorty[72] little things!' 'Ah, the little ducks!' for he was so fond of children. Scarcely had he caught one by the thigh than a quick rush was made by everybody for the succulent limbs; and how they tousled them and mousled them! The children cried out, I can tell you. Of course there were not enough for everybody, so some had to share, and some had simply to go on with what they were doing before.

I must not, by the way, forget to mention the independent attitude taken by six or seven of the party, who sat and stood about with half-closed eyes, inflated nostrils, clenched teeth, and painful, parted lips, behaving like the Duc de Broglio when he watched the amours of the Regent d'Orleans.[73]

Now as Sporion and his friends began to grow tired and exhausted with the new debauch, they cared no longer to take the initiative, but, relaxing every muscle, abandoned themselves to passive joys, yielding utterly to the ardent embraces of the intoxicated satyrs, who waxed fast and furious, and seemed as if they would never come to the end of their strength. Full of the new tricks they had learnt that morning, they played them passionately and roughly, making havoc of the cultured flesh, and tearing the splendid frocks and dresses into ribands. Duchesses and Maréchales, Marquises and Princesses, Dukes and Marshalls, Marquesses and Princes, were ravished and stretched and rumpled and crushed beneath the interminable vigour and hairy breasts of the inflamed woodlanders. They bit at the white thighs and nozzled wildly in the crevices. They sat astride the women's chests and consummated frantically with their bosoms; they caught their prey by the hips and held it over their heads, irrumating with prodigious gusto. It was the triumph of the valley.

High up in the heavens the sun had mounted and filled all the air with generous warmth, whilst shadows grew shorter and sharper. Little light-winged papillons flitted across the stage, the bees made music on their flowery way, the birds were very gay and kept up a jargoning and refraining, the lambs were bleating upon the hillside, and the orchestra kept playing, playing the uncanny tunes of Titurel.

Chapter VI Of the amorous encounter which took place between Venus and Tannhäuser

Venus and Tannhäuser had retired to the exquisite little boudoir or pavilion Le Con had designed for the queen on the first terrace, and which commanded the most delicious view of the parks and gardens. It was a sweet little place, all silk curtains and soft cushions. There were eight sides to it, bright with mirrors and candelabra, and rich with pictured panels, and the ceiling, dome-shaped and some thirty feet above the head, shone obscurely with gilt mouldings through the warm haze of candle light below. Tiny wax statuettes dressed theatrically and smiling with plump cheeks, quaint magots that looked as cruel as foreign gods, gilded monticules, pale celadon vases, clocks that said nothing, ivory boxes full of secrets, china figurines playing whole scenes of plays, and a world of strange preciousness crowded the curious cabinets that stood against the walls. On one side of the room there were six perfect little card tables, with quite the daintiest and most elegant chairs set primly round them; so, after all, there may be some truth in that line of Mr Theodore Watts –

'I played at picquet with the Queen of Love'.[74]

Nothing in the pavilion was more beautiful than the folding screens painted by De La Pine, with Claudian landscapes – the sort of things that fairly make one melt, things one can lie and look at for hours together, and forget that the country can ever be dull and tiresome. There were four of them, delicate walls that hem in an amour so cosily, and make room within room.

The place was scented with huge branches of red roses, and with a faint amatory perfume breathed out from the couches and cushions – a perfume Chateline distilled in secret and called L'Eau Lavante.

Those who have only seen Venus at the Louvre or the British Museum, at Florence, at Naples, or at Rome, can not have the faintest idea how sweet and enticing and gracious, how really exquisitely she looked lying with Tannhäuser upon rose silk in that pretty boudoir.

Cosmé's precise curls and artful waves had been finally disarranged at supper, and strayed ringlets of black hair fell loosely over Venus's soft, delicious, tired, swollen eyelids. Her frail chemise and dear little drawers were torn and moist, and clung transparently about her, and all her body was nervous and responsive. Her closed thighs seemed like a vast replica of the little bijou she held between them; the beautiful *tétons du derrière*[75] were as firm as a plump virgin's cheek, and promised a joy as profound as the mystery of the Rue Vendôme,[76] and the minor chevelure, just profuse enough, curled as prettily as the hair upon a cherub's head.

Tannhäuser, pale and speechless with excitement, passed his gem-girt fingers brutally over the divine limbs, tearing away smock and pantalon and stocking, and then, stripping himself of his own few things, fell upon the splendid lady with a deep-drawn breath.

It is, I know, the custom of all romancers to paint heroes who can give a lady proof of their valliance at least twenty times a night. Now Tannhäuser had no such Gargantuan facility, and was rather relieved when, an hour later, Priapusa and Doricourt and some others burst into the room and claimed Venus for themselves. The pavilion soon filled with a noisy crowd that could scarcely keep its feet. Several of the actors were there, and Lesfesses, who had played Sporion so brilliantly, and was still in his make-up, paid tremendous attention to Tannhäuser. But the Chevalier found him quite uninteresting off the stage, and rose and crossed the room to where Venus and the manicure were seated.

'How tired the poor baby looks,' said Priapusa. 'Shall I put him in his little cot?'

'Well, if he's as sleepy as I am,' yawned Venus, 'you can't do better'.

Priapusa lifted her mistress off the pillows, and carried her in her arms in a nice, motherly way.

'Come along, children,' said the fat old thing, 'come along; it's time you were both in bed.'

Chapter VII How Tannhäuser awakened and took his morning ablutions in the Venusberg

It is always delightful to wake up in a new bedroom. The fresh wallpaper, the strange pictures, the positions of doors and windows – imperfectly grasped the night before – are revealed with all the charm of surprise when we open our eyes the next morning.

It was about eight o'clock when Tannhäuser awoke, stretched himself deliciously in his great plumed four-post bed, murmured 'What a pretty room!' and freshened the frilled silk pillows behind him. He lay back in his bed and nursed his waking thoughts, and stared at the curious patterned canopy above him. He was very pleased with the room, which certainly was chic and fascinating, and recalled the voluptuous interiors of the elegant amorous Baudouin.[77]

He thought of the *Romaunt de la Rose*,[78] beautiful, but all too brief.

Of the Claude in Lady Delaware's collection.[79]

Of a wonderful pair of blonde trousers he would get Madame Belleville to make for him.

Of Saint Rose, the well-known Peruvian virgin;[80] how she vowed herself to perpetual virginity when she was four years old; how she was beloved by Mary, who, from the pale fresco in the Church of Saint Dominic, would stretch out her arms to embrace her; how she built a little oratory at the end of the garden and prayed and sang hymns in it till all the beetles, spiders, snails and creeping things came round to listen; how she promised to marry Ferdinand de Flores, and on the bridal morning perfumed herself and painted her lips, and put on her wedding frock, and decked her hair with roses, and went up to a little hill not far without the walls of Lima; how she knelt there some moments calling tenderly upon Our Lady's name, and how Saint Mary descended and kissed Rose upon the forehead and carried her swiftly to heaven.

He thought of the splendid opening of Racine's *Britannicus*.

Of a strange pamphlet he had found in Venus's library, called 'A Plea for the Domestication of the Unicorn'.

Of the Bacchanals of Sporion.

Of love, and of a hundred other things.

Through the slim parting of the long, flowered window curtains, he caught a peep of the sun-lit lawns outside, the silver fountains, the bright flowers, the gardeners at work, and beneath the shady trees some early breakfasters, dressed for a day's hunting in the distant wooded valleys.

'How sweet it all is,' exclaimed the Chevalier, yawning with infinite content; 'and what delightful pictures,' he continued, wandering with his eyes from print to print that hung upon the rose-striped walls. Within the delicate curved frames lived the corrupt and gracious creatures of Dorat and his school; slim children in masque and domino, smiling horribly, exquisite letchers leaning over the shoulders of smooth doll-like girls and doing nothing in particular, terrible little Pierrots posing as mulierasts,[81] or pointing at something outside the picture, and unearthly fops and huge birdlike women mingling in some rococo room lighted mysteriously by the flicker of a dying fire that throws great shadows upon wall and ceiling. One of the prints showing how an old marquis practised the five-finger exercise, while in front of him his mistress offered her warm *fesses* to a panting poodle, made the Chevalier stroke himself a little.

Tannhäuser had taken some books to bed with him. One was the witty, extravagant *Tuesday and Josephine,* another was the score of *The Rheingold.*[82] Making a pulpit of his knees, he propped up the opera before him and turned over the pages with a loving hand, and found it delicious to attack Wagner's brilliant comedy with the cool head of the morning.

Once more he was ravished with the beauty and wit of the opening scene; the mystery of its prelude that seems to come up from the very mud of the Rhine, and to be as ancient, the abominable primitive wantonness of the music, the talk and movements of the Rhine-maidens, the black, hateful sounds in Alberich's love-making, and the flowing melody of the river of legends.

But it was the third tableau that he applauded most that morning; the scene where Loge, like some flamboyant primeval Scapin, practises his cunning upon Alberich. The feverish insistent ringing of the hammers at the forge, the dry staccato restlessness of Mime; the ceaseless coming and going of the troupe of Nibelungs, drawn hither and thither like a flock of terror-stricken and infernal sheep; Alberich's savage activity and metamorphoses; and Loge's rapid, flaming, tongue-like movements, make the tableau the least reposeful, most troubled and confusing thing in the whole range of opera. How the Chevalier rejoiced in the extravagant monstrous poetry, the heated melodrama, and splendid agitation of it all!

At eleven o'clock Tannhäuser got up and slipped off his dainty nightdress, and postured elegantly before a long mirror, making much of himself.

Now he would bend forward, now lie upon the floor, now stand upright, and now rest upon one leg and let the other hang loosely till he looked as if he might have been drawn by some early Italian master. Anon he would lie upon the floor with his back to the glass, and glance amorously over his shoulder. Then with a white silk sash he draped himself in a hundred charming ways. So engrossed was he with his mirrored shape that he had not noticed the entrance of a troop of serving boys, who stood admiringly but respectfully at a distance, ready to receive his waking orders. As soon as the Chevalier observed them he smiled sweetly, and bade them prepare his bath.

The bathroom was the largest and perhaps the most beautiful apartment in his splendid suite. The well-known engraving by Lorette that forms the frontispiece to Millevoye's *Architecture du XVIIIme siècle*,[83] will give you a better idea than any words of mine of the construction and decoration of the room. Only, in Lorette's engraving, the bath sunk into the middle of the floor is a little too small.

Tannhäuser stood for a moment, like Narcissus, gazing at his reflection in the still, scented water and then just ruffling its smooth surface with one foot, stepped elegantly into the cool basin, and swam round it twice, very gracefully.

'Won't you join me?' he said, turning to those beautiful boys who stood ready with warm towels and perfume. In a moment they were free of their light morning dress, and jumped into the water and joined hands, and surrounded the Chevalier with a laughing chain.

'Splash me a little,' he cried, and the boys teased him with water and quite excited him. He chased the prettiest of them and bit his *fesses*,[84] and kissed him upon the perineum till the dear fellow banded like a carmelite, and its little bald top-knot looked like a great pink pearl under the water. As the boy seemed anxious to take up the active attitude, Tannhäuser graciously descended to the passive – a generous trait that won him the complete affections of his *valets de bain*, or pretty fish, as he called them, because they loved to swim between his legs.

However, it is not so much at the very bath itself, as in the drying and delicious frictions that the bather finds his chiefest pleasures. Venus had appointed her most tried attendants to wait upon Tannhäuser, and he was more than satisfied with the skill that they displayed in the performance of those quasi-amorous functions. The delicate attention they paid his loving parts aroused feelings within him that almost amounted to gratitude; and when the rites were ended, any touch of home-sickness he might have felt was utterly dispelled.

After he had rested a little, and sipped his chocolate, he wandered into the dressing-room. Daucourt, his *valet de chambre*, Chenille, the perruquier and barber, and two charming young dressers, were awaiting him and ready with suggestions for the morning toilet. The shaving over, Daucourt commanded his underlings to step forward with the suite of suits from which he proposed Tannhäuser should make a choice. The final selection was a happy one. A dear little coat of pigeon-rose silk that hung loosely about his hips, and showed off the jut of his behind to perfection; trousers of black lace in flounces, falling – almost like a petticoat – as far as the knee; and a delicate chemise of white muslin, spangled with gold and profusely pleated.

The two dressers, under Daucourt's direction, did their work superbly, beautifully, leisurely, with an exquisite deference for the nude, and a really sensitive appreciation of the Chevalier's scrumptious torso.

Chapter VIII Of the ecstasy of Adolphe, and the remarkable manifestation thereof

As pleased as Lord Foppington[85] with his appearance, the Chevalier tripped off to bid good-morning to Venus. He found her wandering, in a sweet muslin frock, upon the lawn outside, and plucking flowers to deck her little *déjeuner*. He kissed her lightly upon the neck.

'I'm just going to feed Adolphe,' she said, pointing to a little reticule of buns that hung from her arm. Adolphe was her pet unicorn. 'He is such a dear,' she continued; 'milk-white all over, excepting his black eyes, rose mouth and nostrils, and scarlet John. This way.' The unicorn had a very pretty palace of its own, made of green foliage and golden bars – a fitting home for such a delicate and dainty beast. Ah, it was a splendid thing to watch the white creature roaming in its artful cage, proud and beautiful, knowing no mate and coming to no hand except the Queen's itself.

As Venus and Tannhäuser approached the wicket, Adolphe began prancing and curvetting, pawing the soft turf with his ivory hoofs and flaunting his tail like a gonfalon. Venus raised the latch and entered.

'You mustn't come in with me, Adolphe is so jealous,' she said, turning to the Chevalier who was following her, 'but you can stand outside and look on; Adolphe likes an audience.' Then in her delicious fingers she broke the spicy buns, and with affectionate niceness, breakfasted her ardent pet. When the last crumbs had been scattered, Venus brushed her hands together and pretended to leave the cage, without taking any further notice of Adolphe. Every morning she went through this piece of play, and every morning the amorous unicorn was cheated into a distressing agony lest that day should have proved the last of Venus's love. Not for long, though, would she leave him in that doubtful, piteous state, but running back passionately to where he stood, make adorable amends for her unkindness.

Poor Adolphe! How happy he was, touching the Queen's breasts with his quick tongue-tip. I have no doubt that the keener scent of animals must make women much more attractive to them than to men; for the gorgeous odour that but faintly fills our nostrils must be revealed to the brute creation in divine fullness. Anyhow, Adolphe sniffed as never a man did around the skirts of Venus. After the first charming interchange of affectionate delicacies was over, the unicorn lay down upon his side, and, closing his eyes, beat his stomach wildly with the mark of manhood!

Venus caught that stunning member in her hands and laid her cheek along it; but few touches were wanted to consummate the creature's pleasure. The Queen bared her left arm to the elbow, and with the soft underneath of it made amazing movements horizontally upon the tightly-strung instrument. When the melody began to flow, the unicorn offered up an astonishing vocal accompaniment. Tannhäuser was amused to learn that the etiquette of the Venusberg compelled everybody to await the outburst of these venereal sounds before they could sit down to *déjeuner.*

Adolphe had been quite profuse that morning.

Venus knelt where it had fallen, and lapped her little apéritif.

Chapter IX How Venus and Tannhäuser breakfasted and then drove through the palace gardens

The breakfasters were scattered over the gardens in têtes-à-tête and tiny parties. Venus and Tannhäuser sat together upon the lawn that lay in front of the Casino, and made havoc of a ravishing *déjeuner*. The Chevalier was feeling very happy. Everything around him seemed so white and light and matinal; the floating frocks of the ladies, the scarce-robed boys and satyrs stepping hither and thither elegantly, with meats and wines and fruits; the damask tablecloths, the delicate talk and laughter that rose everywhere; the flowers' colour and the flowers' scent; the shady trees, the wind's cool voice, and the sky above that was as fresh and pastoral as a perfect sixth. And Venus looked so beautiful. Not at all like the lady in Lemprière.[86]

'You're such a dear!' murmured Tannhäuser, holding her hand.

At the further end of the lawn, and a little hidden by a rose-tree, a young man was breakfasting alone. He toyed nervously with his food now and then, but for the most part leant back in his chair with unemployed hands, and gazed stupidly at Venus.

'That's Felix', said the Goddess, in answer to an enquiry from the Chevalier; and she went on to explain his attitude. Felix always attended Venus upon her little latrinal excursions, holding her, serving her, and making much of all she did. To undo her things, lift her skirts, to wait and watch the coming, to dip a lip or finger in the royal output, to stain himself deliciously with it, to lie beneath her as the favours fell, to carry off the crumpled, crotted paper – these were the pleasures of that young man's life.

Truly there never was a queen so beloved by her subjects as Venus. Everything she wore had its lover. Heavens! how her handkerchiefs were filched, her stockings stolen! Daily, what intrigues, what countless ruses to possess her merest frippery! Every scrap of her body was adored. Never, for Savaral, could her ear yield sufficient wax! Never, for Pradon, could she spit prodigally enough! And Saphius found a month an interminable time.

After breakfast was over, and Felix's fears lest Tannhäuser should have robbed him of his capricious rights had been dispelled, Venus invited the Chevalier to take a more extensive view of the gardens, parks, pavilions, and ornamental waters. The carriage was ordered. It was a delicate, shell-like affair, with billowy cushions and a light canopy, and was drawn by ten satyrs, dressed as finely as the coachmen of the Empress Pauline the First.

The drive proved interesting and various, and Tannhäuser was quite delighted with almost everything he saw.

And who is not pleased when on either side of him rich lawns are spread with lovely frocks and white limbs – and upon flowerbeds the dearest ladies are implicated in a glory of underclothing; when he can see, in the deep cool shadow of the trees, warm boys entwined, here at the base, there at the branch – when in the fountain's wave Love holds his court, and the insistent water burrows in every delicious crease and crevice?

A pretty sight, too, was little Rosalie, perched like a postilion upon the painted phallus of the god of all gardens. Her eyes were closed and she was smiling as the carriage passed. Round her neck and slender girlish shoulders there was a cloud of complex dress, over which bulged her wig-like flaxen tresses. Her legs and feet were bare, and the toes twisted in an amorous style. At the foot of the statue lay her shoes and stockings and a few other things.

Tannhäuser was singularly moved at this spectacle, and rose out of all proportion. Venus slipped the fingers of comfort under the lace flounces of his trousers, saying, 'Is it all mine? Is it all mine?' and doing fascinating things. In the end, the carriage was only prevented from being overturned by the happy intervention of Priapusa, who stepped out from somewhere or other just in time to preserve its balance.

How the old lady's eye glistened as Tannhäuser withdrew his panting blade! In her sincere admiration for fine things, she quite forgot and forgave the shock she had received from the falling of the gay equipage. Venus and Tannhäuser were profuse with apology and thanks, and quite a crowd of loving courtiers gathered round, consoling and congratulating in a breath.

The Chevalier vowed he never would go in the carriage again, and was really quite upset about it. However, after he had had a little support from the smelling-salts, he recovered his self-possession, and consented to drive on further.

The landscape grew rather mysterious. The park, no longer troubled and adorned with figures, was full of grey echoes and mysterious sounds; the leaves whispered a little sadly, and there was a grotto that murmured like a voice haunting the silence of a deserted oracle. Tannhäuser became a little *triste*. In the distance, through the trees, gleamed a still, argent lake

– a reticent, romantic water that must have held the subtlest fish that ever were. Around its marge the trees and flags and *fleurs de luce* were unbreakably asleep.

The Chevalier fell into a strange mood, as he looked at the lake. It seemed to him that the thing would speak, reveal some curious secret, say some beautiful word, if he should dare wrinkle its pale face with a pebble.

'I should be frightened to do that, though,' he said to himself. Then he wondered what might be upon the other side; other gardens, other gods? A thousand drowsy fancies passed through his brain. Sometimes the lake took fantastic shapes, or grew to twenty times its size, or shrunk into a miniature of itself, without ever once losing its unruffled calm, its deathly reserve. When the water increased, the Chevalier was very frightened, for he thought how huge the frogs must have become. He thought of their big eyes and monstrous wet feet, but when the water lessened, he laughed to himself, whilst thinking how tiny the frogs must have grown. He thought of their legs that must look thinner than spiders', and of their dwindled croaking that never could be heard. Perhaps the lake was only painted, after all. He had seen things like it at the theatre. Anyway, it was a wonderful lake, a beautiful lake, and he would love to bathe in it, but he was sure he would be drowned if he did.

Chapter X Of the Stabat Mater, Spiridion and de la Pine

When he woke up from his day-dream, he noticed that the carriage was on its way back to the palace. They stopped at the Casino first, and stepped out to join the players at *petits chevaux*.[87] Tannhäuser preferred to watch the game rather than play himself, and stood behind Venus, who slipped into a vacant chair and cast gold pieces upon lucky numbers. The first thing that Tannhäuser noticed was the grace and charm, the gaiety and beauty of the croupiers. They were quite adorable even when they raked in one's little losings. Dressed in black silk, and wearing white kid gloves, loose yellow wigs and feathered toques, with faces oval and young, bodies lithe and quick, voices silvery and affectionate, they made amends for all the hateful arrogance, disgusting aplomb, and shameful ugliness of the rest of their kind.

The dear fellow who proclaimed the winner was really quite delightful. He took a passionate interest in the horses, and had licked all the paint off their *petits couillons*![88] You will ask me, no doubt, 'Is that all he did?' I will answer, 'Not quite,' as the merest glance at their *petits derrières* would prove.

In the afternoon light that came through the great silken-blinded windows of the Casino, all the gilded decorations, all the chandeliers, the mirrors, the polished floor, the painted ceiling, the horses galloping round their green meadow, the fat rouleaux of gold and silver, the ivory rakes, the fanned and strange-frocked crowd of dandy gamesters looked magnificently rich and warm. Tea was being served. It was so pretty to see some plush little lady sipping nervously, and keeping her eyes over the cup's edge intently upon the slackening horses.

The more indifferent left the tables and took their tea in parties here and there.

Tannhäuser found a great deal to amuse him at the Casino. Ponchon was the manager, and a person of extraordinary invention. Never a day but he was ready for a new show – a novel attraction. A glance through the old Casino programmes would give you a very considerable idea of his talent. What countless ballets, comedies, comedy-ballets, concerts, masques, charades, proverbs, pantomimes, *tableaux-magiques*, and peep-shows excentriques; what troupes of marionettes, what burlesques!

Ponchon had an astonishing flair for new talent, and many of the principal comedians and singers at the Queen's Theatre and Opera House had made their first appearance and reputation at the Casino.

This afternoon the *pièce de résistance* was a performance of Rossini's *Stabat Mater*,[89] an adorable masterpiece. It was given in the beautiful Salle des Printemps Parfumés. Ah! what a stunning rendering of the delicious *démodée pièce de décadence*. There is a subtle quality about the music, like the unhealthy bloom upon wax fruit, that both orchestra and singer contrived to emphasise with consummate delicacy.

The Virgin was sung by Spiridion, that soft incomparable alto. A miraculous virgin, too, he made of her. To begin with, he dressed the role most effectively. His plump legs up to the feminine hips of him, were in very white stockings, clocked with a false pink. He wore brown kid boots, buttoned to mid-calf, and his whorish thighs had thin scarlet garters round them. His jacket was cut like a jockey's, only the sleeves ended in manifold frills; and round the neck, and just upon the shoulders there was a black cape. His hair, dyed green, was curled into ringlets, such as the smooth Madonnas of Morales[90] are made lovely with, and fell over his high egg-shaped creamy forehead, and about his ears and cheeks and back.

The alto's face was fearful and wonderful – a dream face. The eyes were full and black, with puffy blue-rimmed hemispheres beneath them, the cheeks, inclining to fatness, were powdered and dimpled, the mouth was purple and curved painfully, the chin tiny, and exquisitely modelled, the expression cruel and womanish. Heavens! how splendid he looked and sounded.

An exquisite piece of phrasing was accompanied with some curly gesture of the hand, some delightful undulation of the stomach, some nervous movement of the thigh, or glorious rising of the bosom.

The performance provoked enthusiasm – thunders of applause. Claude and Clair pelted the thing with roses, and carried him off in triumph to the tables. His costume was declared ravishing. The men almost pulled him to bits, and mouthed at his great quivering bottom! The little horses were quite forgotten for the moment.

Sup, the penetrating, burst through his silk fleshings, and thrust in bravely up to the hilt, whilst the alto's legs were feasted upon by Pudex, Cyril, Anquetin, and some others. Ballice, Corvo, Quadra, Senillé, Mellefont, Théodore, Le Vit, and Matta, all of the egoistic cult, stood and crouched round, saturating the lovers with warm douches.

Later in the afternoon, Venus and Tannhäuser paid a little visit to De La Pine's studio, as the Chevalier was very anxious to have his portrait painted. De La Pine's glory as a painter was hugely increased by his reputation as a *fouteur*, for ladies that had pleasant memories of him looked with a biased eye upon his *fêtes galantes merveilleuses*, portraits and *folies bergères.*[91]

Yes, he was a bawdy creature, and his workshop a regular brothel. However, his great talent stood in no need of such meretricious and phallic support, and he was every whit as strong and facile with his brush as with his tool.

When Venus and the Chevalier entered his studio, he was standing amid a group of friends and connoisseurs who were liking his latest picture. It was a small canvas, one of his delightful morning pieces. Upon an Italian balcony stood a lady in a white frock, reading a letter. She wore brown stockings, straw-coloured petticoats, white shoes, and a Leghorn hat. Her hair was red and in a chignon. At her feet lay a tiny Japanese dog, painted from the Queen's favourite 'Fanny', and upon the balustrade stood an open empty bird cage. The background was a stretch of Gallic country, clusters of trees cresting the ridges of low hills, a bit of river, a château, and the morning sky.

De La Pine hastened to kiss the moist and scented hand of Venus. Tannhäuser bowed profoundly and begged to have some pictures shown him. The gracious painter took him round his studio.

Cosmé was one of the party, for De La Pine just then was painting his portrait – a portrait, by the way, which promised to be a veritable *chef d'oeuvre*. Cosmé was loved and admired by everybody. To begin with, he was pastmaster in his art, that fine, relevant art of coiffing; then he was really modest and obliging, and was only seen and heard when he was wanted. He was useful; he was decorative in his white apron, black mask, and silver suit; he was discreet.

The painter was giving Venus and Tannhäuser a little dinner that evening, and he insisted on Cosmé joining them. The barber vowed he would be *de trop*, and required a world of pressing before he would accept the invitation. Venus added her voice, and he consented.

Ah! what a delightful little *partie carrée*[92] it turned out. The painter was in purple and full dress, all tassels and grand folds. His hair magnificently curled, his heavy eyelids painted, his gestures large and romantic, he reminded one a little of Maurel playing Wolfram in the second act of the Opera of Wagner.[93]

Venus was in a ravishing toilet and confection of Camille's, and looked like K****. Tannhäuser was dressed as a woman and looked like a Goddess. Cosmé sparkled with gold, bristled with ruffs, glittered with bright buttons, was painted, powdered, gorgeously bewigged and looked like a marquis in a comic opera.

The *salle à manger* at De La Pine's was quite the prettiest that ever was.

[Here the manuscript ends]

1907

MARCEL PROUST

From *Time Regained* (*Le Temps retrouvé*)

[A late-night encounter with the Baron de Charlus in wartime Paris; his vision of a conquered Paris becoming a second Pompeii; his homosexual interest in soldiers unconvincingly disguised]

But I must return to my narrative. I am walking down the boulevards by the side of M. de Charlus, who has just made a vague attempt to use me as an intermediary for overtures of peace between himself and Morel. Seeing that I made no reply, he went on: 'Anyway, I do not know why it is that he no longer gives concerts. There is no music now, on the pretext that there is a war on, but people dance and go out to dinner and women invent something called Ambrine for their skin. Social amusements fill what may prove, if the Germans continue to advance, to be the last days of our Pompeii. And if the city is indeed doomed, that in itself will save it from frivolity. The lava of some German Vesuvius – and their naval guns are no less terrible than a volcano – has only to surprise these good people at their toilet and to immortalise their gestures by interrupting them, and in days to come it will be part of a child's education to look at pictures in his school-books of Mme Molé about to put on a last layer of powder before going out to dine with a sister-in-law, or Sosthène de Guermantes adding the final touches to his false eyebrows; these things will be the subject of lectures by the Brichots of the future, for the frivolity of an age, when ten centuries have passed over it, is matter for the gravest erudition, particularly if it has been embalmed by a volcanic eruption or by the substances akin to lava which a bombardment gives off. What documents for the future historian if asphyxiating gases, like the fumes of Vesuvius, and the collapse of a whole city, like the catastrophe which buried Pompeii, should preserve intact all the imprudent dowagers who have not yet sent off their paintings and their statues to safety in Bayonne. And indeed, for the last year, have we not already seen glimpses of Pompeii every evening: people burying themselves in their cellars, not in order to emerge with some old bottle of Mouton Rothschild or Saint-Emilion, but to conceal along with themselves their most treasured belongings, like the priests of Herculaneum whom death surprised in the act of carrying away the sacred vessels? Attachment to an object always brings death to its possessor. True, Paris was not, like Herculaneum, founded by Hercules. But how many points of resemblance leap to the eye! And this lucid vision that is given to us is not unique to ourselves, it has been granted to every age. If I reflect that tomorrow we may suffer the fate of the cities of Vesuvius, these in their turn sensed that they were threatened with the doom of the accursed cities of the Bible. On the wall of a house in Pompeii has been found the revealing inscription: *Sodoma, Gomora.*'

Perhaps it was this name of Sodom and the ideas that it evoked in him, or possibly the idea of the bombardment, that made M. de Charlus for an instant raise his eyes to heaven, but soon he brought them back to earth. 'I admire all the heroes of this war,' he said. 'Why, my dear boy, those English soldiers whom at the beginning I rather thoughtlessly dismissed as mere football players presumptuous enough to measure themselves against professionals – and what professionals! – well, purely from the aesthetic point of view they are quite simply Greek athletes, you understand me, my boy, Greek athletes, they are the young men of Plato, or rather they are Spartans. I have a friend who has been to Rouen where their base is, he has seen marvels, marvels almost unimaginable. It is not Rouen any longer, it is another town. Of course the old Rouen still exists, with the emaciated saints of the cathedral. And naturally, that is beautiful too, but it is something quite different. And our *poilus*![94] I cannot tell you how deliciously full of character I find our *poilus*, the young Parisian boys, like that one there, for instance, who is passing us, with his knowing expression, his alert and humorous face. I often stop them for one reason or another and we chat for a moment or two, and what subtlety, what good sense! And the boys from the provinces, how amusing and nice they are, with the way they roll their r's and their regional dialects! I have always lived a lot in the country, I have slept in farms, I know how to talk to them. Still, our admiration for the French must not make us deprecate our enemies: that would only be to disparage ourselves. And you don't know what a soldier the German soldier is; you haven't seen him, as I have, march past on parade, doing the goose-step, *unter den Linden*.'[95]

And returning to that ideal of virility which he had outlined to me at Balbec and which, with time, had assumed a more philosophical form in his mind, but using also absurd arguments which at moments, even just after he had said something out of the ordinary, gave his hearer a glimpse of the mental shallowness of a mere society gentleman, albeit an intelligent one: 'You see,' he said to me, 'that splendid sturdy fellow the Boche soldier is strong and healthy and thinks only of the greatness of his country, *Deutschland über Alles*, which is not so stupid as you might think, whereas, while they were preparing themselves in a virile fashion, we were hopelessly sunk in dilettantism.' This word probably signified for M. de Charlus something analogous to literature, for immediately, doubtless remembering that I was fond of literature and had at one time intended to devote myself to it, he slapped me on the shoulder (taking the opportunity to lean so heavily upon me that the blow hurt as much as the recoil of a '76' against my shoulder in my military-service days) and said, as if to soften the reproach: 'Yes, we were sunk in dilettantism, all of us, you too, you may remember. Like me you may say your *mea culpa*. We have been too dilettantish.' From astonishment at this reproach, from lack of readiness in repartee, from deference towards my interlocutor, and also because I was touched by his friendly kindness, I replied as though I too, as he suggested, had cause to beat my breast – an idiotic reaction, for I could not be accused of the slightest suggestion of dilettantism. 'Well,' he said to me, 'I must leave you here' (the group which had escorted him at a distance had finally abandoned us), 'I am going off to bed like a very old gentleman, particularly as, so it seems, the war has changed all our habits – isn't that one of the imbecile aphorisms which Norpois is so fond of?' I knew, as a matter of fact, that when he went home at night M. de Charlus did not cease to be surrounded by soldiers, for he had turned his house into a military hospital and had done this, I believe, in obedience to the dictates much less of his imagination than of his kind heart.

It was a clear, windless night; I imagined that the Seine, flowing between the twin semicircles of the span and the reflection of its bridges, must look like the Bosporus. And – a symbol perhaps of the invasion foretold by the defeatism of M. de Charlus, or else of the co-operation of our Muslim brothers with the armies of France – the moon, narrow and curved like a sequin, seemed to have placed the sky of Paris beneath the oriental sign of the crescent.

M. de Charlus lingered a few moments more, while he said goodbye to me with a shake of my hand powerful enough to crush it to pieces – a Germanic peculiarity to be found among those who share the Baron's inclinations. For several seconds he continued, as Cottard would have said, to 'knead' my hand, as if he had wished to restore to my joints a suppleness which they had never lost. In certain blind men the sense of touch makes good to a certain extent the lack of sight. I do not exactly know what sense it was taking the place of here. Perhaps he thought that he was merely shaking my hand, as no doubt he thought that he was merely seeing a Senegalese soldier who passed in the darkness without deigning to notice that he was being admired. But in each case the Baron was mistaken: the intensity of contact and of gaze was greater than propriety permitted. 'Don't you see all the Orient of Decamps and Fromentin and Ingres and Delacroix[96] in this scene?' he asked me, still immobilised by the passage of the Senegalese. 'As you know, I for my part am interested in things and in people only as a painter, a philosopher. Besides, I am too old. But to make this scene complete, what a pity that neither of us is an odalisque!'

1927; translated by Chris Baldick, 2011

Notes

1 Arthur Symons, *Selected Letters, 1880–1935*, eds Karl Beckson and John M. Munro (Iowa City: University of Iowa Press, 1989), pp. 44–5 (letter of 16 January 1889).

2 Stephen Calloway and David Colvin (eds), *In Black and White: The Literary Remains of Aubrey Beardsley* (London: Cypher Press, 1998). This work is freely available online at www.cypherpress.com/beardsley/underthehill.

3 A well-known romantic drama by Victor Hugo (1830).

4 Arago was an early nineteenth-century scientist and politician, who is not otherwise known to have uttered this maxim.

5 In the legend of Don Juan, best known from the Mozart-Da Ponte operatic version, *Don Giovanni* (1787), the Commander, Don Pedro, is killed by Juan in a sword-fight while defending his daughter from abduction. Eventually his statue comes to life, apprehends Juan with a chilling handshake and announces his damnation.

6 Charles Jud was the presumed culprit in a famous murder case of 1860, but was never apprehended.

7 In French slang of the time, a card-sharp or similar fraudster.

8 Artists and illustrators of the time (although Archille Deveria had died in 1857), the first two being noted for their modern Parisian scenes.

9 Apollonian. Villiers enjoyed applying this epithet to his golden-haired friend, the writer Catulle Mendès (1841–1909), who was plainly the model for 'C——'.

10 Les Quinze-Vingts ('Fifteen-Score', thus 300, after its original population) was an old Parisian hospital for the blind.

11 In legends of Troy, Penthesilea was an Amazon queen.

12 *Velaria* are veils. Herculaneum, the ancient town south of Naples, had been buried under volcanic ash, along with Pompeii further south, by the eruption of Vesuvius in 79 CE, and rediscovered in successive excavations from 1738.

13 According to the *Babylonian History* (278 BCE) of Barossus, Xisuthros was an Assyrian king who was forewarned by the gods of the impending Great Flood, and instructed to build a great ship to carry his family and livestock. The Biblical story of Noah and the Flood derives from this or similar tales.

14 Jules Oppert (1825–1905) was a German-born philologist, archaeologist and

pioneer Assyriologist who was awarded French citizenship and numerous academic honours for his discoveries, including decipherments of cuneiform inscriptions.

15 Champagne, of a prestigious label.

16 Jean-Léon Gérôme's 1857 painting *Duel After the Masked Ball* shows Pierrot slumped in the arms of his seconds, fatally wounded by Harlequin.

17 Customary title of the Paris executioner.

18 Nasser ed-Din was the reigning Shah of Persia at the time Villiers wrote, and had visited Paris in 1873. In this passage Villiers misattributes to him atrocities committed by his great grandfather Fath Ali Shah's uncle, the notoriously cruel eunuch warlord Agha Mohammad Khan Qajar, after the siege of Kerman in 1794. Hobbs and Egginson are fictional.

19 Tomás de Torquemada and Pedro de Arbues were both leading figures in the Spanish Inquisition in the late fifteenth century. The third Duke of Alba, Fernando Álvarez de Toledo, was nicknamed the 'butcher of Flanders' after his bloody repression of Protestants during his governorship of the Spanish Netherlands (1567–73). The Duke of York mentioned here is King Richard III.

20 Fontenay-aux-Roses, five miles south-west of central Paris. The absorption of this village into the Parisian suburbs was already under way in Huysmans's time.

21 Probably *Scabiosa atropurpurea*, which has flowers of deep purple.

22 The anhydride of santonic acid, a drug used to expel intestinal roundworm, and for some urinary complaints. Its effect on vision is more commonly yellowing.

23 Charles du Fresne du Cange, a French historian and philologist, published his *Glossary of Medieval and Late Latin* in 1678.

24 The last three named were philosophers of the thirteenth century, all later claimed dubiously as pioneers of 'occult' learning. If Des Esseintes has a copy of any work by the fifth-century Athenian natural philosopher Archelaus, it must be an astonishing rarity, since none of Archelaus's writings survived antiquity.

25 In typography, a cursive variety of Gothic font.

26 Jules Barbey d'Aurevilly (1808–89), French critic, novelist, and writer of short stories; a convert to Catholicism from 1846. His works include *Du Dandysme* (1845), the novel *Un Prêtre marié* (1865), and the story-collection *Les Diaboliques* (1874).

27 The German writer E. T. A. Hoffmann's tale 'The Sandman' ('Der Sandmann', 1816) features a life-size clockwork doll that the infatuated hero mistakes for a real young woman. The doll is called Olympia, but is renamed Coppélia in Léo Delibes's ballet *Coppélia* (1870), based on Hoffmann's tale.

28 Literally 'acts of faith', *autos-da-fé* were executions of heretics, usually by burning.

29 The *Malleus Maleficarum* ('Hammer of Witches', 1487) was a treatise on witches, attempting to refute those who denied their existence. It became a widely used handbook for witch-hunters. Its authors were Heinrich Kramer and Jacob Sprenger, although Sprenger's role has sometimes been questioned.

30 Huysmans's admiration for the works of Barbey did not always extend to

recalling their titles accurately. The story mentioned here is correctly 'A un diner d'athées' (1871, reprinted in *Les Diaboliques*, 1874).

31 Members of a Vatican legal tribunal. The blessing of physical objects would never have been part of the Rota's duties.

32 'Lady Tan' would be an approximation; but the name is literally 'faience', i.e. earthenware or pottery.

33 Spanish, 'pleasant retreat': the name is associated especially with the royal summer-palace and park built for Philip IV outside (but now within the centre of) Madrid in the 1630s.

34 The Pincian hill is occupied by scenic public gardens with views over the city.

35 In a mischievous early prose work, the *Selection of Consoling Maxims on Love* (*Choix de maxims consolantes sur l'amour*, 1846), Baudelaire had written 'Never speak ill of mother Nature; if she has assigned to you a flat-chested mistress, say "I have a boyfriend – but with hips!" [*un ami – avec des hanches!*] and go to the temple to offer up thanks to the gods.' D'Annunzio amends *ami* to the feminine *amie* (girlfriend, sweetheart), thereby losing the point of Baudelaire's jest.

36 From P. B. Shelley's poem 'The Magnetic Lady to her Patient' (posthumously published, 1832), lines 26–7: 'And forget me, for I can never / Be thine.'

37 Celebrated French-born landscape painter who lived and worked in Rome from 1625 until his death in 1682, when he was buried close to the scene of this chapter, in the Santa Trinità dei Monti.

38 In Greek mythology, a wise old drunkard who teaches and accompanies the god of intoxication, Dionysus (Latin, Bacchus). In decorative art, he usually appears as a pot-bellied man riding a donkey, and so drunk that satyrs have to support him.

39 'You are to be congratulated.'

40 Little book of secrets.

41 The fictional Jeckyll is clearly modelled upon Dante Gabriel Rossetti (1828–82), the Italian-English poet and painter. Rossetti was an associate of Holman Hunt, with whom he co-founded the Pre-Raphaelite Brotherhood in 1848; he wrote sonnets, painted subjects derived from Dante (author of the *Vita Nuova*), and painted a *Sibylla Palmifera* (Sibyl Bearing a Palm) in 1866–70. Andrea Sperelli here also follows Holman Hunt in attempting a study of Isabella (originally Lisabetta in Boccaccio): Hunt's painting *Isabella and the Pot of Basil* (1868) was inspired by John Keats's version of her story, 'Isabella; or, The Pot of Basil' (1820).

42 *Che pensi?*: 'what are you thinking?' *Chi lo sa!*: 'who knows!'

43 Sperelli and his friends are mocking litanies addressed to the Virgin Mary: 'Handmaid of the Lord, Palm-Bearing Sibyl, pretty girl, pray for us!' The first two titles applied to Clara come from Pre-Raphaelite paintings (the first from Rossetti's study of the Annunciation entitled *Ecce Ancilla Domini*, 1850), the third from Catullus.

44 Spanish, 'girlish but pretty'.

45 Fortuna Publica was a minor Roman goddess embodying the luck of the city-state.

46 Rabelaisian means obscene or racy in language, after the sixteenth-century French comic writer. An *olla podrida* is a miscellany, after the Spanish pork-and-bean stew (literally 'stinking pot').
47 In Balzac's novel *L'Illustre Gaudissart* (1833), the title character is a jovially philistine travelling salesman.
48 Gabrielle Réjane (1856–1920) was one of the most famous French actresses of the time.
49 Tannhäuser was a thirteenth-century German poet, who from the fifteenth century became the subject of a legend in which he appears as a wandering knight who discovers the Venusberg, the secret lair of the love-goddess, and spends a year there worshipping her. He later suffers remorse and unsuccessfully seeks absolution from the Pope, then returns to the Venusberg.
50 Louis de Carmontelle (1717–1806), French artist, designer, and author. In his portrait (1760) of the celebrated author and literary hostess Mme du Deffand, her hands are in fact not visible.
51 Christian Mentzel (1622–1701), German botanist, author of the *Lexicon Plantarum* (1682) under the Latinised form of his name, Mentzelius.
52 These are the *seirō*: luxurious apartments of high-class courtesans in the Yoshiwara district of Edo (now Tokyo), as most famously portrayed by the late eighteenth-century artist Kitagawa Utamaro. La Motte, Nursery Numbers: not identified.
53 The legendary seducer Don Juan. See note 5.
54 A fictitious artist, whose work is described later in this story.
55 Make-up artist.
56 Possibly alluding to the Hôtel Cluny, a fifteenth-century Paris mansion that had become a museum of medieval art in 1833: its collection includes shoes and other artefacts, along with a famous tapestry of a lady with a unicorn.
57 Alfred Delvau's invaluable *Dictionnaire érotique moderne* (1864) explains the meanings of many slang sexual terms, with illustrative quotations. The pages mentioned cover ten different phrases, none of which appears to be alluded to here.
58 Obscenities.
59 Unidentified.
60 Embroidered with a rococo motif, such as a cherub, associated with the style of Antoine Watteau (1684–1721), inventor of the *fêtes galantes* genre of painting, which represents scenes of elegantly sportive leisure.
61 A legendary female saint blessed with a long beard after praying to God to be saved from impending marriage, or rape, according to different versions of her story.
62 A design based on the figure of a humanized monkey.
63 Rambouillet's culinary feat (*tour de cuisine*) comprises dishes based on sea-bream, carp's tongue, wood-pigeon, mixed game, goose paté, lamb's tail, artichokes, apples, and two kinds of ice-cream. Réchale and Mirliton are fictitious.
64 Depilatrix.
65 In Thomas Otway's comedy *The Soldier's Fortune* (1681), Sir Jolly Jumble is an old pimp.

66 Pregnant.
67 Befuddled.
68 A slang expression for cunnilingus. The Two Columns, imagined as the name of a café, are the legs.
69 Before being fictionalised in Edmond Rostand's 1897 drama, Cyrano de Bergerac was a real dramatist and romancer of the seventeenth century; but this comedy is fictitious.
70 Lord Fanny was a nickname applied by Alexander Pope in the first of his Horatian Imitations (1733) to the politician Lord Hervey, who was bisexual and effeminate in appearance. *Love at All Hazards* has not been identified.
71 Another bogus reference. Pénillière is a Rabelaisian word for the pubis.
72 Boisterous.
73 Philippe d'Orléans was Regent of France (1715–23) during the minority of Louis XV, and had many mistresses. The memoirs of the Duc de Saint-Simon mention one of the Broglio family as a participant in the Regent's debauched drinking-parties.
74 Theodore Watts (1832–1914), later known as Watts-Dunton, English critic, poet, and helpmeet to A. C. Swinburne. The line quoted here has not been found in Watts's published poems.
75 Rear tits, i.e. buttocks.
76 The rue de Vendôme, which is mentioned in some of Balzac's novels, had already been renamed the rue Béranger in 1864. The mystery mentioned remains mysterious.
77 Probably the Pavillon Carré de Baudouin, a grand eighteenth-century pleasure-villa overlooking Paris from the twentieth arrondissement. The writers Jules and Edmond de Goncourt had grown up there, but it had become an orphanage in 1836.
78 An unfinished early thirteenth-century French poem of four thousand lines by Guillaume de Lorris, famed for its allegorical presentation of a courtly-love philosophy. It was continued at greater length by Jean de Meun in the later thirteenth century.
79 Claude Lorrain (1600–82), the French-born Roman artist often known simply as Claude, was the most influential landscape painter of his time. Lady Delaware is fictional.
80 St Rose (Rosa) of Lima (1586–1617; canonised 1671 as the first saint of the Americas), noted for her devotion to virginity despite her parents' attempt to marry her. Catholic hagiography presents her as dying of natural causes, Beardsely's account of her assumption being parodic whimsy.
81 'Woman-lovers', i.e. heterosexual men. This coinage, modelled upon 'pederast' but with an inconsistent Latin root, was attributed by Oscar Wilde to his friend Robert Ross.
82 *Das Rheingold* (The Rhine Gold, 1869) is the first part of Richard Wagner's operatic tetralogy *Der Ring der Nibelungen*. *Tuesday, Josephine*: unidentified.
83 Another bogus allusion. A *lorette* is a woman who lives idly on her wealthy lovers; and there is no well-known artist of that name. Charles Millevoye was a minor early nineteenth-century poet, not an architectural historian.

84 Buttocks.
85 The extravagant fop character in John Vanbrugh's comedy *The Relapse* (1696).
86 John Lemprière's *Bibliotheca Classica* (1788) was a standard reference book on ancient mythology, history, and biography.
87 A casino game using a mechanised board on which toy horses rotate randomly, bets being placed on which horse will stop nearest to a marked spot.
88 Tiny testicles.
89 The *Stabat Mater dolorosa* ('The sorrowful Mother stood . . .') is a medieval hymn which the Italian composer Gioachino Rossini set for four principal voices with choir and orchestra (1833; revised 1842).
90 Luis de Morales, sixteenth-century Spanish painter: several of his works are studies of the Madonna and Child.
91 Beardsley here employs the name of the famous Paris music-hall the Folies Bergère, so named after the neighbouring rue Bergère, as though this were a genre of painting equivalent to the *fêtes galantes* (see note 60 above), presumably depicting frolicsome shepherdesses (*bergères*). A *fouteur* is a (male) sexual athlete.
92 Foursome.
93 Victor Maurel (1848–1923) was a French baritone actor-singer who had appeared in the part of Tannhäuser's friend Wolfram in the English première (1876) of Richard Wagner's opera *Tannhäuser und der Sängerkrieg auf Wartburg* (1845). He performed regularly in London in the early 1890s.
94 An affectionate slang term of the First World War period (literally 'hairy ones'), applied to soldiers of the French infantry.
95 German, 'Under the linden trees': the name of the grand avenue that runs through central Berlin.
96 Alexandre-Gabriel Decamps (1803–60), Eugène Fromentin (1820–76), Jean-Auguste-Dominique Ingres (1780–1867), and Eugène Delacroix (1798–1863) were all French painters, some of whose works are devoted to 'oriental' subjects, including nude studies of Turkish harem concubines known as odalisques. The most famous examples are Ingres's *La Grande odalisque* (1814) and *Le Bain turc* (1862), but Delacroix also painted an *Odalisque* (1857).

5

DIAGNOSES AND DENUNCIATIONS

The focus of this section is principally on the critical reception of Decadence in the late 1880s and the 1890s, and its interpretation, or diagnosis, – particularly among English critics – as symptomatic of cultural degeneration. Only Arthur Symons (1865–1945) attempts to keep the focus on the more literary and stylistic innovations of Decadent poetry and the influence of French aesthetics on Decadent poets. In his 'Decadent Movement in Literature', he uses musical and artistic analogies to emphasise the importance of 'nuance' and the 'inexpressibility' of certain sensations, and he defines Decadence as a distinctly European movement. The majority of newspaper hacks and periodical writers, however, like Harry Quilter (1851–1907), take issue with what they regard as the foreignness of Decadence, and they interpret the last phase of the tradition in terms of theories then circulating about cultural degeneration. In the mid-1890s, literary Decadence becomes intertwined with debates about cultural degeneration. Decadent artists and writers, according to the conservative press, are geniuses who are mentally ill. The references to contagion and sickness in Quilter's short article on Aubrey Beardsley, for example, reflect a sense of crisis felt by the old guard in 1895, as they called for a wholesale rejection of Decadent art. Decadence, in their view, was a French imposition, and Quilter's rallying cry indicated a general British hypersensitivity regarding France at this time. Seen against the political background of tension between England and France over North Africa, Quilter's vision of a 'nation of Beardsleys' was less to do with the decadence of his drawings than with his cultural 'collaboration' with the rival power.

Metaphors of health and sickness circulated widely in the nineteenth century, and were used against a range of innovative artists. Friedrich Nietzsche (1844–1900) enthusiastically deploys a psycho-medical rhetoric of degeneration against Wagner in *The Case of Wagner* (*Der Fall Wagner*), in which he describes Wagner's decadent genius as being characterised by pathological manifestations such as hysteria, nervous excitability, histrionics, mendacity, visual restlessness, sensationalism, aesthetic fragmentation, and effeminacy.[1] The use of these metaphors in literature and popular criticism had a visceral impact on the reading public, who were conservative and easily led by opinion-mongers in the newspapers and journals. As Nicole Dubreuil-Blondin has noted, metaphors of 'dirt' ('le sale') and 'disease' ('le malade') had been employed by French critics against Impressionist art in the 1870s.[2] Such hostility reflected a deep-rooted indignation at their innovative work. Their sketchy, plein-air depictions of modern life were a challenge to the painterly ideals of 'high finish' and to the tradition of drawing subjects from mythology and history. Twenty years later, the same emotive metaphors of sickness and hysteria were applied by Hugh E. M. Stutfield in his article 'Tommyrotics' (1895) to the work of Decadent and modern writers and artists for similar reasons:

> That there is a moral cancer in our midst is not to be denied, and that it has roots deep down in morbid hysteria seems equally clear. That such morbidity is directly fed and fostered by the 'new' art and the 'new' literature – themselves symptoms of the disease – is a (to me) self-evident proposition. So far our fiction is only 'gamy': let us see to it that we do not acquire a taste for the carrion of the French literary vulture.[3]

The strongest case for the corruptive influence of Decadent ideas was set out by Max Nordau (1849–1923) in his book *Entartung*, published in German in 1892 and translated into English in 1895 as *Degeneration*. Its publication in England coincided with the trial of Oscar Wilde, who in the public mind was an artist identified with insanity and egomania. Despite its length, *Degeneration* was phenomenally successful; and its impact was far-reaching and pervasive. It was reprinted ten times between 1892 and 1900, and was one of the ten best-selling books in Europe between 1890 and 1900.[4] Nordau's inspiration was the classification of mental abnormality made by the Italian criminologist Cesare Lombroso (1835–1909), and in his dedication Nordau states his debt to his 'honoured master'. He writes

> Degenerates are not always criminals, prostitutes, anarchists, and pronounced lunatics; they are often authors and artists. These, however, manifest the same mental characteristics, and for the most part the same somatic features, as the members of the above-mentioned anthropological family, who satisfy their unhealthy impulses with the knife of the assassin or the bomb of the dynamiter, instead of with pen and pencil.

Nordau's approach was polymathic and all-inclusive. The list of those whom he identified as deviant, insane, and criminal included Ibsen, Wagner, Tolstoy, Ruskin, Burne-Jones, Rossetti, Wilde, Zola, Verlaine, Nietzsche and Baudelaire, to mention a few. These individuals, in his view, represented the decline of European art and he classified their work in terms of its preoccupation with disease, sexual deviancy, amorality, and mysticism.

The diatribe against Decadence properly begins with book three of *Degeneration*, entitled 'Ego-mania', chapter 1 of which outlines the 'organic roots', the bio-chemical changes that take place within both sane and degenerate types. Nordau takes his model from contemporary psychological research and shows how the derangement of the cells in a degenerate or imbecilic individual corresponded to that of an ego-maniac or Decadent. The consciousness of a sane man, he argues, is 'filled with images of the external world, not with images of the activity of his organs', whereas 'the cell of the degenerate is formed a little differently . . . the particles of the protoplasm are otherwise and less regularly disposed; the molecular movements take place, in consequence, in a less free and rapid, less rhythmic and vigorous manner'. All this, he concedes, is difficult to demonstrate and prove in practice, but he argues that the indisputable fact is that 'all the bodily signs or "stigmata" of degeneration . . . have their origin in a bio-chemical and bio-mechanical derangement of the nerve-cell, or, perhaps, of the cell in general'. Nordau continues: 'The degenerate man remains a child all his life. He scarcely appreciates or even perceives the external world, and is only occupied with the organic processes in his own body. He is more than egotistical, he is an ego-maniac'. Inadvertent praise as far as Decadents were concerned, and a perfect description of J.-K. Huysmans's decadent anti-hero, Des Esseintes.

Nordau's accusations of continental decadentism were music to the ears of conservative critics in England, who, as Bernard Shaw commented, 'without half his cleverness or energy of expression, clumsily imitate[d] his sham-scientific vivisection in their attacks on artists whose work they happen to dislike'.[5] The cultural impact of a book such as Nordau's in England was huge; it not only pathologised certain artists and writers but it also prescribed a cure, or at least suggested that a scourge of such degenerates would bring about a return to cultural health. This optimistic forecast was what respectable middle-class society wanted to hear. Confronted with the desensitising aspects of modern life – high-velocity and metropolitan – the English public felt insecure and undermined by the New and the foreign. Nordau's book became the stick with which the British conservative press beat the Decadents for their lack of morality. With some degree of dexterous invention, however, Oscar Wilde used Nordau in an attempt to evade incarceration. While imprisoned in Reading Gaol, he invoked both Lombroso and Nordau in a letter to the Home Secretary asking for leniency on the unconvincing and somewhat immodest grounds that such offences as he had committed were the natural consequences of an insanity that accompanied genius.

The English reception of literary Decadence contrasts with the French treatment of the tradition. In France, Decadence was regarded as a modern sensibility concerned principally with modern ideas about aesthetics (see Raoul Vague's piece for the last number of *Le Décadent,* and Remy de Gourmont's essay 'Stéphane Mallarmé et l'idée de décadence'). In its journey across the English Channel, however, it did not fare well; it was received by the English press as an unwelcome foreign influence signifying moral turpitude and degeneration. It had acquired extra baggage, we might say, of being Latin in origin, French by design, and revolutionary by association. Its marginal status from the 1870s onwards made it a vulnerable and culturally mutable category, and as it accumulated easily the characteristics of other movements and styles, including Pre-Raphaelitism, Aestheticism, Impressionism, and, most notably, Symbolism, it was regarded by English critics as, at best, a silly but harmless fad, and, at worst, a movement undermining the national cultural health.[6]

RAOUL VAGUE

An Article about the Decadents (Un Article sur les Décadents)

Not everybody trivialises and pre-judges the Decadents as our Parisian newspapermen are in the habit of doing. Nowadays we have the pleasure of meeting, even among the most hostile writers, quite a few who do understand us. The following extract is taken from an article on the Decadents that has appeared in La Vie posthume, *a journal of rational philosophy.*[7] *It shows its signatory, Stephanus,*[8] *to be more intelligent or more honest than most of his colleagues in the daily press.*

Their thinking is guided by a formula that can be summed up as: nothing is as important as one's self. More philosophical than literary by inclination, they would subscribe to the most radical proposition of absolute idealism: nothing exists but one's self. Distinguishing themselves from the crowd by their subtle intellect and refined sensibility, they aim to cultivate these superior talents. A soul that is blessed with such gifts is for them a work of art that is obliged to seek its own beauty and perfection: it will draw upon the external world for its moods, it will extend and polish its reflective surface, taking care that it should reflect everything around it.

The decadent analyses the emotions that he experiences. He cultivates them in rapt meditation. He clarifies them, seizing upon their most delicate shades through introspection and memory, often transforming the coarse or sketchy outlines of primitive feelings into complete and distinct images.

He puts into practice the motto of the Roman poet Terence, *I hold no aspect of humanity* (or of the *universe,* even) *foreign to me,* along with that of Socrates, *Know thyself;* albeit to more self-interested purposes.

From Nature, from Art, from Science, and from Woman he requires impressions, these being the elements from which one can fashion one's self. Always in complete command of himself, he will absorb and take in everything but will never give himself away. He is moved by his feelings, not to express the tremors of his soul outwardly as love or pity, but so as to nourish his solitary contemplation. Heedless of any obligation, he cares not to reciprocate. The world is but his laboratory, his fellow men and women are only materials that he will select or discard according to the requirements of his latest sketch or essay. He is coolly cruel, although quite without malice, like a priest who cannot be blamed for the sacrifices demanded by the worship of his God.

Desirous of self-knowledge, he places himself under observation, pursuing his analysis as far as registering the most fugitive feelings, the faintest quiverings, and mere glimpses of emergent states of mind; through the relentless pursuit of this searching and meticulous investigation, he pushes back the frontiers of the unconscious. But here too he is seeking only his own pleasure, and he keeps the fruits to himself, having borrowed the seeds from the world beyond him.

This Eudemonism, this doctrine of seeking happiness in the delights of the mind and heart, is a revival of Greek Epicureanism, although with more fastidious scepticism, more egotistical refinement, more acute insight, more profundity and originality. It supplements it with a kind of formal precept: the necessity of a mental solitude into which the soul in its finest hours may withdraw to contemplate itself in its self-sufficiency.

In order to express itself, a form of spirituality such as this should seek a new language, one that can closely translate the subtly introspective impressions of a soul that reverberates at the slightest touch. And so a style is born, shaping and developing itself in infinite elaboration.

Language is synthetic: it concentrates within a word or phrase every means of expression. It combines in itself all the qualities of harmony, colour-sense, draughtsmanship, rhythm, and symmetry. Its art raises these to the highest level, making from words the most vivid image of the soul in all its varied aspects. The decadents have claimed this as their task. In carrying it out, though, they have rushed ahead of the common reader who understands nothing about their writing, full of new words and unusual turns of phrase, and treats it as some sort of practical joke or as a fearsome mystification of which they should beware. The critics and men of letters often enough have no better understanding of them, and cannot decide whether they are dealing with lunatics, clowns, or artists indulging in a pointless game. Feeling menaced by the incomprehensible, they line up against it as an exclusive brotherhood.

Unqualified as I am to assess the decadents' style, I find it intriguing and stimulating to consider their sensibility, which I have summed up inadequately and perhaps inaccurately from their teachings. It is essentially very difficult to lead that sort of life (though it be one dedicated entirely to pleasure), combining as it does cloistered solitude with a feverish social whirl. It calls for unrelenting vigilance and, whatever people may say, many sacrifices. Repeatedly one has to renew the battle against one's bestial appetites, and their slavish cultivation of new sensations; once these are let loose among the gorgeous temptations of the flesh, their thirst is whetted and they strain and chafe against the bit. And how much more painful (although less often called for) is the spirit's resistance to temptation when it grows weary and half-ashamed of its calculated semi-virtues and semi-passions and seeks to compensate by lavish abandonment.

They must be quite exceptional, then, the true Decadents who can persevere in all this, whether from instinct or sanity or strong will-power. Most of the others play a role which they forget once the passions are inflamed, as in that play about Constantine.[9] For such a role they require a cultivated, critical, and sceptical intelligence disposed to a nihilistic outlook; senses that are delicate yet already satiated; and a heart, persuaded of its own weakness by native wisdom or by deep wounds, submissive to the mind's guidance.

While scepticism provides the philosophical fabric of the decadents' doctrine, its moral foundation is that of Egoism. It occupies the highest peak of Individualism. It is a religion that ordains an idolatry of the self.

What has been said here is not in all respects fair, but it is frankly spoken, which we appreciate just as much.

1888; translated by Chris Baldick, 2011

FRIEDRICH NIETZSCHE

From *The Case of Wagner* (*Der Fall Wagner*)

The ship dashed on to a reef; Wagner had run aground. The reef was Schopenhauer's[10] philosophy; Wagner had stuck fast on a *contrary* view of the world. What had he set to music? Optimism? Wagner was ashamed. It was moreover an optimism for which Schopenhauer had devised an evil expression, – *unscrupulous* optimism. He was more than ever ashamed. He reflected for some time; his position seemed desperate . . . At last a path of escape seemed gradually to open before him: what if the reef on which he had been wrecked could be interpreted as a goal, as the ulterior motive, as the actual purpose of his journey? To be wrecked here, this was also a goal. *Bene navigavi cum naufragium feci*[11] . . . and he translated the 'Ring' into Schopenhauerian language. Everything goes wrong, everything goes to wrack and ruin, the new world is just as bad as the old one: – Nonentity, the Indian Circe beckons . . . Brunnhilda, who according to the old plan had to retire with a song in honour of free love, consoling the world with the hope of a socialistic Utopia in which 'all will be well'; now gets something else to do. She must first study Schopenhauer. She must first versify the fourth book of 'The World as Will and Idea'. *Wagner was saved. . . .* Joking apart, this *was* a salvation. The service which Wagner owes to Schopenhauer is incalculable. It was the *philosopher of decadence* who allowed the *artist of decadence* to find himself. –

5

The artist of decadence. That is the word. And here I begin to be serious. I could not think of looking on approvingly while this *décadent* spoils our health – and music into the bargain. Is Wagner a man at all? Is he not rather a disease? Everything he touches he contaminates. *He has made music sick.*

A typical *décadent* who thinks himself necessary with his corrupted taste, who arrogates to himself a higher taste, who tries to establish his depravity as a law, as progress, as a fulfilment.

And no one guards against it. His powers of seduction attain monstrous proportions, holy incense hangs around him, the misunderstanding concerning him is called the Gospel, – and he has certainly not converted only the *poor in spirit*[12] to his cause!

I should like to open the window a little. Air! More air! – [13]

The fact that people in Germany deceive themselves concerning Wagner does not surprise me. The reverse would surprise me. The Germans have modelled a Wagner for themselves, whom they can honour: never yet have they been psychologists; they are thankful that they misunderstand. But that people should also deceive themselves concerning Wagner in Paris! Where people are scarcely anything else than psychologists. And in Saint Petersburg! Where things are divined, which even Paris has no idea of. How intimately related must Wagner be to the entire decadence of Europe for her not to have felt that he was decadent! He belongs to it: he is its protagonist, its greatest name . . . We bring honour on ourselves by elevating him to the clouds. – For the mere fact that no one guards against him is in itself already a sign of decadence. Instinct is weakened, what ought to be eschewed now attracts. People actually kiss that which plunges them more quickly into the abyss. – Is there any need for an example? One has only to think of the régime which anaemic, or gouty, or diabetic people prescribe for themselves. The definition of a vegetarian: a creature who has need of a corroborating diet. To recognise what is harmful as harmful, to be able to deny oneself what is harmful, is a sign of youth, of vitality. That which is harmful lures the exhausted: cabbage lures the vegetarian. Illness itself can be a stimulus to life: but one must be healthy enough for such a stimulus! – Wagner increases exhaustion: *therefore* he attracts the weak and exhausted to him. Oh, the rattlesnake joy of the old Master precisely because he always saw 'the little children' coming unto him![14]

I place this point of view first and foremost: Wagner's art is diseased. The problems he sets on the stage are all concerned with hysteria; the convulsiveness of his emotions, his over-excited sensitiveness, his taste which demands ever sharper condimentation, his erraticness which he togged out to look like principles, and, last but not least, his choice of heroes and heroines, considered as physiological types (– a hospital ward! –): the whole represents a morbid picture; of this there can be no doubt. *Wagner est une névrose.*[15] Maybe, that nothing is better known to-day, or in any case the subject of greater study, than the Protean character of degeneration which has disguised itself here, both as an art and as an artist. In Wagner our medical men and physiologists have a most interesting case, or at least a very complete one. Owing to the very fact that nothing is more modern than this thorough morbidness, this dilatoriness and excessive irritability of the nervous machinery, Wagner is the *modern artist par excellence*, the Cagliostro[16] of modernity. All that the world most needs to-day, is combined in the most seductive manner in his art, – the three great stimulants of exhausted people: *brutality, artificiality* and *innocence* (idiocy).

Wagner is a great corrupter of music. With it, he found the means of stimulating tired nerves, – and in this way he made music ill. In the art of spurring exhausted creatures back into activity, and of recalling half-corpses to life, the inventiveness he shows is of no mean order. He is the master of hypnotic trickery, and he fells the strongest like bullocks. Wagner's *success* – his success with nerves, and therefore with women – converted the whole world of ambitious musicians into disciples of his secret art. And not only the ambitious, but also the *shrewd*. . . . Only with morbid music can money be made to-day; our big theatres live on Wagner.

[. . .]

7

Enough! Enough! I fear that, beneath all my merry jests, you are beginning to recognise the sinister truth only too clearly – the picture of the decline of art, of the decline of the artist. The latter, which is a decline of character, might perhaps be defined provisionally in the following manner: the musician is now becoming an actor, his art is developing ever more and more into a talent for *telling lies*. In a certain chapter of my principal work which bears the title 'Concerning the Physiology of Art',[17] I shall have an opportunity of showing more thoroughly how this transformation of art as a whole into histrionics is just as much a sign of physiological degeneration (or more precisely a form of hysteria), as any other individual corruption, and infirmity peculiar to the art which Wagner inaugurated: for instance the restlessness of its optics, which makes it necessary to change one's attitude to it every second. They understand nothing of Wagner who see in him but a sport of nature, an arbitrary mood, a chapter of accidents. He was not the 'defective', 'ill-fated', 'contradictory' genius that people have declared him to be. Wagner was something *complete*, he was a typical *décadent*, in whom every sign of 'free will' was lacking, in whom every feature was necessary. If there is anything at all of interest in Wagner, it is the consistency with which a critical physiological condition may convert itself, step by step, conclusion after conclusion, into a method, a form of procedure, a reform of all principles, a crisis in taste.

At this point I shall only stop to consider the question of *style*. How is *decadence* in *literature* characterised? By the fact that in it life no longer animates the whole. Words become predominant and leap right out of the sentence to which they belong, the sentences themselves trespass beyond their bounds, and obscure the sense of the whole page, and the page in its turn gains in vigour at the cost of the whole, – the whole is no longer a whole. But this is the formula for every decadent style: there is always anarchy among the atoms, disaggregation of the will, – in moral terms: 'freedom of the individual', – extended into a political theory: '*equal* rights for all'. Life, equal vitality, all the vibration and exuberance of life, driven back into the smallest structure, and the remainder left almost lifeless. Everywhere paralysis, distress, and numbness, or hostility and chaos: both striking one with ever increasing force the higher the forms of organisation are into which one ascends. The whole no longer lives at all: it is composed, reckoned up, artificial, a fictitious thing.

[. . .]

8

– 'Very good! But how can this *décadent* spoil one's taste if perchance one is not a musician, if perchance one is not oneself a *décadent*?' – Conversely! How can one *help* it! *Just* you try it! – You know not what Wagner is: quite a great actor! Does a more profound, a more *ponderous* influence exist on the stage? Just look at these youthlets, – all benumbed, pale, breathless! They are Wagnerites: they know nothing about music, – and yet Wagner gets the mastery of them. Wagner's art presses with the weight of a hundred atmospheres: do but submit, there is nothing else to do. . . . Wagner the actor is a tyrant, his pathos flings all taste, all resistance, to the winds.

– Who else has this persuasive power in his attitudes, who else sees attitudes so clearly before anything else! This holding-of-its-breath in Wagnerian pathos, this disinclination to have done with an intense feeling, this terrifying habit of dwelling on a situation in which every instant almost chokes one. – –

Was Wagner a musician at all? In any case he was something else to *a much greater degree* – that is to say, an incomparable *histrio*, the greatest mime, the most astounding theatrical genius that the Germans have ever had, our *scenic artist par excellence.* He belongs to some other sphere than the history of music, with whose really great and genuine figure he must not be confounded. Wagner *and* Beethoven – this is blasphemy – and above all it does not do justice even to Wagner . . . As a musician he was no more than what he was as a man: he *became* a musician, he *became* a poet, because the tyrant in him, his actor's genius, drove him to be both. Nothing is known concerning Wagner, so long as his dominating instinct has not been divined.

Wagner was *not* instinctively a musician. And this he proved by the way in which he abandoned all laws and rules, or, in more precise terms, all style in music, in order to make what he wanted with it, *i.e.*, a rhetorical medium for the stage, a medium of expression, a means of accentuating an attitude, a vehicle of suggestion and of the psychologically picturesque. In this department Wagner may well stand as an inventor and an innovator of the first order – *he increased the powers of speech of music to an incalculable degree* – : he is the Victor Hugo[18] of music as language, provided always we allow that under certain circumstances music may be something which is not music, but speech – instrument – *ancilla dramaturgica.*[19] Wagner's music, *not* in the tender care of theatrical taste, which is very tolerant, is simply bad music, perhaps the worst that has ever been composed. When a musician can no longer count up to three, he becomes 'dramatic', he becomes 'Wagnerian.' . . .

Wagner almost discovered the magic which can be wrought even now by means of music which is both incoherent and *elementary.* His consciousness of this attains to huge proportions, as does also his instinct to dispense entirely with higher law and style. The elementary factors – sound, movement, colour, in short, the whole sensuousness of music – suffice. Wagner never calculates as a musician with a musician's conscience: all he strains after is effect, nothing more than effect. And he knows what he has to make an effect upon! – In this he is as unhesitating as Schiller[20] was, as any theatrical man must be; he has also the latter's contempt for the world which he brings to its knees before him. A man is an actor when he is ahead of mankind in his possession of this one view, that everything which has to strike people as true, must not be true. This rule was formulated by Talma:[21] it contains the whole psychology of the actor, it also contains – and this we need not doubt – all his morality. Wagner's music is never true.

– But it is supposed to be so: and thus everything is as it should be. As long as we are young, and Wagnerites into the bargain, we regard Wagner as rich, even as the model of a prodigal giver, even as a great landlord in the realm of sound. We admire him in very much the same way as young Frenchmen admire Victor Hugo – that is to say, for his 'royal liberality'.

Later on we admire the one as well as the other for the opposite reason: as masters and paragons in economy, as *prudent* amphitryons.[22] Nobody can equal them in the art of providing a princely board with such a modest outlay. – The Wagnerite, with his credulous stomach, is even sated with the fare which his master conjures up before him. But we others who, in books as in music, desire above all to find *substance*, and who are scarcely satisfied with the mere representation of a banquet, are much worse off. In plain English, Wagner does not give us enough to masticate. His recitative – very little meat, more bones, and plenty of broth – I christened '*alla genovese*': I had no intention of flattering the Genoese with this remark, but rather the *older recitativo*, the *recitativo secco*.[23] And as to Wagnerian *leitmotif*, I fear I lack the necessary culinary understanding for it. If hard pressed, I might say that I regard it perhaps as an ideal toothpick, as an opportunity of ridding one's self of what remains of one's meal. Wagner's 'arias' are still left over. But now I shall hold my tongue.

1888; translated by J. M. Kennedy, 1911

ARTHUR SYMONS

The Decadent Movement in Literature

The latest movement in European literature has been called by many names, none of them quite exact or comprehensive – Decadence, Symbolism, Impressionism, for instance. It is easy to dispute over words, and we shall find that Verlaine objects to being called a Decadent, Maeterlinck to being called a Symbolist, Huysmans to being called an Impressionist.[24] These terms, as it happens, have been adopted as the badge of little separate cliques, noisy, brainsick young people who haunt the brasseries of the Boulevard Saint-Michel, and exhaust their ingenuities in theorizing over the works they cannot write. But, taken frankly as epithets which express their own meaning, both Impressionism and Symbolism convey some notion of that new kind of literature which is perhaps more broadly characterized by the word Decadence. The most representative literature of the day – the writing which appeals to, which has done so much to form, the younger generation – is certainly not classic, nor has it any relation with that old antithesis of the Classic, the Romantic. After a fashion it is no doubt a decadence; it has all the qualities that mark the end of great periods, the qualities that we find in the Greek, the Latin, decadence: an intense self-consciousness, a restless curiosity in research, an over-subtilizing refinement upon refinement, a spiritual and moral perversity. If what we call the classic is indeed the supreme art – those qualities of perfect simplicity, perfect sanity, perfect proportion, the supreme qualities – then this representative literature of to-day, interesting, beautiful, novel as it is, is really a new and beautiful and interesting disease.

Healthy we cannot call it, and healthy it does not wish to be considered. The Goncourts,[25] in their prefaces, in their *Journal*, are always insisting on their own pet malady, *la névrose*.[26] It is in their work, too, that Huysmans notes with delight 'le style tacheté et faisandé' – high-flavoured and spotted with corruption – which he himself possesses in the highest degree. 'Having desire without light, curiosity without wisdom, seeking God by strange ways, by ways traced by the hands of men; offering rash incense upon the high places to an unknown God, who is the God of darkness' – that is how Ernest Hello, in one of his apocalyptic moments, characterizes the nineteenth century.[27] And this unreason of the soul – of which Hello himself is so curious a victim – this unstable equilibrium, which has overbalanced so many brilliant intelligences into one form or another of spiritual confusion, is but another form of the *maladie fin de siècle*. For its very disease of form, this literature is certainly typical of a civilization grown over-luxurious, over-inquiring, too languid for the relief of action, too uncertain for any emphasis in opinion or in conduct. It reflects all the moods, all the manners, of a sophisticated society; its very artificiality is a way of being true to nature: simplicity, sanity, proportion – the classic qualities – how much do we possess them in our life, our surroundings, that we should look to find them in our literature – so evidently the literature of a decadence?

Taking the word Decadence, then, as most precisely expressing the general sense of the newest movement in literature, we find that the terms Impressionism and Symbolism define correctly enough the two main branches of that movement. Now Impressionist and Symbolist have more in common than either supposes; both are really working on the same hypothesis, applied in different directions. What both seek is not general truth merely, but *la vérité vraie*, the very essence of truth – the truth of appearances to the senses, of the visible world to the eyes that see it: and the truth of spiritual things to the spiritual vision. The Impressionist, in literature as in painting, would flash upon you in a new, sudden way so exact an image of what you have just seen, just as you have seen it, that you may say, as a young American sculptor, a pupil of Rodin, said to me on seeing for the first time a picture of Whistler's, 'Whistler seems to think his picture upon canvas – and there it is!'[28] Or you may find, with Sainte-Beuve,[29] writing of Goncourt, the 'soul of the landscape' – the soul of whatever corner of the visible world has to be realized. The Symbolist, in this new, sudden way, would flash upon you the 'soul' of that which can be apprehended only by the soul – the finer sense of things unseen, the deeper meaning of things evident. And naturally, necessarily, this endeavour after a perfect truth to one's impression, to one's intuition – perhaps an impossible endeavour – has brought with it, in its revolt from ready-made impressions and conclusions, a revolt from the ready-made of language, from the bondage of traditional form, of a form become rigid. In France, where this movement began and has mainly flourished, it is Goncourt who was the first to invent a style in prose really new, impressionistic, a style which was itself almost sensation. It is Verlaine who has invented such another new style in verse.

The work of the brothers De Goncourt – twelve novels, eleven or twelve studies in the history of the eighteenth century, six or seven books about art, the art mainly of the eighteenth century and of Japan, two plays, some volumes of letters and of fragments, and a *Journal* in six volumes – is perhaps, in its intention and its consequences, the most revolutionary of the century. No one has ever tried so deliberately to do something new as the Goncourts: and the final word in the summing up which the survivor has placed at the head of the *Préfaces et Manifestes* is a word which speaks of 'tentatives enfin, où les deux frères ont cherchés à faire du neuf, ont fait leurs efforts pour doter les diverses branches de la littérature de quelque chose que n'avaient point songé à trouver leurs prédécesseurs.'[30] And in the preface to *Chérie*, in that pathetic passage which tells of the two brothers (one mortally stricken, and within a few months of death) taking their daily walk in the Bois de Boulogne, there is a definite demand on posterity. 'The search after reality in literature, the resurrection of eighteenth-century art, the triumph of *Japonisme*[31] – are not these,' said Jules, 'the three great literary and artistic movements of the second half of the nineteenth century? And it is we who brought them about, these three movements. Well, when one has done that, it is difficult indeed not to be *somebody* in the future.' Nor, even, is this all. What the Goncourts have done is to specialize vision, so to speak, and to subtilize language to the point of rendering every detail in just the form and colour of the actual impression. M. Edmond de Goncourt once said to me – varying, if I remember rightly, an expression he had put into the *Journal* – 'My brother and I invented an opera-glass: the young people nowadays are taking it out of our hands.'

An opera-glass – a special, unique way of seeing things – that is what the Goncourts have brought to bear upon the common things about us; and it is here that they have done the 'something new', here more than anywhere. They have never sought 'to see life steadily, and see it whole':[32] their vision has always been somewhat feverish, with the diseased sharpness of over-excited nerves. 'We do not hide from ourselves that we have been passionate, nervous creatures, unhealthily impressionable', confesses the *Journal*. But it is this morbid intensity in seeing and seizing things that has helped to form that marvellous style – 'a style perhaps too ambitious of impossibilities', as they admit – a style which inherits some of its colour from Gautier, some of its fine outline from Flaubert, but which has brought light and shadow into the colour, which has softened outline in the magic of atmosphere. With them words are not merely colour and sound, they live. That search after 'L'image peinte', 'l'épithète rare', is not (as with Flaubert) a search after harmony of phrase for its own sake; it is a desperate endeavour to give sensation, to flash the impression of the moment, to preserve the very heat and motion of life. And so, in analysis as in description, they have found out a way of noting the fine shades; they have broken the outline of the conventional novel in chapters, with its continuous story, in order to indicate – sometimes in a chapter of half a page – this and that revealing moment, this or that significant attitude or accident or sensation. For the placid traditions of French prose they have had but little respect; their aim has been but one, that of having (as M. Edmond de Goncourt tells us in the preface to *Chérie*) 'une langue rendant nos idées, nos sensations, nos figurations des hommes et des choses, d'une façon distincte de celui-ci ou de celui-là, une langue personnelle, une langue portant notre signature.'[33]

What Goncourt has done in prose – inventing absolutely a new way of saying things, to correspond with that new way of seeing things which he has found – Verlaine has done in verse. In a famous poem, 'Art Poétique', he has himself defined his own ideal of the poetic art:

'Car nous voulons la Nuance encor,
Pas la Couleur, rien que la Nuance!
Oh! la Nuance seule fiance
Le rêve au rêve et la flûte au cor!'[34]

Music first of all and before all, he insists; and then, not colour, but *la nuance*, the last fine shade. Poetry is to be something vague, intangible, evanescent, a winged soul in flight 'toward other skies and other loves'. To express the inexpressible he speaks of beautiful eyes behind a veil, of the palpitating sunlight of noon, of the blue swarm of clear stars in a cool autumn sky; and the verse in which he makes this confession of faith has the exquisite troubled beauty – 'sans rien en lui qui pèse ou qui pose'[35] – which he commends as the essential quality of verse. In a later poem of poetical counsel he tells us that art should, first of all, be absolutely clear, absolutely sincere: 'L'art, mes enfants, c'est d'être absolument soi-même.'[36] The two poems, with their seven years' interval – an interval which means so much in the life of a man like Verlaine – give us all that there is of theory in the work of the least theoretical, the most really instinctive, of poetical innovators. Verlaine's poetry has varied with his life; always in excess – now furiously sensual, now feverishly devout – he has been constant only to himself, to his own self-contradictions. For, with all the violence, turmoil, and disorder of a life which is almost the life of a modern Villon,[37] Paul Verlaine has always retained that childlike simplicity, and, in his verse, which has been his confessional, that fine sincerity, of which Villon may be thought to have set the example in literature.

Beginning his career as a Parnassian with the *Poèmes Saturniens*, Verlaine becomes himself, in his exquisite first manner, in the *Fêtes Galantes*, caprices after Watteau,[38] followed, a year later, by *La Bonne Chanson*, a happy record of too confident a lover's happiness. *Romances sans Paroles*, in which the poetry of Impressionism reaches its very highest point, is more *tourmenté*, goes deeper, becomes more poignantly personal. It is the poetry of sensation, of evocation; poetry which paints as well as sings, and which paints as Whistler paints, seeming to think the colors and outlines upon the canvas, to think them only, and they are there. The mere magic of words – words which evoke pictures, which recall sensations – can go no further; and in his next book, *Sagesse*, published after seven years' wanderings and sufferings, there is a graver manner of more deeply personal confession – that 'sincerity, and the impression of the moment followed to the letter', which he has defined in a prose criticism on himself as his main preference in regard to style. 'Sincerity, and the impression of the moment followed to the letter,' mark the rest of Verlaine's work, whether the sentiment be that of passionate friendship, as in *Amour*: of love, human and divine, as in *Bonheur*: of the mere lust of the flesh, as in *Parallèlement* and *Chansons pour Elle*. In his very latest verse the quality of simplicity has become exaggerated, has become, at times, childish; the once exquisite depravity of style has lost some of its distinction; there is no longer the same delicately vivid 'impression of the moment' to render. Yet the very closeness with which it follows a lamentable career gives a curious interest to even the worst of Verlaine's work. And how unique, how unsurpassable in its kind, is the best! 'Et tout le reste est littérature!' was the cry, supreme and contemptuous, of that early 'Art Poétique'; and, compared with Verlaine at his best, all other contemporary work in verse seems not yet disenfranchised from mere 'literature'. To fix the last fine shade, the quintessence of things; to fix it fleetingly; to be a disembodied voice, and yet the voice of a human soul: that is the ideal of Decadence, and it is what Paul Verlaine has achieved.

And certainly, so far as achievement goes, no other poet of the actual group in France can be named beside him or near him. But in Stéphane Mallarmé, with his supreme pose as the supreme poet, and his two or three pieces of exquisite verse and delicately artificial prose to show by way of result, we have the prophet and pontiff of the movement, the mystical and theoretical leader of the great emancipation. No one has ever dreamed such beautiful, impossible dreams as Mallarmé; no one has ever so possessed his soul in the contemplation of masterpieces to come. All his life he has been haunted by the desire to create, not so much something new in literature, as a literature which should itself be a new art. He has dreamed of a work into which all the arts should enter, and achieve themselves by a mutual interdependence – a harmonizing of all the arts into one supreme art – and he has theorized with infinite subtlety over the possibilities of doing the impossible. Every Tuesday for the last twenty years he has talked more fascinatingly, more suggestively, than any one else has ever done, in that little room in the Rue de Rome, to that little group of eager young poets. 'A seeker after something in the world, that is there in no satisfying measure, or not at all', he has carried his contempt for the usual, the conventional, beyond the point of literary expression, into the domain of practical affairs. Until the publication, quite recently, of a selection of *Vers et Prose*, it was only possible to get his poems in a limited and expensive edition, lithographed in fac-simile of his own clear and elegant handwriting. An aristocrat of letters, Mallarmé has always looked with intense disdain on the indiscriminate accident of universal suffrage. He has wished neither to be read nor to be understood by the bourgeois intelligence, and it is with some deliberateness of intention that he has made both issues impossible. M. Catulle Mendès[39] defines him admirably as 'a difficult author', and in his latest period he has succeeded in becoming absolutely unintelligible. His early poems, 'L'Après-midi d'un Faune', 'Hérodiade', for example, and some exquisite sonnets, and one or two fragments of perfectly polished verse, are written in a language which has nothing in common with every-day language – symbol within symbol, image within image; but symbol and image achieve themselves in expression without seeming to call for the necessity of a key. The latest poems (in which punctuation is sometimes entirely suppressed, for our further bewilderment) consist merely of a sequence of symbols, in which every word must be taken in a sense with which its ordinary significance has nothing to do. Mallarmé's contortion of the French language, so far as mere style is concerned, is curiously similar to the kind of depravation which was undergone by the Latin language in its decadence. It is, indeed, in part a reversion to Latin phraseology, to the Latin construction, and it has made, of the clear and flowing French language, something irregular, unquiet, expressive, with sudden surprising felicities, with nervous starts and lapses, with new capacities for the exact noting of sensation. Alike to the ordinary and to the scholarly reader, it is painful, intolerable; a jargon, a massacre. Supremely self-confident, and backed, certainly, by an ardent following of the younger generation, Mallarmé goes on his way, experimenting more and more audaciously, having achieved by this time, at all events, a style wholly his own. Yet the 'chef-d'oeuvre inconnu' seems no nearer completion, the impossible seems no more likely to be done. The two or three beautiful fragments remain, and we still hear the voice in the Rue de Rome.

Probably it is as a voice, an influence, that Mallarmé will be remembered. His personal magnetism has had a great deal to do with the making of the very newest French literature; few literary beginners in Paris have been able to escape the rewards and punishments of his contact, his suggestion. One of the young poets who form that delightful Tuesday evening coterie said to me the other day, 'We owe much to Mallarmé, but he has kept us all back three years.' That is where the danger of so inspiring, so helping a personality comes in. The work even of M. Henri de Regnier,[40] who is the best of the disciples, has not entirely got clear from the influence that has shown his fine talent the way to develop. Perhaps it is in the verse of men who are not exactly following in the counsel of the master – who might disown him, whom he might disown – that one sees most clearly the outcome of his theories, the actual consequences of his practice. In regard to the construction of verse, Mallarmé has always remained faithful to the traditional syllabic measurement; but the freak or the discovery of 'le vers libre' is certainly the natural consequence of his experiments upon the elasticity of rhythm, upon the power of resistance of the caesura. 'Le vers libre' in the hands of most of the experimenters becomes merely rhymeless irregular prose; in the hands of Gustave Kahn[41] and Edouard Dujardin[42] it has, it must be admitted, attained a certain beauty of its own. I never really understood the charm that may be found in this apparently structureless rhythm until I heard, not long since, M. Dujardin read aloud the as yet unpublished conclusion of a dramatic poem in several parts. It was rhymed, but rhymed with some irregularity, and the rhythm was purely and simply a vocal effect. The rhythm came and went as the spirit moved. You might deny that it was rhythm at all; and yet, read as I heard it read, in a sort of slow chant, it produced on me the effect of really beautiful verse. But M. Dujardin is a poet: 'vers libres' in the hands of a sciolist are the most intolerably easy and annoying of poetical exercises. Even in the case of *Le Pèlerin Passionné* I cannot see the justification of what is merely regular syllabic verse lengthened or shortened arbitrarily, with the Alexandrine always evident in the background as the foot-rule of the new metre. In this hazardous experiment M. Jean Moréas,[43] whose real talent lies in quite another direction, has brought nothing into literature but an example of deliberate singularity for singularity's sake. I seem to find the measure of the man in a remark I once heard him make in a café, where we were discussing the technique of metre: 'You, Verlaine,' he cried, leaning across the table, 'have only written lines of sixteen syllables: *I* have written lines of twenty syllables.' And turning to me, he asked anxiously if Swinburne had ever done that – had written a line of twenty syllables.

That is indeed the measure of the man, and it points a criticism upon not a few of the busy little *littérateurs* who are founding new *revues* every other week in Paris. These people have nothing to say, but they are resolved to say something, and to say it in the newest mode. They are Impressionists because it is the fashion, Symbolists because it is the vogue, Decadents because Decadence is in the very air of the cafés. And so, in their manner, they are mile-posts on the way of this new movement, telling how far it has gone. But to find a new personality, a new way of seeing things, among the young writers who are starting up on every hand, we must turn from Paris to Brussels – to the so-called Belgian Shakespeare, Maurice Maeterlinck. M. Maeterlinck was discovered to the general French public by M. Octave Mirbeau,[44] in an article in the *Figaro*, August 24, 1890, on the publication of *La Princesse Maleine*. 'M. Maurice Maeterlinck nous a donné l'oeuvre la plus géniale de ce temps, et la plus extraordinaire et la plus naïve aussi, comparable et – oserai-je le dire? – supérieure en beauté à ce qui il y a de plus beau dans Shakespeare . . . plus tragique que *Macbeth*, plus extraordinaire en pensée que *Hamlet*.'[45] That is how the enthusiast announced his discovery. In truth, M. Maeterlinck is not a Shakespeare, and the Elizabethan violence of his first play is of the school of Webster and Tourneur rather than of Shakespeare. As a dramatist he has but one note, that of fear; he has but one method, that of repetition. In *La Princesse Maleine* there is a certain amount of action – action which is certainly meant to reinvest the terrors of *Macbeth* and of *Lear*. In *L'Intruse* and *Les Aveugles* the scene is stationary, the action but reflected upon the stage, as if from another plane. In *Les Sept Princesses* the action, such as it is, is 'such stuff as dreams are made of', and is literally, in great part, seen through a window.

This window, looking out upon the unseen – an open door, as in *L'Intruse*, through which Death, the intruder, may come invisibly – how typical of the new kind of symbolistic and impressionistic drama which M. Maeterlinck has invented! I say invented, a little rashly. The real discoverer of this new kind of drama was that strange, inspiring, incomplete man of genius whom M. Maeterlinck, above all others, delights to honour, Villiers de l'Isle-Adam.[46] Imagine a combination of Swift, of Poe, and of Coleridge, and you will have some idea of the extraordinary, impossible poet and cynic who, after a life of brilliant failure, has left a series of unfinished works in every kind of literature; among the finished achievements one volume of short stories *Contes Cruels*, which is an absolute masterpiece. Yet, apart from this, it was the misfortune of Villiers never to attain the height of his imaginings, and even *Axël*, the work of a lifetime, is an achievement only half achieved. Only half achieved, or achieved only in the work of others; for, in its mystical intention, its remoteness from any kind of outward reality, *Axël* is undoubtedly the origin of the symbolistic drama. This drama, in Villiers, is of pure symbol, of sheer poetry. It has an exalted eloquence which we find in none of his followers. As M. Maeterlinck has developed it, it is a drama which appeals directly to the sensations – sometimes crudely, sometimes subtly – playing its variations upon the very nerves themselves. The 'vague spiritual fear' which it creates out of our nervous apprehension is unlike anything that has ever been done before, even by Hoffmann, even by Poe. It is an effect of atmosphere – an atmosphere in which outlines change and become mysterious, in which a word quietly uttered makes one start, in which all one's mental activity becomes concentrated on something, one knows not what, something slow, creeping, terrifying, which comes nearer and nearer, an impending nightmare.

La Princesse Maleine, it is said, was written for a theatre of marionettes, and it is certainly with the effect of marionettes that these sudden, exclamatory people come and go. Maleine, Hjalmar, Uglyane – these are no men and women, but a masque of shadows, a dance of silhouettes behind the white sheet of the 'Chat Noir', and they have the fantastic charm of these enigmatical semblances, 'luminous, gemlike, ghostlike', with, also, their somewhat mechanical eeriness. The personages of *L'Intruse*, of *Les Aveugles* – in which the spiritual terror and physical apprehension which are common to all M. Maeterlinck's work have become more interior – are mere abstractions, typifying age, infancy, disaster, but with scarcely a suggestion of individual character. And the style itself is a sort of abstraction, all the capacities of language being deliberately abandoned for a simplicity which, in its calculated repetition, is like the drip, drip, of a tiny stream of water. M. Maeterlinck is difficult to quote, but here, in English, is a passage from Act I, of *La Princesse Maleine*, which will indicate something of this Biblically monotonous style:

> 'I cannot see you. Come hither, there is more light here; lean back your head a little towards the sky. You too are strange to-night! It is as though my eyes were opened to-night! It is as though my heart were half opened to-night! But I think you are strangely beautiful! But you are strangely beautiful, Uglyane! It seems to me that I have never looked on you till now! But I think you are strangely beautiful! There is something about you. . . . Let us go elsewhither – under the light – come!'

As an experiment in a new kind of drama, these curious plays do not seem to exactly achieve themselves on the stage; it is difficult to imagine how they could ever be made so impressive, when thus externalized, as they are when all is left to the imagination. *L'Intruse*, for instance, which was given at the Haymarket Theatre on January 27, 1892 – not quite faithfully given, it is true – seemed, as one saw it then, too faint in outline, with too little carrying power for scenic effect. But M. Maeterlinck is by no means anxious to be considered merely or mainly as a dramatist. A brooding poet, a mystic, a contemplative spectator of the comedy of death – that is how he presents himself to us in his work; and the introduction which he has prefixed to his translation of *L'Ornement des Noces Spirituelles*, of Ruysbroeck l'Admirable, shows how deeply he has studied the mystical writers of all ages, and how much akin to theirs is his own temper. Plato and Plotinus, St. Bernard and Jacob Boehm, Coleridge and Novalis – he knows them all, and it is with a sort of reverence that he sets himself to the task of translating the astonishing Flemish mystic of the thirteenth century, known till now only by the fragments translated into French by Ernest Hello from a sixteenth century Latin version. This translation and this introduction help to explain the real character of M. Maeterlinck's dramatic work – dramatic as to form, by a sort of accident, but essentially mystical.

Partly akin to M. Maeterlinek by race, more completely alien from him in temper than it is possible to express, Joris Karl Huysmans demands a prominent place in any record of the Decadent movement. His work, like that of the Goncourts, is largely determined by the *maladie fin de siècle* – the diseased nerves that, in his case, have given a curious personal quality of pessimism to his outlook on the world, his view of life. Part of his work – *Marthe, Les Soeurs Vatard, En Ménage, A Vau-l'Eau* – is a minute and searching study of the minor discomforts, the commonplace miseries of life, as seen by a peevishly disordered vision, delighting, for its own self-torture, in the insistent contemplation of human stupidity, of the sordid in existence. Yet these books do but lead up to the unique masterpiece, the astonishing caprice of *A Rebours*, in which he has concentrated all that is delicately depraved, all that is beautifully, curiously poisonous, in modern art. *A Rebours* is the history of a typical Decadent – a study, indeed, after a real man, but a study which seizes the type rather than the personality. In the sensations and ideas of Des Esseintes we see the sensations and ideas of the effeminate, over-civilized, deliberately abnormal creature who is the last product of our society: partly the father, partly the offspring, of the perverse art that he adores. Des Esseintes creates for his solace, in the wilderness of a barren and profoundly uncomfortable world, an artificial paradise. His *Thébaïde raffinée*[47] is furnished elaborately for candle-light, equipped with the pictures, the books, that satisfy his sense of the exquisitely abnormal. He delights in the Latin of Apuleius and Petronius, in the French of Baudelaire, Goncourt, Verlaine, Mallarmé, Villiers; in the pictures of Gustave Moreau, the French Burne-Jones, of Odilon Redon, the French Blake.[48] He delights in the beauty of strange, unnatural flowers, in the melodic combination of scents, in the imagined harmonies of the sense of taste. And at last, exhausted by these spiritual and sensory debauches in the delights of the artificial, he is left (as we close the book) with a brief, doubtful choice before him – madness or death, or else a return to nature, to the normal life.

Since *A Rebours*, M. Huysmans has written one other remarkable book, *Là-Bas*, a study in the hysteria and mystical corruption of contemporary Black Magic. But it is on that one exceptional achievement, *A Rebours*, that his fame will rest; it is there that he has expressed not merely himself, but an epoch. And he has done so in a style which carries the modern experiments upon language to their furthest development. Formed upon Goncourt and Flaubert, it has sought for novelty, *l'image peinte*, the exactitude of colour, the forcible precision of epithet, wherever words, images, or epithets are to be found. Barbaric in its profusion, violent in its emphasis, wearying in its splendour, it is – especially in regard to things seen – extraordinarily expressive, with all the shades of a painter's palette. Elaborately and deliberately perverse, it is in its very perversity that Huysmans's work – so fascinating, so repellent, so instinctively artificial – comes to represent, as the work of no other writer can be said to do, the main tendencies, the chief results, of the Decadent movement in literature.

Such, then, is the typical literature of the Decadence – literature which, as we have considered it so far, is entirely French. But those qualities which we find in the work of Goncourt, Verlaine, Huysmans – qualities which have permeated literature much more completely in France than in any other country – are not wanting in the recent literature of other countries. In Holland there is a new school of Sensitivists, as they call themselves, who have done some remarkable work – Couperus, in *Ecstasy*, for example – very much on the lines of the French art of Impressionism. In Italy, Luigi Capuana (in *Giacinta*, for instance) has done some wonderful studies of morbid sensation; Gabriele d'Annunzio, in that marvellous, malarious *Piacere*, has achieved a triumph of exquisite perversity. In Spain, one of the principal novelists, Señora Pardo-Bazan, has formed herself, with some deliberateness, after Goncourt, grafting his method, curiously enough, upon a typically Spanish Catholicism of her own. In Norway, Ibsen has lately developed a personal kind of Impressionism (in *Hedda Gabler*) and of Symbolism (in *The Master-Builder*) – 'opening the door', in his own phrase, 'to the younger generation'.[49] And in England, too, we find the same influences at work. The prose of Mr. Walter Pater, the verse of Mr. W. E. Henley[50] – to take two prominent examples – are attempts to do with the English language something of what Goncourt and Verlaine have done with the French. Mr. Pater's prose is the most beautiful English prose which is now being written; and unlike the prose of Goncourt, it has done no violence to language, it has sought after no vivid effects, it has found a large part of mastery in reticence, in knowing what to omit. But how far away from the classic ideals of style is this style in which words have their colour, their music, their perfume, in which there is 'some strangeness in the proportion' of every beauty! The *Studies in the Renaissance* have made of criticism a new art – have raised criticism almost to the act of creation. And *Marius the Epicurean*, in its study of 'sensations and ideas' (the conjunction was Goncourt's before it was Mr. Pater's) and the *Imaginary Portraits*, in their evocations of the Middle Ages, the age of Watteau – have they not that morbid subtlety of analysis, that morbid curiosity of form, that we have found in the works of the French Decadents? A fastidiousness equal to that of Flaubert[51] has limited Mr. Pater's work to six volumes, but in these six volumes there is not a page that is not perfectly finished, with a conscious art of perfection. In its minute elaboration it can be compared only with goldsmith's work – so fine, so delicate is the handling of so delicate, so precious a material. Mr. Henley's work in verse has none of the characteristics of Mr. Pater's work in prose. Verlaine's definition of his own theory of poetical writing – 'sincerity, and the impression of the moment followed to the letter' – might well be adopted as a definition of Mr. Henley's theory or practice. In *A Book of Verses* and *The Song of the Sword* he has brought into the traditional conventionalities of modern English verse the note of a new personality, the touch of a new method. The poetry of Impressionism can go no further, in one direction, than that series of rhymes and rhythms named *In Hospital*. The ache and throb of the body in its long nights on a tumbled bed, and as it lies on the operating-table awaiting 'the thick, sweet mystery of chloroforms', are brought home to us as nothing else that I know in poetry has ever brought the physical sensations. And for a sharper, closer truth of rendering, Mr. Henley has resorted (after the manner of Heine)[52] to a rhymeless form of lyric verse, which in his hands, certainly, is sensitive and expressive. Whether this kind of *vers libre* can fully compensate, in what it gains of freedom and elasticity, for what it loses of compact form and vocal appeal, is a difficult question. It is one that Mr. Henley's verse is far from solving in the affirmative, for, in his work, the finest things to my mind, are rhymed. In the purely impressionistic way, do not the *London Voluntaries*, which are rhymed, surpass all the unrhymed vignettes and nocturnes which attempt the same quality of result? They flash before us certain aspects of the poetry of London as only Whistler had ever done and in another art. Nor is it only the poetry of cities, as here, nor the poetry of the disagreeable, as in *In Hospital*, that Mr. Henley can evoke: he can evoke the magic of personal romance. He has written verse that is exquisitely frivolous, daintily capricious, wayward and fugitive as the winged remembrance of some momentary delight. And, in certain fragments he has come nearer than any other English singer to what I have called the achievement of Verlaine and the ideal of the Decadence: to be a disembodied voice, and yet the voice of a human soul.

1893

MAX NORDAU

From *Degeneration*: Book 3, 'Ego-Mania', chapter 3, 'Decadents and Aesthetes'

A later disciple, M. Joris Karl Huysmans, is more instructive than all those imitators of Baudelaire who have only developed the one or the other side of him. He has undertaken the toilsome task of putting together, from all the isolated traits which are found dispersed in Baudelaire's poems and prose writings, a human figure, and of presenting to us Baudelairism incarnate and living, thinking and acting. The book in which he shows us his model 'Decadent' is entitled *A Rebours* ('Against the Grain').

The word 'décadent' was borrowed by the French critics, in the fifties, from the history of the declining Roman Empire, to characterize the style of Théophile Gautier, and notably of Baudelaire. At the present time the disciples of these two writers, and of their previous imitators, claim it as a title of honour. Otherwise than with the expressions 'pre-Raphaelites' and 'Symbolists,' we possess an exact explanation of the sense which those who speak of 'decadence' and 'decadents' attach to these words.

'The style of decadence,' says Théophile Gautier,[53] '... is nothing else than art arrived at that extreme point of maturity produced by those civilizations which are growing old with their oblique suns [!] – a style that is ingenious, complicated, learned, full of shades of meaning and research, always pushing further the limits of language, borrowing from all the technical vocabularies, taking colours from all palettes, notes from all keyboards, forcing itself to express in thought that which is most ineffable, and in form the vaguest and most fleeting contours; listening, that it may translate them, to the subtle confidences of the neuropath, to the avowals of ageing and depraved passion, and to the singular hallucinations of the fixed idea verging on madness. This style of decadence is the last effort of the Word (*Verbe*), called upon to express everything, and pushed to the utmost extremity. We may remind ourselves, in connection with it, of the language of the Later Roman Empire, already mottled with the greenness of decomposition, and, as it were, gamy (*faisandée*), and of the complicated refinements of the Byzantine school, the last form of Greek art fallen into deliquescence. Such is the inevitable and fatal idiom of peoples and civilizations where factitious life has replaced the natural life, and developed in man unknown wants. Besides, it is no easy matter, this style despised of pedants, for it expresses new ideas with new forms and words that have not yet been heard. In opposition to the classic style, it admits of shading, and these shadows teem and swarm with the larvae of superstitions, the haggard phantoms of insomnia, nocturnal terrors, remorse which starts and turns back at the slightest noise, monstrous dreams stayed only by impotence, obscure phantasies at which the daylight would stand amazed, and all that the soul conceals of the dark, the unformed, and the vaguely horrible, in its deepest and furthest recesses.'

The same ideas that Gautier approximately expresses in this rigmarole, Baudelaire enumerates in these terms: 'Does it not seem to the reader, as it does to me, that the language of the later Latin decadence – the departing sigh of a robust person already transformed and prepared for the spiritual life – is singularly appropriate to express passion as it has been understood and felt by the modern poetic world? Mysticism is the opposite pole of that magnet in which Catullus and his followers, brutal and purely epidermic poets, have only recognised the pole of sensuality. In this marvellous language, solecism and barbarism appear to me to convey the forced negligences of a passion which forgets itself and mocks at rules. Words, received in a new acceptation, display the charming awkwardness of the Northern barbarian kneeling before the Roman beauty. Even a play on words, when it enters into these pedantic stammerings, does it not display the wild and bizarre grace of infancy?'[54]

The reader, who has the chapter on the psychology of mysticism present to his mind, naturally at once recognises what is hidden behind the word-wash of Gautier and Baudelaire. Their description of the state of mind which the 'decadent' language is supposed to express is simply a description of the disposition of the mystically degenerate mind, with its shifting nebulous ideas, its fleeting formless shadowy thought, its perversions and aberrations, its tribulations and impulsions. To express this state of mind, a new and unheard-of language must in fact be found, since there cannot be in any customary language designations corresponding to presentations which in reality do not exist. It is absolutely arbitrary to seek for an example and a model of 'decadent' expression in the language of the Later Roman Empire. It would be difficult for Gautier to discover in any writer whatever of the fourth or fifth century the 'mottled greenness of decomposition and, as it were, gamy' Latin which so greatly charms him. M. Huysmans, monstrously exaggerating Gautier's and Baudelaire's idea, as is the way with imitators, gives the following description of this supposed Latin of the fifth century: 'The Latin tongue, . . . now hung [!], completely rotten, . . . losing its members, dropping suppurations, scarcely preserving, in the total decay of its body, some firm parts which the Christians detached in order to pickle them in the brine of their new language.'[55]

This debauch in pathological and nauseous ideas of a deranged mind with gustatory perversion is a delirium, and has no foundation whatever in philological facts. The Latin of the later period of decadence was coarse and full of errors, in consequence of the increasing barbarity in the manners and taste of the readers, the narrow-mindedness and grammatical ignorance of the writers, and the intrusion of barbarous elements into its vocabulary. But it was very far from expressing 'new ideas with new forms' and from taking 'colours from all palettes'; it surprises us, on the contrary, by its awkwardness in rendering the most simple thoughts, and by its profound impoverishment. The German language has also had a similar period of decadence. After the Thirty Years' War, even the best writers, a Moscherosch, a Zinkgref, a Schupp,[56] were 'often almost incomprehensible' with 'their long-winded and involved periods', and 'their deportment as distorted as it was stiff';[57] the grammar displayed the worst deformities, the vocabulary swarmed with strange intruders, but the German of those desolate decades was surely not 'decadent' in the sense of Gautier's, Baudelaire's and Huysmans's definitions. The truth is, that these degenerate writers have arbitrarily attributed their own state of mind to the authors of the Roman and Byzantine decadence, to a Petronius, but especially to a Commodianus of Gaza, an Ausonius, a Prudentius, a Sidonius Apollinaris, etc.,[58] and have created in their own image, or according to their morbid instincts, an 'ideal man of the Roman decadence', just as Rousseau invented the ideal savage and Chateaubriand the ideal Indian, and have transported him by their own imagination into a fabulous past or into a distant country. M. Paul Bourget is more honest when he refrains from fraudulently quoting the Latin authors of the Latin decline, and thus describes the 'decadence', independently of his Parnassian masters: 'The word "decadence" denotes a state of society which produces too great a number of individuals unfit for the labours of common life. A society ought to be assimilated to an organism. As an organism, in fact, it resolves itself into a federation of lesser organisms, which again resolve themselves into a federation of cells. The individual is the social cell. In order that the whole organism should function with energy, it is necessary that the component organisms should function with energy, but with a subordinate energy. And in order that these inferior organisms should themselves function with energy, it is necessary that their component cells should function with energy, but with a subordinate energy. If the energy of the cells becomes independent, the organisms composing the total organism cease likewise to subordinate their energy to the total energy, and the anarchy which takes place constitutes the decadence of the whole.'[59]

Very true. A society in decadence 'produces too great a number of individuals unfit for the labours of common life'; these individuals are precisely the degenerate; 'they cease to subordinate their energy to the total energy', because they are ego-maniacs, and their stunted development has not attained to the height at which an individual reaches his moral and intellectual junction with the totality, and their ego-mania makes the degenerate necessarily anarchists, i.e., enemies of all institutions which they do not understand, and to which they cannot adapt themselves. It is very characteristic that M. Bourget, who sees all this, who recognises that 'decadent' is synonymous with inaptitude for regular functions and subordination to social aims, and that the consequence of decadence is anarchy and the ruin of the community, does not the less justify and admire the decadents, especially Baudelaire. This is 'la conscience dans le mal' of which his master speaks.

We will now examine the ideal 'decadent' that Huysmans draws so complacently and in such detail for us, in *A Rebours*. First, a word on the author of this instructive book. Huysmans, the classical type of the hysterical mind without originality, who is the predestined victim of every suggestion, began his literary career as a fanatical imitator of Zola, and produced, in this first period of his development, romances and novels in which (as in *Marthe*)[60] he greatly surpassed his model in obscenity. Then he swerved from naturalism, by an abrupt change of disposition, which is no less genuinely hysterical, overwhelmed this tendency and Zola himself with the most violent abuse, and began to ape the Diabolists, particularly Baudelaire. A red thread unites both of his otherwise abruptly contrasted methods, viz., his lubricity. That has remained the same. He is, as a languishing 'Decadent', quite as vulgarly obscene as when he was a bestial 'Naturalist'.[61]

A Rebours can scarcely be called a novel, and Huysmans, in fact, does not call it so. It does not reveal a history, it has no action, but presents itself as a sort of portrayal or biography of a man whose habits, sympathies and antipathies, and ideas on all possible subjects, specially on art and literature, are related to us in great detail. This man is called Des Esseintes, and is the last scion of an ancient French ducal title.

The Duke Jean des Esseintes is physically an anaemic and nervous man of weak constitution, the inheritor of all the vices and all the degeneracies of an exhausted race. 'For two centuries the Des Esseintes had married their children to each other, consuming their remnant of vigour in consanguineous unions. . . . The predominance of lymph in the blood appeared.'[62] (This employment of technical expressions and empty phrases, scientific in sound, is peculiar to many modern degenerate authors and to their imitators. They sow these words and expressions around them, as the 'learned valet' of a well-known German farce[63] scatters around him his scraps of French, but without being more cognizant of science than the latter was of the French language.) Des Esseintes was educated by the Jesuits, lost his parents early in life, squandered the greater part of his patrimony in foolish carousing which overwhelmed him with ennui, and soon retired from society, which had become insupportable. 'His contempt for humanity increased; he understood at last that the world is composed for the most part of bullies and imbeciles. He had certainly no hope of discovering in others the same aspirations and the same hatreds, no hope of uniting himself with a kindred spirit delighting in a diligent decrepitude [!] as he did. Enervated, moody, exasperated by the inanity of interchanged and accepted ideas, he became like a person aching all over, till at last he was constantly excoriating his epidermis, and suffering from the patriotic and social nonsense which was dealt out each morning in the newspapers. . . . He dreamed of a refined Thebaid, of a comfortable desert, a warm and unmoving ark, where he would take refuge far from the incessant flood of human stupidity.'[64]

He realizes this dream. He sells his possessions, buys Government stock with the ruins of his fortune, draws in this way an annual income of fifty thousand francs, buys himself a house which stands alone on a hill at some distance from a small village near Paris, and arranges it according to his own taste.

'The artificial appeared to Des Esseintes as the distinguishing mark of human genius. As he expressed it, the day of nature is past: by the disgusting uniformity of its landscapes and skies, it has positively exhausted the attentive patience of refined spirits. In sooth, what platitude of a specialist who sees no further than his own line! what pettiness of a tradeswoman keeping this or that article to the exclusion of every other! what a monotonous stock of meadows and trees! what a commonplace agency for mountains and seas!'.

He banishes, in consequence, all that is natural from his horizon, and surrounds himself by all that is artificial. He sleeps during the day, and only leaves his bed towards evening, in order to pass the night in reading and musing in his brightly-lit ground-floor. He never crosses the threshold of his house, but remains within his four walls. He will see no one, and even the old couple who wait on him must do their work while he is asleep, so as not to be seen by him. He receives neither letters nor papers, knows nothing of the outer world. He never has an appetite, and when by chance this is aroused, 'he dips his roast meat, covered with some extraordinary butter, into a cup of tea [oh, the devil!], a faultless mixture of Si-a-Fayun, Mo-yu-tan and Khansky, yellow teas brought from China and Russia by special caravans'.

His dining-room 'resembled a ship's cabin', with 'its little French window opening in the wainscot like a port-hole'. It was built within a larger room pierced by two windows, one of which was exactly opposite the port-hole in the wainscot. A large aquarium occupied the whole space between the port-hole and this window. In order, then, to give light to the cabin, the daylight had to pass through the window, the panes of which had been replaced by plate glass, and then through the water. 'Sometimes, in the afternoon, when by chance Des Esseintes was awake and up, he set in motion the play of the pipes and conduits which emptied the aquarium and filled it afresh with pure water, introducing into it drops of coloured essences, thus producing for himself at pleasure the green or muddy yellow, opalescent or silver, tones of a real river, according to the colour of the sky, the greater or less heat of the sun, the more or less decided indications of rain; in a word, according to the season and the weather. He would then imagine himself to be between-decks on a brig, and contemplated with curiosity marvellous mechanical fish, constructed with clock-work, which passed before the window of the port-hole, and clung to the sham weeds, or else, while breathing the smell of the tar with which the room had been filled before he entered, he examined the coloured engravings hung on the walls representing steamers sailing for Valparaiso and La Plata, such as are seen at steamship agencies, and at Lloyd's'.

These mechanical fish are decidedly more remarkable than Baudelaire's landscapes in tin. But this dream of an ironmonger, retired from business and become an idiot, was not the only pleasure of the Duc des Esseintes, who despised so deeply the 'stupidity and vulgarity of men', although, of all his acquaintance, probably not one would have stooped to ideas so asinine as these mechanical fish with clock-work movements. When he wishes to do himself a particularly good turn, he composes and plays a gustatory symphony. He has had a cupboard constructed containing a series of little liqueur barrels. The taps of all the barrels could be opened or shut simultaneously by an engine set in motion by pressure on a knob in the wainscot, and under every tap stood an 'imperceptible' goblet, into which, on the turning of the cock, a drop fell. Des Esseintes called this liquor-cupboard his 'mouth organ'. (Notice all these ridiculous complications to mix a variety of liqueurs! As if it required all this deeply thought out mechanism!) 'The organ was then open. The stops labelled "flute, horn, voix céleste", were drawn out ready for action. Des Esseintes drank a drop here and there, played internal symphonies, and succeeded in procuring in the throat sensations analogous to those that music offers to the ear. Each liqueur corresponded in taste, according to him, to the sound of an instrument. Dry curaçoa, for example, to the clarionet, the tone of which is acescent and velvety; kümmel brandy to the oboë, with its sonorous nasal sound; mint and anisette to the flute, which is at the same time sugary and peppery, squeaking and sweet; while, to complete the orchestra, kirsch rages with the blast of a trumpet; gin and whisky scarify the palate with their shrill outbursts of cornets and trombones; liqueur-brandy fulminates with the deafening crash of the tuba; while Chios-raki and mastic roll on to the mucous membrane like the thunder-claps of cymbals and kettledrums struck with the arm!' Thus he plays 'string quartettes under the vault of his palate, representing with the violin old eau-de-vie, smoky and subtle, sharp and delicate; with the tenor simulated by strong rum'; with vespetro as violoncello, and bitters as double bass; green chartreuse was the major, and benedictine the minor key,' etc.

Des Esseintes does not only hear the music of the liqueurs: he sniffs also the colour of perfumes. As he has a mouth organ, he possesses a nasal picture-gallery, *i.e.*, a large collection of flasks containing all possible odorous substances. When his taste-symphonies no longer give him pleasure, he plays an olfactory tune. 'Seated in his dressing-room before his table . . . a little fever disturbed him, he was ready for work. . . . With his vaporizers he injected into the room an essence formed of ambrosia, Mitcham lavender, sweet peas, ess. bouquet, an essence which, when it is distilled by an artist, deserves the name by which it is known, viz., "extract of flowery meadow". Then, in this meadow, he introduced an exact fusion of tuberose, of orange and almond flower, and forthwith artificially-created lilacs sprang up, while limes winnowed each other, pouring down upon the earth their pale emanations. Into this decoration, laid on in broad outlines . . . he blew . . . a light rain of human and quasi-feline essences, savouring of skirts, and indicating the powdered and painted woman, the stephanotis, ayapana, opoponax, cypress, champak, and sarcanthus: on which he juxtaposed a suspicion of syringa, in order to instil into the factitious atmosphere which emanated from them a natural bloom of laughter bathed in sweat (!!), and of joys which riot boisterously in full sunshine'.

We have seen how slavishly M. Huysmans, in his drivel about tea, liqueurs and perfumes, follows to the letter the fundamental principle of the Parnassians – of ransacking technical dictionaries. He has evidently been forced to copy the catalogues of commercial travellers dealing in perfumes and soaps, teas and liqueurs, to scrape together his erudition in current prices.

That Des Esseintes should be made ill by this mode of life is not surprising. His stomach rejects all forms of food, and this renders the highest triumph of his love for the artificial possible: he is obliged to be nourished by means of peptonized injections, hence, in a way, diametrically opposed to nature.

Not to be too prolix, I omit many details, e.g., an endless description of tones associated with colours; of orchids which he loves, because they have for him the appearance of eruptions, scars, scabs, ulcers and cancers, and seem covered with dressings, plastered with black mercurial axunge, green belladonna unguents; an exposition of the mystical aspect of precious and half-precious stones, etc. We will only acquaint ourselves with a few more peculiarities of taste in this decadent type:

'The wild spirit, the rough, careless talent of Goya captivated him; but the universal admiration which Goya's works had gained deterred him somewhat, and for many years he had ceased having them framed. . . . Indeed, if the finest tune in the world becomes vulgar, insupportable, as soon as the public hum it and barrel-organs seize upon it, the work of art to which false artists are not indifferent, which is not disputed by fools, which is not content with stirring up the enthusiasm of some, even it becomes, by this very means, for the initiated polluted, commonplace and almost repulsive'.

The reference to barrel-organs is a trick calculated to mislead the inattentive reader. If a beautiful tune becomes insupportable as played on barrel-organs, it is because the organs are false, noisy and expressionless, i.e., they modify the very essence of the tune and drag it down to vulgarity; but the admiration of the greatest fool himself changes absolutely nothing in a work of art, and those who have loved it for its qualities will again find all these qualities complete and intact, even when the looks of millions of impassive Philistines have crawled over it. The truth is, the decadent, bursting with silly vanity, here betrays involuntarily his inmost self. The fellow has not, in fact, the smallest comprehension of art, and is wholly inaccessible to the beautiful as to all external impressions. To know if a work of art pleases him or not, he does not look at the work of art – oh no! he turns his back and anxiously studies the demeanour of the people standing before it. Are they enthusiastic, the decadent despises the work; do they remain indifferent, or even appear displeased, he admires it with full conviction. The ordinary man always seeks to think, to feel, and to do the same as the multitude; the decadent seeks exactly the contrary. Both derive the manner of seeing and feeling, not from their internal convictions, but from what the crowd dictate to them. Both lack all individuality, and they are obliged to have their eyes constantly fixed on the crowd to find their way. The decadent is, therefore, an ordinary man with a minus sign, who, equally with the latter, only in a contrary sense, follows in the wake of the crowd, and meanwhile makes things far more difficult for himself than the ordinary man; he is also constantly in a state of irritation, while the latter as constantly enjoys himself. This can be summed up in one proposition – the decadent snob is an anti-social Philistine, suffering from a mania for contradiction, without the smallest feeling for the work of art itself.

Des Esseintes reads occasionally between his gustatory and olfactory séances. The only works which please him are naturally those of the most extreme Parnassians and Symbolists. For he finds in them 'the death-struggle of the old language, after it had become ever mouldier from century to century, was ending in dissolution, and in the attainment of that deliquescence of the Latin language which gave up the ghost in the mysterious concepts and enigmatical expressions of St. Boniface and St. Adhelm. Moreover, the decomposition of the French language had set in all at once. In the Latin language there was a long transition, a lapse of 400 years, between the speckled and beautiful speech of Claudian and Rutilius, and the gamy speech of the eighth century. In the French language no lapse of time, no succession in age, had taken place; the speckled (*tacheté*) and superb style of the brothers De Goncourt and the gamy style of Verlaine and Mallarmé rubbed elbows in Paris, existing at the same time and in the same century.'

We now know the taste of a typical decadent in all directions. Let us cast another glance at his character, morals, sentiments and political views.

He has a friend, D'Aigurande, who one day thinks of marrying. 'Arguing from the fact that D'Aigurande possessed no fortune, and that the dowry of his wife was almost nothing, he (Des Esseintes) perceived in this simple desire an infinite perspective of ridiculous misfortunes.' In consequence (!) he encouraged his friend to commit this folly, and what had to happen did happen: the young couple lacked money, everything became a subject for altercations and quarrels; in short, the life of both became insupportable. He amused himself out of doors; she 'sought by the expedients of adultery to forget her rainy and dull life.' By common consent they cancelled their contract and demanded a legal separation. 'My plan of battle was exact, Des Esseintes then said to himself, experiencing the satisfaction of those strategists who see their long-foreseen manoeuvres succeeding.'

Another time, in the Rue de Rivoli, he comes upon a boy of about sixteen years old, a 'pale, cunning-looking' child, smoking a bad cigarette, and who asks him for a light. Des Esseintes offers him Turkish aromatic cigarettes, enters into conversation with him, learns that his mother is dead, that his father beats him, and that be works for a cardboard-box maker. 'Des Esseintes listened thoughtfully. "Come and drink," said he, and led him into a café, where he made him drink some very strong punch. The child drank in silence. "Come," said Des Esseintes suddenly, "do you feel inclined for some amusement this evening? I will treat you."' And he leads the unfortunate boy into a disorderly house, where his youth and nervousness astonish the girls. While one of these women draws the boy away, the landlady asks Des Esseintes what was his idea in bringing them such an imp. The decadent answers: 'I am simply trying to train an assassin. This boy is innocent, and has reached the age when the blood grows hot; he might run after the girls in his quarter, remain honest while amusing himself.... Bringing him here, on the contrary, into the midst of a luxury of which he had no conception, and which will engrave itself forcibly on his memory, in offering him every fortnight such an unexpected treat, he will get accustomed to these pleasures from which his means debar him. Let us admit that it will require three months for them to become absolutely necessary to him.... Well, at the end of three months I discontinue the little rente which I am going to pay you in advance for this good action, and then he will steal in order to live here.... He will kill, I hope, the good gentleman who will appear inopportunely while he is attempting to break open his writing-table. Then my aim will be attained; I shall have contributed, to the extent of my resources, in creating a villain, one more enemy of that hideous society which fleeces us.' And he leaves the poor defiled boy on this first evening with these words: 'Return as quickly as possible to your father.... Do unto others what you would not wish them to do to you; with this rule you will go a long way. Good-evening. Above all, don't be ungrateful. Let me hear of you as soon as possible through the police news.'

He sees the village children fighting for a piece of black bread covered with curd cheese; he immediately orders for himself a similar slice of bread, and says to his servant: 'Throw this bread and cheese to those children who are doing for each other in the road. Let the feeblest be crippled, not manage to get a single piece, and, besides, be well whipped by their parents when they return home with torn breeches and black eyes; that will give them an idea of the life that awaits them'.

When he thinks of society, this cry bursts from his breast: 'Oh, perish, society! Die, old world!'.

Lest the reader should feel curious as to the course of Des Esseintes's history, let us add that a serious nervous illness attacks him in his solitude, and that his doctor imperiously orders him to return to Paris and the common life. Huysmans, in a second novel, 'Là-bas', shows us what Des Esseintes eventually does in Paris. He writes a history of Gilles de Rais, the wholesale murderer of the fifteenth century, to whom Moreau de Tours's book (treating of sexual aberrations) has unmistakably called the attention of the Diabolist band, who are in general profoundly ignorant, but erudite on this special subject of erotomania. This furnishes M. Huysmans with the opportunity of burrowing and sniffing with swinish satisfaction into the most horrible filth. Besides this, he exhibits in this book the mystic side of decadentism; he shows us Des Esseintes become devout, but going at the same time to the 'black mass' with a hysterical woman, etc. I have no occasion to trouble myself with this book, as repulsive as it is silly. All I wished was to show the ideal man of decadentism.

We have him now, then, the 'super-man' (*surhomme*) of whom Baudelaire and his disciples dream, and whom they wish to resemble: physically, ill and feeble; morally, an arrant scoundrel; intellectually, an unspeakable idiot who passes his whole time in choosing the colours of stuffs which are to drape his room artistically, in observing the movements of mechanical fishes, in sniffing perfumes and sipping liqueurs. His raciest notion is to keep awake all night and to sleep all day, and to dip his meat into his tea. Love and friendship are unknown to him. His artistic sense consists in watching the attitude of people before some work, in order immediately to assume the opposite position. His complete inadaptability reveals itself in that every contact with the world and men causes him pain. He naturally throws the blame of his discomfort on his fellow-creatures, and rails at them like a fish-wife. He classes them all together as villains and blockheads, and he hurls at them horrible anarchical maledictions. The dunderhead considers himself infinitely superior to other people, and his inconceivable stupidity only equals his inflated adoration of himself. He possesses an income of 50,000 francs, and must also have it, for such a pitiable creature would not be in a position to draw one sou from society, or one grain of wheat from nature. A parasite of the lowest grade of atavism, a sort of human sacculus,[65] he would be condemned, if he were poor, to die miserably of hunger in so far as society, in misdirected charity, did not assure to him the necessaries of life in an idiot asylum.

[. . .]

Hence, as we have seen, not one of the sophisms of the Aesthetes withstands criticism. The work of art is not its own aim, but it has a specially organic, and a social task. It is subject to the moral law; it must obey this; it has claim to esteem only if it is morally beautiful and ideal. And it cannot be other than natural and true, in so far, at least, as it is the offprint of a personality, which is also a part of nature and reality. The entire system takes as its point of departure a few erroneous or imprudent assertions of thinkers and poets commanding respect, but developed by the Parnassians and Decadents in a way of which Lessing, Kant and Schiller never allowed themselves to dream. This is no other than the well-known attempt to explain and justify impulsions by motives more or less obvious and invented *post facto*. The degenerate who, in consequence of their organic aberrations, make the repulsive and ugly, vice and crime, the subject-matter of plastic and literary works of art, naturally have recourse to the theory that art has nothing in common with morality, truth and beauty, since this theory has for them the value of an excuse. And must not the excessive value set upon artistic activity as such, without regard to the worth of its results, be highly welcome to the limitless crowd of imitators who practise art, not from an inner prompting, but from a foolhardy craving for the respect surrounding real artists – imitators who have nothing of their own to say, no emotion, not an idea, but who, with a superficial professional dexterity easily acquired, falsify the views and feelings of masters in all branches of art? This rabble, which claims for itself a top place in the scale of intellectual rank, and freedom from the constraint of all moral laws as its most noble privilege, is certainly baser than the lowest scavenger. These creatures are of absolutely no use to the commonwealth, and injure true art by their productions, whose multitude and importunateness shut out from most men the sight of the genuine works of art – never very numerous – of the epoch. They are weaklings in will, unfitted for any activity requiring regular uniform efforts, or else victims to vanity, wishing to be more famous than is possible to a stone-breaker or a tailor. The uncertainty of comprehension and taste among the majority of mankind, and the incompetency of most professional critics, allow these intruders to make their nest among the arts, and to dwell there as parasites their life long. The buyer soon distinguishes a good boot from a bad one, and the journeyman cobbler who cannot properly sew on a sole finds no employment. But that a book or painting void of all originality is indifferent in quality, and for that reason superfluous, is by no means so easily recognised by the Philistine, or even by the man armed with the critical pen, and the producer of such chaff can apply himself undisturbed to his assiduous waste of time. These bunglers with pen, brush and modelling spattle, strutting about in cap and doublet, naturally swear by the doctrine of the Aesthetes, carry themselves as if they were the salt of humanity, and make a parade of their contempt for the Philistine. They belong, however, to the elements of the race which are most inimical to society. Insensible to its tasks and interests, without the capacity to comprehend a serious thought or a fruitful deed, they dream only of the satisfaction of their basest instincts, and are pernicious – through the example they set as drones, as well as through the confusion they cause in minds insufficiently forewarned, by their abuse of the word 'art' to mean demoralization and childishness. Ego-maniacs, Decadents and Aesthetes have completely gathered under their banner this refuse of civilized peoples, and march at its head.

1893; anonymous translation, 1913

HARRY QUILTER

The Gospel of Intensity

Mr. Beardsley is a young man of decided and original ability, but I do not think there can be any two opinions as to the use he has made of his genius. There is, to the present writer, something absolutely repulsive in this artist's renderings of humanity, and in the general savour of his compositions. By the side of them, the most up-to-datedly improper of Dudley Hardy's young ladies,[66] the most vehemently vulgar of Phil May's 'Arriets[67] are wholesome and cleanly. Much of the form of the drawing has been borrowed from Burne-Jones, and, as I believe Mr. Beardsley himself admits, from Puvis de Chavannes,[68] but the spirit belongs entirely to the artist himself, and I dare express it no more definitely, than by saying that however unnatural, extravagant, and morbid are the stories and poems of the modern decadence, which I shall have occasion to mention in this paper, there is not one of them which is more perverted in what it says and suggests than these grotesques, in which the types of manhood and womanhood are, as it were, mingled together, and result in a monstrous sexless amalgam, miserable, morbid, dreary, and unnatural. Mr. Beardsley says, in defence of his sensual conceptions, that most human faces are sensual, and that he goes for his types to a certain *café*.[69] It is a pity, methinks, that the address of that *café* should not be made public, for very certainly if the men and women in these drawings, with these expressions, are its habitual frequenters, a whiff of grape-shot would do the whole establishment good, and clear the moral atmosphere into the bargain. I am not going to dwell upon this subject, but I beg all readers who may think that my words are upon these points exaggerated, to examine these drawings for themselves and form their own conclusion. And I remind all critics who have tolerated, and even praised, Mr. Beardsley's work for its ingenious eccentricities, that the first duty of a writer upon art is to remember that the worst offenders against the cause of fine and healthy art, are those who seek to exalt debased types of humanity, and to delineate unnatural and unwholesome emotions. Think, for one moment, only of what art has been in the past, of the intense elevating pleasure it has given to millions, and shall yet give in the days to come; and then say whether it is tolerable that we should permit and favour a species of design which is corrupt to the last degree, enfeebling and enervating. Just fancy a nation of Beardsleys! Conceive politics, commerce, law, and religion approached from this stand-point, applied in this manner. And yet, why not? Art is, we are told with sickening reiteration, but a reflection of life; why should we not have a Beardsley bishop addressing a Beardsley congregation, or, say, Mr. Gully,[70] *à la* Beardsley, reproving an emasculated House of Commons? It is easy to see the ridiculous side of this work; easy and, of course, pleasant to disregard it altogether; but the neglect does harm, and the ridicule passes lightly over those who are likely to enjoy such conceptions. And since it is beyond doubt that this art has been made the handmaid of a very morbid species of literature, and has in that service achieved great success and emolument, it is essential that all those who attempt to point out the demoralising effect of the fiction and poetry in question, should point out also this artistic connection.

1895

REMY DE GOURMONT

Stéphane Mallarmé and the Idea of Decadence (Stéphane Mallarmé et L'Idée de Décadence)

> *Decadence: a word highly convenient to ignorant pedants; a vague term behind which our laziness and lack of curiosity about the law may take cover.*
>
> *Baudelaire, Letter to Jules Janin*

I

The idea of decadence made its abrupt entry into French literature in about 1885. At first it served to glorify or to mock an entire group of poets, then it settled upon a single figure: Stéphane Mallarmé was pronounced monarch of that realm – which would have been ironic and almost insulting, had the word itself been used and understood in its true sense. Yet in a typically Latin aberration, the academics, showing their usual queasy horror in the face of any new enterprise, applied this term to the fever of originality agitating a whole generation. Held responsible for the rebellious conduct that he had encouraged, M. Mallarmé appeared to these plodding camp-followers like some fearsome Aladdin, a mortal enemy to their sound principles of universal imitation.

Such, after all, is the true custom of the literary world, and it has been flourishing for nearly three hundred years now. The most famous rebellions have hardly damaged it, and never uprooted it. Ever since the impertinence of the Romantics was seen off, we have been kept stifled, cowering under that ancient birch-rod.

Such, too, is the true custom of the Latin peoples. The Romans, so long as they stayed Roman, knew nothing of individualism. Their civilization proclaimed and exhibited perfectly the social features of the animal kingdom: for them, competition tended towards sameness, where for us it tends towards difference. Once they had produced five or six poets – the lucky offshoots of Hellenic grafting – they would not stand for any more; and it may indeed be the case that not a single original poet was born among them for four or five centuries, their social or racial instincts having overcome the individual instinct for freedom. They had their Emperor and their Virgil, and they gave their obedience to both, until the Christian insurgence and the barbarian invasions jointly prevailed over the Capitol. Literary freedom, like all freedoms, is born from the union of strength with awareness. We should commemorate the day upon which St Ambrose repudiated the principles of Horace in the composition of his hymns,[71] because it clearly indicates the birth of a new mentality.

Just as the Romans' political history provides us with the notion of historical decadence, their literary history provides us with that of literary decadence, these being twin facets of a single concept; for it has been easy to trace the coincidence of these two movements, and easy to give the impression that these were necessarily linked processes. Montesquieu[72] owes his fame to the fact that he more than anyone was taken in by this illusion.

Savages are most reluctant to concede that death is natural: every death for them is a case of murder. They have not the slightest inkling of law, and live in the realm of contingency. By common agreement this state of mind is deemed inferior; and rightly so, although the notion of an inflexible law is just as wrong and dangerous as its opposite. Absolute necessity belongs only to natural laws, which can never vary or change. When we come to the social and political evolution of peoples, not only are there no necessary laws, but there are not even any generally applicable laws. These laws either turn out, once disentangled from the facts they explain, to be nothing more than worthy statements of the obvious, or they simply confirm in more pompous terms the very principle of change.

Empires, then, are born, they mature, and they die; social structures prove to be unstable; the cohesion of human groups varies in strength between one era and another; new relationships emerge and reproduce themselves. From all this a treatise on the mechanism of society could be composed, if one avoided adapting one's philosophy strictly to the reality of unexpected disasters. For the unexpected must be left a place which will sometimes be the very throne from which irony laughs as it sends down lightning flashes.

The idea of decadence is, then, nothing more than the idea of natural death. The historians will not hear of any alternative. To explain why Byzantium was taken by the Turks, they make us listen to the rumblings of theological disputes or to the cracking whip of the Blues' charioteer in the circus. Longchamps takes us to Sedan, no doubt, but then Epsom takes us to Waterloo.[73] The prolonged decadence of fallen empires is one of History's most curious illusions: if some empires have died from illness or old age, on the contrary most have succumbed to violent death at the height of their physical strength and intellectual vitality.

Besides, intelligence is a personal quality, and no relation can reasonably be established between a people's power and the genius of one man. Greek literature and the literatures of the Middle Ages are not matched by stable or powerful political forces, whether Greek, Italian or French; and the Scandinavian kingdoms have been blessed by original talents at the very time when their material power has dwindled. It would perhaps be closer to the truth to say that political decadence is the condition most favourable to the blossoming of the intellect: it is when a Gustavus Adolphus and a Charles XII are no longer possible that an Ibsen and a Björnson arise.[74] By the same token, the fall of Napoleon heralded a springtime of magnificent new growth; and the age of Goethe was that of his country's collapse. Our historically sceptical bent will not be fully satisfied, though, until we have countered these examples with the evidence of those periods of combined glory, of which the sumptuous age of Louis XIV is the revered model. After this, a few moments of reflection will oblige us to form opinions rather different from those still found in textbooks or bandied about in conversation.

Bossuet[75] was the first to imagine that he could pass judgement upon universal history – as he naively called it – according to the principles of Biblical Judaism: as he saw it, all empires crumbled if Jehovah's hand came down upon them. Here we have the idea of decadence explained by the idea of chastisement. Montesquieu's philosophy, although more complex, is perhaps even more childish, distasteful as it is to mention a historian who dates the decadence of Rome from the dawn of its admirable centuries of peace – perhaps the only happy period enjoyed by human civilisation. Once we investigate the meaning of such words, we discover that they make not the slightest sense, and memorable authors used them all their lives uncomprehendingly. But however debatable or at least however vague it may be, the general idea of decadence is clear and distinct by comparison with the more restricted idea of literary decadence.

From Racine's time until Vigny's,[76] France did not produce a single great poet. That is a fact. An interval like that is certainly a period of literary decadence; yet we must not stray beyond the fact itself, nor ascribe to it any implausible appearance of logic or necessity. Poetry hibernated through the eighteenth century for want of poets, but this failure is not the consequence of too fine a flowering in previous times. It is what it is, nothing more. Once we call it by the name of decadence, we are granting the existence of some mysterious organism, some allegorical woman called Poetry, who is born, reproduces herself and dies at regular intervals according to the usual cycle of human generations. It is a pleasing fancy, perhaps as the subject of a dissertation or a lecture, but for the purpose of this discussion, which is only the analysis of an idea, we must set it aside.

The main feature of eighteenth-century poetry is its positively Roman spirit of imitation: it imitated furiously, gracefully, tenderly, ironically, stupidly, or self-consciously, in Chinese as much as in Roman fashion. It adopted 'models' – the term being compulsory. There was no question of a poet giving voice to the impressions life made upon him; instead, he had to keep his eye on Racine and scale those heights. Psychologically speaking, it is very odd. The same thinker who would destroy the notion of deference in politics would devote himself to restoring and smartening it up in literature. There were some critics at the time when Goethe was writing *Werther*, but they were busy comparing the merits of Gilbert and Boileau.[77] Must we seek a cause for this? That would be futile. If we wanted to explain why no poet was born in France for a hundred years (aside from Delille and Chénier), we would then have to go on to explain why Ronsard was born, or Théophile, or Racine, although nothing is known or can be known about it.[78] Peel away its mysticism, its necessity, and all its historical genealogy, and the notion of literary decadence comes down to a purely negative idea, which is simply that of absence. This is so elementary that one hardly dares say it, but when superior minds are lacking in any period, swarms of mediocrities will be more actively visible. And because the mediocrity is an imitator, those periods rightly described as decadent are nothing but periods of imitation. In the final analysis, the idea of decadence and that of imitation are identical.

II

However, in discussions about Mallarmé and his group, the idea of decadence has become assimilated to its direct opposite, the idea of innovation. To men of our generation, no doubt because we too were implicated and stupidly scoffed at by orthodox critics, such judgements appeared startling. But they were simply clumsy and hackneyed versions of the edicts handed down in every age by the elders seeking to curse and stamp out the new serpents as they emerge from their shells under the old, ironic maternal eye. Intelligence laughs devilishly at exorcisms, and the University's holy water has never yet been able to neuter it any more than the Church's. In former times, the man who stepped forth as defender of the faith against newfangled heresies would be the Jesuit, but today it is all too often the Professor who takes his stand as champion of the rules.

Here again we find the contradiction that astonishes us in Voltaire[79] and the Voltairians of more recent times: the man who shows courage in matters of justice and political liberty is the same one who falters and shrinks away when it becomes a question of literary novelty or liberty. When he gets as far as Tolstoy and Ibsen and makes mention of their fame, he will add (in a footnote) 'Are these reputations, especially Ibsen's, firmly established? The question whether the author of *Ghosts* is a hoaxer or a genius is still unresolved at the present time.'[80] Such is the attitude, when faced with original work that has not been seen or read before, of a writer who in the very book just quoted demonstrates an admirable independence of judgement. I need hardly add that he mocks the 'decadents' at every opportunity. After this, how can we be surprised at the clumsy mockery of lesser minds? Any new way of expressing eternal human truths scandalises people at first, especially the over-educated. They feel a kind of terror, so in order to feel safe again they resort to denial, insult, and derision. It is the natural reflex of the human animal faced with physical peril. But how did it come about that all genuine innovation in literature or art is regarded as dangerous? And above all, why has this assumption become one of the disorders peculiar to our time – and one of the worst, since it tends to hamper change and to thwart life?

For years on end, Delacroix and Puvis de Chavannes, so different in genius, were ridiculed and rejected by the juries.[81] From behind the obviously contradictory pretexts for this, just one explanation emerges, which is originality. A work that shows hardly any trace of earlier methods and that cannot instantly be linked with something already known and understood makes the guardians of art feel threatened, and each responds to the provocation according to his temperament. The watchwords also vary from one age to the next: in the eighteenth century, non-imitation was considered a violation of Taste, which was a serious matter at the time when Voltaire was raising his shrine (really only a shrinelet) to that trifling deity. For nearly ten years, until only a few weeks ago, artists and writers who refused to plagiarise the masters were branded as either decadents or symbolists. The latter term of abuse was preferred eventually, being more obscure and so easier to manipulate; and besides, just like the former, it embodies the abhorrent principle of non-imitation.

A long time ago, well before M. Tarde[82] had developed his social philosophy, it was said that 'imitation rules the world of men, as gravitation rules the world of things'. In the special domain of art and literature, this law is especially evident. Literary history can be summed up as nothing more than a list of one intellectual epidemic after another. Some of these have been short-lived. Fashions change or persist according to unforeseeable caprices that are hard to determine. Shakespeare had no immediate influence, while Honoré d'Urfé[83] during and beyond his lifetime for half a century was the master and inspiration of all fictional romance – and would have reigned longer had not *La Princesse de Clèves* been written secretly by a noblewoman.[84] The seventeenth century, part of whose literature is merely translation and imitation, was not averse, though, to cautiously moderate novelty. This is because although it would have been shameful not to imitate the Ancients – or, strange as it seems, the Spanish (but only the Spanish) – in subject-matter and style (Racine shuddered to think what he had done in writing *Bajazet*),[85] one could take pride in being able to treat classical borrowings in a freshly original manner.

This literature, however, very soon became classical itself, providing a second model for imitation. And because this was more accessible, it soon became almost the only spring to which successive generations came to drink, pray, and dilute their ink. Boileau was deified while still alive; and as soon as Voltaire learned to read, he read Boileau. From that point onward, the principle of imitation reigned over French literature.

With some exceptions, however memorable they may be, this principle has continued to be so powerful and well understood – particularly as education expands – that as soon as a critic invokes it, the reader of a new, refreshing work will be shamed into casting it aside. This is how the newspaper critics have prevented the acceptance of Ibsen's work in France. And this is why verse plays, the most imitative works of all, still achieve success even down to the level of the commercial theatres: these theatrical occasions, always boosted by publicity, provide sound illustration for our theory.

The idea of imitation, then, has become the very essence of art or literature. It is just as hard to imagine a new novel that is not derivative from or equivalent to some previous novel as it is to imagine verses that do not rhyme or that have not been scanned meticulously down to the last syllable. When such innovations have none the less been produced, bringing a sudden change to the accustomed prospect of the literary landscape, the experts have been flustered. To hide their discomfort, they began to laugh (the third method), and then they handed down their verdicts: since these specimens of prose or verse are not devoted to imitating prior literary examples or works sanctioned by the textbooks, it follows that they come from goodness knows what abnormal source. Attempts were made to invoke the Pre-Raphaelites[86] as an explanation, but these proved indecisive and even rather ridiculous, so profound and impenetrable was the ignorance displayed on all sides.

At about this time, though, a book appeared that cleared up all these misunderstandings by asserting an inevitable link between the new poets and the obscure versifiers of the Roman decadence highly praised by Des

Esseintes. This was taken up enthusiastically on all sides, so that even those slighted by it welcomed the disparagement as a distinction. Once the principle was accepted, comparisons proliferated. Since nobody, perhaps not even Des Esseintes, had actually read those discredited poets, it was child's play for any columnist to liken Sidonius Apollinarus,[87] of whom he knew nothing, to Stéphane Mallarmé, of whom he understood nothing. Neither Sidonius Apollinarus nor Mallarmé is a decadent, because each possesses in varying degrees his own originality; but that is precisely why the term was applied justly to the author of *L'Après-midi d'un Faune*,[88] because it signified something very obscurely in the minds of these same detractors of his: something little-known, difficult, rare, precious, unexpected, and new.

On the other hand, if we want to restore to the idea of literary decadence its true meaning, along with its true cruelty, then we doubt that any mention should be made of Mallarmé, or of Laforgue,[89] or of any currently practising symbolist. The decadent of Latin literature is neither Ammianus Marcellinus nor St Augustine, each of whom fashioned a language in his own style; nor is it St Ambrose, who created the hymn; nor Prudentius, who invented the literary genre of the lyric biography.[90] We are beginning to become more indulgent towards Latin literature of the second period: tired, perhaps, of ridiculing it without reading it, we have begun at least to glance at it. Before too long, the following quite simple notions will be accepted: that there is no such thing as one good kind of Latin or one bad kind of Latin; that languages are living things that undergo change, not necessarily for the worse; that genius can be found in the sixth century as well as in the second, or in the eleventh century just as in the eighteenth; that classicist prejudices are an obstacle both to the development of literary history and to the comprehensive understanding of the language itself. Had they been better understood, the poets on Des Esseintes's bookshelves would not have been used for the naming of a literary movement, unless the intention – far-fetched and silly as it would be – had been to compare idealist innovators with Christian innovators.

III

My sole intention here has been to attempt the historical (or anecdotal) analysis of an idea, and to indicate by means of a somewhat extended example, how a word comes to have only the meaning that it suits us to give it; so I do not believe it will be necessary to establish in detail the grounds upon which Stéphane Mallarmé may deserve to be hated or mocked.

Among the feelings aroused by literature, hatred is the queen. Literature is, along with religion perhaps, the abstract passion that stirs people the most violently. Granted, we have not yet witnessed literary wars like the religious wars of what we may agree to call bygone times; but this is because literature has never yet reached down instantly to the people. By the time it gets to them, it has lost its explosive force: there is some distance from the opening night of *Hernani*[91] to the point at which Victor Hugo can be bought in illustrated instalments. However, one could well imagine a mobilisation of German sentimentality against English humour or French irony. It is because they are so unfamiliar with each other that nations hate each other so little: when fraternisation sets in, alliances always end in cannon-fire.

The hatred that dogged Mallarmé was never particularly bitter, because even in the literary world men only hate seriously as soon as material interests add a little flavour to the contest for the ideal. But he never offered any target for envy, and put up with injustice and abuse as inevitable burdens of genius. It was only the solitary and undisguised superiority of his mind, then, that was jeered at, under the pretext of his obscurity. Artists, even if undervalued by the herd-instinct of cliques, win commissions and earn money. Poets have the resource of long articles in the reviews and newspapers; and some, like Théophile Gautier, have made their living from them. Baudelaire found little success in that line, and Mallarmé even less. So it was at a poet lacking any social adornments that the sarcasm was directed.

Amid a preposterous collection in the Louvre can be found one accidental marvel, an Andromeda carved in ivory by Cellini.[92] It is a frightened woman, all her flesh atremble with terror at being tied up: where can she flee? And it is the poetry of Stéphane Mallarmé. The emblem is fitting moreover because, like the sculptor, the poet turned out only cups, vases, caskets, and statuettes. He is not colossal, he is perfect. His poetry does not present a generous human bounty displayed to the astonished crowd. It does not express strong, commonly held ideas that easily galvanize popular attention numbed by toil. It is personal, withdrawn upon itself like those flowers that shrink from the sun; it yields no perfume except at dusk; it offers up its thought only to the intimacy of a true and heartfelt fellow-thought. Its excessively coy modesty wraps itself in too many veils, to be sure, but there is great delicacy in this longing to flee the hands and eyes of popularity. Flee? Where could it flee? Mallarmé took refuge in obscurity as if in a cloister, putting the wall of a cell between himself and the understanding of others; he wished to live alone with his pride. But that was the Mallarmé of the last years, when, hurt but not downhearted, he felt possessed by that disgust for idle phrases which had also afflicted Jean Racine long ago; the years when he created a new syntax for his own use, when he employed words according to new occult relations among them. Stéphane Mallarmé was a relatively prolific writer, and the greater part of his work is untainted by any obscurity. But if, in his later and final phases, beginning with the *Prose pour des Esseintes*,[93] we find doubtful phrases or lines that vex us, only a vulgarly inattentive mind will shrink from the delightful task of overcoming them.

There are too few obscure writers in French; and so we become indolently accustomed to liking only those writings that are easy, and soon enough those at an elementary level. Yet books that are blindingly clear are seldom worth re-reading. Clarity establishes the prestige of classic literature; and that is what makes it so clearly dull. Clear minds are usually those that can see only one thing at a time. A brain enriched with ideas and sensations forms a kind of whirlpool, churning the waters as it gushes forth. Like Ximénès Doudan,[94] let us prefer a swamp teeming with life to a glass of clear water. Granted, one does feel thirsty sometimes, but then one can use a filter. Literature that gives immediate pleasure to all men is by definition worthless. It should cascade down from its summits, gushing down through the rocks until it pours into the valley, within reach of all men and all their flocks.

So if a definitive study of Stéphane Mallarmé were undertaken, it would have to treat the question of obscurity solely from a psychological point of view, because there is never an absolutely literal obscurity in anything written in good faith. A sensible interpretation is always possible. It will change according to the evening hour, perhaps, as the shade of a lawn changes at the whim of the clouds, but here and everywhere the truth shall be as our momentary mood will have it. Mallarmé's work is the most marvellous occasion for reverie that has yet been offered to men for whom the superfluity of dull assertions has become wearisome. A poetry full of doubts, of variable nuances, and of ambiguous perfumes is perhaps the only kind in which we can henceforth find pleasure. And if the word 'decadence' were truly to encapsulate all these autumnal twilight charms, we might welcome it so far as to make it one of the keys of our viol. But it is dead, and the master, the last but one, is dead.[95]

1898; translated by Chris Baldick, 2011

Notes

1 See chapter 1, 'Nietzsche's Decadent Philosophy', in Charles Bernheimer, *Decadent Subjects: The Idea of Decadence in Art, Literature, Philosophy, and Culture of the* Fin de Siècle *in Europe* (Baltimore: Johns Hopkins University Press, 2002), pp. 7–32, esp. pp. 12–13.

2 Nicole Dubreuil-Blondin, 'Les Métaphores de la Critique d'Art: le "sale" et le "malade" à l'époque de l'impressionisme', in *La Critique d'Art en France 1850–1900*, ed. J.-P. Bouillon (Saint-Etienne: Centre Interdisciplinaire d'Etudes et de Recherches sur l'Expression Contemporaine [CIE-REC], 1989), pp. 105–20; see especially p. 105.

3 Hugh E. M. Stutfield, 'Tommyrotics', *Blackwood's Edinburgh Magazine*, 157 (1895), 833–45: 843.

4 Hans-Peter Söder, 'Disease and Health as Contexts of Modernity: Max Nordau as a Critic of Fin-de-Siècle Modernism', *German Studies Review*, 14 (1991): 473–87: 474.
5 Bernard Shaw, 'The Sanity of Art: An Exposure of the Current Nonsense About Artists Being Degenerate' (1895/1908), in Sally Ledger and Roger Luckhurst, eds, *The Fin de Siècle: A Reader in Cultural History c. 1880–1900* (Oxford: Oxford University Press, 2000), p. 22.
6 Ruth Z. Temple addresses the problem of labelling in her article, 'Truth in Labelling: Pre-Raphaelitism, Aestheticism, Decadence, Fin de Siècle', *English Literature in Transition*, 17, 4 (1974), 201–22.
7 A monthly spiritualist journal, founded in Marseilles, 1885–89.
8 A pseudonym, which, in ancient Greek, means garland, wreath, or crown.
9 A reference, perhaps, to *La Juive de Constantine* (1846), a drama by Théophile Gautier and Noël Parfait.
10 Arthur Schopenhauer (1788–1860), German philosopher whose *The World as Will and Idea* (*Die Welt als Wille und Vorstellung*, 1818) influenced a number of Decadent writers.
11 'When I have suffered shipwreck, I have navigated well.'
12 An allusion to Matthew 5: 3.
13 A reference to Goethe, whose last words are said to have been 'Light! More light!' See Chapter 1, note 43.
14 An allusion to Matthew 19: 14, Mark 10: 14, Luke 18: 16.
15 'Wagner is a neurosis.'
16 Count Alessandro di Cagliostro (1743–95), Italian occultist and adventurer.
17 A reference to Nietzsche's planned work, *The Will as Power: Attempt at a Revaluation of All Values*.
18 Victor Hugo (1802–85), French Romantic writer.
19 'handmaiden of drama'.
20 Friedrich Schiller (1759–1805), German dramatist and poet.
21 François-Joseph Talma (1763–1826), French actor.
22 Nietzsche here adopts French usage, in which 'amphitryon' means 'generous host'.
23 'Unaccompanied' or 'barely accompanied'.
24 Paul Verlaine (1844–96), French Symbolist poet; Maurice Maeterlinck (1862–1949), Belgian poet and dramatist; Joris-Karl Huysmans (1848–1907), French novelist.
25 Edmond and Jules de Goncourt (1822–96 and 1830–70), French authors who were also brothers.
26 Neurosis.
27 Ernest Hello (1828–85), French Roman Catholic author and mystic.
28 James Abbott McNeill Whistler (1834–1903), American Impressionist painter.
29 Charles Augustin Sainte-Beuve (1804–69), French literary critic.
30 'Endeavours in which the two brothers sought to make something new, and attempted to endow the various branches of literature with something their predecessors had never dreamed of finding.'

31 *Chérie* (1884), a novel by Edmond de Goncourt; 'Japonisme', a term first used in 1872 to describe the influence of Japanese art on Western traditions.
32 Lines from 'To a Friend' by Matthew Arnold (1822–88).
33 'a language portraying our ideas, sensations, and representations of people and things, in a manner distinct from this writer or that; a personal language, a language bearing our signature'.
34 'We would have Nuance once more, not Colour, nothing but Nuance! Oh! Nuance alone matches dream to dream and flute to horn!'
35 'with nothing to it that would stifle or weigh it down'.
36 'J'ai dit à l'esprit vain . . .' (1891), '[The secret of] Art, my children, is to be absolutely oneself'.
37 François Villon (1431–63), French poet.
38 Antoine Watteau (1684–1721), French painter in the rococo style.
39 Catulle Mendès (1841–1909), French poet and critic.
40 Henri François Joseph de Regnier (1864–1936), French Symbolist poet.
41 Gustave Kahn (1859–1936), French Symbolist poet.
42 Edouard Dujardin (1861–1941), French writer.
43 Jean Moréas (Ioannis Papadiamantopoulos, 1856–1910) Greek poet resident in France from 1875 and writing mostly in French. He published a Symbolist manifesto in 1886, and, among other works, *Le Pèlerin passionné* in 1891. See pp. 184–91 for Moréas's story 'La Faënza'.
44 Octave Mirbeau (1848–1917), French journalist, novelist, and playwright.
45 'M. Maurice Maeterlinck has given us the most inspired work of our time, the most exceptional and the most ingenuous too, comparable and – dare I say it? – superior to the finest things in Shakespeare . . . more tragic than *Macbeth*, more wonderful in thought than *Hamlet*.'
46 Philippe-Auguste Villiers de l'Isle-Adam (1838–89), French Symbolist writer. *Contes cruels* appeared in 1883, *Axël* posthumously in 1890.
47 'refined retreat' (the phrase is quoted from *A Rebours*). See pp. 172–84 for extracts from *A Rebours*.
48 Apuleius (*c*. 125–*c*. 180), Latin writer, whose bawdy novel, *The Golden Ass*, was praised by late-nineteenth-century decadents; Gustave Moreau (1826–98), French Symbolist painter; Edward Burne-Jones (1833–98), late Pre-Raphaelite painter; Odilon Redon (1840–1916), French Symbolist painter; William Blake (1757–1827), English poet, painter, and printmaker.
49 Louis Marie-Anne Couperus (1863–1923), Dutch novelist; Luigi Capuana (1839–1915), Italian writer and journalist; Gabriele d'Annunzio (1863–1938), Italian poet, journalist, novelist, and dramatist; Emilia Pardo Bazan (1851–1921), Spanish writer; Henrik Ibsen (1828–1906), Norwegian playwright, theatre director, and poet. See pp. 191–9 for an extract from d'Annunzio's *The Child of Pleasure*.
50 William Ernest Henley (1849–1903), English poet.
51 Gustave Flaubert (1821–80), French Realist novelist.
52 Heinrich Heine (1797–1856), German poet.
53 Nordau quotes from Théophile Gautier's prefatory essay to the third edition of *Les Fleurs du mal* (1868) by Charles Baudelaire (see pp. 79–80).

54 The paragraph quoted is Baudelaire's note appended (in the 1857 edition of *Fleurs du mal* only) to his Latin poem '*Franciscae meae laudes*' (see pp. 80–1).
55 Nordau quotes from J.-K. Huysmans, *A Rebours* (1884).
56 Johann Michael Moscherosch (1601–69), German satirist; Julius Wilhelm Zinkgref (1591–1635), German poet; Johann Balthasar Schupp (1610–61), German pastor and satirist.
57 [Nordau's footnote:] Henri Kurz, in his introduction to the 'Simplician' writings of Grimmelshausen. Leipzig, 1863, Ist part, p. li. See also his remarks on the German of Grimmelshausen (author of *Simplicissimus*), p. xlv. et seq.
58 For the first-century prose satirist Petronius, see p. 43. The other writers listed here were poets of the imperial provinces writing in Latin in the fourth and fifth centuries.
59 Nordau quotes from Paul Bourget, *Essais de psychologie contemporaine* (1883), p. 24. Nordau confuses the term 'Parnassian' with 'Decadent' throughout, but the Parnassians were a group of poets based in Paris and led by Charles Marie René Leconte de Lisle (1818–94), their name deriving from three collections, *La Parnasse Contemporain*, published in 1866, 1871, and 1876. Classical formal precision and impersonality were their ideals.
60 *Marthe: histoire d'une fille* (1876), Huysmans's first novel.
61 Diabolists, devil-worshippers, artists and writers interested in sorcery and witchcraft; Naturalists, a group of writers, commonly associated with Zola, who believed that heredity and social environment determined individual character.
62 Nordau quotes from Huysmans's *A Rebours* (1884).
63 Untraced.
64 Nordau quotes hereon from Huysmans's *A Rebours* (1884).
65 [Nordau's footnote:] The sacculus is a cirripedia which lives in the condition of a parasite in the intestinal canal of certain crustacea. It represents the deepest retrograde transformation of a living being primarily of a higher organization. It has lost all its differentiated organs, and essentially only amounts to a vesicule (hence its name: little bag), which fills itself with juices from its host, absorbed by the parasite with the help of certain vessels, which it plunges into the intestinal walls of the latter. This atrophied creature has retained so few marks of an independent animal that it was looked upon for a long time as a diseased excrescence of its host's intestines.
66 A reference to Dudley Hardy (1867–1922), English painter and illustrator, who rose to prominence through the boom in illustrated magazines and poster art at the *fin de siècle*. His *Gaiety Girl* series of posters were extremely popular in the 1890s and showed the influence of French poster artists like Jules Chéret.
67 Phil May (1864–1903), English caricaturist who worked for *Punch* and *The Graphic* from the 1890s. 'Arriet was one of May's cockney characters for *Punch*.
68 Pierre Puvis de Chavannes (1824–98), French Symbolist painter.
69 Possibly a reference to St James's, Piccadilly, to which Beardsley once turned up as a transvestite.
70 William Court Gully, first Viscount Selby (1835–1909), Speaker of the House of Commons, 1895–1905.

71 St Ambrose, Bishop of Milan 374–97.

72 Charles-Louis de Secondat, baron de la Brède et de Montesquieu (1689–1755), French political historian. In fact, Montesquieu's *Considérations sur les causes de la grandeur des Romains et de leur décadence* (1734) attributes the decline of the empire largely to military over-extension, making little attempt to seek cultural or moral causes for it.

73 Both Longchamps and Epsom are racecourses, Gourmont's point being that attributing a civilisation's political decline to its frivolous pursuits (as with Byzantium's obsession with Blues v. Whites chariot-races) and thus ascribing the crushing defeat of the French armies at Sedan (1870) to the French elite's love of horse-racing, puts you at a loss to account for the English victory at Waterloo, the English being notorious for devoting themselves to exactly the same idle follies.

74 Gustav II Adolf, known in English as Gustavus Adolphus (1594–1632), founder of the Swedish empire; Charles XII (1682–1718), King of Sweden 1697–1718; Henrik Johan Ibsen (1828–1906) and Bjørnstjerne Martinius Bjørnson (1832–1910), acclaimed Norwegian writers of the nineteenth century.

75 Jacques-Bénigne Bossuet (1627–1704), French bishop and theologian.

76 Jean Racine (1639–99), French dramatist; Alfred de Vigny (1797–1863), French poet, playwright and novelist.

77 *The Sorrows of the Young Werther* (1774) by Goethe; Gabriel Gilbert (*c.* 1620–*c.* 1680), French poet and dramatist; Nicolas Boileau-Despréaux (1636–1711), French poet and critic.

78 Jacques Delille (1738–1813); André de Chénier (1762–94); Pierre de Ronsard (1524–85); Théophile de Viau (1590–1626); Jean Racine (1630–99).

79 François-Marie Arouet (1694–1778), essayist and philosopher, better known as Voltaire.

80 Gourmont is here quoting from Paul Stapfer, *Des Réputations littéraires: essais de morale et de l'histoire*, first series, Paris, 1893, p. 178, fn. 1: 'Sont-ce là des gloires bien établies, celles d'Ibsen surtout? La question de savoir si l'auteur des *Révenants* est un mystificateur ou un génie n'est pas résolue à l'heure où nous sommes.'

81 Eugène Delacroix (1798–1863), French Romantic painter; Pierre Puvis de Chavannes (1824–1898), French painter.

82 Jean-Gabriel de Tarde (1843–1904), French sociologist, who derived his model of society from chemistry.

83 Honoré d'Urfé (1568–1625), French author of lengthy prose romances, much admired throughout the seventeenth century.

84 *La Princesse de Clèves*, French novel, published anonymously in 1678, thought to be the work of Madame de la Fayette, and often identified as the first French novel.

85 Racine's tragedy *Bajazet* (1672) was unusual in being set not in ancient or mythological times but in modern Turkey, albeit in a sultan's palace.

86 The Pre-Raphaelite Brotherhood, a group of young artists in England who set up a breakaway group from the Royal Academy in 1848.

87 Gaius Sollius Apollinarus Sidonius, later canonised as St Sidonius Apollinarus,

fifth-century Latin poet of Gaul (France) and bishop of Augustonemetum (Clermont-Ferrand).

88 Poem by Mallarmé about the relationship between the real and the ideal.

89 Jules Laforgue (1860–87), French Symbolist poet.

90 Aurelius Prudentius Clemens, fourth-century Latin poet and hymnodist of Spain, known for his widely imitated *Psychomachia* ('Battle for the Soul').

91 The first night of Hugo's verse play (25 February 1830) witnessed the 'Battle of Hernani' in which a group of the dramatist's young supporters, led by the red-waistcoated Théophile Gautier, formed a Romantic bodyguard to protect the performance from expected disruption by Classicist hecklers. The Romantic faction claimed a famous victory in the ensuing brawl.

92 Benvenuto Cellini (1500–71), Italian sculptor in the Mannerist style.

93 'Prose pour des Esseintes', a tribute poem by Mallarmé, published in *La Revue Indépendante* in 1885.

94 Ximénès Doudan (1800–72), French journalist.

95 Mallarmé had died on 9 September 1898, de Gourmont's article serving in part as an obituary tribute. The suggestion that one of his literary masters survives is perhaps a salute to Mallarmé's friend Catulle Mendès (1841–1909).

6

PARODIES AND PASTICHES

A significant consequence of the publishing boom in France in the early 1880s was a proliferation of periodicals and literary reviews, especially satirical illustrated periodicals and new Symbolist magazines, including *La Plume* and *La Revue Blanche.* An 'esprit de blague' (jocular spirit) characterised the new output, and Decadent poetry became an obvious target. Anatole Baju's journal, *Le Décadent,* for example, contained a variety of spoof contributions, from sonnets supposedly written by General Boulanger and Louis II of Bavaria to a series of poems allegedly written by Arthur Rimbaud. The fake Rimbaud poems generated an outraged response from the conservative critics, but the two forgers, Laurent Tailhade and Georges Fourest, refused to reveal their identities. Instead, and inspired by their success, they created a caricature poet-figure, Mitrophane Crapousin, who enjoyed a short-lived but glittering literary career.

These lively parodies of Decadence in the 1880s prompted the revival of an eighteenth-century corollary term to 'decadence' and 'decadentism' – 'déliquescence' – meaning a state of slow liquefaction and decay. It was popularised as a term through various parodies and pastiches, particularly in a collection of poems entitled *Les Déliquescences: Poèmes décadents d'Adoré Floupette avec sa vie par Marius Tapora* (1885), the most celebrated Decadence spoof of the period. Published in two editions in May and June 1885, and printed in a run of one hundred and ten copies, *Les Déliquescences* was received warmly by its unwitting readers, reassured by the serious, glowing reviews in *Le Temps,* which praised 'Floupette' (who was, in fact, the minor poets Gabriel Vicaire (1848–1900) and Henri Beauclair (1860–1919)) for his comic interpretation of decadent excess. In both the form and the subject of the poem, 'Decadents', Floupette declares the limitations of Decadent verse, rhapsodising over the vacuous nature of Decadent poetry ('We gape like puppets in a fairground booth') and the preoccupation of Decadent poets with base sensations ('Aromas of a marchioness we share / Whose undergarments reek of chamber-pot'). *Les Déliquescences* parodied the work of Verlaine and Mallarmé and the cult that had grown up around them, and it traded on the major themes of

Decadence – pessimism, morbidity, mysticism, sensuality and the imagery of perfumes, gem-stones, and hot-house flowers. Exploiting the contemporary vogue for decadent *noms de plume*, Beauclair and Vicaire created the poet Adoré Floupette. Inspired by Baju's so-called school of Decadence, referred to jokingly as the 'école de flou' ('woolly school'), 'Floupette' was a satire on the Decadents' vague, impressionistic techniques and their tendency to collapse. In the poem 'Decadent Ball' ('Bal Décadent'), the description degenerates or deliquesces from a romantic dance-floor encounter with all the decadent trappings to a coarse but exuberant come-on. The dance of Decadence, according to Floupette, is a flimsy pretext for penetrative sex and moral dissolution, and, at the end of the poem, the speaker loses all self-possession, ejaculating both rhetorically and physically.

Self-mockery characterises late nineteenth-century Decadence both in England and France, but, whereas in France it signals a softening or deliquescence of the movement, in England it is a key constituent part of the artifice and exaggeration of the Decadent pose, and among the Decadents themselves there were many public displays of frivolous wit and teasing. The example we provide here is Max Beerbohm's (1872–1956) 'A Defence of Cosmetics', which appeared in the first number of *The Yellow Book* when Beerbohm was still an undergraduate at Oxford. It can be read alongside Baudelaire's 'In Praise of Make-Up' of 1863 (see pp. 22–4), but, unlike the French poet's more serious observations about the role of artifice in modern culture, Beerbohm's intentions were highly satirical. Beerbohm was sending up the Decadents' celebration of artifice, their preoccupation with what was known then as the 'lady's toilet' (that is, the feminine processes of dressing and making up), and the tendency among some male Decadents to use cosmetics. His real intentions escaped the notice of the critics, who, taking him at his word, attacked him viciously in the popular press. Beerbohm's response to all this was typical of the publicity-seeking Decadent: 'So long as I attract notice', he wrote to his friend Reggie Turner, 'I am happy'.

'As a guide to middle-class prejudice throughout the second half of the nineteenth century', claims Matthew Sturgis in *Passionate Attitudes*, 'there is no surer index than *Punch*.'[1] In its lampoons upon the effete and indolent avant-garde, *Punch* not only encapsulated the general disapproval of the Victorians towards aesthetic types and dandies, but it brought a kind of relief because it caricatured (and thereby clarified) Decadence to the contemporary reader.[2] Between about 1873 and 1882, *Punch* was relentless in its satire of Aestheticism, an art movement which it regarded as ridiculous and pretentious, and representative of the moral 'flabbiness' of the *fin de siècle*.[3] George du Maurier pilloried the Aesthetic movement by creating Jellaby Postlethwaite, an Aesthetic poet, and Maudle, an Aesthetic painter, two figures intended as caricatures of Oscar Wilde and his association with the limp and languid gestures of the Aesthetic movement. By the mid-1890s, however, when English Decadence was beginning to crystallise around Oscar Wilde and Aubrey Beardsley, the attacks of *Punch* on Aestheticism and the fashionable excesses of Decadence were less frequent. The 'New' was now its target. Occasionally the self-indulgent lassitude of the Decadents was revived as a subject in cartoons, spoofs, mock-interviews and reviews of plays and exhibitions, but Decadence was diminished in the view of the satirical press. In 'A Ballad of a Bun', in *The Battle of the Bays* (1894), Owen Seaman (1861–1936; editor of *Punch* between 1906 and 1936), mocks poets who might have succeeded Tennyson in the Laureateship with a parody of Davidson's 'A Ballad of a Nun' (see pp. 121–5). In 'To any Boy-Poet of the Decadence', Seaman conflates Decadent with New and patronisingly puts down the aspirations of young poets: 'For your dull little vices we don't care a fig'. In general, *Punch* preferred to satirise Decadent individuals and the non-naturalistic Decadent style rather than the broader movement itself, and in the 1890s its main concern was the way that British culture was being undermined by the avant-garde's interest in continental ideas. French affectation is sent up in the sketch between the 'Decadent Guys', in *Punch* of 1894, in which the conversation of two abandoned Guy Fawkes dummies, Lord Raggie Tattershall and Fustian Flitters, parodies the pretentious dialogue of two Victorian upper-class dandies. As they anticipate their 'performance' on the bonfire, they extol the exquisite beauty of each others' rags in a series of vacuous and contradictory statements. 'The true *impromptu* is invariably premeditated', says Flitters to Tattershall, 'Does not consistency solely consist in contradicting oneself? But I suppose I *am* a trifle *décousu*.'

The attention to matters of form by English Decadent writers and artists received much attention from the newspaper and periodical press in the 1890s. Critics attributed this tendency to the influence of modern French art, and they resented its intrusion in English art. A non-naturalistic style was, they argued, the sign of a declining sense of tradition and an all-pervasive moral laxity. The visual parodies of Beardsley's illustrations by Edward T. Reed (1860–1933) in *Punch* between 1894 and 1895 reflect the unease of cultural patriots. In Reed's image titled *Britannia à la Beardsley*, for example, in the *Punch Almanack* for 1895, Reed illustrates how the influence of foreign ideas (French and Japanese in particular) undermines British values. The drawing appeared at a time when hostility towards the Decadent movement was at its height, but Reed's clever imitation of his black-and-white style implicitly acknowledges Beardsley's skill. An evil-looking Boadicea is seated on her chariot on the breezy English south coast, surrounded by emasculated symbols of British pride and glory. The detail in the caricature is well-observed, and Reed satirises the medieval and Japanese influences in Beardsley's drawings for *Salome*. 'Otherness' is invoked in a variety of ways. The image is supposed to represent the dangerous consequences of being receptive to French influence, but only a few details signify a concern with France. The overriding impression is a pastiche of Japanese art. Anti-French sentiments, here, are harnessed to incorporate all foreign influence, and France is presented as only one danger among many.

The prevalence of parody and satire in the literature and art of the Decadence signal its demise in both France and England, an observation first made by Jackson, who in *The Eighteen Nineties* (1913), noted that, just as the end of the Aesthetic movement had been registered by W. H. Mallock's *The New Republic* (1878), W. S. Gilbert's opera *Patience* (1881), and George du Maurier's drawings in *Punch*, so the end of Decadence in England coincided with the publication of Robert Hichens's *The Green Carnation* (1894) and G. S. Street's *The Autobiography of a Boy* (1894). However, these observations, while true, obscured the complexity of the relationship between Decadence and parody, for, to some significant extent, Decadence *is* parody. We might reflect here on the contribution of Lionel Johnson (1867–1902) to the Decadent movement. His prose parody, 'The Cultured Faun' (published anonymously in the *Anti-Jacobin*), targeted the Decadent art he also promoted. In 'A Decadent's Lyric', Johnson produces such a faithful imitation of Arthur Symons's Decadent verse that, as Jackson commented, 'it might easily have passed for the real thing'.[4] The parodying of Decadents for their superficiality was not so much a negation as an endorsement of their aesthetic. Part of the innovation of the Decadents was to mix up the public's preconceptions about the real and the artificial, and as we have remarked in the cases of Adoré Floupette and Beerbohm's 'Defence of Cosmetics', the public could not always see the joke, proof that in spite of *Punch*'s attempts, literary Decadence was difficult to ignore.

GABRIEL VICAIRE AND HENRI BEAUCLAIR

From *The Deliquescences of Adoré Floupette: Decadent Poems*

Editors' Notice

Of all the works inspired by so-called Decadent or Symbolist poetry, the most amusing and most genuine is without the slightest doubt *The Deliquescences of Adoré Floupette*. Written by two poetical wits as a kind of amusement, this slender tome achieved an unsought success. Published anonymously at first in an edition of one hundred and ten copies,[5] then reprinted in greater numbers with a 'Life of Floupette by Marius Tapora',[6] this curious booklet provoked a general burst of laughter which further intensified the indignant protests from a writer at the newspaper *Le Temps*.

Once we learn that this solemn critic (to avoid giving offence, we shall not name him) had devoted a long and earnest article to the minute analysis of *The Deliquescences* and to challenging its supposed authorship, the notoriety earned by this innocent hoax will not surprise us. In fairness, we should add that others who were better informed than our journalist were taken in by the wilfully naive tones of the *Deliquescences* and credited these new authors with a literary production of scarcely conceivable imagination and originality. Gabriel Vicaire's and Henri Beauclair's collection was made up of short, distinctive pieces bearing an uncanny resemblance to the forms, rhythms, and imagery used by the poets of the Left Bank's little magazines and reviews. It served the cause of poetry better, perhaps, than the kind of works it parodied.

A great rarity, eagerly sought after by bibliophiles, *The Deliquescences* has until now enjoyed the singular luck of being highly esteemed while few have been able to confirm for themselves what exactly is amusing about them. This is why we are now offering to connoisseurs of curiosities an unexpurgated edition of it, 'purified', as we would formerly have said, from any typographical errors that might alter its meaning.

Now that the evolution of Symbolist art has run its course, and its recognised representatives have attained the standing of their literary elder brothers (the late Romantics and Parnassians), anybody who chose to take offence at these agreeable fancies would be blind to the comical lesson that they contain.

For our part, we prefer to take their side rather than to mock.

1885; translated by Chris Baldick, 2011

ADORÉ FLOUPETTE

Decadents (Les Décadents)

Our mighty fathers had such dreams in youth
That sped them winging to the Light's true land.
But we, with drooping hollyhocks in hand,
Have no more heart, nor one remaining tooth!

We gape like puppets in a fairground booth
At rustic scenes we cannot understand,
While common duties seem to us so bland,
We simple jokers, Decadents forsooth.

Oh graveyard of Desire! Distaste most rare!
Aromas of a marchioness we share
Whose undergarments reek of chamber-pot.

Incontinence, indeed, is our philosophy;
Our flesh and blood are scarcely worth a jot:
A summer breeze would melt our brains like toffee!

1885; translated by Chris Baldick, 2011

Decadent Ball (Bal décadent)

I'm off!

– Tristan Corbière

It was a dance
Of decadence,

A graceful yet
Morose minuet,

Tuberculosis
And lots of roses.

No jumping about,
No twist and shout,

But the spinning stuff
Was daft enough.

Chandeliers flared,
Breasts were bared;

Beside the band
I saw this blonde,

Her eyes dense
With experience;

A book-illustration
Air of damnation,

An angel defiled,
A dubious child

Wan as the moon
But looking for fun,

Flower of opopanax,[7]
Shadow of anthrax,

Crimson and pale,
Very young, very frail,

She suddenly smiled,
Driving me wild.

'Parisian pick-up,
Your floury make-up

Blows my mind
Like a candle-end.

Your eyes are green,
My thoughts obscene,

Your desperate air
Sets me on fire,

So let me ride you
And die inside you',

Said I; and we dance –
Am I in with a chance?

Take it easy and slow . . .
But, whoops, there I go

Losing my essence
In deliquescence!

1885; translated by Derek Mahon, 2011

MAX BEERBOHM

A Defence of Cosmetics

Nay, but it is useless to protest. Artifice must queen it once more in the town, and so, if there be any whose hearts chafe at her return, let them not say, 'We have come into evil times', and be all for resistance, reformation or angry cavilling. For did the king's sceptre send the sea retrograde, or the wand of the sorcerer avail to turn the sun from its old course? And what man or what number of men ever stayed that reiterated process by which the cities of this world grow, are very strong, fail and grow again? Indeed, indeed, there is charm in every period, and only fools and flutter-pates do not seek reverently for what is charming in their own day. No martyrdom, however fine, nor satire, however splendidly bitter, has changed by a little tittle the known tendency of things. It is the times that can perfect us, not we the times, and so let all of us wisely acquiesce. Like the little wired marionettes, let us acquiesce in the dance.

For behold! The Victorian era comes to its end and the day of *sancta simplicitas*[8] is quite ended. The old signs are here and the portents to warn the seer of life that we are ripe for a new epoch of artifice. Are not men rattling the dice-box and ladies dipping their fingers in the rouge-pots? At Rome, in the keenest time of her *dégringolade*,[9] when there was gambling even in the holy temples, great ladies (does not Lucian[10] tell us?) did not scruple to squander all they had upon unguents from Arabia. Nero's mistress and unhappy wife, Poppaea, of shameful memory, had in her travelling retinue fifteen – or, as some say, fifty – she-asses, for the sake of their milk, that was thought an incomparable guard against cosmetics with poison in them. Last century, too, when life was lived by candle-light, and ethics was but etiquette, and even art a question of punctilio, women, we know, gave the best hours of the day to the crafty larding of their faces and the towering of their coiffures. And men, throwing passion into the wine-bowl to sink or swim, turned out thought to browse upon the green cloth. Cannot we even now in our fancy see them, those silent exquisites round the long table at Brooks', masked, all of them, 'lest the countenance should betray feeling', in quinze masks, through whose eyelets they sat peeping, peeping, while macao brought them riches or ruin? We can see them, those silent rascals, sitting there with their cards and their *rouleaux*[11]and their wooden money-bowls, long after the dawn had crept up St. James' and pressed its haggard face against the window of the little club. Yes, we can raise their ghosts – and, more, we can see manywhere a devotion to hazard fully as meek as theirs. In England there has been a wonderful revival of cards. Roulette may rival dead faro[12] in the tale of her devotees. Her wheel is spinning busily in every house and ere long it may be that tender parents will be waiting to complain of the compulsory baccarat[13] in our public schools.

In fact, we are all gamblers once more, but our gambling is on a finer scale than ever it was. We fly from the card-room to the heath, and from the heath to the City, and from the City to the coast of the Mediterranean. And just as no one seriously encourages the clergy in its frantic efforts to lay the spirit of chance, that has thus resurged among us, so no longer are many faces set against that other great sign of a more complicated life, the love for cosmetics. No longer is a lady of fashion blamed if, to escape the outrageous persecution of time, she fly for sanctuary to the toilet-table; and if a damosel, prying in her mirror, be sure that with brush and pigment she can trick herself into more charm, we are not angry. Indeed, why should we ever have been? Surely it is laudable, this wish to make fair the ugly and overtop fairness, and no wonder that within the last five years the trade of the makers of cosmetics has increased immoderately – twenty-fold, so one of these makers has said to me. We need but walk down any modish street and peer into the little broughams that flit past, or (in Thackeray's phrase)[14] under the bonnet of any woman we meet, to see over how wide a kingdom rouge reigns. We men, who, from Juvenal down to that discourteous painter[15] of whom Lord Chesterfield tells us, have especially shown a dislike of cosmetics, are quite yielding; and there are, I fancy, many such husbands as he who, suddenly realising that his wife was painted, bade her sternly, 'Go up and take it all off', and, on her reappearance, bade her with increasing sternness, 'Go up and put it all on again.'

But now that the use of pigments is becoming general, and most women are not so young as they are painted, it may be asked curiously how the prejudice ever came into being. Indeed, it is hard to trace folly, for that it is inconsequent, to its start; and perhaps it savours too much of reason to suggest that the prejudice was due to the tristful confusion man has made of soul and surface. Through trusting so keenly to the detection of the one by keeping watch upon the other, and by force of the thousand errors following, he has come to think of surface even as the reverse of soul. He supposes that every clown beneath his paint and lip-salve is moribund and knows it, (though in verity, I am told, clowns are as cheerful a class of men as any other), that the fairer the fruit's rind and the more delectable its bloom, the closer are packed the ashes within it. The very jargon of the hunting-field connects cunning with a mask.[16] And so perhaps came man's anger at the embellishment of women – that lovely mask of enamel with its shadows of pink and tiny pencilled veins, what must lurk behind it? Of what treacherous mysteries may it not be the screen? Does not the heathen lacquer her dark face, and the harlot paint her cheeks, because sorrow has made them pale?

After all, the old prejudice is a-dying. We need not pry into the secret of its birth. Rather is this a time of jolliness and glad indulgence. For the era of rouge is upon us, and as only in an elaborate era can man by the tangled accrescency of his own pleasures and emotions reach that refinement which is his highest excellence, and by making himself, so to say, independent of Nature, come nearest to God, so only in an elaborate era is woman perfect. Artifice is the strength of the world, and in that same mask of paint and powder, shadowed with vermeil tinct and most trimly pencilled, is woman's strength.

For see! We need not look so far back to see woman under the direct influence of Nature. Early in this century, our grandmothers, sickening of the odour of faded exotics and spilt wine, came out into the daylight once more and let the breezes blow around their faces and enter, sharp and welcome, into their lungs. Artifice they drove forth, and they set Martin Tupper[17] upon a throne of mahogany to rule over them. A very reign of terror set in. All things were sacrificed to the fetish Nature. Old ladies may still be heard to tell how, when they were girls, affectation was not; and, if we verify their assertion in the light of such literary authorities as Dickens, we find that it is absolutely true. Women appear to have been in those days utterly natural in their conduct – flighty, gushing, blushing, fainting, giggling and shaking their curls. They knew no reserve in the first days of the Victorian era. No thought was held too trivial, no emotion too silly, to express. To

Nature everything was sacrificed. Great heavens! And in those barren days what influence was exerted by women? By men they seem not to have been feared nor loved, but regarded rather as 'dear little creatures' or 'wonderful little beings', and in their relation to life as foolish and ineffectual as the landscapes they did in water-colour. Yet, if the women of those years were of no great account, they had a certain charm and they at least had not begun to trespass upon men's ground; if they touched not thought, which is theirs by right, at any rate they refrained from action, which is ours. Far more serious was it when, in the natural trend of time, they became enamoured of rinking[18] and archery and galloping along the Brighton Parade. Swiftly they have sped on since then from horror to horror. The invasion of the tennis-courts and of the golf-links, the seizure of the tricycle and of the type-writer, were but steps preliminary in that campaign which is to end with the final victorious occupation of St. Stephen's.[19] But stay! The horrific pioneers of womanhood who gad hither and thither and, confounding wisdom with the device on her shield, shriek for the unbecoming, are doomed. Though they spin their tricycle-treadles so amazingly fast, they are too late. Though they scream victory, none follow them. Artifice, that fair exile, has returned.

Yes, though the pioneers know it not, they are doomed already. For of the curiosities of history not the least strange is the manner in which two social movements may be seen to overlap, long after the second has, in truth, given its deathblow to the first. And, in like manner as one has seen the limbs of a murdered thing in lively movement, so we need not doubt that, though the voices of those who cry out for reform be very terribly shrill, they will soon be hushed. Dear Artifice is with us. It needed but that we should wait.

Surely, without any of my pleading, women will welcome their great and amiable protectrix, as by instinct. For (have I not said?) it is upon her that all their strength, their life almost, depends. Artifice's first command to them is that they should repose. With bodily activity their powder will fly, their enamel crack. They are butterflies who must not flit, if they love their bloom. Now, setting aside the point of view of passion, from which very many obvious things might be said, (and probably have been by the minor poets), it is, from the intellectual point of view, quite necessary that a woman should repose. Hers is the resupinate sex. On her couch she is a goddess, but so soon as ever she put her foot to the ground – lo, she is the veriest little sillypop and quite done for. She cannot rival us in action, but she is our mistress in the things of the mind. Let her not by second-rate athletics, nor indeed by any exercise soever of the limbs, spoil the pretty procedure of her reason. Let her be content to remain the guide, the subtle suggester of what *we* must do, the strategist whose soldiers we are, the little architect whose workmen.

'After all,' as a pretty girl once said to me, 'women are a sex by themselves, so to speak', and the sharper the line between their worldly functions and ours, the better. This greater swiftness and less erring subtlety of mind, their forte and privilege, justifies the painted mask that Artifice bids them wear. Behind it their minds can play without let. They gain the strength of reserve. They become important, as in the days of the Roman Empire were the Emperor's mistresses, as was the Pompadour[20] at Versailles, as was our Elizabeth. Yet do not their faces become lined with thought; beautiful and without meaning are their faces.

And, truly, of all the good things that will happen with the full renascence of cosmetics, one of the best is that surface will finally be severed from soul. That damnable confusion will be solved by the extinguishing of a prejudice which, as I suggest, itself created. Too long has the face been degraded from its rank as a thing of beauty to a mere vulgar index of character or emotion. We had come to troubling ourselves, not with its charm of colour and line, but with such questions as whether the lips were sensuous, the eyes full of sadness, the nose indicative of determination. I have no quarrel with physiognomy. For my own part, I believe in it. But it has tended to degrade the face aesthetically, in such wise as the study of cheirosophy[21] has tended to degrade the hand. And the use of cosmetics, the masking of the face, will change this. We shall gaze at a woman merely because she is beautiful, not stare into her face anxiously, as into the face of a barometer.

How fatal it has been, in how many ways, this confusion of soul and surface! Wise were the Greeks in making plain masks for their mummers to play in, and dunces we not to have done the same! Only the other day, an actress was saying that what she was most proud of in her art – next, of course, to having appeared in some provincial pantomime at the age of three – was the deftness with which she contrived, in parts demanding a rapid succession of emotions, to dab her cheeks quite quickly with rouge from the palm of her right hand, or powder from the palm of her left. Gracious goodness! why do not we have masks upon the stage? Drama is the presentment of the soul in action. The mirror of the soul is the voice. Let the young critics, who seek a cheap reputation for austerity, by cavilling at 'incidental music', set their faces rather against the attempt to justify inferior dramatic art by the subvention of a quite alien art like painting, of any art, indeed, whose sphere is only surface. Let those, again, who sneer, so rightly, at the 'painted anecdotes of the Academy', censure equally the writers who trespass on painter's ground. It is a proclaimed sin that a painter should concern himself with a good little girl's affection for a Scotch greyhound, or the keen enjoyment of their port by elderly gentlemen of the early 'forties. Yet, for a painter to prod the soul with his paint-brush is no worse than for a novelist to refuse to dip under the surface, and the fashion of avoiding a psychological study of grief by stating that the owner's hair turned white in a single night, or of shame by mentioning a sudden rush of scarlet to the cheeks, is as lamentable as may be. But! But with the universal use of cosmetics and the consequent secernment of soul and surface, which, at the risk of irritating a reader, I must again insist upon, all those old properties that went to bolster up the ordinary novel – the trembling lips, the flashing eyes, the determined curve of the chin, the nervous trick of biting the moustache – aye and the hectic spot of red on either cheek – will be made spiflicate, as the puppets were spiflicated[22] by Don Quixote. Yes, even now Demos[23] begins to discern. The same spirit that has revived rouge, smote his mouth as it grinned at the wondrous painter of mist and river,[24] and now sends him sprawling for the pearls that Meredith[25] dived for in the deep waters of romance.

Indeed the revival of cosmetics must needs be so splendid an influence, conjuring boons innumerable, that one inclines almost to mutter against the inexorable law by which Artifice must perish from time to time. That such branches of painting as the staining of glass or the illuminating of manuscripts should fall into disuse seems, in comparison, so likely; these were esoteric arts; they died with the monastic spirit. But personal appearance is art's very basis. The painting of the face is the first kind of painting man can have known. To make beautiful things – is it not an impulse laid upon few? But to make oneself beautiful is an universal instinct. Strange that the resultant art could never perish! So fascinating an art too! So various in its materials from *stimmis*, *psimythium* and *fuligo* to bismuth[26] and arsenic, so simple in that its ground and its subject-matter are one, so marvellous in that its very subject-matter becomes lovely when an artist has selected it! For surely this is no idle nor fantastic saying. To deny that 'make-up' is an art, on the pretext that the finished work of its exponents depends for beauty and excellence upon the ground chosen for the work, is absurd. At the touch of a true artist, the plainest face turns comely. As subject-matter the face is no more than suggestive, as ground, merely a loom round which the *beatus artifex*[27] may spin the threads of any gold fabric:

> 'Quae nunc nomen habent operosi signa Myronis
> Pondus iners quondam duraque massa fuit.
> Multa viros nescire decet, pars maxima rerum
> Offendat, si non interiora tegas,'[28]

and, as Ovid would seem to suggest, by pigments any tone may be set aglow on a woman's cheek, from enamel the features take any form. Insomuch that surely the advocates of soup-kitchens and free-libraries and other devices for giving people what providence did not mean them to receive, should send out pamphlets in the praise of self-embellishment. For it will place Beauty within easy reach of many who could not otherwise hope to attain it.

But of course Artifice is rather exacting. In return for the repose she forces – so wisely! – upon her followers when the sun is high or the moon is blown across heaven, she demands that they should pay her long homage at the sun's rising. The initiate may not enter lightly upon her mysteries. For, if a bad complexion be inexcusable, to be ill-painted is unforgivable; and when the toilet is laden once more with the fulness of its elaboration, we shall hear no more of the proper occupation for women. And think, how sweet an energy, to sit at the mirror of coquetry! See the dear merits of the toilet as shown upon old vases, or upon the walls of Roman dwellings, or, rather still, read Böttiger's alluring, scholarly description of 'Morgenscenen im Putzzimmer Einer Reichen Römerin.'[29] Read of Sabina's face as she comes through the curtain of her bed-chamber to the chamber of her toilet. The slave-girls have long been chafing their white feet upon the marble floor. They stand, those timid Greek girls, marshalled in little battalions. Each has her appointed task, and all kneel in welcome as Sabina stalks, ugly and frowning, to the toilet chair. Scaphion steps forth from among them, and, dipping a tiny sponge in a bowl of hot milk, passes it lightly, ever so lightly, over her mistress' face. The Poppaean pastes melt beneath it like snow. A cooling lotion is poured over her brow and is fanned with feathers. Phiale comes after, a clever girl, captured in some sea-skirmish in the Aegean. In her left hand she holds the ivory box wherein are the phucus[30] and that white powder, psimythium; in her right a sheaf of slim brushes. With how sure a touch does she mingle the colours, and in what sweet proportion blushes and blanches her lady's upturned face. Phiale is the cleverest of all the slaves. Now Calamis dips her quill in a certain powder that floats, liquid and sable, in the hollow of her palm. Standing upon tip-toe and with lips parted, she traces the arch of the eyebrows. The slaves whisper loudly of their lady's beauty, and two of them hold up a mirror to her. Yes, the eyebrows are rightly arched. But why does Psecas abase herself? She is craving leave to powder Sabina's hair with a fine new powder. It is made of the grated rind of the cedar-tree, and a Gallic perfumer, whose stall is near the Circus, gave it to her for a kiss. No lady in Rome knows of it. And so, when four special slaves have piled up the headdress, out of a perforated box this glistening powder is showered. Into every little brown ringlet it enters, till Sabina's hair seems like a pile of gold coins. Lest the breezes send it flying, the girls lay the powder with sprinkled attar.[31] Soon Sabina will start for the Temple of Cybele.[32]

Ah! Such are the lures of the toilet that none will for long hold aloof from them. Cosmetics are not going to be a mere prosaic remedy for age or plainness, but all ladies and all young girls will come to love them. Does not a certain blithe Marquise, whose *lettres intimes* from the Court of Louis Seize are less read than their wit would merit, tell us how she was scandalised to see '*même les toutes jeunes demoiselles émaillées comme ma tabatière?*'[33]

So it shall be with us. Surely the common prejudice against painting the lily can be based on mere ground of economy. That which is already fair is complete, it may be urged – urged implausibly, for there are not so many lovely things in this world that we can afford not to know each one of them by heart. There is only one white lily, and who that has ever seen – as I have – a lily really well painted could grudge the artist so fair a ground for his skill? Scarcely do you believe through how many nice metamorphoses a lily may be passed by him. In like manner, we all know the young girl, with her simpleness, her goodness, her wayward ignorance. And a very charming ideal for England must she have been, and a very natural one, when a young girl sat even on the throne. But no nation can keep its ideal for ever and it needed none of Mr. Gilbert's delicate satire in 'Utopia'[34] to remind us that she had passed out of our ken with the rest of the early Victorian era. What writer of plays, as lately asked some pressman, who had been told off to attend many first nights and knew what he was talking about, ever dreams of making the young girl the centre of his theme? Rather he seeks inspiration from the tried and tired woman of the world, in all her intricate maturity, whilst, by way of comic relief, he sends the young girl flitting in and out with a tennis-racket, the poor εἴδωλον ἀμαυρόν[35] of her former self. The season of the unsophisticated is gone by, and the young girl's final extinction beneath the rising tides of cosmetics will leave no gap in life and will rob art of nothing.

'Tush,' I can hear some damned flutterpate exclaim, 'girlishness and innocence are as strong and as permanent as womanhood itself! Why, a few months past, the whole town went mad over Miss Cissie Loftus![36] Was not hers a success of girlish innocence and the absence of rouge? If such things as these be outmoded, why was she so wildly popular?' Indeed, the triumph of that clever girl, whose début made London nice even in August, is but another witness to the truth of my contention. In a very sophisticated time, simplicity has a new *dulcedo*.[37] Hers was a success of contrast. Accustomed to clever malaperts like Miss Lloyd or Miss Reeve,[38] whose experienced pouts and smiles under the sun-bonnet are a standing burlesque of innocence and girlishness, Demos was really delighted, for once and away, to see the real presentment of these things upon his stage. Coming after all those sly serios, coming so young and mere with her pink frock and straightly combed hair, Miss Cissie Loftus had the charm which things of another period often do possess. Besides, just as we adored her for the abrupt nod with which she was wont at first to acknowledge the applause, so we were glad for her to come upon the stage with nothing to tinge the ivory of her cheeks. It seemed so strange, that neglect of convention. To be behind footlights and not rouged! Yes, hers was a success of contrast. She was like a daisy in the window at Solomons'.[39] She was delightful. And yet, such is the force of convention, that when last I saw her, playing in some burlesque at the Gaiety, her fringe was curled and her pretty face rouged with the best of them. And, if further need be to show the absurdity of having called her performance 'a triumph of naturalness over the jaded spirit of modernity', let us reflect that the little mimic was not a real old-fashioned girl after all. She had none of that restless naturalness that would seem to have characterised the girl of the early Victorian days. She had no pretty ways – no smiles nor blushes nor tremors. Possibly Demos could not have stood a presentment of girlishness unrestrained.

But with her grave insouciance, Miss Cissie Loftus had much of the reserve that is one of the factors of feminine perfection, and to most comes only, as I have said, with artifice. Her features played very, very slightly. And in truth, this may have been one of the reasons of her great success. For expression is but too often the ruin of a face; and, since we cannot as yet so order the circumstances of life that women shall never be betrayed into 'an unbecoming emotion', when the brunette shall never have cause to blush, and the lady who looks well with parted lips be kept in a permanent state of surprise, the safest way by far is to create, by brush and pigments, artificial expressions for every face.

And this – say you? – will make monotony? You are mistaken, *toto coelo*[40] mistaken. When your mistress has wearied you with one expression, then it will need but a few touches of that pencil, a backward sweep of that brush, and lo, you will be revelling in another. For though, of course, the painting of the face is, in manner, most like the painting of canvas, in outcome it is rather akin to the art of music – lasting, like music's echo, not for very long. So that, no doubt, of the many little appurtenances of the Reformed Toilet Table, not the least vital will be a list of the emotions that become its owner, with recipes for simulating them. According to the colour she wills her hair to be for the time – black or yellow or, peradventure, burnished red – she will blush for you, sneer for you, laugh or languish for you. The good combinations of line and colour are nearly numberless, and by their means poor restless woman will be able to realise her moods in all their shades and lights and dappledoms, to live many lives and masquerade through many moments of joy. No monotony will be. And for us men matrimony will have lost its sting.

But be it remembered! Though we men will garner these oblique boons, it is into the hands of women that Artifice gives her pigments. I know, I know that many men in a certain sect of society have shown a marked tendency to the use of cosmetics. I speak not of the countless gentlemen who walk about town in the time of its desertion from August to October, artificially bronzed, as though they were fresh from the moors or from the Solent. This, I conceive, is done for purely social reasons and need not concern me here. Rather do I speak of those who make themselves up, seemingly with an aesthetic purpose. Doubtless – I wish to be quite just – there are many who look the better for such embellishment; but, at the hazard of being thought old-fashioned and prejudiced, I cannot speak of the custom with anything but strong disapproval. If men are to lie among the rouge-pots, inevitably it will tend to promote that amalgamation of the sexes which is one of the chief planks in the decadent platform and to obtund that piquant contrast between him and her, which is one of the redeeming features of creation. Besides, really, men have not the excuse of facial monotony, that holds in the case of women. Have we not hair upon our chins and upper lips? And can we not, by diverting the trend of our moustache or by growing our beard in this way or that, avoid the boredom of looking the same for long? Let us beware. For if, in violation of unwritten sexual law, men take to trifling with the paints and brushes that are feminine heritage, it may be that our great ladies will don false imperials, and the little doner[41] deck her pretty chin with a Newgate fringe! After all, I think we need not fear that many men will thus trespass. Most of them are in the City nowadays, and the great wear and tear of that place would put their use of rouge – that demands bodily repose from its dependants – quite outside the range of practical aesthetics.

But that in the world of women they will not neglect this art, so ripping in itself, in its result so wonderfully beneficent, I am sure indeed. Much, I have said, is already done for its full renascence. The spirit of the age has made straight the path of its professors. Fashion has made Jezebel surrender her monopoly of the rouge-pot. As yet, the great art of self-embellishment is for us but in its infancy. But if English-women can bring it to the flower of an excellence so supreme as never yet has it known, then, though Old England may lose her martial and commercial supremacy, we patriots will have the satisfaction of knowing that she has been advanced at one bound to a place in the councils of aesthetic Europe. And, in sooth, is this hoping too high of my countrywomen? True that, as the art seems always to have appealed to the ladies of Athens, and it was not until the waning time of the Republic that Roman ladies learned to love the practice of it, so Paris, Athenian in this as in all other things, has been noted hitherto as a far more vivid centre of the art than London. But it was in Rome, under the Emperors, that unguentaria[42] reached its zenith, and shall it not be in London, soon, that unguentaria shall outstrip its Roman perfection? Surely there must be among us artists as cunning in the use of brush and puff as any who lived at Versailles. Surely the splendid, impalpable advance of good taste, as shown in dress and in the decoration of houses, may justify my hope of the preëminence of English-women in the cosmetic art. By their innate delicacy of touch they will accomplish much, and much, of course, by their swift feminine perception. Yet it were well that they should know something also of the theoretical side of the craft. Modern authorities upon the mysteries of the toilet are, it is true, rather few; but among the ancients many a writer would seem to have been fascinated by them. Archigenes, a man of science at the Court of Cleopatra, and Criton at the Court of the Emperor Trajan, both wrote treatises upon cosmetics – doubtless most scholarly treatises that would have given many a precious hint. It is a pity they are not extant. From Lucian or from Juvenal, with his bitter picture of a Roman *levée*,[43] much may be learnt; from the staid pages of Xenophon and Aristophanes' dear farces. But best of all is that fine book of the *Ars Amatoria*[44] that Ovid has set aside for the consideration of dyes, perfumes and pomades. Written by an artist who knew the allurements of the toilet and understood its philosophy, it remains without rival as a treatise upon Artifice. It is more than a poem, it is a manual; and if there be left in England any lady who cannot read Latin in the original, she will do well to procure a discreet translation. In the Bodleian Library[45] there is treasured the only known copy of a very poignant and delightful rendering of this one book of Ovid's masterpiece. It was made by a certain Wye Waltonstall, who lived in the days of Elizabeth, and, seeing that he dedicated it to 'the Vertuous Ladyes and Gentlewomen of Great Britain', I am sure that the gallant writer, could he know of our great renascence of cosmetics, would wish his little work to be placed once more within their reach. 'Inasmuch as to you, ladyes and gentlewomen,' so he writes in his queer little dedication, 'my booke of pigments doth first addresse itself, that it may kisse your hands and afterward have the lines thereof in reading sweetened by the odour of your breath, while the dead letters formed into words by your divided lips may receive new life by your passionate expression, and the words marryed in that Ruby coloured temple may thus happily united, multiply your contentment.' It is rather sad to think that, at this crisis in the history of pigments, the Vertuous Ladyes and Gentlewomen cannot read the *libellus*[46] of Wye Waltonstall, who did so dearly love pigments.

But since the days when these great critics wrote their treatises, with what gifts innumerable has Artifice been loaded by Science! Many little partitions must be added to the *narthecium*[47] before it can comprehend all the new cosmetics that have been quietly devised since classical days, and will make the modern toilet chalks away more splendid in its possibilities. A pity that no one has devoted himself to the compiling of a new list; but doubtless all the newest devices are known to the admirable unguentarians of Bond Street, who will impart them to their clients. Our thanks, too, should be given to Science for ridding us of the old danger that was latent in the use of cosmetics. Nowadays they cannot, being purged of any poisonous element, do harm to the skin that they make beautiful. There need be no more sowing the seeds of destruction in the furrows of time, no martyrs to the cause like Georgina Gunning, that fair dame but *infelix*,[48] who died, so they relate, from the effect of a poisonous rouge upon her lips. No, we need have no fears now. Artifice will claim not another victim from among her worshippers.

Loveliness shall sit at the toilet, watching her oval face in the oval mirror. Her smooth fingers shall flit among the paints and powder, to tip and mingle them, catch up a pencil, clasp a phial, and what not and what *not*, until the mask of vermeil tinct has been laid aptly, the enamel quite hardened. And, heavens, how she will charm us and ensorcel our eyes! Positively rouge will rob us for a time of all our reason; we shall go mad over masks. Was it not at Capua that they had a whole street where nothing was sold but dyes and unguents? We must have such a street, and, to fill our new Seplasia,[49] our Arcade of the Unguents, all herbs and minerals and live creatures shall give of their substance. The white cliffs of Albion[50] shall be ground to powder for loveliness, and perfumed by the ghost of many a little violet. The fluffy eider-ducks, that are swimming round the pond, shall lose their feathers, that the powder-puff may be moonlike as it passes over loveliness's lovely face. Even the camels shall become ministers of delight, giving their hair in many tufts to be stained by the paints in her colour-box, and across her cheek the swift hare's foot shall fly as of old. The sea shall offer her the phucus, its scarlet weed. We shall spill the blood of mulberries at her bidding. And, as in another period of great ecstasy, a dancing wanton, la belle Aubrey,[51] was crowned upon a church's lighted altar, so Arsenic, that 'green-tress'd goddess', ashamed at length of skulking between the soup of the unpopular and the test-tubes of the Queen's analyst, shall be exalted to a place of highest honour upon loveliness's toilet-table.[52]

All these things shall come to pass. Times of jolliness and glad indulgence! For Artifice, whom we drove forth, has returned among us, and, though her eyes are red with crying, she is smiling forgiveness. She is kind. Let us dance and be glad, and trip the cockawhoop! Artifice, sweetest exile, is come into her kingdom. Let us dance her a welcome!

1894

OWEN SEAMAN

A Ballad of a Bun

A Decadent was dribbling by;
  'Lady,' he said, 'you seem undone;
You need a panacea; try
  This sample of the Bodley bun.

'It is fulfilled of precious spice,
  Whereof I give the recipe; –
Take common dripping, stew in vice,
  And serve with vertu; taste and see!

'And lo! I brand you on the brow
   As kin to Nature's lowest germ;
You are sister to the microbe now,
   And second-cousin to the worm.'

1894

To any Boy-Poet of the Decadence (Showing curious reversal of epigram – 'La nature l'a fait sanglier; la civilisation l'a réduit à l'état de cochon.')[53]

But my good little man, you have made a mistake
   If you really are pleased to suppose
That the Thames is alight with the lyrics you make;
   We could all do the same if we chose.

From Solomon down, we may read, as we run,
   Of the ways of a man and a maid;
There is nothing that's new to us under the sun,
   And certainly not in the shade.

The erotic affairs that you fiddle aloud
   Are as vulgar as coin of the mint;
And you merely distinguish yourself from the crowd
   By the fact that you put 'em in print.

Youre a 'prentice, my boy, in the primitive stage,
   And you itch, like a boy, to confess:
When you know a bit more of the arts of the age
   You will probably talk a bit less.

For your dull little vices we don't care a fig,
   It is *this* that we deeply deplore;
You were cast for a common or usual pig,
   But you play the invincible bore.

1894

ANONYMOUS

The Decadent Guys (A Colour-Study in Green Carnations)

They were sitting close together in their characteristic attitudes; the knees slightly limp, and the arms hanging loosely by their sides; Lord Raggie Tattersall in the peculiar kind of portable chair he most affected; Fustian Flitters in a luxurious sort of hand-barrow. The lemon-tinted November light of a back street in a London slum floated lovingly on their collapsed forms, and on the great mass of weary cabbage-stalks that lay dreaming themselves daintily to death in the gutter at their feet.

They were both dressed very much alike, in loosely-fitting, fantastically patched coats. Lord Raggie was wearing a straw hat, with the crown reticently suggested rather than expressed, which suited his complexion very well, emphasising, as it did, the white weariness of his smooth face, with the bright spot of red that had appeared on each cheek, and the vacant fretfulness of his hollow eyes; he held his head slightly on one side, and seemed very tired. Fustian Flitters had adopted the regulation chimney-pot hat, beautiful with the iridescent sheen of decay; he was taller, bulgier, and bulkier than his friend, and allowed his heavy chin to droop languidly forward. Both wore white cotton gloves, broken boots, and rather small magenta cauliflowers in their button-holes.

'My dear Raggie,' said Mr. Flitters, in a gently elaborate voice, and with a gracious wave of his plump straw-distended white fingers towards his companion's chair; 'you are looking very well this afternoon. You would be perfectly charming in a red wig and a cocked-hat, and a checked ulster with purple and green shadows in the folds. You would wear it beautifully, floating negligently over your shoulders. But you are wonderfully complete as you are!'

'That is so true!' acquiesced Raggie, with perfect complacency. 'I am very beautiful. And you, Fustian, you are so energetically inert. Are you going to blow up to-night? You are so brilliant when you blow up.'

'I have not decided either way. I never do. It will depend upon how I feel in the bonfire. I let it come if it will. The true *impromptu* is invariably premeditated.'

'Isn't that rather self-contradictory?' said Raggie, with his pretty quick smile.

'Of course it is. Does not consistency solely consist in contradicting oneself? But I suppose I *am* a trifle *décousu*.'[54]

'You are. Indeed, we are both what those absurd clothes-dealing Philistines would call "threadbare" – you and I.'

'I hope so, most sincerely. There is something so hopelessly middle-class about wearing perfectly new clothes. It always reminds me of that ridiculous Nature, who will persist in putting all her poor little trees into brand-new suits of hideous non-arsenical green every spring. As if withered leaves, or even nudity itself, would not really be infinitely more decent! I detest a coat that is what the world calls a "fit!"'

'Clothes that fit,' observed Lord Raggie, gravely, 'are the natural penalty for possessing that dreadful deformity, a good figure. Only exploded mediocrities like Tupper and Bunn and Shakspeare ought to have figures.'

'*Had* Shakspeare a figure? I thought it was only a bust.'

'We shall have *our* little bust by and by, I suppose,' said Raggie, pensively. 'I wonder *when*. I feel in the mood to sally forth and paint the night with strange scarlet, slashed with silver and gold, while our young votaries – beautiful pink boys in paper hats – let off marvellous pale epigrammatic crackers and purple paradoxical squibs in our honour.'

'See, Raggie, here come our youthful disciples! Do they not look deliciously innocent and enthusiastic? I wish, though, we could contrive to imbue them with something of our own lovely limpness – they are so atrociously lively and active.'

'That will come, Fustian', said Lord Raggie, indulgently. 'We must give them time. Already they have copied our distinctive costume, caught our very features and colouring. Some day, Fustian, some day they will adopt our mystic emblem – the symbol that is such a true symbol in possessing no meaning whatever – the Magenta Cauliflower! And then – and then – .'

'– It will be time for Us to drop it,' continued Mr. Fustian Flitters, with his pecular smile of inscrutable obviousness.

'Beautiful rose-coloured children!' murmured Lord Raggie, dreamily; 'how sad to think that they will all grow up and degenerate into pork-butchers, and generals, and bishops, and absurdly futile persons of that sort! But listen; it is so sweet of them – they are going to sing an exquisite little catch I composed expressly for them, a sort of mellifluously raucous chant with no tune in particular. That is where it is so wonderful. True melody is always quite tuneless!'

One by one the shrill, passionate young voices chimed in, until the very lamp-posts throbbed and rang with the words, and they seemed to wander away, away among the sleeping pageant of the chimney-pots, away to the burnished golden globes of the struggling pawnbroker.

'Please ter remember. The Fifth o' November. For Gun Powder Plot.
Ter-blow up the King and 'is Porliment. Shall never. Be. Forgot!
'Oller, Boys, 'Oller!'

Lord Raggie, with his head bent, listened with a smile parting the scarlet thread of his lips, a smile in his pretty hollow eyes. 'I wonder why people should be exhorted to remember such a prosaic and commonplace crime as that,' he meditated aloud: 'a crime, too, that had not even the vulgar merit of being a success!'

'Only failures ever do succeed, really.' said Fustian, leaning largely over his barrow. 'How deliciously they are joggling us! Don't you like having your innermost shavings stimulated, Raggie?'

'There is only one stimulating thing in the world,' was the languid answer; 'and that is a soporific. But see, Fustian, here comes one of those unconsciously absurd persons they call policemen. How stiffly he holds himself. Why is there something so irresistibly ludicrous about every creature that possesses a spine? Perhaps because to be vertebrate is to be normal, and the normal is necessarily such a hideous monstrosity. I love what are called warped distorted figures. The only real Adonis nowadays is a Guy.' And the shrill voices of the young choristers, detaching themselves one by one from the melodic fabric in which they were enmeshed, grew fainter and fainter still – until they slipped at last into silence. 'Fustian, did you notice? Our rose-white adherents have abandoned us. They have run away – "done a guy", as vulgarians express it.'

'They have done two,' said Mr. Flitters correctively; 'which only proves the absolute sincerity of their devotion. Is not the whole art of fidelity comprised in knowing exactly when to betray?'

'How original you are to-day, Fustian! But what is this crude blue copper going to do with you and me? Can we be going to become notorious – *really* notorious – at last?'

'I devoutly trust not. Notoriety is now merely a synonym for respectable obscurity. But he certainly appears to be engaged in what a serious humourist would call "running us in."'

'How pedantic of him! Then shan't we be allowed to explode at all this evening?'

'It seems not. They think we are dangerous. How can one tell? Perhaps we are. Give me a light, Raggie, and I will be brilliant for you alone. Come, the young Shoeblack bends to his brush, and the pale-faced Coster watches him in his pearly kicksies; the shadows on the mussels in the fish-stall are violet, and the vendor of half penny ices is washing the spaces of his tumblers with primrose and with crimson. Let me be brilliant, dear boy, or I feel that I shall burst for sheer vacuity, and pass away, as so many of us have passed, with all my combustibles still in me!'

And with gentle resignation, as martyrs whose apotheosis is merely postponed, Lord Raggie and Fustian Flitters allowed themselves to be slowly moved on by the rude hand of an unsympathetic Peeler.

1894

EDWARD T. REED

Britannia à la Beardsley

BRITANNIA À LA BEARDSLEY.

(*By Our "Yellow" Decadent.*)

LIONEL JOHNSON

A Decadent's Lyric

Sometimes, in very joy of shame,
Our flesh becomes one living flame:
And she and I
Are no more separate, but the same.

Ardour and agony unite;
Desire, delirium, delight:
And I and she
Faint in the fierce and fevered night.

Her body music is: and ah,
The accords of lute and viola!
When she and I
Play on live limbs love's opera!

1897

Notes

1 Matthew Sturgis, *Passionate Attitudes: The English Decadence of the 1890s* (London: Macmillan, 1995), p. 211.
2 R. K. R. Thornton makes this point in *The Decadent Dilemma* (London: Edward Arnold, 1983), p. 21: 'it is in the parodic and satirical writings about Decadence that the ideas and characteristics become clarified into caricature'.
3 For a summary of *Punch*'s attitude towards the Decadents and the 1890s, see Sturgis, pp. 211–27.
4 Holbrook Jackson, *The Eighteen Nineties* (Harmondsworth: Penguin, 1950), p. 161.
5 [Vicaire and Beauclair's footnote:] *The Deliquescences: Decadent Poems of Adoré Floupette*. Byzantium: Lion Vanné, publisher, 1885, small 12mo (the final page reads: Printed at the press of Lutetia, the second of May, eighteen hundred and eighty-five, for Adoré Floupette, by Léon Épinette, printer, 16 Boulevard Saint-Germain, Paris). There are ten copies bearing the authors' names on the cover.
6 [Vicaire and Beauclair's footnote:] *The Deliquescences: Decadent Poems of Adoré Floupette, together with His Life by Marius Tapora*. Byzantium: Lion Vanné, publisher, 1885, small 12mo (the printer's colophon gives the date as the twentieth of June, eighteen hundred and eighty-five). There are ten copies on Dutch paper bearing the authors' names on the cover.
7 Acrid resin from the umbelliferous plant, found in Turkey and the East Indies. One of Des Esseintes's favourite essences.

8 (Latin:) 'Holy simplicity'.
9 French, 'downfall' or 'collapse'.
10 Syrian-Greek prose writer of the second century CE. The allusion is to a prose dialogue known as the *Erotes* (or in Latin the *Amores*), doubtfully attributed to Lucian, in which the love of boys is preferred to that of women, in part because each morning women disguise their true ugliness under cosmetics while boys wash decently.
11 Quinze and macao are both card games. Brooks' was a London gentlemen's club. Rouleaux are rolls of gold coins.
12 Faro is a card game, by this time considered 'dead', i.e. out of fashion among gamblers.
13 A casino card game.
14 In W. M. Thackeray's novel *Vanity Fair* (1847–8) one character is described not peering but 'leering under the bonnets of passers by' (ch. 28).
15 Jean Etienne Liotard (1702–89), Swiss-French portrait-painter, who was said to have forbidden ladies to wear make-up when sitting for him, on the grounds that he only painted Nature.
16 In hunting jargon, the face of a fox is called its 'mask'.
17 Martin Tupper (1810–89), English writer, whose best-selling collection of semi-poetic platitudes, *Proverbial Philosophy* (4 series, 1837–76), made him for Beerbohm's generation an easily mocked representative of early Victorian moralising.
18 Ice-skating.
19 Outdated metonym for the House of Commons, from the name of the former royal chapel of the Palace of Westminster in which the Commons assembled until the building was destroyed by fire in 1834.
20 Mme de Pompadour (Jeanne-Antoinette Poisson, 1821–64), principal mistress to King Louis XV from 1745, exercised extensive political influence, despite her bourgeois origins.
21 The science of the hand, here identified with chirognomy, which purports to read character from features of the hand as physiognomy does with faces.
22 Jocular slang term for 'overwhelmed' or 'crushed'. In the second volume (1615) of Miguel de Cervantes's *Don Quixote*, the deluded hero attends a puppet show, and decapitates some of the puppets, whom he mistakes for real-life villains (ch. 26).
23 A personification of the People, or the common man.
24 The wondrous painter may be the French Impressionist Claude Monet (1840–1926).
25 George Meredith (1828–1909), English poet and novelist.
26 *Stimmis* (properly *stimmi*) is the Greek word for kohl eye-shadow; *psimythium* is Greek for ceruse, a white lead-based face-powder; *fuligo* the Latin for soot; bismuth is the chemical base for a pearl-white cosmetic powder.
27 (Latin:) 'Blessed artist'.
28 Ovid, *Ars Amatoria* book III (*c.* 1 CE) 219–20 and 229–30, from a pertinent passage about the feminine toilet as art. 'The now-famous works signed by the busy Myron were once a dead weight of hard rock. It is right that many things

should be kept from our knowledge: most things would be offensive if their inner secrets were not covered.' Myron of Eleutherae was a noted fifth-century Greek sculptor.

29 Karl Böttiger (1760–1835), German author and archaeologist. His *Sabina oder Morgenscenen im Putzzimmer einer reichen Römerin* ('Sabina, or Morning Scenes in the Dressing-Room of a Wealthy Roman Lady') appeared in 1803. Beerbohm's summary is based on an English version that appeared in *Blackwood's Magazine* in October 1818.

30 Properly *fucus* (Latin:) rouge.

31 Essence of rose-petal.

32 The earth-mother goddess of the Phrygians in ancient Anatolia.

33 'even the young women enamelled like my tobacco case'. Both the quotation and the marquise appear to be invented, possibly modelled loosely upon the Marquise du Deffand (1697–1780), whose letters to the English writer Horace Walpole were published in 1810.

34 *Utopia Limited; or, The Flowers of Progress*, a comic opera by W. S. Gilbert and Arthur Sullivan, premiered in 1893.

35 (Greek:) 'faint image', i.e. pale shadow. The phrase appears twice in the fourth book of Homer's *Odyssey*.

36 Cissie Loftus (Cecilia Loftus Brown, 1876–1943), Scottish actress, made her London music-hall debut in 1893, at the age of seventeen, and soon after eloped with Beerbohm's friend, the Irish writer and former MP Justin Huntly McCarthy.

37 (Latin:) sweetness; thus 'sweetheart'.

38 Marie Lloyd (Matilda Wood, 1870–1922), English singer and comedienne, the most famous music-hall artiste of her age, notorious for her winkingly suggestive renditions of seemingly innocent lyrics. Ada Reeve (Adelaide Reeve, 1874–1966), English actress and singer, a music-hall artiste from the age of fourteen, famed in the 1890s for the innuendo of her hit songs 'She Was a Clergyman's Daughter' and 'What Do I Care?'.

39 A reference perhaps to Israel Solomon's, an expensive florist on Piccadilly.

40 (Latin:) 'by all of heaven', i.e. utterly.

41 Lady or sweetheart (late Victorian slang, from Spanish 'Dona').

42 (Latin:) perfumery, here applied to the cosmetic arts generally.

43 The allusions are to the *Erotes*, attributed to Lucian (see note 10 above); and a passage in Juvenal's Second Satire in which he rails against men who paint their faces. A *levée* is a morning ritual of washing and dressing.

44 The third book of the *Ars Amatoria* (see note 28 above), in which Ovid advises women on the best use of cosmetics.

45 The great library of the University of Oxford, founded by Thomas Bodley in 1600. The translation by the Elizabethan author 'Wye Waltonstall' is Beerbohm's invention.

46 (Latin:) 'little book'.

47 (Latin:) 'ointment box'.

48 The *infelix* (unfortunate) lady was not Georgina but Maria (*née* Gunning), Countess of Coventry (1733–60), a celebrated beauty of her day, whose

persistent use of lead-based cosmetics damaged her face and caused fatal blood-poisoning.

49 Capua: ancient southern Italian city renowned in antiquity for its luxuries, especially its trade in perfumes and cosmetics, based in the Seplasia, a street (or possibly larger marketplace) in the city centre.

50 England.

51 This could be Beerbohm's joke against Aubrey Beardsley (1872–98), who illustrated Oscar Wilde's play *Salome* (1893).

52 The 'unpopular' here are individual victims of domestic poisoning, while the 'Queen's analyst' is Beerbohm's inaccurate title for the Government Chemist, responsible for investigating nationally significant cases of food and drink adulteration.

53 'Nature made him a wild boar; civilisation turned him into a (mere) pig'.

54 Incoherent; literally 'unstitched'.

SELECT BIBLIOGRAPHY

Anthologies of Decadent writing

Beckson, Karl, *Aesthetes and Decadents of the 1890s: An Anthology of British Prose and Poetry* (Chicago: Academy, 1982)

Blyth, Caroline (ed.), *Decadent Verse: An Anthology of Late-Victorian Poetry, 1872–1900* (London: Anthem, 2009)

Hustvedt, Asti (ed.), *The Decadent Reader: Fiction, Fantasy, and Perversion from Fin-de-siècle France* (New York: Zone Books, 1999)

Rodensky, Lisa (ed.), *Decadent Poetry from Wilde to Naidu* (London: Penguin, 2006)

Schoolfield, George C., *A Baedeker of Decadence: Charting a Literary Fashion, 1884–1927* (New Haven, Conn.; London: Yale University Press, 2004)

Secker, Martin (ed. with introduction by John Betjeman), *The Eighteen Nineties: A Period Anthology in Prose and Verse* (London: Richards Press, 1948)

Showalter, Elaine (ed.), *Daughters of Decadence: Women Writers of the Fin de Siècle* (New Brunswick: Rutgers University Press, 1993)

Stableford, Brian (ed.), *The Dedalus Book of Decadence: Moral Ruins* (Sawtry: Dedalus, 1990)

Stableford, Brian (ed.), *The Second Dedalus Book of Decadence: The Black Feast* (Sawtry: Dedalus, 1992)

Stableford, Brian (ed.), *The Dedalus Book of Femmes Fatales* (Sawtry: Dedalus, 1992)

Stanford, Derek (ed.), *Writings of the 'Nineties: From Wilde to Beerbohm* (London: Dent, 1971)

Thornton, R. K. R. and Marion Twain (eds), *Poetry of the 1890s* (London: Penguin, 1997)

General studies of Decadence

Beckson, Karl, *London in the 1890s: A Cultural History* (New York: W. W. Norton, 1992)

Bernheimer, Charles, *Decadent Subjects: The Idea of Decadence in Art, Literature, Philosophy, and Culture of the* Fin de Siècle *in Europe* (Baltimore, MD: Johns Hopkins University Press, 2002)

Birkett, Jennifer, *The Sins of the Fathers 1870–1914* (London: Quartet Books, 1986)

Bristow, Joseph, '"Sterile Ecstasies": The Perversity of the Decadent Movement', *Essays and Studies*, 48 (1995): 65–88

Carter, A. E., *The Idea of Decadence in French Literature (1830–1900)* (Toronto: University of Toronto Press, 1958)

Cevasco, G., *A Breviary of the Decadence: J.-K. Huysmans'* A Rebours *and English Literature* (New York: AMS Press, 2000)

Charlesworth, Barbara, *Dark Passages: The Decadent Consciousness in Victorian Literature* (Madison: University of Wisconsin Press, 1955)

Constable, Liz, Dennis Denisoff, and Matthew Potolsky (eds), *Perennial Decay: On the Aesthetics and Politics of Decadence* (Philadelphia: University of Pennsylvania Press, 1999)

Daly, Nicholas, *Modernism, Romance and the Fin de Siècle: Popular Fiction and British Culture, 1880–1914* (Cambridge: Cambridge University Press, 1999)

Denisoff, Denis, 'Decadence and Aestheticism', in Gail Marshall (ed.), *The Cambridge Companion to the Fin de Siècle* (Cambridge: Cambridge University Press, 2007), pp. 31–52

Dowling, Linda, *Aestheticism and Decadence: A Selective Annotated Bibliography* (New York: Garland, 1977)

Dowling, Linda, *Language and Decadence in the Victorian Fin de Siècle* (Princeton, NJ: Princeton University Press, 1986)

Ellis, Tracey (ed.), *Decadence and Danger: Writing, History and the Fin de Siècle* (Bath: Sulis Press, 1997)

Fletcher, Ian (ed.), *Decadence and the 1890s*, Stratford-Upon-Avon Studies series (London: Edward Arnold, 1979)

Gagnier, Regenia, *Individualism, Decadence and Globalization: On the Relationship of Part to Whole 1859–1920* (Basingstoke: Palgrave 2010)

Gerber, Helmut E., 'The Nineties: Beginning, End, or Transition?', in *Edwardians and Late Victorians*, ed. Richard Ellmann (New York: Columbia University Press, 1960)

Gilman, Richard, *Decadence: The Strange Life of an Epithet* (New York: Farrar, Straus and Giroux, 1975)

Gye, Joengmeen, 'Journey into Modern Literature: Realism, Naturalism, Pre-Raphaelitism, Aestheticism, and Decadence', *British and American Fiction to 1900*, 9 (Summer 2002): 165–80

Hannoosh, Michèle, *Parody and Decadence, Laforgue's Moralités légendaires* (Columbus: Ohio State University Press, 1989)

Hanson, Ellis, *Decadence and Catholicism* (Cambridge, MA: Harvard University Press, 1997)

Harris, Wendell V., 'Identifying the Decadent Fiction of the 1890s', *English Literature in Transition*, 5, 5 (1962): 1–13

Harris, Wendell V., 'John Lane's Keynotes Series and the Fiction of the 1890s', *PMLA*, 83, 5 (October 1968): 1407–13

Harris, Wendell V., 'Innocent Decadence: The Poetry of the Savoy', *PMLA*, 77, 5 (December 1962): 629–36

Hurley, Kelly, *The Gothic Body: Sexuality, Materialism, and Degeneration at the Fin de Siècle* (Cambridge: Cambridge University Press, 1996)

Jackson, Holbrook, *The Eighteen Nineties* (London: Grant Richards, 1913)

Jouve, Sévérine, *Obsessions et Perversions dans la littérature et les demeures à la fin du dix-neuvième siècle* (Paris: Hermann, 1996)

Ledger, Sally and Roger Luckhurst (eds), *The Fin de Siècle: A Reader in Cultural History c. 1880–1900* (Oxford: Oxford University Press, 2000)

MacLeod, Kirsten, *Fictions of British Decadence: High Art, Popular Writing and the Fin de Siècle* (Basingtoke: Palgrave, 2006)

Marquèze-Pouey, Louis, *Le Mouvement décadent en France* (Paris: Presses Universitaires de France, 1986)

Marshall, Gail (ed.), *The Cambridge Companion to the Fin de Siècle* (Cambridge: Cambridge University Press, 2007)

Munro, John M., *The Decadent Poetry of the Eighteen-Nineties* (Beirut: American University of Beirut, 1970)

Nalbantian, Suzanne, *Seeds of Decadence in the Late Nineteenth-Century Novel* (London: Macmillan, 1983)

Navarette, Susan J., *The Shape of Fear: Horror and the Fin de Siècle Culture of Decadence* (Lexington, Kentucky: University Press of Kentucky, 1998)

Palacio, Jean de, *Figures et formes de la décadence* (Paris: Seguier, 1994)

Palacio, Jean de, *Le silence du texte: poétique de la décadence* (Louvain; Dudley, MA: Peeters, 2003)

Pierrot, Jean, *L'Imaginaire décadent*, [1977], trans. Derek Coltman as *The Decadent Imagination, 1880–1900* (Chicago: University of Chicago Press, 1981)

Praz, Mario, *The Romantic Agony* (trans. Angus Davidson) (Oxford: Oxford University Press, 1970)

Prungnaud, Joëlle, *Gothique et Décadence: Recherches sur la continuité d'un mythe et d'un genre au XIXe siècle en Grande-Bretagne et en France* (Paris: Honoré Champion, 1997)

Reed, John, *Decadent Style* (Athens: Ohio University Press, 1985)

Ridge, George R., *The Hero in French Decadent Literature* (Athens, GA: University of Georgia Press, 1961)

Spackman, Barbara, *Decadent Genealogies: The Rhetoric of Sickness from Baudelaire to d'Annunzio* (Ithaca: Cornell University Press, 1989)

Stableford, Brian, *Glorious Perversity: The Decline and Fall of Literary Decadence* (Rockville, MD: Wildside Press, 1998)

St John, Michael (ed.), *Romancing Decay: Ideas of Decadence in European Culture* (Brookfield, VT: Ashgate, 1999)

Sturgis, Matthew, *Passionate Attitudes: The English Decadence of the 1890s* (London: Macmillan, 1995)

Swart, Konrad W., *The Sense of Decadence in Nineteenth-Century France* (The Hague: Nijhoff, 1964)

Temple, Ruth Z., *The Critic's Alchemy: A Study of the Introduction of French Symbolism into England* (New York: Twayne, 1953)

Temple, Ruth Z., 'Truth in Labelling: Pre-Raphaelitism, Aestheticism, Decadence, Fin de Siècle', *English Literature in Transition*, 17, 4 (1974): 201–22

Thornton, R.K.R., *The Decadent Dilemma* (London: Edward Arnold, 1983)

Weir, David, *Decadence and the Making of Modernism* (Amherst: University of Massachusetts Press, 1995)

Weir, David, *Decadent Culture in the United States: Art and Literature against the American Grain, 1890–1926* (Albany: State University of New York Press, 2008)

INDEX

Page numbers for works or extracts from the listed author or source appear in **bold** type.

EU authorised representative for GPSR:
Easy Access System Europe, Mustamäe tee 50,
10621 Tallinn, Estonia
gpsr.requests@easproject.com

www.ingramcontent.com/pod-product-compliance
Lightning Source LLC
Chambersburg PA
CBHW051100030726
47504CB00006B/1717

* 9 7 8 0 7 1 9 0 7 5 5 1 3 *